Final Score: LOVE ALL!

TEACHINGS BY SWAMI CHINMAYANANDA

Published by

Chinmaya Mission West

P.O. Box 129, Piercy, CA 95587, U.S.A.

Tel. (707) 247-3488

Email: publications@chinmayamission.org

Website: www.chinmayamission.org

First Edition: December 2016, 5000 copies

Concept: Pūjya Gurudev Swami Chinmayananda (see Preface)

Compiled and edited by Anjali Singh

Assisted by Swami Advayananda, Christine Grimmer, Cauvery Bhalla, and Jujhar Singh

Editorial Support by the Mananam Team

Swami Shantananda, Margaret Dukes, David Dukes, Neena Dev,

Rudite Emir, Rashmi Mehrotra, Arun Mehrotra,

Padmashree Rao, and Aarthi Ramalingam

Design & Layout

Zoe Collington Modgill

InDesign Formatting

Preeti Pahwa

Credits: See Preface

Special thanks to Pūjya Guruji Swami Tejomayananda

for his loving support and guidance.

Printed by

Silverpoint Press Pvt. Ltd., Mumbai, India

Library of Congress Control Number: 2016948982

ISBN: 978-1-60827-018-7

THE MANANAM SERIES

CHINMAYA BIRTH CENTENARY CELEBRATION SERIES

Final Score: LOVE ALL!

TEACHINGS BY SWAMI CHINMAYANANDA

CHINMAYA PUBLICATIONS
CHINMAYA MISSION WEST PUBLICATIONS DIVISION

Contents

Foreword

Whenever we take up a project and it reaches the point of its successful completion, it gives us the immense joy of fulfillment — that same joy I am feeling while writing this foreword for the twelfth and final issue of the Chinmaya Birth Centenary Celebration Series of the Mananam Series publications. The book is rightly titled, *Final Score: Love All*.

We all know how fond Pūjya Gurudev was of tennis. He loved to play and watch others playing. In this present issue, Anjali Singh, in her inimitable style, has presented the teaching of Pūjya Gurudev through the analogy of tennis. In tennis, the game begins with 'Love All' and, interestingly, the game of Pūjya Gurudev begins and concludes with 'Love All.' All those who came in contact with him experienced his unconditional love.

Anjali deserves all compliments for this beautifully brought out final issue. I take this opportunity to record my deep appreciation to the Mananam team — Margaret and David Dukes, Rudite Emir, Neena Dev, Rashmi and Arun Mehrotra, Padmashree Rao, Aarthi Ramalingam — for their exemplary commitment to editing all issues of this very special series. My heartfelt thanks to them all!

This entire series of twelve books is our offering of love and reverence to Pūjya Gurudev. May he be pleased with our sevā and bless us all with the fulfillment of life.

Swami Tejomayananda
Head, Chinmaya Mission Worldwide

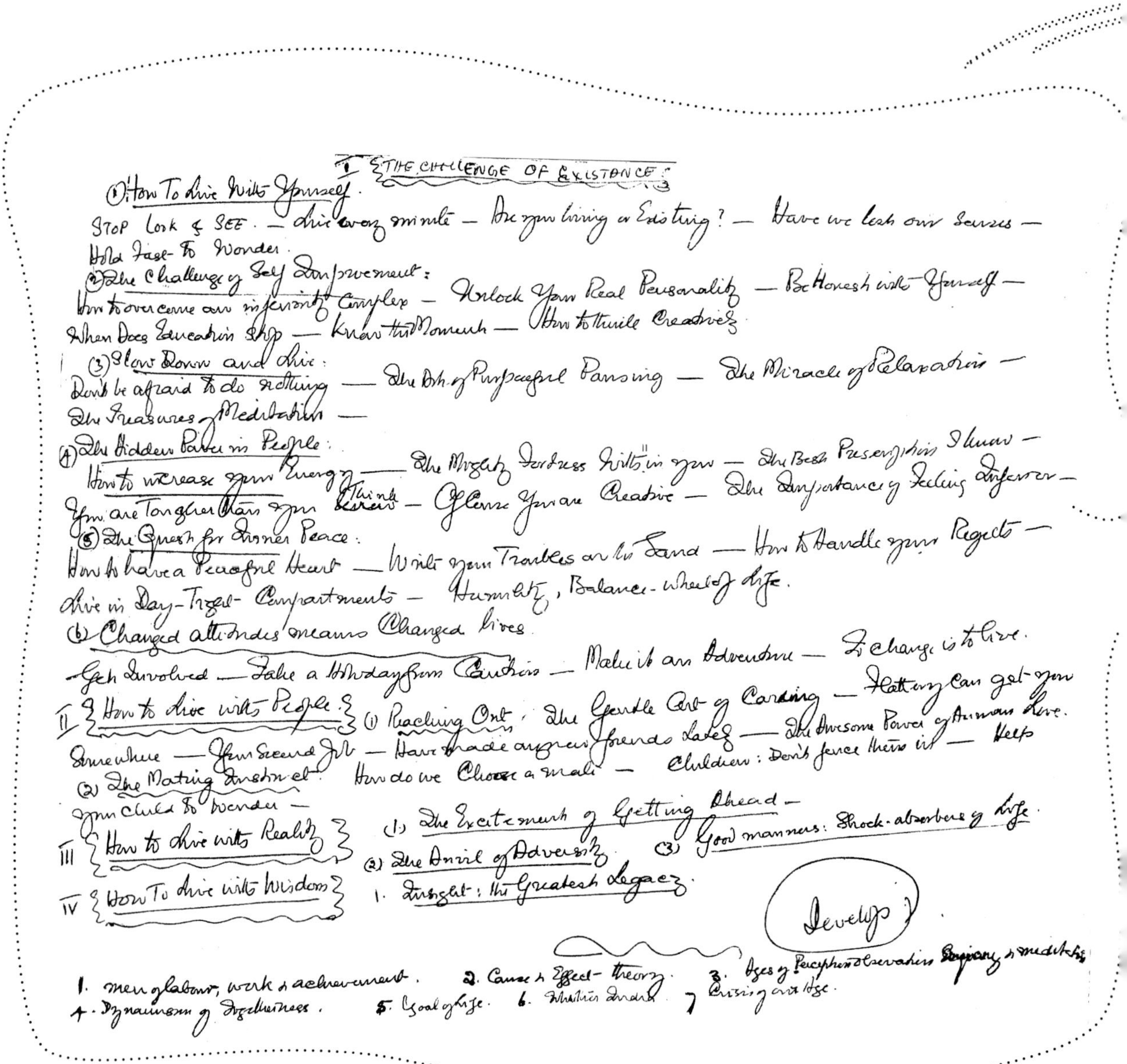

I THE CHALLENGE OF EXISTENCE

(1) How To Live With Yourself.
STOP Look & SEE. — Live every minute — Are you living or Existing? — Have we lost our Senses — Hold fast to Wonder.
(2) The Challenge of Self Improvement:
How to overcome an inferiority Complex — Unlock Your Real Personality — Be Honest with Yourself — When Does Education Stop — Know the Moment — How to think Creatively
(3) Slow Down and Live:
Don't be afraid to do nothing — The Art of Purposeful Pausing — The Miracle of Relaxation — The Treasures of Meditation —
(4) The Hidden Power in People:
How to increase your Energy — The Mighty Forces Within you — The Best Prescription I know — You are Tougher than you Think — Of course You are Creative — The Importance of Feeling Inferior —
(5) The Quest for Inner Peace:
How to have a Peaceful Heart — Write your Troubles on the Sand — How to Handle your Regrets — Live in Day-Tight Compartments — Humility, Balance-wheel of Life.
(6) Changed attitudes means Changed lives
Get Involved — Take a Holiday from Caution — Make it an Adventure — To change is to live.

II { How to Live with People: } (1) Reaching Out: The Gentle Art of Caring — Flattery can get you Somewhere — Your Second Job — Have made any new friends lately — The Awesome Power of Human Love.
(2) The Mating Instinct: How do we Choose a mate — Children: Don't fence them in — Help your child to wonder —

III { How to Live with Reality } (1) The Excitement of Getting Ahead — (2) The Anvil of Adversity (3) Good manners: Shock-absorbers of Life.

IV { How To Live with Wisdom } 1. Insight: the Greatest Legacy.

Develop

1. men of labour, work & achievement. 2. Cause & Effect-theory. 3. Ages of Perception & observation & meditation
4. Dynamism of Togetherness. 5. Goal of life. 6. Mother India. 7 Crisis of our Age.

Handwritten note found in Swamiji's kuṭiyā in Sidhbari in 2015
(See inside front cover for a readable display of the note.)

Preface

The aim of this culminating book in the Chinmaya Birth Centenary Celebration Series is to bring out the core teachings of Pūjya Gurudev Swami Chinmayananda — and the unique way in which he delivered his teachings.

When we started planning the book, my daughter Nanki and I considered many options. But none of them really clicked with us. One evening, Cauvery Bhalla happened to call me from Sidhbari, where she had gone on behalf of CCMT Archives to scan all the books, diaries, and papers in Gurudev's rooms in the āśrama. I requested her to pray to Gurudev on my behalf at the Samadhi Mandir for help with this book.

The very next morning, an amazing thing happened! Cauvery called me excitedly to say that she had found a page among Gurudev's papers which had fifty-two topics written in his own handwriting! She read out the topics, suggesting that they seemed the perfect guideline for the book. No one had come across this small document in the last twenty-two years, lying there in Gurudev's cottage (see inside front and back covers). We could not have been given a better concept! My request for help had been answered within fourteen hours!

Meanwhile, I happened to have written an article on the uniqueness of Gurudev's teaching methods by recalling how he taught meditation through his remarks on tennis matches he used to watch on TV. Thus, on Cauvery's prompting, we developed a final format for this book. Gurudev watching tennis on TV in Sidhbari is the backdrop, and his core teachings are captured under the fifty-two headings that he himself had listed. And in keeping with his instruction in that small document to 'develop,' we have added several additional topics as well.

Pūjya Guruji Swami Tejomayananda has shown constant interest in and anticipation about this book and has encouraged us every time he was in Delhi. In our final brainstorming session with Guruji, Mitul Seth suggested a title along the lines of 'The Score Is Love All.' Later, some U.S.A. devotees added the word 'Final' to it. This is how we got the book's title Final Score: Love All!

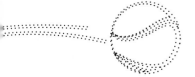

Over the years, I had marked on the back pages of Gurudev's books, certain passages and quotes that I had found inspiring, together with the relevant page numbers and topics. This habit has proved to be very useful as an organized source of Gurudev's core teachings. We are grateful to the many devotees who have sorted out the marked passages and quotes — Cauvery Bhalla, Kalpana Vaswani, Aishna Sharma, Madhu Bawa, Indu Shrikent, Sumir Chaudhry, Trishna Gulrajni, Radha Chawla, Mona Malkani, and Neera Sharma.

Powerful and hard-hitting quotes from Gurudev's books and discourses form the main parts of this book. They are a call to us from Gurudev, beyond time and space, out of his endless love, so that we may reflect on them and move onward and upward on our journey home.

All handwritten quotes and those beginning with a capital letter
in the quotes sections are the actual words of

Pūjya Gurudev Swami Chinmayananda.

Everyone who has had the great fortune of spending time in Gurudev's physical presence has stories to tell. The stories recalled by devotees may be inspiring, funny, embarrassing or life changing. But all the stories contain profound teachings — guiding devotees at key stages of their lives. We are grateful to many devotees all over the world who wrote out many pages of their experiences with Gurudev. Kum Kum Bhatia lovingly shortened articles sent by devotees. Because the concept for the book changed, the contributions could not be used in full. But relevant portions have been incorporated under the key topics. Please see the back of the book for the list of devotees who have contributed their experiences with Gurudev.

Some of Gurudev's letters to devotees have been sourced from the letter archives of CCMT, and extracts have been used where relevant. Devotees whose letters have been used are also listed at the back of the book.

Ācārya Vilasini Balakrishnan, who was secretary to Gurudev for seven years, sent two collections of invaluable correspondence with devotees and Chinmaya Lesson Course students; Gauri Rana typed these out in full.

Swami Advayananda, head of Chinmaya International Foundation (CIF), graciously found time in his busy work schedule to read the introductions to the topics concerned with meditation to ensure that they are aligned with the key teachings of Vedānta; Swami Prakarshananda from Delhi reviewed the rest of the introductions.

It had not only been my request that was answered by Gurudev, but Christine Grimmer's also. In faraway Australia, Christine had been praying to Gurudev to give her some work which would keep Gurudev in her mind all the time! When I needed someone to continue the editing of the introductions to the topics, so skillfully commenced by Shivani Choudhary, I approached Christine. She was ecstatic, as Gurudev had answered her prayer as well! And Christine put in her best between her job and house-changing duties and in attending to her mother during her illness.

The comments made by Pūjya Gurudev while he was watching tennis on TV or video have been used to draw out their philosophical meanings — as we understood them. The conversations relating to tennis were actual exchanges as recorded in a diary. Rudite Emir and my son Jujhar Singh gave invaluable advice, especially for the tennis-related narrative.

Throughout the book, Pūjya Gurudev Swami Chinmayananda is referred to as either 'Swamiji' or 'Gurudev.'

Swamiji watching tennis on TV in Sidhbari with devotees

Swamiji playing tennis with Dwaraknath Reddy

Swamiji playing tennis

Final Score: LOVE ALL!

TEACHINGS BY SWAMI CHINMAYANANDA

Swami Chinmayananda noticed a lady devotee who was looking lost while watching a tennis match on television and asked, "You don't know this game?" "No, Swamiji!" replied the devotee. "Similarly, if you don't know the game of life," said Swamiji, "there is no 'maza' (joy) in it! Play the game of life, play whatever part you have been called upon to play. But never forget your greater mission in life and the ultimate goal you want to achieve. Life becomes a sport once you have learned the art of adding silver edges around the clouds that float in and out of your life's path. Sorrow turns into smiles, pain into pleasure, discord into melody — when the mind is silent in unshaken faith in Him, who always protects, who alone really IS in everything, everywhere, ever."

The game of tennis is being played in the courtyard of life. The coach (Guru) is Pūjya Gurudev Swami Chinmayananda. The scene is Sidhbari, in Himachal Pradesh, India. Swamiji makes comments about the tennis match, and the players are seen on the television screen, but he is actually addressing the devotees sitting around him!

As a young person, Swamiji played tennis, rode horses, and loved sports in general. Later, after he became a Swami, when he was ill and was commanded by doctors to rest and avoid talking, he would watch tennis on television or on video. But he always remained a teacher and would employ whatever he was watching to teach Vedānta. It was — and is — a new way to understand Vedānta — through tennis!

> "A literature which has a deeper meaning of the sublime, other than the superficial word meaning, is called mystic literature. All scriptures successfully communicate the Truth (God) by employing this type of mysticism." – Swami Chinmayananda

> "I am by training a religious man, by experience a Vedāntin, by inclination a Bhakta, in temperament a Karma Yogi, and in practice an Integral Yogī. I am committed to the impossible theory of *Love All*." – Swami Chinmayananda

STEP 1

HOW TO LIVE WITH YOURSELF

*S*ilent calls from the depth of man to achieve, to fulfill, to identify with entire life is called the cry of the Spirit.

-Swami Chinmayananda

1

Wake Up, Sampras!

"Wake up, Sampras!" Swamiji advised the tennis player in December 1991, while watching him lose a game on television in Sidhbari. But Sampras did not wake up. He went on to lose another game! Swamiji then gave him some philosophical advice, which Sampras did not even hear! "Why are you so sleepy?" He asked Sampras. Exasperated, Swamiji almost gave up on Sampras, except for one last try. "Oh, Sampras! Why are you so sleepy? What can your Guru do if you are like that? It is not so difficult. Wake up!" It was a match between Pete Sampras and Guy Forget.

When Pūjya Gurudev Swami Chinmayananda uttered the word 'Guru,' instead of 'coach,' it dawned on us that through his tennis commentary, he was speaking to all of us sitting there! We, the devotees, were the Sampras he was addressing! Sampras, Lendl, or Wheaton and Courier, who were the greats of the time, stand for each one of us whose alertness had temporarily gone!

We were not supposed to talk too much to Swamiji, as doctors had forced a three-month rest period due to his heart condition, but we wanted to sit in his presence. So almost all of us were either watching the tennis matches with him or were sitting in meditation. Many of us used to sit in that hall for long periods in a cross-legged position. From his enforced silence, Swamiji was coaching us in our match against the mind. From his periodic tennis commentaries, we were getting direct instruction on how to win in spiritual life and, particularly, in meditation.

This section — 'Wake Up, Sampras!' — is a call to man to follow the spiritual path. If you want to win (in any game, and especially in this game of life), you have to be awake, alert, and vigilant. Here, in the night of the senses, where man is so caught up in its ensnaring dreams, a wake-up call is imperative — and the greatest blessing.

Commenting on the *Kaṭha Upaniṣad* mantra (1.3.14) — "Arise and Awake" — Pūjya Gurudev Swami Chinmayananda says, "In this mantra, we have the world-famous call of the spiritual kingdom — the call of hope and glory — to man rotting in his dejections and sorrows. Arise, awake — O Man! Turn toward the brilliant sunlit land of perfection. Walk the path and reach the glorious summit from where you can experience that your sense of limitations and imperfections, hopes and desires, successes and failures, loves and hatreds, birth and death were all but a gruesome midsummer night's dream!

"Rude shocks in life, such as loss of property, sudden bereavements, disappointments in love, and such other causes may temporarily make us realize the falsity of the values lived by us in our day-to-day lives of competition and selfishness. Man, under this stress in life, comes to feel the hollowness of life and, for the time being, comes to entertain a seemingly healthy detachment! But this is only a passing mood.

"Hence the sages cry out, 'Awake,' meaning that the one who has, under the lash of circumstances, come to accomplish the command 'Arise,' should try his best to come to a fuller realization of what has actually happened within him in his personality, and thus fully get himself awakened. Challenges come in life and they should not cow us down. They are meant to sharpen our abilities and make us wake up.

"Wake up and dance in joy! The dull relief of sleep is not the cure we are demanding."

THE CALL TO PLAY

We do not need to await a 'call' from the Divine. The Divine is forever calling. But, sadly, we rarely 'hear' the call. This call can only be heard in the quietude of an integrated heart. "Come one step forward — I will take a hundred toward you!" says the Lord. That one step means, "Take the time to listen," but generally we have no time, no inclination. Vedānta tells us that Self-realization is the birthright of every one of us under the Divine Constitution — not the result of imagination. But we don't have the time or the correct means to inquire. When the spiritual urge in man begins to take shape, invariably God's guidance comes in the form of a teacher or sublime literature. The guidance of the teacher is a 'call' to us to play the game of life in the spirit of dedicated action with Self-unfoldment as the goal!

Swami Chinmayananda:

Of all the living creatures, man alone can gain here intimations from Perfection, imperceptible but compelling, and in the irrepressible enchantment of which he revolts against the weaknesses of his flesh, the wanderings of his mind, and the brutalities of his intellect. No doubt, at this moment, he is a hapless victim of these saboteurs within himself. But at the same time, he listens in himself to a constant whispering of a deeper call — a sad enchanting tune of an unearthly harmony somewhere deep within himself, a voiceless tune, a wordless song, a dumb whisper, a passionless thirst which goads him, almost whipping him to walk an unknown righteous path to reach again an unknown Goal! Even so, mightier forces of denser appeal and grosser satisfactions of greater urges drive him down to walk consciously a different path, which is away from the great goal that constantly beckons him from afar… far… afar!

The Lord is our own heart. To deny Him is to deny ourselves. You may leave Him, but He will not leave you. Even that rejection of Him is a stage through which all of us must go to purify our thoughts to ultimately reach Him within us!

One who feels charmed by the call of Vedānta, who can appreciate its arguments, who feels a sympathetic understanding of the ideal indicated, is indeed at the very end of his transmigrations, the product of an entire evolutionary past. If he makes use of his present chance with diligent and careful application, Vedānta guarantees success to him. This is a call to man to throw off his lethargy, his dejections, his sentiments of self-pity, and to wake up to face life and, through understanding, to grow fast to reach the Goal.

Listen. Just Listen. The Eternal Flute plays nonstop to those who know how to listen. You can. Try.

As soon as the student reaches the Master, he is washed clean of all his traditional beliefs. This is, indeed, a kind of shock therapy by which the student is brutally shaken out of the deep ruts into which he may have fallen and shown new dimensions of thought along the right, straight path.

A thousand learned pandits in a hundred years can perhaps bring about what only a true Guru can accomplish with a smile, a wink, for the devotees around him. The spiritual journey is not a revolution, but an evolution.

Letter to ***Gauri Menon:*** When the world is weeping in rains, when blind despair is darkening our bosom, in the prison house of the body, the Divine is born … the spiritual urge is born.

When a sincere student meets his or her teacher, the flame that is ignited, perhaps with one sentence, is instantaneous:

Swamini Shivapriyananda: Coming from the secular Western environment, I did not seek spirituality, and, moreover, carried a strong aversion to religion. But wonder of wonders! In 1981, looking for a holistic approach to life, I landed at Gurudev's camp. Ten days later, inspired and intellectually infatuated, I was ready to go to India. As the time to leave was approaching, the fear was creeping in. "Where was I going? Is it a trap? Am I getting into a cult, or some strange Indian religion?" With those doubts in mind a day before I was to leave, I approached Gurudev. "What is this Vedānta? Is it philosophy, or is it religion?" He answered: "Vedānta is the science of life. It is the art of living. It is philosophy. It is religion. It is 'tat tvam asi' and much, much more." What a reply!

Sometimes it is the development of ideas and, finally, a sentence that hits home:

Swamini Umananda: I met Swamiji in France, in August 1983, during a spiritual retreat organized by a Franco-Indian Cultural Center, which had invited Swamiji. I had been trained as a yoga teacher in that center and I was working there as a volunteer. The director introduced me: "Swamiji, this is Christiane; she will translate." I joined hands in the Indian way. He did not say a word; he just looked at me deeply and gravely. I felt the penetrating gaze reading far into me, like in an open book. What an experience! To be seen as we are by someone who nevertheless continues to love us! Throughout the week I was commissioned to look after Swamiji. Every moment, every contact, every interaction with him was a seed of change. This is as true for the lectures as for the 'ordinary' moments of everyday life. I remember the shock that the lectures had been: sitting at the foot of the dais, I was not losing a single word, thrilled by the ideas Swamiji developed, captivated by the beauty of the message he delivered, filled up with joy by his jokes. I then felt that I had been waiting all my life for such an elevating message, such a positive and dynamic vision of life, such words of hope and freedom, such a sublime thought. I did not understand everything, far from it, but what I understood was uplifting.

While listening to his teaching, I felt a very strong call to the spiritual life. He invited us enthusiastically to spirituality: "Turn your heart to God!" These words are etched in my heart and were the seeds of a new life. The impact was very strong, renewed at each lecture, and this determined the choices taken afterward.

Personal transformation is the essence of the relationship between teacher and student. The depth of this transformation depends simply on our faith in the Master. The more we have faith, the more we are willing to change. This process of transformation is based on: love, transparency, commitment, and surrender.

Sometimes his way of life inspires:

Ācāryas Gaurang and Darshana Nanavaty: In April 1975, we attended Gurudev's talks in Seattle. The way he explained [Vedānta] was so inspiring — deep down, we had a thirst to learn about Hinduism. Still I thought, "A Swami who jokes so much must surely be here only for the money." Sure enough, just before the final day of the lecture series, they passed out the Guru-dakṣiṇā envelopes (student's offering to the Teacher). I told Darshana, "See, what I thought is turning out right." Anyhow, we could not deny that we were getting drawn and were totally absorbed in his teachings. Then, on another day, we saw Chuck Schuetz, a devotee, preparing an afternoon snack for Gurudev — he was applying mirchi powder and butter to the bread. I told myself, "If this Swami wants spicy food, he should have stayed in India." So, when we came to know that we could invite the Swami for bhikṣā, we did not offer to host Gurudev. The next time we met Gurudev and on our first trip with him, I eagerly asked him, "Can I bring you tea in the morning?" I was envisioning a 6:00 A.M. teatime; then he took me by surprise, "Okay, bring it to me at 4 o'clock." A little taken aback, I again foolishly persisted: "Should I then wake you up at 3:30 A.M.?" not knowing how early Gurudev began his days! The next morning, when we went to his room a little before 4:00 A.M., we saw the door to his room ajar. There he was at his desk, with a stack of letters already written and waiting to be mailed. It dawned on us, "Here is a Swami who lives what he teaches." Our respect for him grew.

Sometimes it is the penetrating look that sees within and touches one's heart:

Swamini Amritananda: As a young seeker of the Truth, I traveled to India in search of a Guru, but did not find one. However, someone gave me a copy of Gurudev's *Gītā*. Back in Australia, Gurudev was giving talks at Melbourne University, and I attended two of them. I had made plans to return to India and decided to attend his camp in Sidhbari. When I reached there, the camp had been canceled due to Indira Gandhi's assassination. There were just a handful of people there. Soon, Gurudev arrived and I had the opportunity to meet him and spend time with him. I was ushered into his kuṭiyā where he sat alone with his eyes closed, relaxing. He opened his eyes, and with a penetrating look, asked me a few questions. I plucked up courage to ask him a question: "I know that everything is impermanent in this world. Is there a possibility that even God could be impermanent?" He replied, "You have a yacht in the ocean, and on it are various objects — the helmsman, a dog, a bicycle, a torch, and a green parrot. What upholds them?" "The yacht?" I replied. "What upholds the yacht?" "The ocean." "What is the substratum for the ocean?" "The earth." "And what upholds the earth? Know that the Lord is the substratum of everything." This is the teaching I received in that first meeting with Gurudev. (Incidentally, I grew up yachting with my family, had a dog, a bicycle, and a green parrot!) He told me about the Vedānta course in Mumbai and asked me to go there. He said I would meet an exquisite teacher who would remove all my doubts. That teacher was Pūjya Guruji Swami Tejomayananda.

Swamiji knew exactly where to find a person's heart and how to touch it:

Swami Prashantananda: It is a cold, bleak, foggy day. I am sitting by a bright fire. I pick up a twig and throw it, but it falls a few inches short of the flame. Nothing seems to happen; then suddenly, the twig is aflame. Something similar happened to me about fifty-three years ago. My father had been asked to listen to a young Swami who spoke about the *Gītā* in English. He drafted me to drive him to the hall. He told me to sit and wait for him. After suffering nearly an hour of boredom in the 1950 Ford, I became curious. I went inside and saw an orange-clad figure sitting on the dais. I have absolutely no recollection of what I heard. Did this twig burst into flame? It appears so. Early next morning I hunted him down. Swamiji was sitting on a mat in a small upstairs room of a huge house. He asked me my name and where I lived. When I said that I was from Rewa, he wondered whether I had visited Khajuraho. On my replying in the affirmative, he inquired if I had any small sculpture from there. By a fortunate coincidence, my younger brother had just returned and brought a beautiful Urvashi (angel) head from Khajuraho. I rushed home to get it. He looked at it for a while and asked, "Can I keep it?" I happily handed it over even as the shadow of an impending fraternal clash loomed in front of me. If you visit Tapovan Kuti in Uttarkashi, you will see the Urvashi head on the low parapet wall of the veranda. After that, Swami Chinmayananda became a part of my life, a part that has grown bigger and bigger. The firewood just burns. Divinity just shines.

If the mind is not closed, but 'listens' to a teacher, one's life is changed:

Sarv Singh: Gurudev had come to Cypress College in California for a yajña. I did not know much about 'this Swami,' but my wife, Rashmi, insisted that I must accompany her. I sat in the last row near the door, intending to leave for a soda after the five 'promised minutes' were over. The lecture was inspiring, mesmerizing, and very scientific. Here was a Swami providing so much information about the body–mind–intellect that it appealed to my engineering mind. Where had I been all these years? He was talking science. I told my wife that I was coming back the next day! On Day 2, I sat in the front row, taking notes, totally focused on every word he said. In just three days, I found out that the Vedas offer so much knowledge about life that I did not know. On Day 3, I went looking for him and prostrated at his feet. He ignored me and kept on walking. Several years later at Sidhbari, he told Rashmi, "Sardarji surrendered first." That encounter at Cypress College changed the direction of my life.

STOP, LOOK, AND SEE

As human beings, we tend to look outward, to be extrovert, and to see the forever-changing world as real, and to see ourselves as limited. Not to know our true nature is ignorance. Most of us do not realize the implications of this great ignorance. We see the paradox of life around us, the comfort and misery, the intelligence and destruction, but life passes by without us even wanting to inquire about the world, ourselves and God – who we really are, or if there is a remedy or a higher purpose in life other than sleeping, eating, and enjoying.

Swami Chinmayananda:

Human life has been given to us unasked. We are blasting it and blaspheming it in a thousand different ways.

Life's beauty depends upon the beauty of the philosophy upon which life is built. If the foundations are false, the edifice, however strongly built, will prove to be in no way better than a castle of cards.

The ideal of ourselves is wonderful. The actuality of ourselves is despicable. Religion is a challenging call to dynamic living.

There is no harm if we possess things of the world, but it would be a tragedy if the things of the world possess us. We think we can gain our physical, mental, and intellectual satisfaction from various things and their arrangements. But there is a touch of sorrow in the greatest joy in this world. He who seeks happiness outside himself will never find satisfaction. It is an illusion to think that more comfort means more happiness. Life looked at through distorted equipment naturally gives a distorted vision.

Prosperity with no peace within is a calamity, gruesome and terrible. Amid the sirens of our industries, the thuds of our modern missiles, the devastating powers of nature that we have discovered and released for our destruction, we do not lend our ears to the thundering truths declared by wise men.

Each today is an added link in the endless chain of dead and gone yesterdays. The lengthening chain continues growing, by adding to itself link after link all the yesterdays. In the stream of time, years roll by one after another. Caught in the flow, we move with it, age with it, and die in time. If only you touch the ground, position yourself firmly and bathe therein, with every dip you come out cleansed, purified, and breathe freshness and dynamism. When you search for the ground, the Lord, you reach That which does not move with the flow, but supports it all the same.

There is a purpose, definite and sure, in each one's arrival here, be it a worm or be it a king. The entire universe with all its happenings is a university educating the ego to grow and evolve into the ultimate realization of its essential Reality, but people want to forget their sorrows, not remove their sorrows.

This ego, thoughtlessly assuming an independent and separate existence for itself, naturally sees the whole world as a mighty, endless array of things and beings, of circumstances and situations — all of them inimical to itself. It feels lonely; in its loneliness it is overwhelmed by fear. A mind that is not evolved will have these five: misapprehension, fear, grief, despondency, and conceit.

Don't flounder your entire life on flimsy things, on passing fancies of eating well and clothing well or showing off of indulgences. This is not the goal and purpose of life. Learn to expand your mind. Experience the grandeur of the world in which you are living and learn to be of service to mankind, even at the risk of starvation and death, if necessary!

It is much better to starve and fly about wherever you want, than to be very well fed in a cage. Open your eyes. Burst your shell. Spread your wings and fly.

You alone can do it!

The issue is not whether one is an atheist or a believer, the problem arises from not having the boldness to see all sides of life clearly and inquire into the purpose of one's existence.

Swami Tejomayananda: Gurudev saw the aristocratic life, but it never fascinated him. On one hand, he had many doubts and questions about religion, yet there was always the thirst to know what the Truth is. One may feel that he was an atheist, which may be true in some sense, but not completely, because if he was, he would not have inquired. Gurudev always had great interest in understanding life and its various facets, in being able to identify with different strata of people. As a journalist, he also wrote thought-provoking articles under the pseudonym 'Mochi,' which means cobbler.

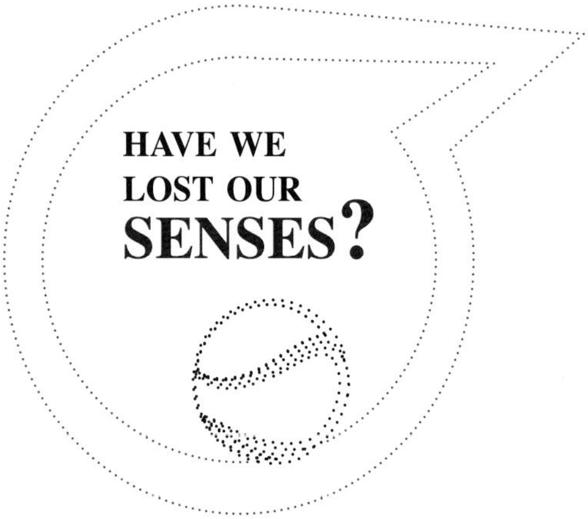

Unfulfilled desires are the root cause of anger. Anger is related to the other negative emotions of fear, despondency, and sorrow. Negative emotions are harmful at all levels of our personality, especially anger when it is expressed toward other beings. At the physical level, anger causes health problems; at the emotional level, it causes anxiety and anguish, and at the intellectual level, it disrupts peace and internal balance. If we give in to anger, we are harming ourselves instead of helping ourselves. The example of anger can be applied to all negative emotions. Giving in to negative emotions leads us to our descent on what is called 'the ladder of fall.'

Swami Chinmayananda:

Man's definition of likes and dislikes is not permanent. He moves from object to object. From the joy of today springs forth the sorrow of tomorrow. The very thing that gives you joy putrefies in your pocket.

The more we gratify our desires, the more they multiply. Desire for the possession of anything becomes an obsession when it grows out of proportion.

Desires are never quenched by enjoyment. At the intellectual level, it is a desire. At the mental level, it is a thought, and at the physical level, it is an action. Satan is not an inexplicable force but our own animal urges expressing themselves as desires in our hearts. Desire does not, in itself, execute its follies; it deludes the sense organs, or the mind, or the intellect, and orders them to do the mischief. We think we can gain our physical, mental, and intellectual satisfaction from various things and their arrangements. When an individual's mind, as a result of its false philosophy, gets dissipated in dreams, his intellect also falls into a deplorable condition. Poignancy of sorrow is felt when the frequency of thoughts is too much. Beyond a certain frequency the mind goes crazy. Dissipation is today the world's mental disease. When you allow yourself to see and think about the tragic life you are leading, then changes begin to happen.

Where desire is throttled, anger is natural. When you are in such a situation, at least after the wave of anger has subsided, reconsider the entire situation and try to mentally live and relive a hundred times the same situation — all the time see that you keep yourself smiling. Where ego is arrogantly high, the anger constantly lashes in and destroys your inner peace. Learn to surrender. Learn not to worry what others say about you. Your glory is not dependent upon the words of others. If you are good and others are not able to recognize it, it is their foolishness; why should you get disturbed by it? That would be absurd. To be angry is to revenge the faults of others on ourselves.

Suppose you have got the value of 'I hate.' You have got the freedom to hate anybody. The person you hate sleeps well, eats well, but it is you who gets exhausted by hating. Most educated people love humanity; it is the next-door neighbor that they hate and detest. The sense of angry vengefulness can bring endless disturbances into us, but the moment we forgive those who have done harm to us, mental calm prevails.

In response to a despondent plea for guidance, ***Swamiji*** *wrote this lovingly firm reply:*

I read through your miserable letter indicating and clearly reflecting how you have managed to blast your life's possibilities merely because of your unsteadiness. To such an individual, life can only be a tragedy, reaching nowhere. To fulfill your great desires and visions, and in order to translate your ideas into action, you must have perseverance — to meet all challenges that might arise *en route*. Never can the path of success be spread with carpets. This requires a lot of personal discipline in you. If you learn the art of wanting to fulfill every fancy in your life, you become a slave to your mind, and a slave can only struggle and never succeed. In order to cultivate this willpower in you, you better start living a rigid life of taming yourself. One meal a day; give up coffee, tea; I do not know whether you are smoking, give up the consumption of every toxin. Every day, go to the nearest temple, pray, and return. After one month of this regimen, start seriously studying the book *Self-Unfoldment*, which is published by Chinmaya Publications. Study only about five pages a day and give a lot of thought to it. So far, I was trying to hold a mirror to show you in all your ugliness and error in judgment. If you follow the positive system that I have now indicated above, it is a guaranteed path to come out of the mental cloud in which you are now lurking. If and when you undertake this self-discipline, you may start writing to me every month of your progress and your difficulties.

*Before allowing anger to take hold, one should pause the mind and count to ten, to calculate whether the anger is even justified. In this context, **Swami Ramananda** recalls an anecdote:*

Gurudev would often narrate memorable anecdotes during his yajñas. One such story was about a family in suburban Mumbai — consisting of a husband, wife, and their eight-year-old daughter. The man was an executive in a well-known company. His lunchbox from home came through the efficient *dabba* system. One day, on opening it, he found the contents totally unsatisfactory. He reached home in great rage and angrily inquired where his wife was. He was met by his little girl, who told him that mother was ill. The mother feebly informed him that their eight-year-old daughter, under her direction, had cooked his lunch. The man immediately felt ashamed of his outburst and of having lost a golden opportunity to appreciate his daughter. He became a victim of his own anger and felt sorrowful, but the damage was done.

ARE YOU LIVING OR EXISTING?

From sunrise to sunset, we are confronted with choices. Often, we fear that the choice may turn out to be wrong, so we hesitate to act, and therefore don't move forward. This is called existing, not living. With every sunset, one day of life is gone. In fact, even if our choice turns out to be wrong, we move forward rather than just existing like a stone. As our understanding deepens, we learn by mistakes, and learn the knack of making right choices. The easiest rule to follow is to live up to whatever convictions we have and make choices in line with those convictions. It is our convictions that have the power to fulfill, that supply the fuel and energy to achieve.

Swami Chinmayananda:

Life means activity. Where activity has ended, death has entered. In active life alone can we progress or deteriorate. Therefore, activity is the very cornerstone of life. Life is a piece of art which can be made beautiful and polished, chiseled and shaped, by our own careful self-effort. This is the way. Periods of activity create man. This creative period depends upon the type of activity we venture upon. Moment to moment you have a choice: to create a thought or destroy a thought in you. Every one of you has a value for something — certain convictions that you have reached in your intellect as to what should be the direction of your life. Everybody exists. It is only a few who live. To live, you should have an ideal.

Due to the poverty of our own intellectual convictions, we are forever living other people's ideas. Knowledge no doubt comes from another person or books, but once having assimilated it, it becomes our own. Read and understand the higher life through your own independent thinking. Let the scriptures guide your thoughts. Take your own time in building up your convictions and, thereafter, let the Lord enrich you with the heroism to live up to them. Die if necessary for your convictions; there is nothing more sacred for the rational man than his own convictions.

We, the desirers, are beggars in the world for happiness. Come out of the womb of plurality into a new birth. In outer space the sun is burning away. Window gazing satisfies an idler alone. Walk out into the world. Sweat and toil. Earn and save. And, rich with the fruits of your own honest labor, return to the shop. Push open the door. Walk in. Approach the counter. Order the thing of your fascination. Come to possess it as your own. So, too, never allow yourself to feel satisfied by recognizing glories in somebody's life. When you admire the meekness of Christ, the compassion of Buddha, the gorgeous joys of Kṛṣṇa, the dignified sufferings of Rāma, the wisdom of Vaśiṣṭa, or the dynamic philosophy of Śaṅkara, never sit back only to gaze at them and in futile wonderment merely come to believe in them, but feel the urge to cultivate such a noble and divine personality in yourself.

A life of dynamic action is always superior to a passive life of slothful inaction. A person who does not work is a misery to himself, a tragedy to his community and a liability to his nation. Man is not born to revel in idleness. Life will whip the idle on the road of right or wrong activity, and thereby evolve him steadily to a state of joy, characterized by dynamic outer activity yet inner calm and peace. To be moody and to drag yourself through life is a painful, unproductive existence.

The Lord has created and given us perfect equipment, but as we grow, we neglect our inner equipment, and it gets clogged with false values and imaginary discontentment. To retune the equipment is living a spiritual life.

There is a preponderance of your own tendencies in early morning. A sāttvika man is sāttvika at that time. He will do japa or studies. A rājasika one will jog and exercise. And a tāmasika one will sleep at that time. The sleeper is a slave to negative living, while the knower is the master in a positive existence. Tāmas is born of ignorance. Under the influence of tāmas, man's intellectual capacity to discriminate between right and wrong gets veiled, and he starts acting as if under some hallucination or stupefaction. Such a man lives in indolence, heedless of higher purpose, and asleep to the nobler and divine aspirations of life. There is no consistency of purpose, brilliance of thought, tenderness of emotion, or nobility of action in an individual who comes under the influence of tamoguṇa.

Millions and trillions of spermatozoa and ova are produced, but only a few of them are united to create a human being. Of all the countless possibilities, to be born a human is a rare chance, indeed. Humans are, to an extent, free from nature, in evolving themselves. Human beings alone, of all the species of the living kingdoms, can hasten their own evolution by cooperating with the great eternal scheme of things around them. Physically, they have evolved to perfection, and nature has nothing more to do to improve them. Their next lap of evolution awaits them at the level of their mind and intellect, and this is a process in which nature cannot help them at all. The program for progress in yourself as an individual is called spirituality.

What sort of achievers are these men of detachment? — asks a Postal Lesson Course student:

Q: When man identifies with Consciousness, his intellectual pursuits, emotional attachments, and physical cravings wither and fall away. Is it not the creation of another 'stone' man, please?

Swamiji: Your question is obviously answered by the dynamic and beautiful life of a Jesus, of a Mohammed, of a Buddha, of a Vivekananda. I am sure if every man of realization can be as productive as Vyāsa, the world needs at least a half dozen of such men of dynamic activity!

A question was asked: "What if the intellect could not decide and come to a judgment about the ethical course of an action. What should one do at such a juncture?" ***Swamiji:*** Like the infant, the intellectual entity in you also must learn slowly through the discipline of life to come to a right decision through a series of conscious, deliberate, and perhaps sorrowful wrong decisions. The scriptures advise us: When in doubt, implicitly follow what other Masters have decided when encountering similar problems, or follow implicitly what other cultured and decent people around would do under similar circumstances.

On seeking sources of guidance, Swamiji expanded on advice given in the Taittirīya Upaniṣad:

Do as the scriptures say.

In case the scriptures are silent about the situation: Do as other cultured people are doing. One should follow the advice of those wise people in society who are the accredited champions of our culture. A wise man should be a man capable of independent thinking and correct judgment. He must be one who is not merely secular in his concept of things, but who has respect for the sanctity of the sacred. He must not only be a man of independent, unbiased judgment and be truly religious, with nothing to gain, but he must also be a man with full freedom to express his ideas. Such fearless men of dedication, firmly established in their ideas and stoutly independent, are the true guides of our culture, and you may follow them whenever there is a doubt regarding either your action or your conduct.

If that does not resolve the problem: Ask your Guru.

If your Guru is not there: Close your eyes and ask yourself, and then act according to your own conviction. Why are you afraid? With whatever data is before you, go ahead and choose an action and carry it through. Even if the action chosen turns out to be a mistake, what does it matter? What do a few mistakes matter in one's long span of life? From the experience of the mistakes, learn to discriminate more keenly.

When our
motives and
intentions are
noble all our actions become
brilliant & good.

2

Focusing on the Goal

One morning, as we watched tennis games with Swamiji during his period of recuperation, he said, "Silence the fellow from talking unnecessarily, and bump him off!" He was referring to the commentator who went on talking between two tennis games, while the players wiped themselves with their towels and changed sides. Swamiji would ask us to fast-forward the commentators' portion each time, saying, "It will do away with the useless chattering. They talk of all sorts of things not connected to the game!"

The commentary during tennis matches is supposed to entertain viewers watching on television. It contributes nothing to the players or the game. For the seeker, the "useless chattering" represents all kinds of thoughts not conducive to spiritual living. By turning the mind to the goal, and avoiding dissipating thoughts, the chatter of the extroverted mind is eventually 'bumped off'!

*O*ne single ideal can transform a listless soul
into a towering leader of men.

GOAL OF LIFE

When we are inspired by a goal, we outperform our own abilities. Gurudev encouraged individuals to pursue a goal no matter what it was, secular or sacred. As a person evolves, so do the goals. He often humorously said that an average lawyer, Mohandas Karamchand Gandhi in South Africa, after being inspired by the ideal of independence for India from British rule, became a Mahātmā whom millions followed! The activity put forth in achieving a goal helps in purifying and focusing the mind. The higher the goal, the greater is the purification, and the greater is the price to be paid in terms of effort and sacrifice. The highest and final goal of human life is Self-realization. In the beginning our activities are inevitably selfish, but selfish activity is better than no activity. When our vision expands to include our family and then the community, the mind gets purified further, and our hearts and minds expand to think of the national interests and then world interests. The highest is when a person sees that the Self in him is the Self everywhere. This is Self-realization. Listening to the words of the Guru and saints helps us to understand that central message of the scriptures.

Swami Chinmayananda:

Let a man of intelligence earn as much as he can, distribute according to his abilities, and enjoy as much as is his desserts — popularity, affection, consideration, and even reverence from others. But let him not misunderstand this to be the very goal of life. At the same time, let him also earn inner peace and self-sufficiency, and let him savor the inner peace and tranquility, totally independent of the entire clamoring crowd around him, which is ever trying to fatten his vanities! The real achievement is to be gained in one's own personal inner contemplation, long before the world comes to reject him.

It is very necessary to discover a great purpose or goal in life. Having gained that goal or ideal for which you have concentrated all your education — apply yourself to it, whether it be political or economic. It should be an ideal that you have chosen according to your heart, not an ideal that somebody has given you, but that which appeals to you the most; then from it, a new enthusiasm comes to you. When there is enthusiasm, then sincerity, ardor, and consistency of purpose automatically follow and a new column of energy arises in you. The goal has to be something higher than yourself, your family, or worldly comfort. If there is a social vision that moves us forward, we discover within ourselves a new source of energy. Dynamism is generated when we discover for ourselves a goal and dedicate ourselves to it with reverence and love. So, with tireless enthusiasm, strive on to reach your goal. Without a goal, the best in you can never come out.

By acting and thinking in consistency with your goal you will surely reach it, just as Napoleon Bonaparte did when he asserted that he would become emperor of France [and actualized it].

If you can dream things, in you lies also the power to make them true. If you can constantly think of them, the splendid things will come, through you, at last, to you. You can pass through all obstacles, clear all hurdles. Let your faith in the Highest drive you on to success — to gain the impossible. If you can continuously dream of a thing and act, it becomes yours. Let your dreaming be a flight of steps to the very sun — for dreams do become reality, at the magic touch of faith and work. The ideal you can realize, the promise you can fulfill. The yawning gulf that seems to widen between you and your goal, you can always leap across. When faith is firm, you can move mountains.

To channelize the resources of youth — the energy to work, the daring to plan, the enthusiasm to conceive and a shy impatience to act — the heroic youth must be trained to study the problems of life and to evaluate each of them correctly. Each one of these can release an avalanche of power and strength, energy and vitality, thought and action. This calls for a special mental balance in each and an unerring intellectual self-application. With such a balanced mind and intellect, the youth will be able to arrive at potentially creative judgments and constructive conclusions. In the very midst of confusing situations, how does one train the mind and intellect to evaluate and judge explosive conditions, threatening challenges, and suffocating situations? This know-how is explained exhaustively in the *Bhagavad-gītā*.

All spectacular successes were achieved in little courageous steps taken with self-confidence and faith in the nobility of the final goal chosen. Dedicated work is a means for the inner purification of one's vāsanās.

Because we are immortal, we cannot accept the happening of death. Because we are of the nature of ānanda (happiness), we cannot accept any sorrow or pain in our life. Permanent happiness can only come from that which is permanent. From the futile things or limited and temporary things, we can expect only temporary happiness.

Return back on the road by which from the Supreme you reached here and realize thy own Self.

To one who has a clear notion of the goal, the purpose, and the teachings of meditation, this immutable state can be reached with no effort or obstacles.

Self-realization is the unveiling ceremony of the Divinity within. To realize the Self is itself the greatest worship that one can offer to the Self. The greatest adoration that we can give to the Supreme, or to a Teacher, is to become It. Beyond the ordinary goals of life, beyond all metaphysical speculations, transcending all concepts of time and space, far removed from the tumults of life and death dwells the majestic glory of the infinite Self in Its own unique majesty.

Self-realization is not an impossibility. It is the heritage of humans. Fulfill your human birth and your goal of life. Fulfill the very program of evolution. Proceed to your next stage, and thereafter proceed again. Let the ultimate end be in the background, to enthuse, to direct, to guide. Think over these ideas. It is immaterial whether you are a Hindu, Christian, or Muslim. What we are searching for is this vital center in ourselves — call it Paramātman, Father in Heaven, Allah, Buddha, or Life. Names may be different, but the State of Consciousness is one.

Swamiji answers a question from a student of the Postal Lesson Course[1] about how to develop sincere dedication to the goals and ideals outlined in Vedānta.

Q: How should we set an ideal for ourselves without first appreciating such an ideal? For example, Gandhi's work was based on the service of the Lord. I cannot, however, serve the Lord because I cannot appreciate Him to such an extent. I can, however, appreciate myself, and therefore I would like to set an ideal based on the understanding of myself. Is this a selfish ideal?

Swamiji: Nobody can have an ideal without first appreciating it. Appreciation comes as a result of study and understanding. You can never appreciate what you don't know. The Lesson Course and the studies that will follow prepare the student to appreciate the ideals. At this moment, you appreciate your ego; all of us — plant, animal, and human — live centered in the ego. This creates unnecessary tension because, as an ego, I have the endless responsibilities of protecting myself from the endless phenomenal universe spread around me. Harmonious living with the universe is not possible where there is selfishness. Then we can only live in endless tensions, stresses, and strains.

Q: The ideal of serving the community gives greater satisfaction than serving yourself. Why is it nobler to serve others rather than oneself?

Swamiji: In order to serve another, you will have to expand yourself to find accommodation for the other in your mind. The more the mind expands and discovers its identity with others around, not only the efficiency of the mind increases, but the joy content in the mind expands. The larger the field of your identification — with child, family, society, country, and the world, and so on — the greater is the sense of satisfaction and inner harmony. The moment you become self-centered in selfishness, then fear, confusion, despair, and a thousand other hosts that disturb the mind flood into your bosom. The above are some of the ideas. Think for yourself. Continue the Lesson Course.

The following personal account by Gurudev, in an interview with Will Noffke and Tom March in the U.S.A. in 1975, illustrates the centrality of a goal to the spiritual journey:

Interviewer: We have many listeners who see Indians coming from India wearing orange robes and don't have the kind of understanding or cannot relate to really what you're trying to do. … What is the spiritual life and how did people like yourself get into it, because you were very active in the world? I think you were a newspaper reporter at one time, you operated in daily life and business, and somehow or the other, you got into spiritual life?

Swamiji: But then you can't say that I'm not active now (laughter)… I am 365 days on my toes. … People expect that I must have had a terrible disappointment in life, a total failure in existence, and therefore I ran to religion as a last recourse of a useless guy. I did not. I was on the search for happiness as any other young man would be, but I had

---

1 Now the Postal Lesson Course is available via email. Contact Administrator, CIF Home Study Courses, at homestudycourses@chinfo.org, or visit www.chinfo.org for the Home Study Courses.

a kink in my mind that after every experiment that I did for happiness — let us say in the evening — my intellect would immediately ask me, "All right, you did it, but what did you get out of it?" ... Then I thought I must score at the university. I tried; I did score. That didn't do it either. Then I thought I must have some power, and I therefore joined the university student movement union and all that. I tried; I became president. There was nothing in it. I joined the political movement, and ultimately I found myself in a jail,[2] and I started thinking, "What is it all about? What did you get, mister, after all your activities?" I thought that this was also a failure.

It was at such a time in my mental mood that I happened to read some spiritual literature. The more I read, the more some bell rang in me. I thought, "This seems to be quite an intelligent affair; let us try to see what it is all about." So I went to an āśrama and started living there as any other student. All the time I was trying to find out the defects and the faults therein. My intention was to write a damning article on how religion is dangerous to society, because I was a socialist. But what happened was that I felt that it was a more intelligent way of living than the other way. So, slowly, slowly, I got myself sucked into it.

So with eyes open, with no blind faith, questioning every step of mine, I reached there because I was honestly seeking that happiness for myself in my life. But generally what happens is that we take it for granted that to do this is happiness: to have a little drink or go to a dance or go to a nightclub or go about having friends — these are all happiness, we think. We take it for granted. ... But if you ask yourself, "Last night I did this: what did I get out of it all?" You are an unhappy man. You got nothing out of it. Ordinarily, people start searching for happiness in the outer world: if I get that girl, if I get that job or that much money... and so on. Now, all these things may be necessary, but ultimately, what you want is peace and joy in your mind. To a smoker, a cigarette may be the means by which he can get happiness; to an alcoholic, it is a drink that gives him that happiness.

So that is how I reached. It's a strange way to reach, but this is how I reached the spiritual life. Thereafter, I started studying, practicing. I found my peace, my happiness. And then I remembered, "Hey, other students of the university must be there, confused and confounded as I was. Why not try to rub a little on them?" Thus, I came down to discuss it with the students, the younger generation, to give them a glimpse of what I had gathered out of it. And thus I started. I thought, I'll do it for a few years, and then I'll go back to my quiet retreat. I have not yet gone back; twenty-three years are over. There's been more and more demand coming. So this is the story. The story is rather disappointing in one sense of the term because there is no girl in it, no son died, no money was lost — which might have led me to surrender myself to the Lord.

---

2 Gurudev was imprisoned during India's freedom struggle for challenging British rule.

***Swami Siddhananda** overheard a conversation, which triggered life-changing insight in a devotee from Delhi, who met Gurudev in the U.S.A. after many years.* "Gurudev, I have been here now for the past many years." "So, what did you come here to do?" asked Gurudev. "I got my bachelor's degree ... " After every sentence, Gurudev asked, "Then?" So he explained all his achievements of getting a doctorate, getting married, getting a big bungalow, children, wealth, and so on. Finally, after everything was exhausted, Gurudev asked him, "Anybody can do those, but what really did you achieve as your own?" He kept quiet and started thinking. After a few months, he left the U.S.A. and went back to New Delhi for his spiritual inquiry. His son related this story.

Swamiji also encouraged people to pursue the goal that they had chosen to help them to grow:

Anil Sachdev: I always wanted to contribute to the holistic economic development of India. I visualized working for industry for fifteen years, and then setting up an organization to assist in creating wealth in an ethical and ecologically sensitive way. When the time came to follow my dream, I found it a new and risky path. I shared my plans with Gurudev and wanted his advice. Before he responded, my mother voiced her anxieties: "Gurudev, Anil is getting a good salary with very good perquisites. Should he set up a consulting business and walk away from a secure future?" Gurudev laughed and said, "Amma, do not worry; one day he will give cars to many others! Anil is inspired to do the Lord's work. So please surrender all your worries to Him." My mother and I knew that we no longer needed to worry even for a moment.

Swamiji was clear and uncompromising about his vision and purpose in life:

Swami Siddhananda: Sacrifice all else for the goal — that is how Gurudev looked at it. Gurudev had siddhis, which he kept under wraps. Many times he performed miracles for his devotees but never paid too much attention to them; neither did he encourage his devotees to pay attention to them. Somebody once asked him why he did not reveal these siddhis. He replied, "Then I cannot teach! That is not my goal! If I start doing miracles, a different crowd comes. My purpose is teaching, which will then stop."

The 'prize' of Realization is infinite and perpetual happiness:

Anjali Singh: When the winner's cup was being presented, I said to Swamiji that my son, Jujhar, thought it was worth spending several years of training for just two minutes of glory. Swamiji said, "That's because Juju is still a child (spiritually young). He is like Edward. When the prince was a boy, he told the King, his father, that he wanted to be a traffic policeman when he grew up. 'Why?' asked the father. 'Because even your car has to stop when I put my hand up!' But Realization is forever. It is not just a two-minute glorious glimpse."

3

Achieving Excellence

"Don't stand there like a sleepy one. Be fully conscious when you come out into the world," said Swamiji to Pete Sampras, who missed some shots. Swamiji always insisted, "The mind should be where the hands are working."

Swamiji insisted that to cultivate this habit, one's attention should be fully on the work at hand, at all times and places. The mind should not be at home when we are sitting in thc office, and it should not be in the office when we have come home. There should be integration of the body and mind in whatever we are doing.

*I*f you bring the entire mind to what you are doing at any given moment, it is yoga, it is pūjā (worship). Each thought, word, and deed should emerge from you bearing the seal of your own recognition.

LIVE EVERY MINUTE

Life is a very precious gift. We are most alive when we are aware of each lived moment. A little reflection confirms that we do not really live the moments of sleep or the moments when our mind is not on what we are doing. While sleeping is necessary for health, inattention in the waking state is time wasted. We truly live only when we make optimum use of our waking hours by being alert. If we are at home and thinking of the office, or at the office and thinking of home, intellectually we are not honoring the precious gift of life in the context of place. When we live in regrets of the past or anxieties about the future, emotionally, we are not honoring or enjoying the gift of life in the context of time.

Swami Chinmayananda:

No hand can make the clock strike for the hours that have passed.

The chariot of Time has no reverse gear. Time lost can never be retrieved. Life is short; the path is long; the pinnacle is very high. The time is little.

Learn to bring your mind to where your hands are working and then see the results: actions then become excellent. Success is the tribute life pays to excellence. Be alert and vigilant. That is the greatest sādhanā.

The present is such a narrow line, where one side of it is in contact with the future and the other side is in contact with the past. The present alone is the time when we can work and achieve, gain and gather, give and serve. In the past, we can now do nothing; in the future, we can now accomplish nothing.

To strive in the present, becoming the architect of the future, is creative living. In this, we employ time. We become the masters of time. To live weeping for the past, wasting the present moments, shuddering with imaginary fears for the future, is self-destructive, suicidal living. In this, time employs us. We then become slaves of time. Measuring time with enjoyments is the privilege of birds and animals. Hunger is their clock. To evaluate time with achievements in life is the glory of dynamic men. Gains point the passage of time. In spite of discomforts to me, how much I served others around me is the secret measure of spiritual life. Nārāyaṇa sevā (serving the Lord) is our watch.

Advice to a young man:

You are growing up to be a man. This is a time in one's life when one can very easily slip into irresponsible enthusiasm of an extrovert life. Be careful. Remember mother, father, and Guru. Let their pure life and love for you inspire you to live always as a master of all temptations around you.

*Advice to **Jujhar Singh**:*

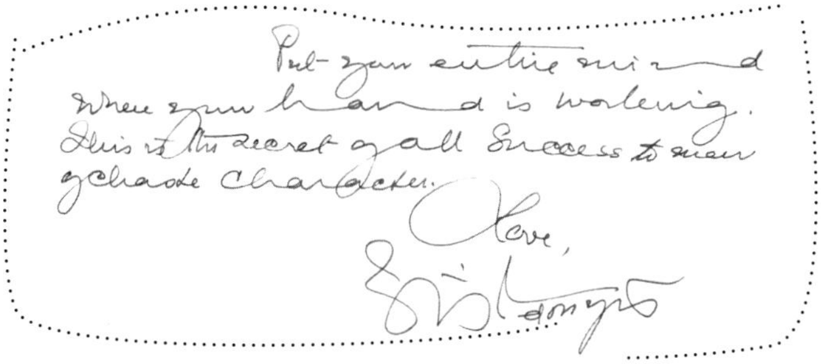
Put your entire mind where your hand is working. This is the secret of all success to man of character.
Love,

A scriptural 'consolation' that the idiosyncrasies of the mind are the mind's own creation:

Swami Tejomayananda: As a brahmacāri, I had gone to Uttarkashi with Gurudev. During the classes, Gurudev expected me to answer all the questions, and that, too, immediately. Mostly I was able to, but sometimes I was not. Gurudev would say, "Are you sleepy?" In order not to feel bad, I would take recourse to verse 33 of *Ātma Bodhaḥ*, which declares that I am not the intellect!

Living in alertness leads to heightened awareness:

Rudite J. Emir: A car chase through the roads of rural California became a key lesson for my spiritual journey. We had just left the small town of Napa, to head out to a Unitarian church some distance away, where Gurudev was to give a lecture. Since I did not have the directions, Gurudev's driver said: "Why don't you just follow my car?" The journey started out well enough, but with each turn Gurudev's car speeded ever faster. I had difficulty keeping up, but I persisted. I arrived on time, feeling thankful that I had survived the frenzied drive. Seldom had I been so attentive at a lecture: with the speedy car chase behind me, my mind was buzzing with heightened alertness. Afterward, Gurudev gave me a long, knowing look. Then I understood the heightened awareness that was expected from me all the time. In his own inimitable way, Gurudev had achieved an unprecedented alertness of mind in me. And he had imparted the lesson with his characteristic touch of humor, as revealed by the driver after the trip: "Swamiji turned the rear-view mirror away from me, toward himself, so he could witness, amid peals of laughter, your attempts not to lose sight of his car!" Gurudev showed us, time and again, the fruits of staying alert. "To listen is not merely to hear," he said. "We in life hear, but very rarely do we know how to listen. To listen is to hear with an intellectual alertness and the attention of awareness."

Ācāryas Gaurang and Darshana Nanavaty: Gurudev often pointed out our errors with humor. For instance, he would write back, "Received your letter with no date..." to people who wrote inattentively.

LIVE IN day-tight COMPARTMENTS

What does living in the 'now' really mean? What is the power of 'now'? Is there no future or past? Or is there only a future that turns into a past and no such thing as 'now'? And what does it mean to live in the 'present'? Answers to questions such as these, offered by Swamiji, are a great means to achievement and a wonderful exercise in contemplation.

Swami Chinmayananda:

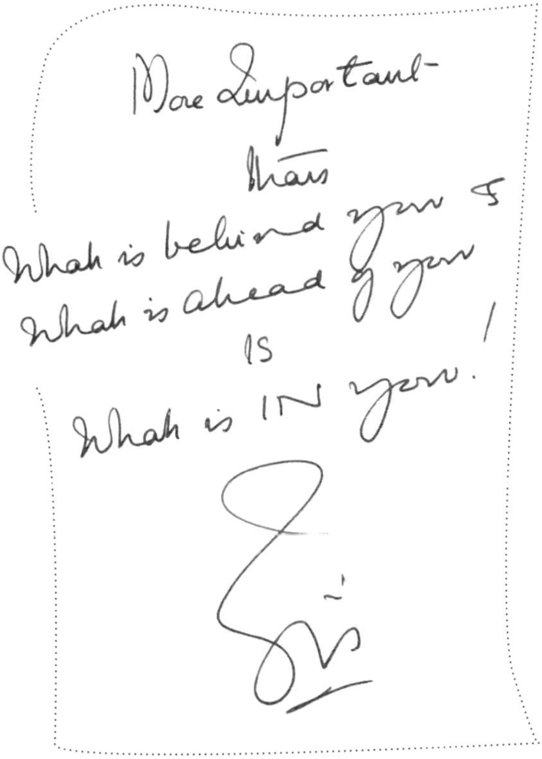

The future tumbling down into the past — that 'tumbling' portion, that point of merger, is called the 'present.' The present, then, may be said to be the future cascading into the past. Really speaking, if you try to capture the present, there is no present; it is ever moving. Before we can grasp the present, it is already the past. But the present alone is the time when we can work and achieve, gain and gather, give and serve. In the dead moments of the past and in the unborn moments of the future, we can never act. These living dynamic present moments are the only fields to be hammered at, wherein are all the glories of life, all the gains in existence. Moment to moment, engage the outgoing mind to live in the present. Completely reject the past. Renounce the future totally.

In meditation, when you are detached from the thoughts, you reach the present; and if you can stay on, the thought flow has already stopped. The content of the present moment is the absolute fullness of the Infinite. "All that was in the past is Brahman; all that will be in the future is also Brahman." That threshold at which the future merges with the past to become the present, that marginal line, that frontier line of the ridge, is not seen now because of the flood of thoughts in the mind. One should try to reach that crucial ridge and *stay there*. In order to do so, I have to allow past thoughts to get exhausted, and I must not allow new thoughts to come. That halt in the thought-current would be the end of the mind (manonāśa). So, where mind is thus annihilated, there is the experience of the Infinitude.

Now the last thought has ended and no new thought is rising. What am I then? — pure, objectless Awareness. Objectless Awareness, or pure Consciousness, is the Present. When I am in the present, there are no thought waves. Allow the present thought to die away. The next thought may be ready to come, but I have no time for it; I am too interested in being in the present. I dive, as it were, between the two waves. Thereafter, at the point where I dived, even if a mountainous wave comes, it will not affect me; I am one with the ocean now.

Eternity is experienced at the sacred depth of the present moment. To live the present, independent of the past and the future, is to experience samādhi, the revealing culmination of meditation. How? It can be reached only through meditation by halting the mind, when you realize the merger of the Universe into yourself. Thereafter, when you come back to the awareness of the body, mind, and intellect, you see the same old world of objects, emotions, and thoughts! But in that dirty world, there is now an aura of divinity: you recognize everything as an expression of the same mighty Self. By the experience of Oneness alone can you realize the ultimate Reality, and not by any other means. He is the Substratum. He is all that was, and He is all that will be. He is this Life within you. This universe is an extension of yourself. This experience is called the highest Reality, the moment of Realization.

Letter to ***Tarachand Chawla:*** "Thank you for your sweet letter full of your foolish, laughable, silly problems. Yes — suppose the sky falls, what will happen? Suppose the sea walks up to your third floor and floods the area — oohh!! What will happen? Stupid. Live today, NOW. Future is in His hands. Just as He, so lovingly looked after you, nurtured and nourished you in the past, He will be your sole protector in the future. So, to worry about it is to doubt His Love!"

Letter to ***Neeru Mehta:*** "Though memories belong to the past, they are in you now. Though hopes and expectations are of the future, they are for you here. In fact, every experience is but here and now. Be that and live in the dynamic present — that is the Law. So fighting against the Law is sin: the specimen or species will be wiped out!! Live the Law and evolve in peace and joy, and rejoice. HA! HA! HA!! HA!! The A-mātra OM!!

Advice for those who want to achieve excellence:

Swami Swaroopananda: I was watching the semifinals of the Wimbledon Tennis Tournament in 1992 with Gurudev in Sidhbari. Looking at Andre Agassi, Gurudev said, "So what if you have not won Wimbledon before? Give up your memories of the past — do not have anxiety for the future — just play the game and be in the present!" Before the tournament finished, I had to leave for Singapore. Andre Agassi was playing Goran Ivanisevic in the finals, and it was night in Singapore when the live match was being relayed. The Singapore ladies, who loved Agassi, were very keen that he win. One of the ladies asked me if I thought whether Agassi would win. "Sure!" I replied. "How can you say that?" she asked. "Because Gurudev has advised him how to win!" After saying that, I comfortably went to sleep, confident that he would. That was the first time Agassi won in Wimbledon!

Perfection, dedication, motivation, and steadfastness connect us to the Higher:

Ruchi Nanavati: It was in 1991 that Gurudev fell ill in Sidhbari and was flown to Jaslok Hospital in Mumbai for treatment. I was fortunate enough to get exclusive time with him through an instrument called TENNIS. For three consecutive days, I watched matches with him. I was totally disinterested in the game, but in the next twenty-seven hours, he taught me all the terms, rules, and scores, and successfully managed to cultivate a lifelong passion for the sport. What stayed with me in and through my life is priceless. His teaching was: *"Give your 100% to everything you are doing, without allowing your mind to wander even for a single moment."* Even though the work may not always be interesting, it has to be done perfectly all the time. Only through perfection, dedication, motivation, and steadfastness will we be able to connect to the Higher.

Advice to senior citizens:

Bharati Sukhtankar: We were at satsaṅga with Swamiji when an elderly man and his wife walked in. "Hanhanh!" said Swamiji. "Tell me, what is the news?" "Nothing much, Swamiji," said the man. "I have retired. My children are settled and my responsibilities are over. But life seems to be dragging. I seem to be just waiting for the final call." Swamiji narrowed his eyes and gave the man a long look. Then he spoke in an even tone. "Your children are settled… you appear to be in good health. And you say life seems to be dragging? Look here, life has just started! Live vigorously a spiritual life. Read the śāstras. Increase your time for japa and contemplation. Serve those around you in whatever capacity you can. Ayyayyayyaaa! The possibilities are endless." He turned to the wife, "Amma, loosen your apron strings. Hand over the running of the household to the youngsters. Go on a pilgrimage. Experience firsthand the beauty, the vitality, the holiness of the places blessed by our avatars and sanctified by our saints and sages. Travel light! Travel right! Tie yourself to the Infinite and let go your identification with 'me' and 'mine.' Like a caterpillar, 'attach' and 'detach.' This is the way to live like a vānaprasthi."

The moment-to-moment spontaneity of Gurudev:

Swamini Radhikananda: It was in a small Christian chapel that I saw Gurudev for the first time in 1978. As I sat in the front of the chapel at American University in Washington, D.C., the moment finally came: I turned to see Gurudev enter from the back of the chapel, and my mind stood still in wonder as I saw the most majestic being, with an aura of power and light, walking slowly and gracefully like a king up the center aisle! Gurudev reached the front row of the chapel, where two little children came up to greet him, and he spontaneously stooped down to speak to the children and embrace them. It struck me as utterly amazing that an internationally known speaker about to give a public speech could be so simple and unselfconscious. His attention was only on the children though he was about to deliver his lecture. He was always spontaneous and childlike. Gurudev, like the children, didn't carry the baggage of the past, and lived spontaneously from moment to moment.

OF COURSE, YOU ARE CREATIVE

In truth, Vedānta is a radical philosophy. It asks us, moment by moment, to question and sometimes reject the usual and the routine and to consider with a fresh mind a different view of reality. This is creative thinking. Creativity is one of the potencies of God. And we are made in the image of God. If one's entire life is spent thinking and reacting in a mundane way, accepting the stereotypical values and attitudes of the times without question, there will be little room for fresh perspectives and alternative views. Every aspect of life needs to be considered in novel ways. In fact, this enthusiasm to experiment with every action of our daily life harnesses the spiritual dimension of our personality. How? Enthusiasm and inspiration are generated by a goal or an ideal. Swamiji invited us to add that extra creative touch to all our actions — mundane and special — and act with inspiration.

Swami Chinmayananda

An inspired man outshines his own abilities. Man is capable of a tremendous amount of effort. This is possible only when we are inspired, otherwise our ability remains dormant. Love transforms work into inspiration with efficiency as its result. If our head and heart are working where the hands are working, there comes artistic perfection. Inspired action is sure to bear fruit and is immediately its own reward.

To live in a routine will never yield the secret of living in inspiration. To get habituated to any method is to get into a rut and balk from all progress. We must have the freedom, at every moment, to change our pattern of living and seek new

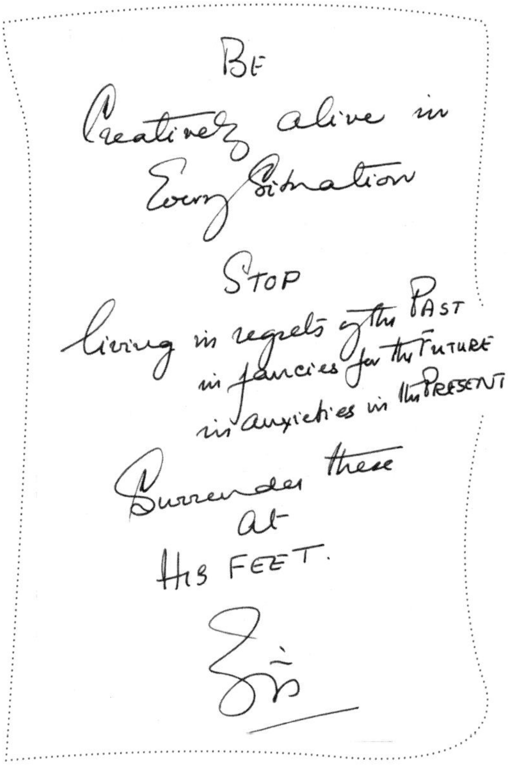
Be
Creatively alive in
Every Situation
Stop
living in regrets of the Past
in fancies for the Future
in anxieties in the Present
Surrender these
at
His Feet.

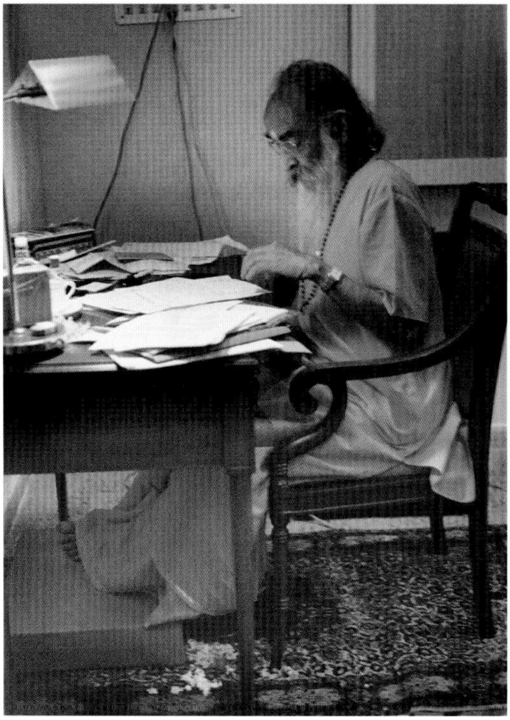

methods of keeping the mind and intellect occupied in lively warmth of love and cheer, or else even our worship becomes mechanical and, in the end, stultifying. Don't keep going from place to place routinely going through the same thing. Let there be a quantum leap!

To live weeping for the past, wasting the present moments, shuddering with imaginary fears for the future is self-destructive, 'suicidal' living. In this, time employs us. We then become slaves of time. To strive on in the present, becoming the architect of the future is 'creative living.' In this, we employ time. We become the masters of time. To repair the mistakes of the past and create a better beauty for the future is the program in the present in all-creative progress.

In this sense, Vedānta is heretical and revolutionary: The attitude with which one should do the 'hearing' of the scriptures is totally different from the attitude with which one is asked to do 'reflection' upon what one has heard. Again, neither the 'faith' nor 'hearing' nor the intellectual freedom of 'reflection' is permitted to poison the deep serenity of the thought-less meditation hours. Thus, a Vedānta student is taught, from the very beginning, to be original at every moment and to live ever in the white heat of inspiration, at once thrilling, divine, and ennobling.

Letter to ***Vrinda Chidambaram:*** Your aggressive shyness must end for the art in you to bloom forth. Art flow is blocked if you are shy. Shyness comes when you are too preoccupied with yourself. This self-consciousness is a play of the subtle ego. Give it up. Else inspiration cannot bubble up in you. Art needs consistent and daily courting.

All one needs is a focused mind to fulfill any desire:

Q: Not all men use their mind for the invocation of the Supreme. There are scientists, artists, politicians, economists, authors, and others — each producing spectacular results, often products of some subtle inspiration. How do people in general get their inspiration?

Swamiji: Subjectively, from the standpoint of man's personality reconstruction, whatever be the mode of invocation, he gains the fulfillment of his desires, if the conditions are all fulfilled. With single-pointed intense consistency, one may invoke war and another peace; both shall have their desires gratified. There is nothing impossible for man — only he must be able to steady his mind and intelligently apply it with the required intensity and constancy; he shall gain what he wishes, be it spiritual unfoldment or material gain in this world. Every success and any splendid performance, anywhere and at any time, are all sparks from pure inspiration, which is a State of Self-hood.

Swamiji explains to a student how negative emotions can be given a new creative direction:

Q: In day-to-day life, how does an individual, trying to live a peaceful, meaningful life, cope with and react to strong negative emotions such as anger, cruelty, hatred, and so on, for other people? Should anger be expressed or repressed?

Swamiji: To act in the world without ego should be the secret of using these emotions of the mind for your spiritual unfoldment and personality rehabilitation. Discover a goal or an ideal. Surrender unto it and then act. You shall discover that even when you experience anger, it becomes creative and not self-destructive. For example, if I am angry at an injustice to a community or a country, or even at myself for my own weaknesses and mental garbage, the anger emotion in these instances becomes creative and it will contribute to the progressive unfoldment of myself. The 'ego-centered' life is negative. While surrendering our ego at a nobler altar, or to the Divine, when we act, the personality and the mind become positive and dynamic. Let our lust or anger be directed toward the Lord, who, we might erroneously feel, is not reaching to help us out in spite of our sincere efforts. Let there be complete miserliness when it comes to giving away your principles and moral values! Let there be almost a delusory fascination for God. Let there be pride that 'I-am-His-devotee.' Let there be competitiveness with other seekers and beautiful souls existing and functioning around you in the community. Let us make our life God-centered. The process of sublimation is changing the center of your life from the ego to the Altar-of-God in you.

How the mundane can be made creative:

Rudite J. Emir: On one occasion a small group of us had stopped at a roadside restaurant while driving between Gurudev's engagements. As we chatted quietly, Gurudev took in the surroundings with a piercing gaze, not saying a word. Suddenly, he pointed to a nearby booth and said, "Take a close look. See that? See that intricate pattern? Imagine something so fine in a simple roadside restaurant!" He was pointing out a detail in some wooden latticework. Once again, he had illustrated the meaning of his words: "Always be quiet, alert, vigilant." He had shown us how to absorb the simple beauty of the present moment from the mundane surroundings of a roadside restaurant, which we had taken for granted and therefore ignored.

Vedānta is all-inclusive — there is nothing undivine:

Bharati Sukhtankar: I was young and in a euphoric state, having worked closely with Swamiji over the last few months writing the Bala Rāmāyaṇam. I felt that the ochre robe was the goal of life. Living a worldly life seemed degrading and mundane. I must have written this to him, for I received a decisive letter. "What is mundane?" Gurudev wrote. "It is not in the world — it is in us. You live in continuous inspiration uplifted by your devotion, your vision. Then all work, in all conditions, wherever you are, becomes divinized. If your mind is not inspired, then even in the noblest temple, in the holiest monastery, in the most sacred valley, your life is mundane! Dear girl, sannyāsa is not the color of the cloth. It is a state of the mind. Live like Janaka — in the world, but not of it." He went on to write, "Never say that worldly life is unholy. Vedānta is all-inclusive. There is nothing in it that is not divine — sarvaṃ khalvidam brāhman neha nanāsti kiñcana. Have some ice cream! Have some more ice cream!" I did. Loads of it! It was prasāda from the Guru!

*L*ook back, judge, and walk ahead.

4

Face the Volley

"It is your own Double Fault. You gave one point to him," Swamiji said to Krickstein, while watching a match between Krickstein and Woodbridge on television.

There were several devotees who had the impression that Swamiji liked to have them chat with him while he was watching tennis on television. But one of Swamiji's overanxious devotees suggested that we should not engage Swamiji so much, as this would make him tired. One devotee took the suggestion to heart and made a resolve to keep silent while in that room. Swamiji dealt with this little trick of the ego in an interesting way.

Sometimes during his recuperation, when he was not watching tennis, Swamiji would watch the Mahabharata serial along with the ashramites. On one such occasion, Swamiji remarked in reference to the vow Bhishma Pitamah took never to marry, "Everywhere it is seen that whenever there is a vow, it leads to their collapse. Even those who (and Swamiji put a finger on his lips) take a vow that they will not speak to Swamiji!" He turned around and looked at the devotee who had resolved to keep silent. Unwittingly breaking her vow, she responded, "Having taken a vow, should a person give it up?" He answered, "That is why Bhishma was suffering! What right has anyone to take a vow? He asserts his ego when he does that."

"What if a person has taken a vow and realizes he should not have done it, but continues. Then what?" someone asked. Swamiji responded, "Then suffer!" Hearing this, the devotee who had taken the vow earlier quickly dissolved her resolve not to speak to him.

The first fault was listening to someone who was not in charge of Swamiji's health instead of following the deep instinct to remain in communion with the Guru while remaining sensitive to Swamiji's condition. The second fault was taking a unilateral vow not to talk to Swamiji, without finding out what he wanted. This was the kind of 'double fault' he was talking about.

MAKE IT AN ADVENTURE

Let life be an adventure in self-expression. An adventurous spirit comes from an amalgamation of confidence and fearlessness. And these come from the feeling of well-being that gets generated from right living. Dreaming big — that is, creating a saṅkalpa (resolve, willing) is the beginning of success. Therefore, it is important to cultivate moral values so that our mind is freed from reacting to our delinquencies, and we have a mind that is courageous, strong, and free to dream big and visualize success in the game of life.

Swami Chinmayananda:

Life is spent in meeting challenges. To meet them efficiently is the game. Sometimes you win, sometimes you lose. Meet them we must: there is no choice. If you meet them with courage and faith in yourself, you win; if you neglect to be dynamic and diligent all the time, and sulk, or try to avoid meeting them, they will, with merciless aggressiveness, roll on and crush you in their blind fury. This is the law of life. Meet them we must. You may win here and may lose there. It becomes a sport, exhausting but exhilarating no doubt, and one can enjoy it all if it is taken as a lifelong sport.

In order to be on the field of life's sport, you must have a mind full of reserve energy and inexhaustible inner stamina. An exhausted and fatigued sick mind gets hit by situations, crushed by problems, and mercilessly tortured by a powerful and tyrannical life. This is not because the outer life has the strength to persecute you, but you are too weak and so allow life to play havoc upon you. In order to stick to our convictions, we need spiritual energy to nurture and nourish our fatigued morale. This inner energy welling up in a well-integrated personality is called fortitude or forbearance.

Be strong — not merely a physical strength of a bull, but the subtle vitality of a calm mind, diligent in its application, consistent in its logical thinking, replete with a will to win over all negative tendencies that poison and weaken the mind. In fact, a strong mind is seriously cultivated by living moral values. Never yield readily to the endless demands of the body; never come under the irresistible charms of the sensuous objects around you. If your intellect is not alert, your mind will run out seeking some immediate pleasure by hugging some object of false magic in the outer world.

In Life, the glory lies not in the quarry, but in the chase … the success is not in the trophy won, but in the race run.

Now and then allow the mind to beat you down and smile away the defeat with a sportsman's spirit of fairness and ease. Be cheerful. Be confident in the Lord's grace and in the ultimate victory.

Letter to ***Nanki Singh (BeBe)*** *when she wanted to go to the same school as her brother:*
Never think negatively. Think always positively. There should be never any 'ifs' in your sankalpas. 'Must,' 'will,' 'shall,' 'can' must be your positive verbs and not 'if I go to Aiglon.'

Letter to ***Jujhar Singh:*** Study hard. Score. In sports, games, art, adventure – score everywhere! Learn to suffer the fools around you. Make use of them!

Never compromise discipline and respect for Vedānta — even for national VIPs:

R. Krishnamoorthy: We had invited the Vice President of India to inaugurate Swamiji's talk and requested the Hon. V.P. to arrive at 6:28 P.M. Two minutes before the start, at 6:25 P.M., I learned that he had not yet left. At 6:29 P.M., when Swamiji arrived, I informed him that the V.P. might be a few minutes late. He ignored it, took his seat, and indicated with his eyes to 'start the talks.' We began with the prayer song at 6:30 P.M., but postponed the traditional garlanding. Swamiji started his speech. When the V.P. arrived, at 6:45 P.M., I did not escort him to the stage, fearing Swamiji's disciplinary wrath, but to a seat in the front row instead, hoping he would not feel slighted. Swamiji continued his talk till a suitable break in the topic occurred; only then did he inform the audience that our Hon. V.P. had arrived and requested him to give the inaugural speech. Trembling, I guided the V.P. to the stage. Thereafter, what he said or what Swamiji said was all like a dream. Surprisingly, the V.P. came down and sat in the front row for twenty-odd minutes instead of going away. As I escorted him back, I heard him telling his personal private secretary that he liked Swamiji's talk. I heaved a sigh of relief. Swamiji's action was a vivid example of courage in action and conviction.

There are many ways to tackle an opposing situation; one is the surprise element:

Swami Siddhananda: Once, when Gurudev entered the Tellicherry Brunner College auditorium, some of the students were creating an uproar by shouting and clapping in disrespect. Gurudev immediately climbed up onto the table and started clapping. Nobody expected this. After a few minutes, they slowly stopped. Then, he gave a thundering talk and the entire auditorium became absolutely silent.

A creative and positive mind will always find a solution:

R. Krishnamoorthy: During one of the camps, there was barely an hour to serve tea between breakfast and the next class. Even with two extra tea caddies, the time taken was too long. Swamiji came to know about it. He entered the kitchen and told the head cook, "Put the table of glasses near the tea caddy and bring extra glasses piled on top of each other." He then dexterously filled one tumbler after another, without closing the tap. Within just three minutes, twenty-odd tumblers were filled and kept on the right side of the caddy! The time taken to open and close the tap after filling each tumbler was totally eliminated. That day, I learned a lesson in time and motion study, which I have used on numerous occasions for many other activities!

Good and bad news is to be expected in the journey of life:

Anjali Singh: During the climb up the mountain road to Uttarkashi in 1985, I asked Swamiji, "When would you like to eat lunch?" Mrs. Leela Nambiar nudged me, warning me to keep off the topic of lunch. "We can eat at Tehri," replied Swamiji. "That's good," said I, feeling excited about the prospect. Mrs. Nambiar again nudged me and whispered softly that the tiffin box containing the lunch had been shifted to the other car by mistake. "We have some good news and bad news for you, Swamiji!" "What is the good news?" he asked. "It's going to be lunchtime soon!" "Do you want to hear the bad news now, Swamiji?" "What is that?" "The lunch was left behind in the other car that broke down!" "Yes, I saw Chopra Sahib taking it away at Rishikesh!" He had known long ago that the lunch was not there, and treated it as part of the adventure of traveling!

YOU ARE TOUGHER THAN YOU THINK

In our adventure through life, success is not always the outcome. Many challenges have to be faced, and the worst strategy would be to run away from it all or to succumb to depression. Failures are not always a bad thing. They are the guiding lights to success. We have within us all the strength we need to recover from failure and to rise above the impulses of the body–mind–intellect.

Swami Chinmayananda:

Challenges come in life and they should not cow us down; they are meant to sharpen our abilities and make us wake up. In order to face challenges, a lot of courage is necessary. Do not run away. Face the world and get hit by the world. Let the world drop you again and again. It is the means to destroy the ego! The courage to face the situation comes when the mind is strong and poised; only then can it rediscover its own efficiency, ability, and beauty of performance — all of which ensure success in life.

God never created you to fail in life. You may slip. You will fall. These are all expected. So what? Get up each time you slip and fall! Learn from your own failures! Fall if you must, never like a huge boulder from the hill, but like a rubber ball, bounce back again to heights the moment you hit the base. Drive yourself back in the path and cheerfully march ahead. Just forget to remember the fall! If you have real faith in Him, where will you fall? From His shoulder into His lap! Keep smiling; all falls are a rise in the total.

Fall, if you must! But,
Stay not where you have fallen!
Get up each time you fall,
and limp on, till you are
able to run again.
Fall, if you must: never
like a huge boulder from the
hill, but like a rubber-ball.
Bound back again to heights
the moment you hit the base.

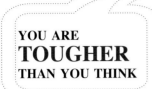

Have the courage to accept whatever comes in life as a result of your actions. Take responsibility for what comes. Have the courage to face the consequences of the past. Collect all the dues; pay up all that you owe the world. Be free in life. If there is an unjust tax on the building, who else can freely fight but a devotee? Every effort you put forth is a step taken toward the Truth. When dispirited — sing His glories. When totally disgusted — surrender to Him. Help comes! Help surely comes!! Invoke the power of Śiva to destroy an undesirable thought. It is with the power of the creator, Brahma, that any kind of thought is created. With the power of Viṣṇu it is sustained, and can be destroyed with the help and the power of God. Destroy it. Refuse to recognize it! Success is our birthright; happiness our heritage; joy our wealth. Peace is ours by the status of manhood. It is up the mountain, no doubt. But are there not steps to lead us? Don't we have legs to climb? And for the small effort, what an elevation, what a view!

Do just as Mother Gaṅgā does every time she comes down from the white peaks to serve the whole of mankind. She has decided to go to the Bay of Bengal. Do you think that on her path there are no obstacles? Where there are no obstacles, Gaṅgā has no beauty: she is a silent river. A slight obstacle — and glug, glug, glug — she begins to sing. A somewhat greater obstacle, she begins to laugh; a little more, and she starts thundering. When she is near the mountain, she giggles all the way until she goes around the mountain, and then — utter silence. Why? The plain is not worthwhile talking about. In the same way, you must be able to circumambulate any obstacle — or else do not enter into any field of activity. This quality is called fortitude, consistent application of your energy, to reach your goal, whatever be the obstacles. Face them smilingly!

Weak persons often feel dejected and tempted to leave work half done when faced with many obstacles. As a result, they miss the chance to achieve their goal when victory may be just around the corner. All psychological cowards often unconsciously live a life of escapism. This sense of escapism is detrimental to any great achievement. There is nothing in the world that we cannot win by honest and consistent work.

When the going gets tough, it is the tough who keep going. History is full of instances, wherein victory would have been for the vanquished if only they had battled a little longer! We often fail for lack of perseverance in our efforts. We leave our work half done in our impatience. Every job demands its quota of efforts. Never give up too soon. Strive on until you win. If you compromise due to lack of courage, you must have the heroism to suffer for it.

Caesar would not be a wolf if Romans were not sheep. It is we who give the might and power to objects to persecute us with their joys and sorrows. Situations can hurt us only if the mind is weak enough to be hurt. It is the desire and craving for something that creates this weakness in the mind. Our attachment to the objects makes the objects powerful, and then the objects come to rule over our mind. Withdraw your grace from the mind. The mind is the devil that has invoked you and received your blessings, and it is now threatening to annihilate you! Man is a master of circumstances. To the extent he comes to assert this mastery, to that extent he is evolved. Be a master of all situations. Don't be a slave to every passing uncertain happening. Be strong. Be bold. Refuse to be unhappy.

Encouragement to a man in his seventies:
Congratulations, young man! You are only just 72 on March 4th, and don't tell me that you are tired and exhausted, because you are talking to one who is 76 and going strong. Work tirelessly till death for the benefit of the community.

Challenge to a mother of two young children, who would worry each time they fell ill:
My dear girl! A little obstacle and you perspire — become nervous — shattered! Why!? Develop depth and height to your mind. Learn to grow strong to face the world. Outside the books you read is a wide-awake world to be reckoned with.

A student wanted to know Swamiji's thoughts on suicide and whether it was allowed by religion:

Q: Why do individuals get depressed and wish to do away with themselves? Does the *Gītā* refer to suicide? What are your thoughts on the subject?

Swamiji: Depression, which is a psychological term now in fashion among us, is nothing but despondency, and it arises in an individual when he wants to do something that he believes is right and appropriate, but the circumstances conspire to cheat him of the chance to act. When this shattering reverberates in an individual, his discrimination gets lost, and waves of despair lash him. In the resultant medley of insane restlessness, the individual foolishly feels that a bullet in his head or jumping down from the Golden Gate Bridge can end all problems. God cannot be cheated so easily; the Law of Nature holds good and has her sway even beyond the grave. The burial ground is only a frontier for the laws of a country and not for the Laws of Existence. Destroying the body is suicide, but the mind and intellect survive the body; even now, it is your mind and intellect that are despairing in your body. Therefore, even after suicide, you survive as a personality, of course, without a body, and so with no means of expressing yourself. How sad! How terrible! Can you imagine a man supremely thirsty brought near water and not allowed to drink? Can you imagine a poet with his eyes plucked? A musician with his ears gorged? A painter with his fingers chopped off? This will be you, the suicide without a body. How tragic! Therefore, all religions of the world declare unanimously that suicide is escapism from life, which does good to no one!

Bitter experiences can purify:

Bharati Sukhtankar: One day over lunch, Gurudev said, "This gourd may be bitter, but it will cleanse your system. Don't reject it. Learn to relish its bitter taste. Certain experiences in life may also be bitter. Learn to accept them with grace. They will cleanse and purify the mind. Just as the bitter gourd will not turn your insides bitter, don't allow bitter experiences in life to poison the serenity and beauty of your mind."

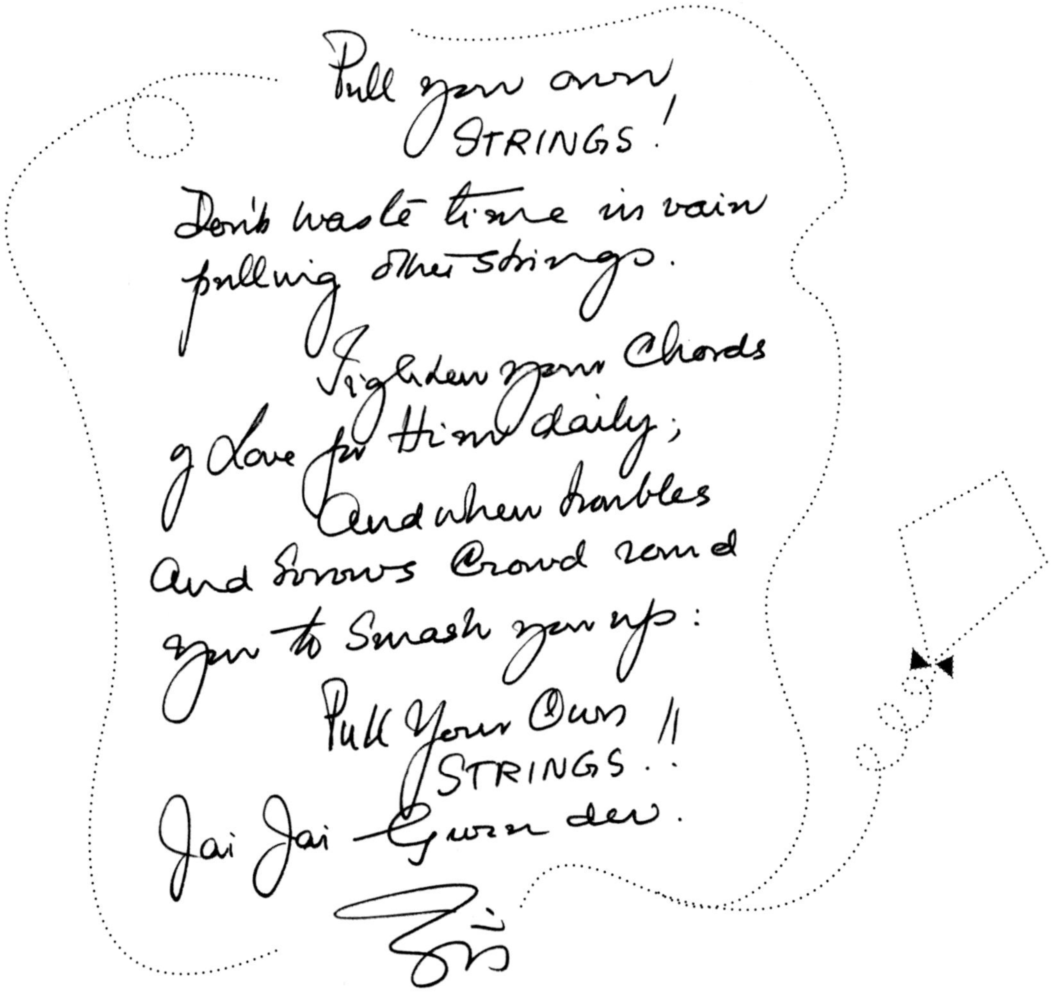

Pull your own
STRINGS!
Don't waste time in vain
pulling other strings.
Tighten your chords
of Love for Him daily;
And when troubles
and Sorrows crowd round
you to Smash you up:
Pull Your Own !!
STRINGS!!
Jai Jai Gurudev.

5

The Challenge of Self-Improvement

During the final between Wheaton and Becker at Wimbledon, Swamiji said, "Never mind! It was lack of experience. You did well. Better luck next time, even though you did concentrate and all that." "Swamiji, is lack of experience a fault?" someone asked. "Of course it is. The physical ability is there, the technique was all right, but the mental self-confidence was lacking. Therefore, you are not able to get it right. Have faith in yourself. Don't get yourself psychologically upset. That is why you are here; otherwise, you will be with Brahman. Look at the other player — he is not reacting to any of the emotions because he has just this one goal in mind."

In tennis, if a player lacks confidence or has a preconceived notion that he won't win because he lacks experience, it will not be helpful to him. Similarly, in spiritual life, and particularly in the practice of meditation, if a person is not confident about his ability to achieve the goal just because he has not attempted to reach it before, the necessary inner dynamic push will not be generated. There may be lack of experience, because a steady spiritual life has not been lived before, yet self-confidence can be generated when one has discovered a deep and sincere inner urge to evolve and has faith in one's Guru and determination to reach the goal. The most important aspect of experience is learning that self-confidence and an inner conviction, not experience with technique as such, are what determine final success in reaching the goal.

HOW TO OVERCOME AN INFERIORITY COMPLEX

An inferiority complex is the result of thinking that we are lesser than what we really are. When we worry about what people will think of us, we give them the prerogative of deciding our status. The truth is that we are all, in essence, the mighty infinite Reality, the supreme Divinity, who is the substratum of this universe. If we were to recognize our true nature, these complexes — inferiority and superiority — would be nullified! We need to remind ourselves, moment to moment, that we are not the limited entity, the paltry little PFT (perceiver–feeler–thinker) that we think we are. Then, what others think of us will be their problem, not ours.

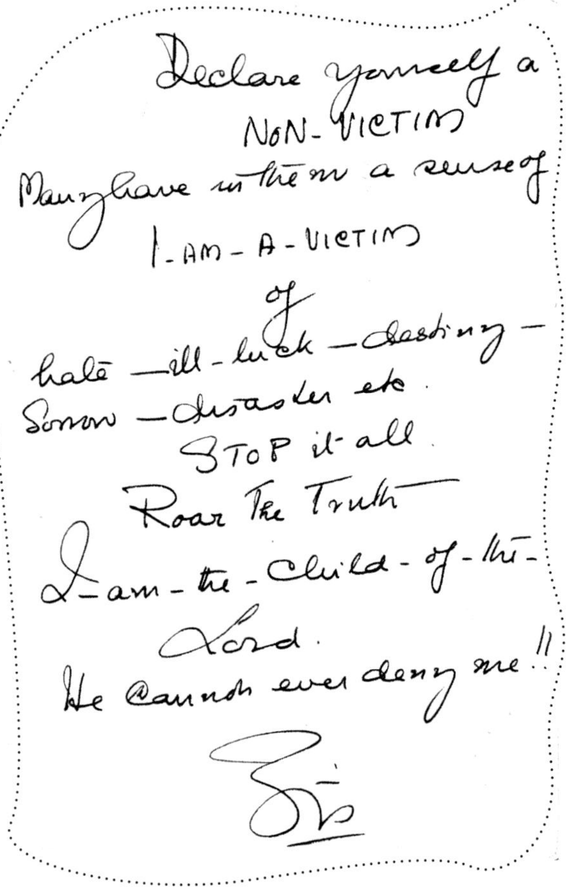
Declare yourself a
NON-VICTIM
Many have in them a sense of
I-AM-A-VICTIM
of
hate — ill-luck — destiny —
sorrow — disaster etc.
STOP it all.
Roar the Truth
I-am-the-Child-of-the-
Lord.
He cannot ever deny me!!

Swami Chinmayananda:

Do not tell the world what you can do; show it. Mind cannot practice not to do; it can only practice 'what to do.' Therefore, do not give negative commands to the mind. It is the fear complex that taxes us thc maximum and punishes us the most with the largest doses of our sorrows and failures in life.

Being very egocentric or thinking oneself useless, both are expressions of the ego. This ego, thoughtlessly assuming an independent and separate existence for itself, naturally sees the whole world as a mighty, endless array of things and beings, of circumstances and situations — all of them inimical to itself. It feels lonely; in its loneliness it is overwhelmed by fear. To assure its own security, the ego thereafter builds mighty, phantom fortresses around itself with frail wealth, impermanent name, flimsy fame, disloyal relations, and undependable friends, and maintains a thousand treacherous relationships with a million things and beings. But still, the ego feels insecure, frightened, lonely, unhappy, and altogether entirely cheated! Fear is always born of the recognition of the 'other.' You are never afraid of yourself. Disassociate yourself from the ego when it falls beneath your contempt.

To consider yourself as 'just this little me' — who has 'come into this world' and lives temporarily in a bag of skin — is a hoax and a fake. No single thing or being is separable from the whole. The only real you, the Self, is the whole. Infinite are your capacities and abilities, because you are Brahman. As you think, so you become.

It is not others, but *you* who is to judge whether you have done your duty. Every night you must congratulate yourself and say, "Well done." It does not matter if others do not appreciate you. It is not for their appreciation that you are living. Do not live in the world as a doormat for everything that is happening.

Live, not as a victim of the universe, but as the substratum. God has not made a dull fellow. Everybody has been made a genius. Einstein was a genius because when he would enter the laboratory no other thought came to him. You and I — our minds are at least ten kilometers away. "Where did I keep the key?" For the next half hour, you make everybody search for the key that was in your pocket! This is how our minds function.

The greatness is not *what* we do, but it is always in *how* we do. Our present work may be great or small, yet the important thing is to do it well. If you cannot do great things, remember that you can do small things in a great way. Perseverance is positive and creative; obstinacy is negative and destructive.

None is eternally condemned nor does one deserve a perpetual hell. It is illogical, unphilosophical. Even the greatest wretch sings His song, sung through a bad reed!

You cannot force open a bud and make it a flower. It must take its own time. A forcibly opened-up flower will not have real beauty, or true fragrance. Never hurry up. Let it take its own time. All that we have to do is to put ourselves on the rails, on the right track, running in the right direction. We shall reach, in time, our coveted destination.

*Letter to **Padma Jaisinghani,** who was nervous to speak on stage:*

Take courage: He is just behind us always when our actions are soaked in love and sincerity. Why then fear or become nervous!! Remember that the Lord is always with you and He alone is the audience. Relax and talk to the 'crowd' as though you are talking to your little sister! It is, after all, only one and one-half minutes — maybe five-to-seven sentences! Nervousness comes when you have no faith either in yourself or in Him who is the Sole Doer. Surrender unto Him who is ever in your own heart: the Witness of everything in you and around you.

A suggestion for someone who could not come up to the mark in her performance:

"...even though she knows everything. She needs more *japa* to grow out of her fear complex."

Having pride in one's culture and values helps to overcome an inferiority complex. The pride can come only when one understands the greatness of one's culture:

Swami Tejomayananda: By making the Scriptures and their knowledge available to all — to the classes and the masses — Gurudev demystified everything. So many people were trying to make everything mystical and secretive, but he made it available to everybody. At this time, we may not appreciate this much; but remember, when the British were ruling, they systematically destroyed our pride in our own religion, culture — everything. Soon after independence, when Gurudev started his work, he created pride in India and her culture. People had started thinking that everything that comes from outside — the West — alone is the best, and everything from India is useless and a waste. But that was not true. He would say, "I don't seek to convert people belonging to other religions to Hinduism; I want to convert Hindus to Hinduism. They themselves do not know." Years later, our Mission youth organized a national quiz called "Awakening Indians to India." Sooner or later, we will organize a quiz for Mission members: "Do you know your Mission?" Only when we know what we truly are ourselves can we do something. If we have such a low opinion of ourselves, what can we do? One should not look down on oneself or degrade oneself.

If one can recognize one's weaknesses and accept them, one can remain free of complexes:

Viji Sundaram: Gurudev was flying through Boston in 1984 with a two-hour delay between flights. My parents and I decided to drive in to meet with him at the airport. Mimi Robins drove in from Brookline. Then, to Mimi, he gave the assignment of driving him from one terminal to another. My parents and I stood with Gurudev at the curb, waiting for Mimi to bring her car from the parking garage. "Here she comes," said Gurudev, picking up his briefcase. Instead, she missed the turnoff and drove past the terminal. Without a word, Gurudev put down his briefcase. Minutes passed and, once again, we spotted Mimi's car approaching. Again she missed the turnoff and just drove by. Again Gurudev put down his briefcase. When she did it for a third time, Gurudev picked up his briefcase and walked to a waiting shuttle bus. "Let's go," he said, jumping into the bus, the three of us in tow, heading to the other terminal for his departing flight. Just a minute or two before Gurudev was to depart, a flustered-looking Mimi, feeling obtuse, came running up. Gurudev smiled warmly at her and laughingly remarked: "Good, you finally found your way." He turned, waved goodbye, and left through the gate. I reassured Mimi that both she and I were directionally challenged.

THE ART OF PURPOSEFUL PAUSING

What is it that enables us to make more right choices than wrong ones? Each of us, based on past experience, feels for oneself what the right action is and what the inner subjective reaction would be if one took this course of action. However, many of our actions are impulsive and lead to regret. To correct this, we need to pause the mind a little and reflect. Call it an 'art' or a 'knack' — it is a simple thing to learn, which can often prevent us from landing into trouble!

Swami Chinmayananda:

The action of today becomes the destiny of tomorrow. Let not your choice leave behind a sense of guilt. We can never correct one mistake by committing another one. Character is formed from the repeated choice of thoughts and actions. Make the right choice and you shall have a firm and noble character. One step back, and you are a master of the situation. One step forward, and you are dancing with the mind. Desire does not in itself execute its follies; it deludes the sense organs or the mind or the intellect and orders them to do the mischief in our lives.

Just as you know how much you have to eat or drink, so, also, by your past actions you get a third sense, a "sixth" sense as it were, and you know what would be your reaction to an action. There are certain common standards which religion talks about and gives guidelines for. But each person will have to feel for himself what is right for him, what is going to be his particular specific reaction based on his past experience. Even in an ordinary conversation, you ask yourself whether you should say such a thing or not. You know it from your experience. Cultured people, they pause for a moment: "Shall I say this? I may be joking, but will it be understood as a joke?" All in a split moment you calculate and decide.

When you get really mad with anger, is it not a fact that you lose sight of yourself — your ideals, your values, your culture — and behave as though you are not yourself? Sometimes you do something very serious, like a crime, in the spur of the moment wherein thought agitations in you, for the moment, veiled your understanding and your knowledge. It is in this sense of the term that the Vedānta masters declare that, unless the mind is quietened, it will not have the necessary poise to contemplate and awake into the higher State of Reality.

We should encash every difficulty by not retaliating. If we retaliate, we build up more vāsanās to be exhausted later. By retaliation we may make our point, but we keep on suffering because the inner peace gets disturbed. A kind of self-condemnation comes within us. Many difficulties, with their consequent unpleasantness and discord, could be smoothed over by patience. We need it, not only with others but also with ourselves.

The person who can pause the mind more, whose judgment is without prejudice or favor, as in the case of Jesus, is correct. When the judgment is serene and calm, you won't make any mistake. Look at the judgment of Jesus when serious charges were brought on Mary Magdalene. According to the Old Testament, she should have been stoned to death. Jesus did not revolt against the rule. Yes, it should be done, that is what is said in the scriptures. You must do it. But who has the birthright to do so? Only the individual who had never sinned could throw the first stone. And Jesus walked away. What a precise, beautiful, discriminative judgment! Nobody dared touch a stone. The woman walked behind the Lord and became his great follower. So, you can say, right judgment is intuitional, because Jesus had neither prejudice against nor favor for that woman or the act. Therefore, the judgment turned out to be perfect.

The power in man that judges actions, you cannot just call it intuition because it is with the help of what he knows that he judges the situation. You could also call it intuition, but it is more the discriminating power within the intellect's faculties. For one who can pause the mind more, his judgment or discriminating power is more. Judgments become wrong because of the mood of the mind. "Had I been at that time quieter, I would not have made that mistake."

Mahābhārata is not life idealized. It is only giving an honest slice of life as it is: a cross section of life brought to the vivid recognition of the average person, because he does not have a total vision of the vulgar things around. In the midst of it all is one vibrant character, always in equipoise, whether in the warfront, while telling a lie, while hugging his wife, or while kicking somebody: he is always balanced. That fellow alone has the butter, the final goal in hand!

THE MIGHTY FORTRESS WITHIN YOU

What is it that protects us from the onslaughts of worldly situations and keeps us ever smiling? It is God's innate nature within us, our intrinsic Goodness. All other aspects of our being — body, mind, and intellect — have instrumental value only. In order to be able to draw sustenance from this hidden Divinity within us, we need to learn how to gain access to it. This capability comes when our minds are not fragmented with conflicting viewpoints that cause confusion. When one's intellect knows the right thing to do, and the mind agrees with the intellect, and the body executes it, then the personality gets integrated. This integration of the body–mind–intellect is achieved when the noble values of life are practiced, which are like a balm to our ulcerated life, which enables the intrinsic Good to shine out.

Swami Chinmayananda:

Why should human affairs be such a complicated affair? Perhaps that is the very reason why dharma is prescribed and, due to it, society is sustained in happiness. Revolutionize your attitude to the world outside by bringing about a total reorientation of your life.

We can revive and strengthen the mind by living the discipline of moral values. Reduce ego and selfish desires, and cultivate love and concern for others. Feel an unending need to help others, even at the expense of your own comfort, security, or welfare. These are lived laboriously at first, but soon they become the most enjoyable lifestyle. Not only do they provide a cheerful and joyous life for yourself and to others around you, but also in a year or two the discipline brings your discriminative power out of its clouds of dullness and incompetency, to shine forth brightly. An awakened intellect makes worldly life more readily successful, and it also reveals the deeper significances of the very existence. Spiritual search starts for that person. He questions and he successfully seeks. Glimmerings of the larger contents of life come to his recognition. He is well set in study and contemplation. All outer actions start gathering a dazzling polish when the mental values change. A moral man automatically lives his moral values, just as a musician ever keeps faith in his voice to tone or tune in while singing!! With effortless ease, he becomes gracious and loving toward others, as he has no selfish motive in his dealing with others. A morally strong person spends less of his mental powers in facing the day-to-day problems in his life. Therefore, he conserves his potential mental vitality, which he spends in his creative pursuits of study, reflection, and meditation.

The company that we keep is very important. Worldly seekers carelessly choose their friends and are indiscriminate in choosing their associations. The chances are that they, in spite of their knowledge and determination, will be snatched away by bad company through the powerful waves of blind passions. To be in the 'company of the good' is to be with those who are devotees of the Lord and are themselves seekers of the Highest. In such an assembly, there is a power created which, in the congregation, erects a powerful fortress against the magic of the world outside.

The values that you uphold in life determine the quality of the thoughts; the quality of thoughts determines, in turn, the quality of actions. Unless the values of life are changed, the contours of our national life cannot change. A value is valuable only in relationship with achievements. It is instrumental. It is not absolute. Only Brahman, the supreme Reality, has absolute value, the only intrinsic value. All others are instrumental or contributory to reaching that highest intrinsic value. By pursuing negative values, you go away from Him. By pursuing positive values, you go toward Him. So, values to be acquired by the seeker are only to take you to that intrinsic value, the absolute value that is Brahman.

Make a success out of the failures of today; this is the highest art to work on yourself. The values to be practiced are love, tenderness, forgiveness, truthfulness, and goodness. Knowing a thing and living up to it are totally different things.

Having performed an action, if a person reacts to it in the form of agitations, disturbances, self-criticism, or accusations, it shows that the action was wrong. And the action that in its perpetration brings peace, contentment, or self-congratulations to the mind is a good action. That which gives you sorrow, do not give to others, but do unto others as you would do to yourself.

To be able to not do what you feel like doing is freedom.

Crookedness in our relationship with others can bring unending tensions to the mind. Therefore, straightforwardness is recommended as a healthier value of life.

Live in the minimum; create the maximum; give the entire thing to the world outside.

Don't underwrite away your whole life — hanging down all the time on a thin thread of some grace of love given or shown to you by somebody. Be a grown-up giant of spiritual strength who can give love to the whole world and bathe the world in love.

Even fasting for a day in the name of the Lord is tapas; facing insult and honor equally is tapas; loving and serving all are also tapas.

A positive mind does not merely eschew jealousy, but rejoices in the prosperity of others; it does not merely refrain from hating, but it loves; it does not just tolerate, but it forgives; it does not merely desist from telling lies, but it always speaks the truth; it is not only free of greed, but it is generous.

Kindness and a sense of cheerfulness can always bring the mind to poise and grandeur.

Truthfulness, meaning intellectual honesty, is an unavoidable requisite for every spiritual seeker. To think one way and to feel differently and ultimately to act belying one's own convictions is to live a dishonest life, which brings disintegration of one's inner personality. Truth is intellectual conviction expressed honestly. Falsehood creates a self-cancellation of one's convictions and leads to a split personality.

Non-injury means never having cruel intentions. Non-injury is the spirit that should dominate all our motives. Our intentions should not be polluted by even a trace of cruelty or hatred. Harmlessness consists not so much in never causing physical injury to a being as in never contemplating to do harm of any sort.

Charity is acceptable only when it toes the line of our own independent intellectual beliefs and convictions. Every benefactor has the right and the duty to inquire into the bona fides of the cause he is trying to patronize.

Cleanliness indicates not only the inner purity of thoughts and motives, but it also suggests the purity of the environment and the cleanliness of habit and personal belongings.

Contentment with whatever has come to one, as one's just share, is the motto of all serious seekers.

The art of practicing harmony is to be applied in the din of the marketplace while we are sweating with exertion.

Purifying our ways of making money:

K. P. Daswani: In the late 1970s, I had made a deal for Nigeria where I was required to make a wrong declaration for the goods that we were shipping there, so that our customer could save the taxes. I was getting a good profit of $100,000 and we were struggling in those days, so I succumbed to the temptation. Gurudev happened to come at that time and I told him about it. He turned around and said, "Just stop it!" I was shocked because he had never shouted at me before! I said, "Swamiji, what is wrong? Everyone works on this basis of corruption of saving taxes." He said, "Don't you understand that you are destroying the economy of a nation which has only twenty-five million people? They live on these import taxes and duties. Who do you think will pay for it?" This made me think anew. I went and canceled the order. It was the way he looked at it — that we are destroying the economy of a nation when we do wrong things — that changed my heart and thinking.

Practicing moral values purifies our inner personality and sharpens our intellect by making it more sāttvic, and thereby more fit to understand Vedānta:

Swami Chidrupananda: In one of the spiritual camps at Sidhbari, a person went to Gurudev and said, "Swamiji, in our group discussion, there was this thought put forward that there is no need for the higher philosophy or Vedānta; just being good and doing good is enough. Nothing beyond this is required." Gurudev responded by saying, "How long you want to do only good? There is something beyond. But let him be good and do good first; later on, he will ask, 'What next?' He will realize that there is still something more. Then he will turn toward Vedānta."

An antidote to fear:

Cate Hallpike: It was so refreshing: "God is Love." These words I had heard so often shouted with full force from high up in a pulpit by priests over many years, who said "God is Love" but who only inspired fear, so that the words had made no sense to me. Now, thanks to Gurudev, I know that Love is the antidote to all feelings of fear and guilt — not soppy emotional love, but love born of a higher knowledge. I recall sitting with him once while he was reading a newspaper, and some junk started to come up in the mind, and then the fear and doubt started to gather. Quietly, from behind the newspaper, I heard, "Drop it, drop it!" Gurudev showered His love on us, day in and day out, "Love! Love! Love! Why are you afraid to love? It is your birthright to love everybody," he said.

HOLD FAST TO WONDER

In the rush of life and our current frantic culture, we have forgotten to enjoy the wondrous beauty of nature. Those who live amidst nature live nearest to God, because their minds are not fragmented and agitated by divergent thoughts caused by the hustle and bustle of life. The calming beauty of nature lifts the mind and expands it easily. Very little effort, thereafter, is required to be quiet in the presence of God.

Swami Chinmayananda:

Accept the mysteries of life. Stop asking how or why. Accept the inexplicable, the Self, the sea, the sky, and the stars that dance through space. Watch. Admire with joy and wonder in the heart. These riddles must remain unsolved to remind us of the supreme Intelligence, who is the Creator Himself. In the presence of this vivid miracle — be silent, humble, and devoted. Observe the beautiful. While there is light, see it! ... And before the shadows fall, stand back and meditate upon the glory and wonder of it all.

The rains came, but the rains passed — and when the floods flowed away, a wonderful thing happened. The grass grew wild and flowered in endless colors. Every year it happens, yet each year it is a wonder to watch the yellow flowers against the rocks, brought into the fields by the flood. This re-creation of life; transforming everything, brings the joyous tidings of His mad munificence to us. There come the jasmines again, free and gay, to nod and dance among their tendrils, to a world crushed under the pressure of its own stress and strain. They know when to come — they never miss their right time. They dance in the breeze, in tune with the bees and birds, to sing without words, the glory of the Lord of all beings — Jagadīśvara (Lord of the World).

Submit to the feet of your Master and render yourself receptive. Submit to the will of the Lord and draw a lesson from every event. Submit to the grandeur of nature and listen to every silent message it offers.

When eyes rest upon peaks, which form a park bench for the tired clouds to rest on for a while, the inner mind of the observer gets hushed, rejuvenated. Let him in silence watch those peaks mirrored in the lakes where calm blue waters lie; the mind chastens and gets burnished into the very Beauty of the Lord of Lords. Help comes. There is a strengthening. The Peace Infinite fills the mind of all who call upon the Lord, who made the mountains and who actually dwells in them.

*S*ymmetry in the object or objects brings into the perceiver's mind a great quietude and peace. And to this inner experience of peace and quietude, we have given the name 'Beauty.' Beauty is the name of God. Man, provided with an intellect and mind, is the only being who can understand this unwritten script of nature's language.

In the heart of the Himalayas lies the Sanctum of Reality. To discover and contact this Sanctum, you will have to become the Himalayas. The girth, the height, the width, the mass of the Himalayas are constituted of motionless vibrancy — life hushed in stones — and every square inch of it is pulsating with life, and yet itself the sustainer of life, rock and soil, tumbling one over the other, rises into the clouds and stands majestic in still inertia! From the heart of the Himalayas flows the eternal Ganges, gushing perpetually in its sacred waters. Realize the center, and let activities for the welfare of all others flow out of you into the world all around you. Sit down and become the Himalayas. You be an actionless mass, spreading all over, and completely motionless. Let Life and Its activities emanate from you, on your surface, and get reabsorbed into you — as the forests in the Himavat. If you can stay thus for ten minutes, you become the Himalayas! And in your core is the Sanctum of the Self!!

When the sea has cast the foam on the shore, go and ask it, "Where are your swirling onrush and maddening dance?" It can only answer, "Ask the ocean!" How can the foam dance without waves? How can dust rise without the wind? See the ocean through the dancing foam; see the wind through the wafting dust. See God through the world of actions and achievements.

Man does not usually like to share the objects of the world, but the pleasures of aesthetic things, like a sunset, he wants to share with others. All moral enjoyments and aestheticism are stepped up in enjoyment when shared with others.

Profound lessons can be learned through the simplicity of nature:

Bharati Sukhtankar: Swamiji was in Uttarkashi with the first batch of brahmacārīs in the summer of 1968. There was an almond tree just outside Tapovan Kuṭiyā and the steps leading down. The sun was sending the long arms of its rays over the eastern mountains. The air was still and fragrant. Swamiji, in his deep stentorian voice, chanted the invocation. Just then, a tiny bird alighted on a branch of the almond tree. It opened wide its beak and trilled away till it seemed as though its heart would burst. Swamiji was quiet. We all listened intently to the bird that was in no hurry to stop its song. The seconds trailed into minutes. Finally, with a dramatic flutter of its wings, it flew away into the blue sky. Swamiji opened his eyes, looked at us, and then closed his *Vivekacūḍāmaṇi*

Beauty can be seen everywhere when the mind is quiet, even through pain:

Rudite J. Emir: Swamiji developed a severe toothache during a camp. Several of us were in his room, along with my young daughter, who ended up in his lap. Swamiji was in great pain, but there was no sign of it on his face. With the child in his lap, he was gazing out the window, watching the sunset together with her, his face aglow with inner peace and joy. Witnessing his unearthly beauty, we sat in awe, immersed in his blissful presence. The glow on his face was unforgettable. The toddler in his lap sensed the ecstatic mood and sat unmoving.

Trishna Guljarajni: Tatha (R. Krishnamoorthy) and Shivpriya Amma were remembering the sky in Sidhbari and what Gurudev said about it: "The sky is Nārāyaṇa's umbrella. Those bright spots — you think they are stars, but they are holes through which Nārāyaṇa is pouring His grace upon us."

One can be in meditation even without shutting one's eyes:

Bharati Sukhtankar: One day, approaching Swamiji with some temerity, I said, "Sometimes I find my mind gliding into stillness, with no conscious effort on my part. It could be brought on by the sight of sunlight filtering through the leaves of a plant, the red round sun dropping down at the horizon at sunset, or a kitten gamboling on the grass. Why does that happen, Swamiji?" Swamiji closed his eyes and leaned back in his chair. "That," he said, "is open-eyed meditation. Sights of nature can frequently be catalysts in bringing about a stillness of the mind. Remember, all of creation is an expression of His divinity. When your mind is relatively calm and unagitated, when there is no mad clamoring of thoughts, and when you carry this state with you through the day, then the stillness can come any time. What brings it about is merely an excuse. It may come from nature or an evening class... keep your mind open for open-eyed meditation at all times." Another day, he stood before a pot of purple-magenta fuchsia flowers. "See that!" he said, "From dull brown earth come these brilliant flowers and lush green leaves. How does this happen? Use this for your meditation today."

THE MIRACLE OF RELAXATION

A relaxed mind is able to see the deeper beauty and wonder all around. Such a mind lends poise and focus to our actions. In relaxation, the joy that we experience expands our mind and the ego slips off with ease. The question is: How can we develop a relaxed mind? We take holidays to relax, so that the mind can experience the joy within, helped by the change of scene outside. For those who live in the cultural world of music, dance, and poetry, the focused mind takes a holiday through art and literature from the distractions of the world. Artists' minds are concentrated, and, depending upon their ability to sublimate their attitudes and inclinations, they can easily get flashes of the Divinity within. Taking a holiday from the ego brings an inner change, and poise in action follows naturally.

Swami Chinmayananda:

Take your time, or time will take you and drain away your strengths. Take a minute, maybe two, throughout your busy day for slowing down to meditate on something beyond the worldly problems and things. Find a quiet place and wait with a receptive heart. Why the worry? What is the hurry? Take your time and roam — picking from the wayside fields that which heals your within. Take some time to walk on grass, to look at flowers, to admire the trees, wondering and pondering upon the wonders stretched around you, up to the horizon! Slacken your pace just so that you may see the view. Take your time, or time takes you. Employ time, or else time will employ you; in the former, you are the master of time; with the latter, you are a slave of time, your employer.

Life becomes a sport once you have learned the art of adding silver edges around the clouds that float in and out of your life's path. Sorrow turns into smiles, pain into pleasure, and discord into melody — when the mind is poised and silent in its unshaken faith in Him who always protects: who alone really IS in everything, everywhere, ever.

Expose yourself to aloneness. When a person is left alone he starts thinking of the higher reality about death, life, soul, God, and the mystery of all. Aloneness is different from loneliness. By remaining lonely, at a place where there is nobody else, realization is not guaranteed. Even in the midst of a crowd you can be alone — being all alone is being with Brahman, the One-without-a-second. Aloneness is not in the surroundings, but it is in one's attitude within — to remain with one end or goal, to remain with all attention fixed upon that one goal. The habit of constantly remaining alone, even in a busy marketplace, is to be cultivated.

Man, when left alone, will become spiritual. The secular, materialistic world will not allow you to think. Therefore we have radio, television, dance, and so on — all to distract the mind. The fit environment for aloneness is not on the mountaintop or in a quiet cave. Be at your meditation seat where you renounce all your relationships with the world around. For the time being, you are to be neither a brother nor a sister; neither a father nor a mother, not a Hindu or a Christian. These are only relationships. 'Short-tall,' 'fat-lean' — these belong to the body. 'Happy–unhappy' — these belong to the mind. 'A believer-a nonbeliever' — these are of the intellect. Detach, detach — be alone. And when you are alone, you are with the Ātman — that is the alone place. You are afraid of loneliness because you do not have the courage to meet yourself and see the parade of your past — recognize that hobbies are your values. You discover that you have a great image of yourself, but the real you is something else. You need not search for God. Be with yourself, and you will turn to God! Prayer is a silent mind. Prayer should be done in the depth of your mind, in the silence of your personality.

Hurry is unknown to all creative expressions in nature outside — the sun rising, the moon setting, the blossoming of the buds, the arrival of the fruits, the germination of the seeds, the fetus in the womb, the bird in the egg — each takes its own time to grow and emerge out. 'Haste is waste' on the Path of Truth. The various disciplines at the mental, intellectual, and physical levels are to be undertaken with an artistic poise, with a literary delicacy, a poetic finish. Force will create only suppressions and deformities of personality. There cannot be any hurry in the natural unfoldment of one's personality.

Music is the ornamentation of silence. The art of listening to Indian classical music itself is a meditation. In India, the ṛṣis have involved all arts in the service of our spiritual culture. Art in every form was made to serve the cause of meditation. The themes, composition, movement, color, dress, and form were all very delicately selected, mixed, and coordinated to create an atmosphere of divine serenity. The audience is wafted into a delicate inner world of joy, at once divine and exhilaratingly peaceful. The melody, beat, and rhythm in our music, the mellifluous orchestra of our purely Indian instruments, bring a magical quietude to the discerning mind. These arts were never played except in temples. The scenario brought a sense of holiness, and thus the sensuous in us and the voluptuous in art are both liquidated to become a stream of a refreshing inner flow of contemplation. Bhāratanātyam is considered by some enthusiasts as a highly evolved form of Indian dance, and the girl has to discipline all her movements, steps, poses, looks, smiles, emotions — in short, everything in her personality, to a pitch of meditation in herself. This mood of the dancer gets broadcast to the receptive and alert minds of the composed and relaxed audience. The Lord dances, and His dance is creation. His dance is the dance of the cosmos. The dancer and the dance are not the same. They are separate, yet the dance has no existence without the dancer. So, too, nothing in the entire universe can exist without the Creator. Music and dance are the throbbing rhythms of His creation. Without Him, mankind will not be.

Poets in their poetic moods, scientists in their laboratory, artisans at their work — all of them discover a joy that is not typical of what we usually experience in the mind. This joy arises subjectively from the steadiness of the mind.

*In a letter to **Sharda Chawla**, Swamiji commended going to spiritual camps:*

"Such short retreats can create a very effective 'Change for the better' in an individual's inner nature and also in her outer personality."

To make optimum use of music, Swamiji advised a certain attitude of listening:

Swamini Gurupriyananda: Many of our saints teach truth through singing their hearts out for the Lord. How to listen to classical music, our devotional songs? Gurudev gave the answer as a message for our Bhakti Sandhya performance: "When the great heart of Smt. M. S. Subbulakshmi opens up to Him, in true, deep devotion, the melody that shall burst forth from her lips can spread the fragrance of His vana-mālā-tulsī garland, perhaps with a suspicion of a slender smell of some clean cowshed and fresh butter. The audience must arrive with its mind well prepared for the great Take-off. See that you are all in your seats before time and fasten the seat belts on your speaking. Calm your mind; remember the Lord of your hearts, iṣṭa devatā (devotee's chosen or favorite deity); sit completely relaxed, both physically and mentally — surrendering totally to Him who is the sole Protector of this universe. To listen to music, adoring the Divine by a deeply devoted person of character and dedication with a worshipful heart, is to transport all devoted hearts listening to it, most effortlessly, in a pleasant spontaneity, into an ecstasy of an inexplicable state of bliss and beatitude." For the concert by Śrī Bala Murali Krishna, Gurudev wrote: "It is not frequently that a nation discovers vocalists like Bala Murali Krishna in its history. They are very rare, to be born with music in their heart." Then, before the performance, he said to the audience: "Learn to listen, relax, allow the music to lift you, throw you down, and lift you up; let its rhythm glide you into adventurous caves of silence and fly you over peaks of melody.... Let go! Let Sangita Lakshmi rock your heart into her magical world of living silence, noisy peace, and flameless light of joy. Don't resist. Keep quiet. Forget everything else. Yield to the graciousness of the pure flow of the music. When it flows from Bala Murali Krishna, you can realize what the crazy gopīs felt in their ecstasy of divine love. Let the blue boy of Vrindavan, in this comforting embrace, melt you into the melody of His Flute."

Breaking people's resistance in a calm way rather than storming their barricades:

Ācārya Vilasini Balakrishnan: Swamiji used humor to point out our attachments in such a way that, in modern psychological terms, 'broke through our defenses.' Swamiji would say that to give a resistant child a pill, just make him laugh, and when his mouth is open wide, pop in the pill before he knows it! Swamiji did this again and again, in every discourse, pointing out human attachments and popping in so many pills of truth that even the most resistant, ego-puffed people could not resist. Slowly he chipped away at our egos, our pride, our stubborn refusal to change. He slowly relaxed our defenses through laughter and compassion. It was all with the goal of freeing us!

Swamiji showed how we can be relaxed in a busy schedule, rather than stressed and harassed:

Swami Shantananda: Toward the end of the Vedānta Course, Gurudev asked me to travel with him as his secretary. His daily routine was to get up at 3:30 A.M. and by 4:30 A.M. he was ready for work. Every day, from 4:30 to 6:30 A.M., he would dictate or himself write over a hundred letters. Since we had only manual typewriters, typing was really hard. Gurudev would be thrilled to receive letters, and it was a pleasure to observe how he replied. When he read and replied to a letter, it was as if the person was in front of him and he was talking to him or her. He wrote the letter, and until it was typed, signed, folded properly, put in the envelope... he was there until it was completed. He would receive letters of great variety: some asked for an article by him, many held queries on Vedānta, and many others asked for help with a problem. The moment he read the letter, he did not have to think for a while like we have to do. He just read the letter and started dictating, sometimes five pages, sometimes ten. While writing, he was very relaxed. He would put his feet up on the table and sometimes suddenly stop talking and close his eyes. In my three years as his secretary, he never asked me to repeat anything. Sometimes, he would stop at a preposition, at half a sentence, or even a word half done, but he would always pick up from where he left off and complete the topic. It was a constant, daily challenge, because the language, the diction, and the vocabulary were those of a Master.

Masters can teach with or without words:

Swamini Shivapriyananda: At one of the camps in the U.S., when I was taking care of the Bala Vihar programs, I hardly had a chance to meet Gurudev or attend lectures. The only session I could regularly attend was morning meditation. The door needed to be open for him to enter the building, and I took the privilege of doing so. It became a very sacred routine. Just he and I, and the deep silence every morning. Day after day, not a word was spoken, only his all-penetrating look as he passed me. If I ever learned about silence that speaks, it was then, and only then.

In self-forgetfulness, one becomes a conduit for the Lord's song:

Rudite J. Emir: Gurudev not only spoke eloquently about the creativity of the artist, but also supported performing arts with a passion. On one trip to India, I accompanied him to a concert by a well-known male singer, who at the beginning of his performance filled the hall with one unbelievably long note that issued forth from deep within him. I was spellbound. Gurudev looked at me knowingly, smiling, understanding my awe, as if to say (as he had on many occasions): "When a true artist sings, there is only the song. When a true dancer dances, there is only the dance. He or she no longer exists. Totally alert, the artist has become a conduit for His song. And no matter how glorious the execution, there can be no reminiscing about the success just achieved."

When we surrender to Him, He takes care of us:

Anil Sachdev: M. S. Subbulaksmi performed at the Bhakti Sandhya function organized by us in Delhi. She had high fever and yet mesmerized one and all by her amazing performance! After dinner, I asked Gurudev: "How was it possible for M. S. to sing so brilliantly despite her high fever and bodily discomfort?" Gurudev laughed and said, "When you are chosen as the instrument by Him, He takes care of you — fever or no fever! When we sing to the Lord, music lifts us beyond all our knowing and doing, to that special place of Being, one with the Lord."

Sensitivity to detail is sensitivity to beauty:

Swamini Gurupriyananda: Gurudev blessed me saying, "Good that you came to visit Ādi Śaṅkarācārya's birthplace at Adi Sankara Nilayam in Veliyanad. It is a very inspiring place of enormous spiritual presence. I know you will do the interior decoration of Śaṅkara's room, where he was born." Gurudev designed the whole room with details of a birth room for the mother [of Śaṅkara] Aaryambha and sent them to me, which was later completed by His grace. Gurudev blessed us to see the divinity and joy in all of Nārāyaṇa's work: "To be sensitive to beauty at all places, all the time, is also the way of yoga. We see beauty only when our mind is quiet and peaceful."

Beauty is the catalytic agent that leads to the culmination of art:

Rudite J. Emir*:* During a satsaṅga at Krishnalaya, California, Gurudev talked about the purpose and definition of art: "To seek beauty and express it is the goal and function of art," he said, while the tape recorder next to him recorded every word. "The common man may not know why he feels happy and peaceful when looking at a sunset; he does not know that it's the beauty that elicits the happy mood." He leaned back in the upholstered chair in which he usually sat while talking to us in the living room of his kuṭiyā at Krishnalaya, closed his eyes, and continued in a subdued voice: "Beauty is the catalytic agent that brings about this mood of the mind … the atmosphere of tranquility." His face shone with a meditative glow as he continued: "One stands aghast because the mind is quiet, fully immersed in the present moment. Stay there. Don't initiate a new thought.… You will dissolve into total self-forgetfulness.… You become beauty. This is the culmination of art."

6

Lendl, Take a Deep Breath!

During a match at Wimbledon between Boris Becker and Ivan Lendl, Swamiji commented, "Lendl, take a deep breath. Let it all go out. Shake off the past. Forget it! Live in the present. Lendl, you are still living in the memory of the past (of not having won Wimbledon). This is psychologically affecting the efficiency of your present action. In this world of ever-changing happenings, of people coming and going, the real essence, the real I, never dies. Holding on to this ever-present 'I,' learn to let go of the past."

The advice to Lendl was also for us — about how to move forward in any endeavor, spiritual or secular. Swamiji famously said, "Refuse to have regrets over the past, fancies for the future, and anxieties in the present. Surrender the present problems to His care, "Nārāyaṇa–Nārāyaṇa." Live in the confidence of His guiding support. Quietly, sincerely, continuously strive on, as best as you can, to live in the awareness of the infinite Self."

HOW TO HANDLE REGRETS

The past can be a very heavy burden to carry, especially if it manifests as negative feelings such as regret for actions we have done and can't change, disappointments over relationships gone sour, frustrations about not having been able to achieve our ambitions, distress about losing the love of our life, and many other memories of failure or injustices of others not having done enough for us, or anything which take our thoughts to dwell in the past. For all these, there is one remedy: like releasing a balloon, let go of the past. Then, if one determinedly stops engaging in actions that are likely to result in regret, that in itself is the best progress. It is a much more powerful way of atoning than getting caught in a cycle of repeated mistakes and expiation.

Swami Chinmayananda:

Let go — where it goes! Stop remembering and craving for things bygone; entertain no joy or sorrow as they reach you in the present. You are carrying a bundle of dead memories of the rotten past. The more we remember the past, those very vāsanās get more deeply fixed into our personality structure. The past is made up of dead moments, and to unearth the buried moments is to live with the dead. Throw away the bundle — walk ten steps and breathe fresh air. Contemplation then comes automatically. Every happening, every experience, is a necessary step toward the great, grand goal. Life supplies experiences, but we never make full use of them. In fact, we always carry a corpse on our shoulders! Embracing this decaying filth, we can never enter the holy sanctum of Truth. We carry bundles of dead moments, which smell!

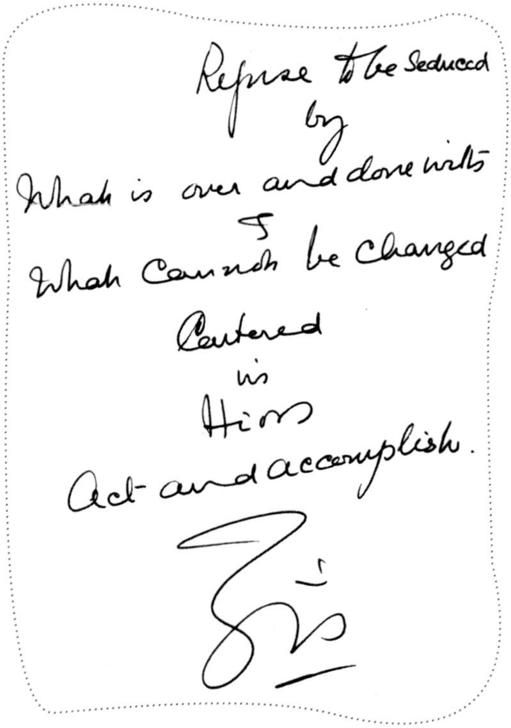

Unload the past, square your shoulders, loosen your muscles, and joyously face your day-to-day problems. When you drag your past memories into the present and try to act with a mind shackled with its hang-ups from the past, you become inefficient, incompetent, and sincerely handicapped in meeting your problems.

Thoughts have a tendency to repeat themselves, and when they do, they create thought-channels that deepen into rivers of thought. Vāsanās are created by us thought by thought, action by action. The less one thinks of a thing, the less one gets attached to it. The opposite is also equally true: the more one thinks of a thing, the more one gets attached to it.

We waste our energies in unproductive and wasteful regrets over things we have already committed. The more we remember them, those very vāsanās get more deeply fixed into our personality structure. Repetition of thinking brings about attachment. With a dose of pure forgiveness, learn to ignore the foolish ways of living you had in your ignorant past. Surrender it all to Him. You forgive yourself: then only can He forgive you!!

To face problems dynamically and to act diligently is any day nobler than escaping passively from the problems and retreating into a hole of bitterness, self-reproach, and self-condemnation.

When an action comes back to me to accuse me, 'Why did you do it?' it is a sin.

Look back, judge, and walk ahead.

Atonement for sins is nothing. Just STOP doing the action. Sins are the negative footprints or vāsanās left in the mind as a result of our wrong actions, which mature to become agitations in the mind. It is because of these agitations that we are not able to meditate and realize the Infinitude.

The core of meditation involves letting go each time we find we have become dependent or addicted. The process of letting go has the quality of a flower that is opening, and this creates a very beautiful feeling of joy, purity, and innocence. It is not necessary to give up the object outwardly. Letting go mentally of your dependency on the object, the clinging attitude, is sufficient to create a feeling of completeness within yourself and within the moment. Simply have the attitude, "I don't have to have it in order to be whole. I can let go and still be full and complete."

Be independent. All relationships will be tossing up and down and can never be steady. Your relationship with Him in your heart alone can be the same.

Let us think BIG and rise above the ripples created by the tragic ego in others.

Never brood over things that have happened or worry over things yet to happen. Live in the present. Intelligently face life with a tranquil mind full of prayer and Īśvara smaraṇa (remembrance). Everything will straighten itself in time. Only we need patience, faith, and sincere self-surrender. The Lord is great; He knows best the purity of every thought, action, and their motives. If the surrender were full, dedication complete, and motives pure, every action becomes a great yajña.

It is a strange bridge from your stupid ego to the infinite Reality. Each time you take two steps, the bridge behind you is burned.

One can remain bitter or move ahead:

Swami Tejomayananda: In the early days, when Gurudev started his work, British rule had just come to an end. So many people were orthodox or in a most confused state. But Gurudev's courage of conviction and fearlessness could not be matched. So many were opposed, but he did not become bitter; he just went on doing his work. Remaining steadfast in your work without becoming bitter is a great quality. And if he felt that he had made a mistake or was wrong, he was magnanimous enough to apologize.

How to atone for sins:

Dr. Shailaja Nadkarni: While he was staying with us, one day Gurudev's heart rate went up and the doctors advised him to have a heart-rhythm check by the HolterMonitor. We got one of the young hospital technicians to come home and place the HolterMonitor on Pūjya Gurudev. The young lady said to me, "I have never met anyone like him." She was a Christian. The next day when she came to the house, she wanted to ask Gurudev a question. He replied, "You can ask anything." She said, "I have committed many mistakes in my life and I have sinned. What should I do to cleanse myself?" Pūjya Gurudev replied, "Take a picture of Christ, keep it in front of you in a clean place, and light a candle in front of it. Then confess, and, after that, never repeat the same mistakes."

When an object of attachment is taken from us, or when we are put into an unconducive situation, it is an opportunity for spiritual growth; but Swamiji knew how to show compassion when the devotee was filled with regret:

Dr. Kshama Mehtre: Gurudev had given me a beautiful ring, which he transferred from his finger to mine quietly while a group photograph was being taken, saying, "You will remember the photograph." I wondered why he had said that about the photograph rather than the ring. The ring was slightly loose on my finger; before I could get it tightened, I lost the ring and I was very upset. Next time when Gurudev came to the Sidhbari āśrama, even before I told him, he said to me "Don't be sad. It was just an object." However, I was dumbfounded by his compassion during the next visit to Sidhbari. He called me to his room and put another ring on my finger.

Words alone are not enough:

Anjali Singh: When I put forward a grievance to Swamiji and found him unsympathetic, I said, "Forget it!" to which he replied: "The very fact of saying 'forget it' means that you have not forgotten it!"

A sāttvika mind cannot be realized while the ego is fully intact:

Rudite J. Emir: Gurudev found many inventive ways to remind us that the ego is the culprit, the one who blocks our journey to fulfillment. One brief but piercing bit of teaching about the ego took place during a yajña in San Francisco. After the lecture, I had just arrived at Gurudev's hotel room and was approaching him, when he looked at me intensely and said: "Drop it!" Without a moment's hesitation, I let go of the shawl around my shoulders. As it was falling to the floor, I realized what Gurudev had meant: "Drop the ego!" He nodded his head in agreement, knowing, as he always did, what had just transpired in my mind.

Vāsanās have to be sublimated, not suppressed:

***Ācārya Vilasini Balakrishnan*:** Gurudev warned us that sublimating our attachments does not mean suppressing them. Suppression will never last and will lead to an eventual eruption of desires. Sublimation, on the other hand, is a natural vairāgya, detachment born of understanding how attachment restricts us and prevents our awakening. Once we see how our mental attachments restrict us — as Gurudev said, "How long will we keep a dead rat in the cupboard? We will throw it out immediately!" Swamiji pointed out that we could reduce the vāsanās behind our mental conditionings only if we are aware of them. The vāsanās that we become aware of we can overcome. The vāsanās that are deeply buried will persist until we become conscious of them, and, by viveka (discrimination) and vairāgya, are dropped.

The sure way to shed our dependencies:

Anjali Singh: Shefali Saran and I were seeing Swamiji off to the airport. I said in the car, "Swamiji, you are going away and I will again become addicted to Prarthna Saran (Shefali's mother) in your absence. I can't do without you, and now I won't be able do without her when you are not here!" Swamiji said, "Don't worry! I am going to unhang you from all your hang-ups and hang you on the Self!

TAKE A HOLIDAY FROM CAUTION

Sometimes we get very serious about the world and take upon ourselves many tensions unnecessarily. Unintelligent attachment to things and beings keeps the mind chained to the world and opens the door to anxiety and tension. At the heart of this is a lack of understanding about the distinction between love and attachment and how this lack of understanding distorts our relationship with our body, mind, and intellect. Our attachments create undue emphasis on worldly interests and prevent us from appreciating the better, more intelligent option. The way forward is to understand this distinction.

Swami Chinmayananda:

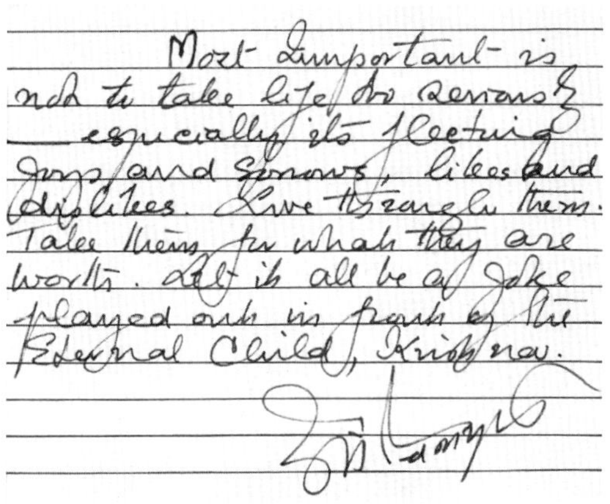

Let your life in the world be no more than a minor disturbance in you, the infinite Self. Nothing in this world is permanent; the disturbing factors also cannot remain permanently with you to give you perpetual disturbance. They, too, are finite. Then why worry? The more a seeker unintelligently worries over his mind and its caprices, the more the mind grows in grossness and asserts itself upon the seeker's inner world. Ignore the mind. Conquer it with understanding. Never create a stalemate in your confrontation with the mind. Where you cannot at this moment directly meet the mind and win it over, ignore it in that field and attack it where it is weak. Observe and understand its weaknesses and its usual strategies. Outwit it by diplomatic moves, by assertion of your essential lordship over it.

Attachment is a mental knot with which you have tied yourself to things and beings all around, which is a self-made slavery. Attachments are not to be renounced, but our relationship is to be chastened by changing the attitude of our love toward them. Detachment doesn't mean love-less-ness. Attachment is a mental conditioning of all of us wherein we start feeling, "I cannot live without a particular thing or a specific person." Attachment means, "I want." I = ego, want = desire. The entire *Gītā* is a cry to end the ego and egocentric desires, and then relate yourself with things, beings, and situations. Then you are free to give love, show anger, to express tendencies without getting involved, bound, tied down, and gagged by emotions.

Silently hear everyone. Accept what is good and reject and forget what is bad. The world is a mixture. Accept all and take only what you want, reject the rest and live happily.

***Query** from a Postal Lesson Course student: I read and learn that attachments are bad, yet how is it possible to live with the family members and not get attached to them?*

***Swamiji**:* You are misunderstanding the exact content of the terms 'attachment' and 'love.' When we come to depend upon things and beings for our sense of security and fullness, it becomes attachment; attachment shackles and makes us a prisoner. Love is an expansion of ourselves to embrace in our identification with things and beings; here we don't need them for our fullness and therefore we are free. Love liberates our mind. Attachment compels us to be a slave to the world outside, and we feel shattered without those beings and things. The urgency of the mind to feel 'I' plus 'I want'— meaning, when I feel that I cannot live without it — this becomes attachment. In short, ego + egocentric (selfish) desire = attachment. Please THINK.

*In a letter to **T. N. Parthasarathy:*** Learn to live like a cracked pot. Receive everything, but in a short time, let it all leak out and make your mind clean for contemplation. Don't get involved with the children or their ups and downs. Surrender them and their future to the Great Protector.

A light-hearted way to begin a letter:

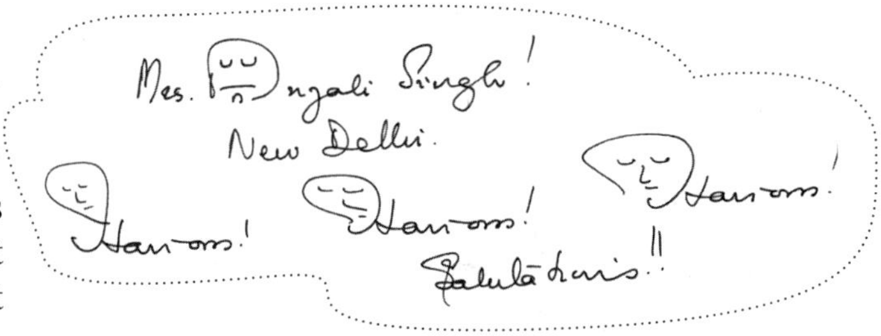

Opting for the optimistic view of life:

Swami Tejomayananda: Doctors said that a person with a heart condition like Gurudev's couldn't even go from place A to place B! Yet Gurudev was constantly traveling internationally, conducting programs and meetings; it was simply a miracle. He was a diabetic patient and losing all sensation in his feet. Some people would show concern and say, "Oh, Swamiji's legs and feet have become numb...." In reply, he would say, "But my brain is working, no? What is working, why don't you pay attention to that?"

Braving physical challenges daringly:

Ācārya Vilasini Balakrishnan: In every city that Swamiji visited, a new doctor would arrive to be his personal physician during the yajña. Each doctor would offer new advice, but even though doctor after doctor advised Gurudev to travel less and rest more, he would smile and nod benevolently. Then he would not change a single thing on his schedule! He would say, "My children are calling me; I must go." He also joked, "Why, I never travel at all. I merely go up on the plane, then the world turns under me, and then the plane comes down! I am not moving anywhere!" Our Gurudev was truly the Motionless!

Continuing to play the game of life under the most severe circumstances:

Dr. Rashmi Singh: During the 1991 yajña in Piercy, Gurudev had several episodes of congestive heart failure, and I was called to treat his condition. He needed intravenous injection of Lasix immediately. I was nervous, sweating, and emotional. How could I puncture my revered Guru with a needle? He looked at me, despite breathing heavily with an oxygen mask on, and extended his arm. He uttered, "Umm, do it!" Half an hour after I had successfully injected him, he got up and went to the next class. He roared like a lion in his usual style and continued all his classes. After class, while I was still shivering from the incident, he said, "Play your role. When you need to be a doctor, be a doctor; when you need to be a wife, be a wife. The world is a stage; play your role to perfection and the Lord will free you."

A holiday from caution every now and then!

Ācārya Vilasini Balakrishnan: After Gurudev's bypass surgery in 1980, he finally gave in to taking insulin twice a day for his diabetes and taking the new sweetener, Equal, in his tea and desserts. When Swamiji started traveling to yajñas again, and going out for bhikṣās three times a day, each bhikṣā host was notified to prepare sweet dishes with Equal and not to serve any high glycemic foods. The challenge to monitor this fell on me. Most devotees insisted on serving their best dishes, including sweets and fried foods. Some would argue: "Swamiji is God Himself and can eat anything." When Swamiji sat down to eat, he uncannily knew exactly which hostesses were upset. He would start asking, "Amma, where is my pāyasam?" When she served pāyasam made with Equal, he would say, "Where is the real pāyasam? I know you made it. You have it hidden in the kitchen!" And the hostess would joyfully bring out the real sweet. Gurudev would take each bite of the forbidden food with great relish. Her face would beam and she would cast disapproving looks at me. Later, Swamiji wrote to me, "Try to keep your mind always in an atmosphere of surrender to the Lord, and keep an awareness of Him as your own Self." So how could I get upset about what Gurudev ate or didn't eat!?

What would be the reaction if the object or person one is attached to were taken away?

Prarthna Saran: A group of devotees sitting with Gurudev before dinner were discussing clinging attachment. Anjali Singh asked, "Swamiji, Prarthna keeps telling me that I am too attached to my children." Even before Gurudev could respond, Pranav, my thirteen-year-old son, rose to Anjali's defense saying, "Swamiji, Anjali Aunty is only attached to her children. Mummy may not be so attached to hers, but she was very attached to her dog!" There was laughter all around. Then Anjali elaborated, "Swamiji, Prarthna's dog died recently and she cried so much that she had severe heart palpitations and a doctor was called. She thought she was going to die of sorrow." Loud laughter again as Anjali continued, "And you know, Swamiji, she had to stop crying, because she was horrified to think that if she died, everyone will say that she died crying for a dog!?" Since it was my turn to offer bhikṣā to Gurudev, I was busy in the kitchen. Unable to control my curiosity, I went to see what the great joke was about, only to discover that it was about me!!

How to overcome a strong sense of attachment:

Purnima Daulet Singh: I have always been worried about being too attached to my children. In Sandeepany, Mumbai in March 1984, I mentioned to my friend, "I have a big problem. I wish I could meet Swamiji." Gurudev would be called 'Swamiji' then. I had been attending his lectures at Powai but had never met him one to one. The headquarters of Chinmaya Mission is in Mumbai, so whenever he came he was always busy at his desk, and there would be a long queue of devotees waiting to meet him just to be able to greet him personally. Anjali kindly arranged a meeting for me, telling him that I had a 'big' problem. I was overawed by him and went in hesitantly. I did my praṇāms and sat quietly because he was busy writing. No words would come out because I was so nervous. He looked at me and patiently asked me what I wanted to say. I hesitatingly told him about my strong attachment to my children and asked how I should deal with it. He continued writing for a few minutes and then just pointed his pen upwards, looked up, and said, "Attach!" I got my answer that one has to practice what he called 'the yoga of attachment–detachment.'

Making God the center of one's life:

Anjali Singh: In 1992 in Sidhbari, the biggest worry for many of us was Swamiji's health. There was this fear of physically losing him. But Swamiji found ways to console us. While looking at the green mustard fields that terraced the valley at Sidhbari, he said, "It is all a delusion. When the sarso (mustard) was born, I was there. When the sarso grew, I was there. When the sarso became green, I was there. When the sarso flowered, I was there. When was I not there?" He wanted us to live our life centered in 'I,' the Self, which never dies.

7

Breakpoint

When one of the players got a breakpoint, one of the devotees said, "Oh! He could win the game! He has got a breakpoint." But Swamiji responded, "He could lose the game, because he has got a breakpoint." Swamiji gave a different meaning for 'breakpoint.'

A breakpoint occurs in tennis if the receiver, and not the server, has the chance to win the game. It is an opportunity to break the service of the player who is serving the ball. Swamiji gave his own opposite meaning and insisted that it meant the receiver would get a break from winning!

In spiritual life there are two types of breakpoints. Spiritual practice is not always smooth. It has its ups and downs. When the mind gets disturbed or when vāsanās embedded in the subconscious rise to the forefront, then there is a break in the bliss experienced by a quiet mind and it gets overshadowed. One need not get worried about this. This is the normal process of the mind till it reaches its goal and abides in the Self. These breaks are natural. So to get perturbed by them and leave the practice is not prudent.

Breaking our routine and missing out on our practice is not advised. Says Swamiji, "Breaks in spiritual practices are not advisable. They not only destroy the effects of the past practices, but often they can cause some positive bad effects — hence, the necessity for the uninterrupted bhajana [worship, seeking the Lord, service]. If bhakti is the emotional accompaniment, bhajana represents the joy-dance of activities in the life of the diligent devotee. When bhajana is practiced for a long period of time, the seeker discovers that the devotion for the Lord has taken root in him. Practice becomes easy when it is ceaselessly carried out with reverence for a sufficiently long period of time."

ANVIL OF ADVERSITY

Each of us has to face adverse situations in life. No one is exempt. While each person's problems come in different wrappings, the essential contents are common — disease, deformities, accidents, separation, non-fulfillment of desires, loss or lack of wealth, losing loved ones, problems of old age, bereavement, natural calamities. Though these are part and parcel of the world of change, when they happen, our mental reactions in the form of anxiety, fear, grief, worry, anger, and dejection, and sometimes even madness, are the problem. Adversity is complex and has the potential for manifold outcomes — not all of which are negative. For example, it can 'finish off our vāsanās' — what in Christianity is called 'forgiveness of sins.' Adversity is the anvil on which the mind is tested and purified. It also hastens the pace of spiritual growth if we maintain the attitude that everything, including adversity, is God's gift.

Swami Chinmayananda:

The world in which others and I live — and unfortunately in which you also have to live — is full of pains and diseases, deaths and sorrows. One or the other has to go earlier. Who knows what all endless sorrow a person might have to suffer due to his illness. Be assured that what He does is always for the best.

Life is full of ups and downs. Things change. Even Śri Rāma and Lord Kṛṣṇa, Christ and Mohammed had to face them. Their glory was that even while facing them all, they smilingly lived fully, fulfilling their duties in life. Those who have faith in God are not guaranteed that they will have none of the worldly tragedies. The world will remain the same whether you are a devotee or not. The devotee finds in herself more equilibrium and balance in meeting the world. The true nature comes out in us only when we are crushed. The fragrance of chandan emerges only when rubbed. Tulsī leaves leave their fragrance on the very fingers that crush them.

Tragedies come from the world; don't worry about them. He gives. He takes away. Don't lose your faith in Him. You offered your worldly and spiritual wealth to the Lord. When trouble comes, you want it back. You want something that the Lord decides not to give you. It is ultimately for your good. He will protect you. How dare you worry about it? In any adversity, there is in its depth a treasure of spiritual blessings secretly hidden.

The Lord sends you disturbance so that you can discriminate between consciousness and thoughts, even in that experience of disturbance. With every disturbance, the Lord is sending you a reason for meditation. The art of practicing harmony is to be applied in the din of the marketplace while we are sweating with exertion upon the narrow path of adversities.

Illness and pain are the dharmas of the body. Whoever has a body will have these. The courage is to suffer them with peaceful joy in spite of them, pray ardently to the Lord for His Love. Never pray for a cure. Lord will never give anyone — even His enemy — more pain than he deserves. Pray only for giving us the strength and courage to suffer and, yet, pray with all love. Keep on smiling, always, at all times, under all conditions. When situations are not conducive, it is pāpa kṣaya, exhaustion of sins, taking place. When they are conducive, it is puṇya kṣaya (exhaustion of merits) taking place. Use the good times for contemplation.

Is there not a Great Master who protected you all along? Do not worry how He will come, that is His job. He will manifest Himself before you and make you realize it. He can give you the power to experience Him. The Lord Himself has assured us in the *Gītā* most positively: "O son of Kunti! Declare from the housetops that My devotee shall never come to ruin." The world, even if you hold on to it, will slip; and God, even if you want to leave Him, will not abandon you. The Lord can smile and make, unmake, remake, and do everything. Wait and watch the divine jokes — peacefully, joyously! The Lord alone is the Sole Protector. One who has surrendered to Him has nothing to fear. All we get is His precious loving prasād back to us.

When God gives pain, God again gives us the power to suffer and provides people to look after us. Never worry. Everything will in the end serve only in taking your mind nearer to Him. Be assured of this. Pain is the Lord's kindest means to wake us up the quickest. There is nothing at any time in any circumstance to worry over, "Why this to me?" What you have is His gift to you. What you do with what you have is your gift to Him. Convert every experience to being His will and humbly surrender to Him. Accept whatever environment you get in life as his prasād.

Among the wondrous phenomena of this universe, the human system, which is self-repairing, appears to be the most unique machine.

In a train, we meet people and make their acquaintance, or we quarrel with them, and so on. When the station comes, we part never to meet again. It is the same in this world. This is the lot for every one of us: that, as we live longer, we have to meet the experience of parting with those who fall in the pilgrimage of life. But if we have lived our life intelligently and have gathered enough philosophical understanding of the nature of the Lord and His actions and His play, we shall watch them all with extreme compassion.

In this letter, Swamiji provides consolation and encouragement for the devotee to use adversity as an opportunity to strengthen his faith and spiritual growth:
Very sorry to understand that … had an accident. May He protect us all. And He does — or else who brings the doctor at the right time to the spot?! Please let me know that it is nothing and she is progressing well. How far were you shot off your balance when this impact of the news came to you? And how quickly could you find your balance? This in itself is an intense sādhanā. Live in the present, without wasting your time and energy trying to relive the past …. Remember, none of us is Nārāyaṇa, and it is His job to nourish, nurture, feed, clothe, and preserve. He is not an unjust God.

Gurudev's consolation and encouragement to a full-time Chinmaya Mission sevikā who had to face the demise of a healthy grown-up son in an accident:
Hari Om! Hari Om! Hari Om! I am shocked! Such sudden tragedy, when it bursts very near us, we cannot but get shocked. It is natural. Despairing and weeping are the outlets through which the ordinary man releases the inner tensions. With knowledge, our return to balance within becomes quick and the sooner. I had to withstand the sudden departure of Brahmacārini Pillani. Now this news from you! We have to live thro' them all; with wisdom and faith, it becomes easier… yet it is painful. Your wife must be most inconsolable. You convey to her my sympathies and prayers. Now stop all mourning. Think. The Lord of Guruvayoor is not a vengeful, cruel power; He is Love incarnate. Therefore, whatever is with us are all His. He gave. He took away. He has every right — the boy is His. The Lord had been confident that you both will be the best parents for him, and so He gave him to you. You did your best to the boy. He came for his growth. The Lord, the Law, demanded now for him a different field to express. Let us not hold him up — let him go from glory to glory. Both of you go and visit our temple ārati for ten continuous days. Thanks. Write to me after this vratam [vow, commitment].

Letter to bereaved person when death was sudden:
I am glad that he did not suffer like other people — he had an effortless death (anāyāsena maraṇam), that which even the ṛṣis desire.

"Whose destiny caused the death?" – questions a student from the Postal Course:

Q. A friend of mine lost his five-year-old son today. Applying the Law of Karma, the following questions came to my mind: 1) Is it caused by the destiny of the boy? 2) Is it caused by the destiny of the parents who have to face the grief?

Swamiji: The doubt arose in your mind only because you recognize the universe as constituted of individuals separate from each other. The entire world is an integral whole. You sitting there in New Jersey are now making me sit down here and dictate this reply and, because of me, you are the Postal Lesson student. Thus, even though I don't know you directly, here are two of us interacting and reaching out to each other. One Hitler can shake all moral values and ethical concepts out of the era. One Jesus influenced all living human beings. It is your prārabdha (destiny) that you are the son of your father, the husband of your wife, and perhaps the father of your children. But at the same time, is it not also true that it is the destiny of your father, wife, and your children that you are what you are. Considering this life as a web of mutual reactions constantly between each being with all others … now the questions become clear:

Q: 1. Is the incident caused by the destiny of the boy?

Swamiji: Surely, the child had no more need for his body in that particular environment to exhaust his residual vāsanās and therefore he quit.

Q: 2. Is the incident caused by the destiny of the parents who have to face the grief?

Swamiji: At the same time, it is also that the destiny of the parents that they have to go through the sorrows of the bereavement. Meet the parents, talk to them, and tell them that I have sent them a message: "Children come through us. They don't belong to us. When an arrow comes out of a bow, it is not for the bow to decide where the arrow should go; the bowman knows it. He decides. The job of the bow is to bend according to the will and demand of the bowman. Each arrow has a different flight in its direction, purpose, and distance. Our job is to bend as the Lord wants us to do. Ours cannot be the responsibility of how far our children should go or in what direction they should go. Since we have got an intelligence, unlike the bow, it is valid that we maintain in ourselves, at all times, good wishes for our children and do our best toward them as long as the chance is given to us."

In reply to ***Dr. Kambham Suhasini:*** *Whether death due to accidents, too, is preordained:*

There are no 'accidents.' This is a cosmos, not a chaos. Everything is happening in nature for the onward surge of evolution. Each one of us will have our share of joys and sorrows during our life, and one day we each snap off from the Manifest Play. Don't try to judge the Justice of such happenings. It can be the greatest Blessing to the departed. We do not know what else was in store for her/him in life!

To a devotee in whose house there was a bereavement of an elderly family member:
When anyone leaves, we, in our selfishness, cry, and despair — the thought is: "How happy I would have been if she or he remained." The phenomenon obeys only its own laws and not our individual whims or fancies or needs. Such sudden tossings in our life's journey shatters those who have no ideal to hold on to. ... Understand the flimsiness of life, which is a field to create joy for others, however meager it may be. Instead of demanding your comfort and happiness in life, try to give comfort and happiness to others in life. Don't waddle in your own pit of sorrow, demanding pity and sympathy from others. Learn to rise up and walk your way. Cry it out quickly and take up the strings of life.

Letter to ***Neeru Mehta:*** Lord does that which is best for us always. Even sorrows mold us into better beings. Your unsaid complaint reminds me of an intelligent fish trying to bite its own tail so that it may be safe from any chance of slipping and falling into endless depths of the ocean. The fool did not realize that it exists in, and is ever supported by, the Lord of the ocean. You are not expected to remain ever in that 'state': now and then agitations must lash at you. Yet, if you have devotion to the Lord, who is ever at your beck and call, who supports you always, there is a golden streak of inner peace threading thro' all worries, anxieties, and agitations. Everything happening to every one of us all the time during a lifetime is to educate us — they are learning occasions. Some learn — some do not. Those who fail to learn are put through the same whirl in different patterns. We must learn to move with alternate Consciousness. There alone is peace and joy, true and enduring.

Letter to ***Srichand Krishnani*****:** Life is difficult. Sometime it becomes too harsh. But still do not lose interest. The only shelter is the Lord alone. Hold on to Him.

Letter to ***Vinita Asrani:*** Nothing in life happening to us is by accident. A very loving and kindly Power is exposing us to different types of joys and sorrows for our own inner growth. Learn to accept them cheerfully even when you cry for the pains!! Obstacles in the form of pain, illness, bereavement, losses would come in everyone's life. That is the nature of life here. They are not permanent. So with patience in silent dignity, face them all cheerfully, these two-night guests. When they move away, let us cheerfully pursue our life's work.

One never knows all the factors that cause the worst and then cause it to be over:
Swami Tejomayananda**:** Gurudev joined national politics as a freedom fighter. He was captured and sent to jail. Since his health was precarious, the jail authorities left him outside. A Christian woman, passing by, took him and nursed him back to health. Gurudev mentioned that she remembered her son when she saw him, because his nose resembled her son's. So, even a nose can save you! What can save you — you do not know.

SHOCK ABSORBERS OF LIFE

When tragedies come to us, we are shocked by them and lose our balance. But if we have prepared our minds in advance and gathered spiritual stamina through philosophical thinking reinforced by conviction and an unshakeable faith in God, then these become our shock absorbers in life. They help to cushion the trauma. Luckily, Vedānta offers this solution. If one can counteract negative effects on the mind through faith and right thinking, these very adversities can become the stepping-stones to achieving a state of equipoise, which in turn is a springboard to knowing the ultimate Truth.

Swami Chinmayananda:

The inner heart that has spun a web of silence around itself can easily sweep all turmoil in, and will absorb all shocks from the outer world of happenings. There can be no greater gift to yourself than a life wherein your mind is quiet and silent, even in the face of imminent calamity.

People say, "God has forsaken me!" Is there an ornament forsaken by gold? Can a mud pot be forsaken by mud? In every experience of yours, He is ever with you. Consciousness flares forth and shines through every thought, but our attention is on the theme of the thoughts and not on the content that illumines the thought. How far is water from the waves? How far is the waker from the dreamer? So, how far is God from you? Who paints the sky blue? Who changes the formation of the clouds and the décor of the sky every minute? The shades change, patterns change, so, also, your thinking changes. You may not like the changes. From experience to experience, even in a tragedy, shift your attention from the sorrow to the One who illumines it. Go back to Consciousness. When the attention is not on the object, there is no experience of sorrow.

Pray. Prayer has strength, unbelievable indeed, until we start praying. Prayer is not asking; it is a longing of the soul. If man prays in prosperity as fervently and wholeheartedly as he does in adversity, how easily would he realize Brahman! Worship the Lord; he is the only one who will never disappoint you. In our life, we refuse to come to the axle, to Nārāyaṇa. We live ever on the circumference and get crushed by the very wheel of life to which we are hanging on for security! Without spiritual stamina, no one can stand up to the threats and onslaughts of circumstances in life.

When your expectations are false, disappointments are natural. Against a dark background alone a Jewel of Light will shine better. There must be deluded ones rejecting the good, so that the good will have its unique value and preciousness. You must learn to smile away their ignorance and the consequent confusions in them. Even Lord Kṛṣṇa will have a śiśupāla (foe)!! The companionship of the good gives the necessary lift for the mind to maintain its height and balance.

Many are the thinkers who have been tantalized by the horrid beauty of the tearful incident in life called death. Even today, death is a fascinating idea with all writers and thinkers, authors and philosophers, of all climes and conditions. It is only the sages of old, who in their quietude had prepared their instruments of understanding and feeling to the required efficiency to soar into the sublime realms of the Beyond, that have really succeeded in analyzing scientifically and in concluding truly the what, how, and why of the phenomenon called death. Death is only one of the incidents in a human existence, and tomorrow has no accidental or arbitrary beginning, but it is only a perfect continuation of today. To die is not anything unique. He is but one in the endless march of the dying crowd, first of many who will come after, one in the midst of his contemporaries. The great Mahātmās go beyond this continuous birth-death experience in their lifetime itself. Why should a sincere seeker ever feel afraid of death? The body has nothing to do with the Self, which is man's true nature.

Up to a point, we feel that this ideal state of constant bliss is just within our reach. But some misery from the world, or some inner grief, always comes to shake up our mind, destroying even the vague comprehension of bliss, which we had gained from the study of the scriptures. How then can a devotee practice his devotion when he is distressed by bereavement, when he suffers loss of wealth, when he is shorn of name and fame? The cardinal attitude of heroism in our Hindu philosophy is: "Refuse to weep; keep smiling." Then even the sorrow that reaches us gets ashamed and retires in its incompetency to make us suffer. It has then to go away; it cannot stay with such a heroic heart.

There are very many things in life which you and I may plan, but they may happen differently. That need not be considered as a great tragedy. All that we get in life are the exact prescriptions of the Lord of Lords — meant solely for our own evolutionary progress.

There is no sin greater than getting oneself upset at life's turns and twists. To lose our balance, self-poise, or equanimity is a crime against the Self. There is nothing really worth worrying about, nor for feeling elated about, in the ever-changing phenomenon called life. Catch hold of the Lord's angavastram (a long shawl covering the upper portion of the body); never go any farther than its length allows. Play the life out around Him in tune to His flute.

To a sincere seeker, nothing untoward happens. The body then becomes His responsibility. To a devotee who turns toward Him entirely, no insurance is needed. He will look after His bhakta.

Q. *If we have to suffer the consequences of our actions, what is the role of prayer?*
Swami Chinmayananda: The stream of happenings comes and goes irresistibly around and above you, and that which gives the balance to face them steadily is prayer. Prayer is not to change the pattern around you but to give you protection from it. We do not travel in a boat to stop waves, but the sides of the boat do protect us from the raw, direct hits of the waves. Think. When personal problems come, you get into the Arjuna sthiti. Hence, you feel confused. At all times, try to maintain the attitude that you are existing and moving about in an atmosphere of His grace, and whatever situations that rise are all situations and challenges prescribed by Him for your own inner purification.

Letter to ***Kamala Chidambaram:*** Lord plans all our encounters, every moment, for our growth. It is foolish to expect what we must have. He decides to what lots we must be exposed.

Letter to ***Madhuri Jhala:*** Surrender to the Lord is the greatest remedy for depression. Expect nothing. Be satisfied with what He gives. Where can there be depression?

Letter to ***Pravin Gandhi:*** Don't try to end ego and a sense of insecurity. But turn to Him, who is ever present in your own heart. He alone is the Sole Protector and most dependable Guide. Surrender and follow Him, and may His grace be an umbrella for you always.

Letter to ***Dr. Kambham Suhasini:*** He is not hearing you because you have a selfish interest somewhere in your depth. Without any personal desire, when you whole-heartedly pray, it is 'heard' and 'accepted.' Don't waste your inner energies in such [selfish] prayers. Serve Him. Be confident that what He accomplishes is always for the good of all. In His infinite wisdom, He never makes any mistakes. Let us learn to surrender to His will and act nobly with humble joy that we are allowed to serve at all.

Letter to ***Anjali Singh:*** Life and its happenings reach us through our mind, and so our interpretation of it all is as our mind decides. Keep your mind calm and serene, unperturbed by what is happening around you. With a clean, quiet mind, it is difficult to detect any fault or defect in the world. All is beautiful and peaceful, pure, and noble. The rest is all His sport. Everything changes. That is saṁsāra — to teach you this simple observable fact that you are exposed to the world of plurality. Study your own life: changes!! Around you, changes!! If everything is changing, the Knower of the change, you, must be changeless. Be that Changeless, your own Self. Try to realize that change seen is a delusion. Birthless Deathless Self alone IS. Never think of the "two things that can happen." Let only one thing happen. Reach the supreme Oneness. Shamelessly embrace, in Love Divine, the most Glorious, in a mood of total meditation. Let Him pervade you, penetrate your 'stone,' and give the pulsations He wants. Reach the joyous Peak of the Bliss Beatitude. You have heard enough. Now reflect — and 'live,' please.

Giving the mind a positive direction:

Swami Tejomayananda: Once, a girl who had a problem with her knees went to see Gurudev. She now had an artificial leg. Most feel pity when they see people with such ailments, but Swamiji laughed and said, "Thank God, you have got good brains! There are so many people who have no brains." The idea was to turn her energies in a positive direction.

Keeping God in our life:

Cate Hallpike: Swamiji was full of love and devotion to those he served and always with his head at the feet of Lord. He carried his simple hand mālā wherever he went. While journeying between events, he would pull it out and chant quietly, but loudly enough so we could learn by example. He was forever reminding us through his own actions that, for forty minutes each day, meditation was not an 'eyes closed event.' Rather, meditation is a 24/7 State of Being.

Vedānta helps to mitigate sorrow due to tragic circumstances:

***Dr. Rashmi Singh**:* Gurudev has been a beacon of light, guiding and supporting us with kindness, love, and compassion. Gurudev first advised me on the occasion of my husband's critical condition, which was due to an angiogram-induced complication. He wrote, "Be a Hindu wife, and your husband will come out of it as easily as he has fallen into it. In life, there will be ups and downs; Pandavas suffered even with Kṛṣṇa at dinner with them every day, Sītā suffered, even though Rāma was her supreme lover, husband. But, with philosophy, we gain the inner strength to stand the shocks of life."

The 'heart' of the matter:

***Ācārya Vilasini Balakrishnan**:* Before his bypass surgery, Gurudev told the doctors that they would be surprised at how large-hearted he was! If he had high sugar levels, he would tell people that he was just too sweet.

Accepting everything as the Lord's gift:

Ācāryas Gaurang and Darshana Nanavaty: We stayed with Gurudev in a motel in Vancouver. It so happened that Gurudev had a small corner room, while Darshana and I were allotted a big room. During satsaṅga, everyone would crowd around Gurudev in his small room; people would even sit on his bed. Seeing this, I offered, "Shall we switch rooms?" He looked straight at me and asked, "Do you think I am suffering? Nārāyaṇa has put me here, only He may be suffering." That was when I realized that he was living the phrase in the *Bhagavad-gītā,* 'nimitta-mātraṁ bhāva,' only working as an instrument of Nārāyaṇa.

When the Guru gives advice, it is to help us prepare ourselves for the shocks of life:

Anjali Singh: I was quite sure that I was right about what a breakpoint was in tennis terminology, that it was an opportunity for the one receiving the ball to break the service of the opponent. But Swamiji kept insisting that it meant that it was a break from winning! I almost wanted to bet with him that if the tennis dictionary proved me right he would have to give me a 'breakthrough' in meditation! Then I restrained myself, remembering that Swamiji made these 'tennis' statements when he wanted to teach something. Sure enough, a letter from home came with some really upsetting news, and my mind, which had been reveling in bliss, tumbled into sorrow. I should have listened to Swamiji and expected this when he had warned me.

8

Deuce!

While watching a match between Steffi Graf and Gabriela Sabatini played earlier that year at Wimbledon, someone asked Swamiji whose side he was on. "Graf," he replied. "I like her attitude." The person who asked the question was supporting Sabatini and said, "I don't want only the Germans to win every year!" To this, Swamiji said, "It is beyond caste or creed or nationality! It is not that. It is the attitude, the character that matters. The other one has it, too. It is a bit of luck against her. But it is neck to neck. It could be a photo finish!" Sure enough, a photo finish it was. Sabatini was two points away from winning Wimbledon, when Graf wrested the match away from her and the final set went to 8–6!

What is the "attitude, the character" Swamiji is talking about? Clearly, he was referring to the inner attitude and character required to walk the path toward Realization — an inner attitude of equipoise, which is gained after a heroic effort to slowly, but gradually, root out our negative traits and replace them with positive ones. This has to be an active effort to change — within one's self.

TO CHANGE IS TO LIVE

Change is inevitable in life. It happens even without our consent. The world keeps changing, and we constantly find ourselves in different environments. What we often haven't realized is that we create environments for ourselves according to the unconscious impulses of our inner drives and desires. For example, at seven o'clock in the evening, one person might be found in a bar and another in a prayer hall. So the real direction of where we find ourselves is driven from within. Though we change inevitably from environment to environment, the important question is: Are we moving in the right direction?

Swami Chinmayananda:

Through individual perfection alone, world perfection can be aspired to. When the people change, the country changes. In our modern world, we are doing the opposite. We try to change the world without changing the people.

Since we live as we are living, we are what we are. If you want to lift your life into a greater ambit, you have to **change** your ways of living.

The type of body, mind, and intellect that you have at this present moment, and the environments created around you with the specific qualities of objects, emotions, and thoughts, are all ordered by your own vāsanās that you predominantly have at this moment. Thus, your mental sluggishness and the environment of drunkards, bottles, and the drinking booth around you are all ordered by your own vāsanā to drink. By your own effort, when you stop drinking the bottles, the other drunkards' bottles, the drinking booth all change around you, and your liver rebuilds its vitality. The mental sluggishness disappears and the intellectual nausea lifts itself. Destiny can be changed, not by readjusting the world outside but by changing your own inner nature. You order your destiny — ***You*** change! — and the world around you must change. Each one of us is the center of the universe. When you change, the world will change. Change the texture of your thoughts, and your life will change.

If you are not willing to change, do not enter the path of spirituality. When you allow yourself to see yourself and think about the tragic life you are leading, then changes begin to happen.

The river of thoughts is the mind. When the water is slow, fast, dirty, flooded, the river is slow, fast, dirty, or flooded. *As the thoughts, so the mind!* The thought flow can be controlled in its quantity, quality, and direction. When the mind's pattern is changed, the man is changed. If any of them — quality, quantity, or direction of thoughts — is changed, the other two are automatically changed. You have to give up imitating the false values of others around you, meaning, stop living blindly a stamped blueprint of life, supplied by the fashions of the times, or by the sensuous men who seek their fulfillment in sense indulgences. Just living the routine life of unintelligent imitation of others in society is the surest way to a life of sensuality. For spiritual purposes, a most intelligently replanned way of life is to be followed. If you want to take up sincere practice, you will have to redirect your life's flow. Hence the first thing to be renounced is the blind following of the patterns of the time.

Death of a previous condition and the birth of a new condition are called change. This is constant in the realm of time. No growth is possible unless we are willing to drop out of our previous condition and accept the ampler status of the new condition. Childhood must end in the youngster; youth must end in the grown man. If a bud is not ready to end its present state, how can it grow and unfold itself to become a flower? All progress is leaving the present state and moving to reach a greater goal, to attain a greater purpose. The only known method for climbing a ladder is to leave the lower rung and get onto the next higher one. To wait for a time when none of the disturbances, external and internal, may visit us, is an impossible ideal.

Excerpts from an interview and a ***Q&A*** *session on why a person would want to change and whether the efforts by Mahātmās have shown any results:*

Wadsworth: Why should a man want to change himself?

Swamiji: When do we go to the doctor? It is not that I, in my flat, got tired of my little apartment and therefore thought, "Why not go to a luxurious hospital?" I don't go there for a holiday. When I feel that in my present way of life I am not as happy as I should be, meaning, I begin to revolt against pain, it makes me go to a spiritual life.

Wadsworth: So man won't get to the spiritual life until it starts hurting?

Swamiji: Certainly, because at a lower plane of consciousness, he feels very happy. That is why animals never seek spiritual life, because they don't feel the need.

Wadsworth: What result have you seen from your teaching?

Swamiji: To try to seek results is not to work inspiredly. A real painter, when he is painting, is not thinking in terms of how many rupees or dollars he can make. His is an inspired work. I don't care what results are left over. Had Christ thought of the results, he would not have opened his mouth. Nobody would have opened his mouth!

***Question** from a Postal Lesson Course student:* You have been bringing out in the papers that modern man is living a life of worry, anxiety, and dissatisfaction. My doubt is: Was it any better ever in the history of mankind? The period was dark when Lord Kṛṣṇa was born, was dark when Jesus Christ was born, and still darker when Prophet Mohammed was born. If this is the state of affairs after God Himself was born as Rāma and Kṛṣṇa, I start doubting the efficacy of the religious path. I think we are making a wrong observation somewhere. Religion may not be the answer at all.

Swami Chinmayananda: Your conclusions are rather hasty. The ordinary man who is not in the habit of diagnosing the disease and conditions of the world generally rambles in a private route exactly as you have argued here. This is excused in an ordinary man, but it is inexcusable in a student of Vedānta capable of reflection. Religion by itself is not a remedy, as the medical science itself is not a remedy and comfort to all the suffering patients. But for those patients who faithfully follow the treatment and live the life prescribed, they are generally found improving in health and get cured of their diseases. Religion is a science of living, and it can only help those who are able to live exactly according to its instructions. It is true that many Masters in the past had again and again influenced the animal man and had succeeded to bring into his life a bit of sanity and civilization. Under the influence of living Masters, many had struggled to the Noble Life and a new cultural beauty was gained within the community. Even after their departure, for some time their influence functioned, and, thereafter, man started learning to compromise and, consequently, he entered again into an era of confusions.

I have been wondering in spite of the developments made in medical science, in spite of the increase in medical colleges, in spite of the availability of thousands of doctors, in spite of the hundreds of hospitals in each state, I find that the number of patients is only increasing and the diseases are multiplying. Will I be right if I suggest, "Let us burn all the medical colleges, bomb out all the hospitals, and hang all the doctors" so that this society may become healthy? If this is acceptable to you in the land where you live, we shall abolish religion, bang the Saints, and bulldoze the temples to build cinema theaters! In spite of all these temples and scriptures, man is still vulgar, and what would have been his condition had there not been in him the lingering touches of beauty added to the human mind by the hands of a Jesus, the blessings of a Buddha, the grace of a Kṛṣṇa, and the dynamic call of Nanak.

If one has an open mind to know what is the truth of the matter, then one can be a skeptic or an atheist, his thirst for true knowledge will find him the way:

Swami Tejomayananda: As a journalist, Gurudev went to Rishikesh to Swami Sivanandaji, who was a most wonderful person and a great sādhu (mendicant), for he had goodness in his heart. He always encouraged and blessed anyone who had even the slightest inclination for spirituality — that was his nature. He was also highly learned and well educated, and he attracted many intelligent university graduates and students. Gurudev went there as a skeptic, but whatever work he undertook, he did it sincerely. Had he been an ordinary journalist, he would have gathered his data for the article, written it, and forgotten about it. But it did not happen like that, for there was an unexpected transformation. He was so inspired by what he saw and heard, and realized that these sādhus (mendicants) were not wasting their time and lives, that they were not escapists or cheats. It was a different life altogether. And so, he decided to become a sannyāsī! His father also blessed him to do so, and Swami Sivanandaji gave him sannyāsa along with some other young sādhakas (spiritual students).

The teaching is available, but are we?

Swami Chidrupananda: Once, Gurudev said in a lecture, "We, the Mahātmās, are willing to shape you and mold you, if you are available for it." Most people were sleeping.

The essence of Gurudev's teachings can be summed up thus:

Swami Tejomayananda: If someone asks what Gurudev's teaching was, can you answer, "Give the whole *Gītā* to everybody"? Yes, that was his teaching, so when I discussed this with others and we brainstormed, we summarized these to be his teachings:

1. "*You change!*" He told us many times, "You are not here to change others." The most humorous thing I remember was when I conducted the first Vedānta course in Sidhbari, and on its conclusion, I requested Swamiji to meet the students and to please address them. The first thing he said to them was, "You have learned this knowledge to go and teach, but don't think you are going to change the world. You cannot change anyone." Then he looked at them and asked, "Could I change you?" and laughed.

2. "*World perfection through individual perfection.*" You can only try to be perfect. After all, the individual is a unit. Don't go on complaining about the imperfections of this world; try to perfect and improve yourself.

3. "*Keep smiling!*" One of our brahmacārīs once asked, "Swamiji, what do you expect from us?" He replied, "Nothing. Just smile when we meet."

4. "*Active resistance to evil.*"

5. And the most beautiful is: "*We can! We must!*"

When total caring attention is given to someone, it has more of an impact:

Swami Siddhananda: One of the boys in a Christian family decided to invite Gurudev to their house to advise their alcoholic son. Gurudev spoke to the boy separately in another room. He showed him a bottle and then asked him to pour from it and drink. Surprised, the boy looked at Gurudev and said, "No." Gurudev said, "I am giving it to you, why don't you drink it? The boy again said, "No." Then Gurudev said, "See, you have the ability to control your addiction. Now you love drinks, and it is available and somebody is offering you some, and yet you say, "No." Why? That means you can do that! Then why don't you continue doing that? He also said that this was the time to study, get a good job, family, and so on. By spending a short period of time with the boy, he completely changed his life.

UNLOCK YOUR REAL PERSONALITY

The turning point, if it comes in life, comes as a great blessing. It is like a river that is flowing downward and decides to take a turn back to its source. This seems to go against everything a river is supposed to do. Usually, it is noted that this inner awakening and urge to expose oneself to the Higher comes unplanned, even unconsciously, when one has made some sort of an effort to seek a way out of life's repetitive and disappointing patterns that don't offer any viable solutions. When this defining moment happens, one automatically meets a Teacher, or begins to seek God in some other way. One's personality begins to find the right direction to unlock itself.

Swami Chinmayananda:

The moment one questions the validity of the pursuits one has been following, one becomes a seeker.

The very fact that a person has decided that he wants to be free from all his weaknesses, that he wishes to walk out into the boundless fields of perfection, has made him blessed.

All scriptures are a road map for the final destination, the higher State of Consciousness. For the man who wants to walk the path of knowledge, neither a blind faith in the Scriptures nor in the Teacher can supply a sufficient motive force. He needs a conviction that rises from within him, born out of his own intelligent thinking and intellectual absorption of ideas.

When thus the student is ready to receive the divine message, a casual instruction from the teacher is more than sufficient to set the student on the flight to the State of Pure Consciousness. A Teacher is necessary to inaugurate us into the mysteries of truth and to show us what exactly the truth is and how exactly we come to lead a miserable life of incompetency and misapprehensions. But the development of the student will entirely depend upon the student's own self-effort. He must be able to digest and absorb the ideas given out by the Teachers. Spiritual growth is possible only when the scriptures are rightly understood, assimilated, and practiced.

"Liquids find their level" is a proven scientific truth; yet, water in two separate vessels need not seek to establish the same level. It is a necessary condition that the containers be connected together; then this scientific truth comes into play. Unless he establishes his contact with God, no divinity can flow into the seeker.

If you create the necessary conditions in the mind and if the conditions are fulfilled, you will be sucked into that State of Supreme Consciousness.

Inner reformation always comes with revelation. When you have detected the weaknesses and are ashamed of them, at that moment those traits are dead. This stage is known as negation. As soon as you apprehend and defeat a weakness, substitute its opposite virtue in your personality. Thereafter, look for its play during each day's dealings, and you will find how the new virtue grows to be a natural trait in you. This stage is called substitution. Introspection, detection, negation, and substitution — these constitute the preliminary processes in the purification and tempering of the seeker.

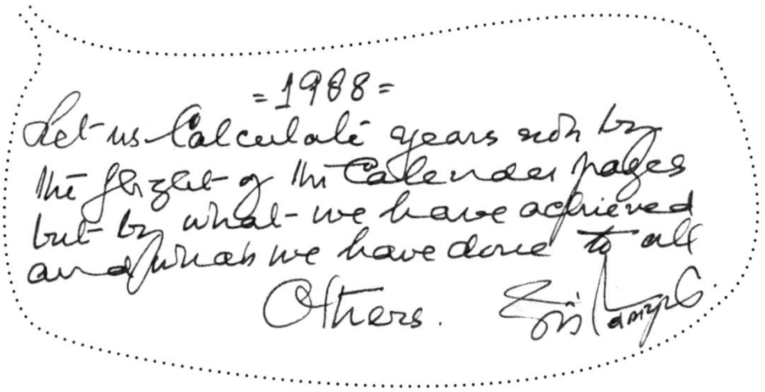

True spiritual stamina is the quality to endure and to suffer for a cause, which the individual has accepted as the ideal and the perfect. This finds a place in every great philosophy, whether it is religious or secular. In order to bring about a revolution even in the world outside, the revolutionaries are called upon to make silent sacrifices in order to establish it in life. How much more essential is it then in the inner revolution of an individual who is trying to free himself from his psychological and intellectual confines?

Freedom is not in doing what you like but in liking what you do.

If one can give up likes and dislikes, then the world becomes double its space for us to move about. Then we do not go about chasing half the things and running away from the other half. Whatever heights of spiritual beauty, culture, or mental integration that you have acquired and developed in your lifetime, they can be looted away in one instance if you allow yourself to be overpowered by your likes and dislikes. So don't come under their influence. Recognize that they are there, but refuse to come under their sway.

The world always supplies us with situations. It is our evaluation that makes it a problem or a crisis. Things will happen around you. Tell yourself in unconducive situations that it is good for your growth for the ego to be hurt; and if it is, and you don't react, you will go one step up!

We must live in self-respect, refusing to insult ourselves even the least bit. Let us always have a well-guarded personal dignity about ourselves in all our transactions with the world.

The intellect loses clarity when instructions are viewed only from the ego's viewpoint:

Christine Grimmer: Secunderabad, I missed a talk because of my inhibition of waiting to be asked to accompany Gurudev. Later he said, "You stick with the Swami." Right! This became my mantra and I went everywhere — crammed into cars, catching taxis — to get to the talks and bhikṣās. One evening, we were told that it was a private bhikṣā and we could not attend. I was having none of it. 'I' would stick with the Swami. 'I' would make it happen. I squeezed the address from someone and, with some fellow devotees (victims), took a taxi and pounded on a large, heavy door. A bewildered servant showed us to chairs at a very formal table. Gurudev sat at its head with members of the royal family of Travancore seated on either side. It was the second time I experienced a Śiva-like look from Gurudev that might have shriveled a more sensitive creature. Next day, I wrote Gurudev a card filled with feeble apologies, begging his forgiveness. He called me, flung the card at me with raised eyebrows, and said one word: "Buddhu!" (Fool!) If you remain a slave to the intellect–ego on the spiritual path, it will make a fool of you. If you are lucky and open to growth, you will soon receive painful advice. I came to understand that 'sticking with the Swami' meant letting my own demands recede, making myself available, being attentive, tuning up to him — not gate-crashing at palace dinner parties.

When one works on letting go of desires, it happens:

Ācārya Vilasini Balakrishnan: At an informal satsaṅga at the camp, one person suggested, "Swamiji, why don't we record all your talks? Vilasini could operate the video camera and travel with you." Swamiji took a fair amount of time to reply, "Why not? Not a bad idea." This was a dream come true and my whole being jumped with joy at the thought. "Swamiji, shall we get a plane ticket to India for Vilasini?" someone asked the next week. On hearing this, my mind was racing in anticipation. Swamiji, however, slowly said, "What's the hurry? If not this year, next year will be fine…." Disappointment came in a huge wave. A week later, the topic was raised again. This time, Gurudev said, "Yes, let's look into it." So once more my mood shot up! This back and forth went on several times during the next two months of his U.S. tour.

Before, my mind had been reasonably quiet and peaceful. Now, it was completely shaken by this desire to go to India. Gurudev played with it all summer long. Each week, it was, "Yes, Vilasini should go to India," and then casually, "No, what's the hurry...?" In one lecture, Gurudev talked about the beauty of how a pendulum swings strongly at first but gradually slows down, swings out less and less, and slowly comes to rest ... Finally, Swamiji's message hit me! As long as my mind was filled with attachment and desire, my mood would swing about recklessly. I began to put myself back on track! So I meditated and prayed to let go of my desire to travel to India. Finally, I reached a place where I could, internally, say, "Okay, Swamiji, I give up. I surrender! Whatever you decide is fine." And then an amazing thing happened. Swamiji told someone to book my ticket to India. Testing and blessing! I was off. I had three more years of joy in serving a Master... and three more years for Gurudev to expose all my mental impurities!

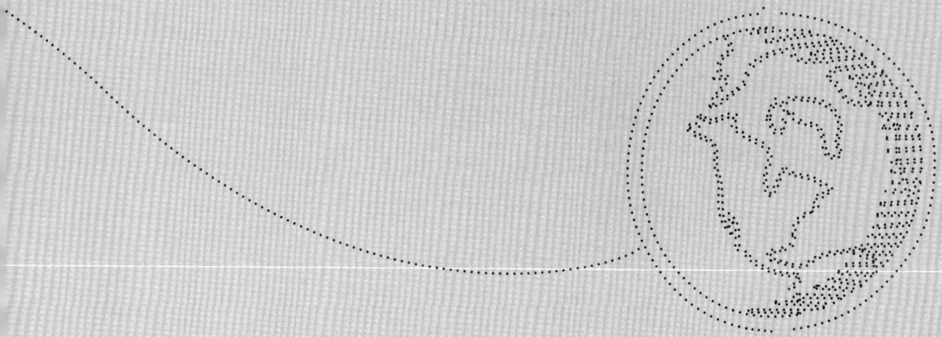

STEP 2

HOW TO LIVE WITH PEOPLE

*I*f you can surrender the results of your actions to the Altar of your dedication, be it God or a nation or a profession, the action becomes a worship. You have to surrender your anxieties and fears so that your work will come out efficiently. Your work will have quality, beauty, fragrance, and perfection. You, too, will become a genius. This is called karma yoga.

-Swami Chinmayananda

9

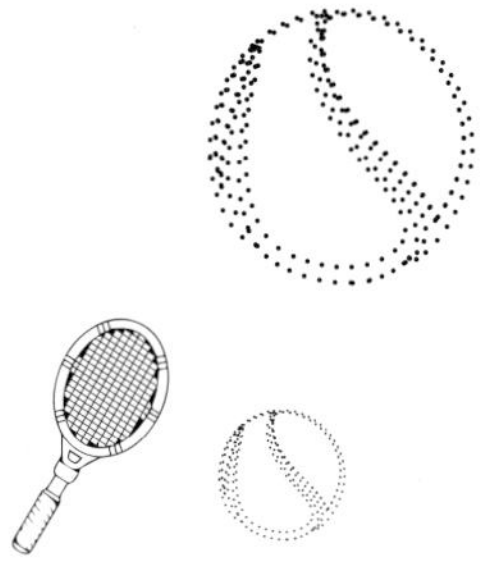

A True Sportsman

A devotee asked, "Swamiji, do you know who will win this match?" Swamiji replied, "It is the game that matters, and not who wins! Play the game! Never mind if you win or lose. The experience of playing is necessary. A game is played in the true spirit of sportsmanship, when a player is least worried about the results of the game. He plays the game neither for winning nor for losing. The play is natural for the player and it is a recreation for him. The game is itself his fulfillment, irrespective of the laws of the game. It does not matter if he wins; what matters is the quality with which he plays. Even if the other is scoring the points 40–LOVE, you don't worry. One stroke can change it all! The ball is now in your court. Let us play the game! And serve with 'LOVE ALL' in your mouth! A Man of Perfection thus works in the world as a true sportsman, and he is inspired by the very game, which he plays truly in whatever field he finds himself engaged!"

Whatever actions we do in life, if we can simply change the attitude in the mind and perform those actions for the joy of it without anxiety about outcomes or expectation of results, then we will be able to play the game of life spontaneously and free of tensions. This happens easily when we perform actions as a service to God, the Totality of existence. Then the action itself becomes a mighty purifying factor. Naturally, when it is performed for God it will also inspire us to put in our best. Whatever be the result of our best effort — success or failure — it will be received as His gift.

Whether it is eating food, working in the office, or serving others, all of them can become worship by a simple change of attitude. This spiritual art of dedicated action is called karma yoga. We can dedicate our actions to any noble cause which is greater than our little self. The wider or greater the goal, the greater is the purification. If I serve others with the attitude that I am serving God, I will begin to notice the all-pervading Reality in everyone. I will be serving with "Love All" in my mouth!

Swamiji gave us lots of work to do during his three months' stay in Sidhbari. He asked one devotee to code all the books in his library. He gave another person several pages of his handwritten notes on the tennis video cassettes he had already watched. He asked her to make an inventory of all the cassettes and paste labels on them. He had already started making the list himself, but it was not complete. Fulfilling these tasks with attention kept us busy for the rest of the stay. Purification of the mind takes place when an action is offered at a higher altar.

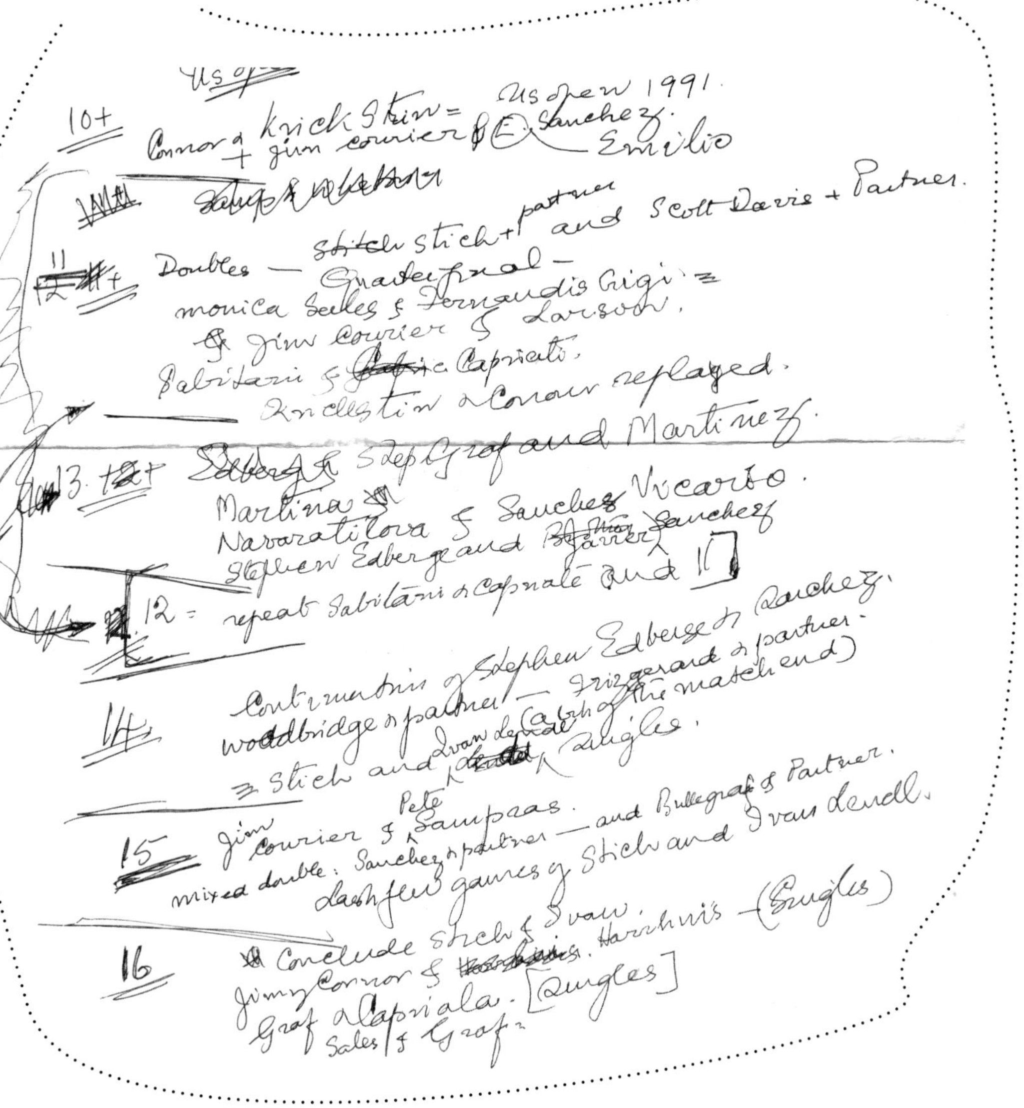
US open
10+ Connor & Krick Stein = US Open 1991.
+ Jim Courier & E. Sanchez. Emilio
Stich + partner and Scott Davis + Partner.
11 Doubles — Quarterfinal —
Monica Seles & Fernandis Gigi =
& Jim Courier & Larson.
Sabitini & Capriati.
Krickstein & Connor replayed.
13. 12+ Edberg & Steph Graf and Martinez.
Martina & Navaratilova & Sanchez Vicario.
Stephen Edberg and Mac Jarrer Sanchez
12 = repeat Sabitini & Capriati and 11
14 Continuation of Stephen Edberg & Sanchez.
Woodbridge & partner — Fitzgerald & partner (Catch of the match end)
= Stich and Ivan Lendl singles.
15 Jim Courier & Pete Sampras.
mixed double: Sanchez & partner — and Bollegraf & Partner.
last few games of Stich and Ivan Lendl.
16 Conclude Stich & Ivan. Haarhuis — (Singles)
Jimmy Connor & Haarhuis.
Graf & Capriati. [Singles]
Sales & Graf.

YOUR SECOND JOB

Our first job in this world is to realize our real Self. Our second job is to handle correctly the circumstances we are placed in by so many factors — birth, environment, our inclinations, innate tendencies, education, and the results of our past actions. Wherever we find ourselves — as influenced by any of these factors — is now our starting point: the 'gift' of God. We have to do justice to this gift by accepting it gracefully and performing all the duties that come within the parameters of our situation, which means doing our second job well. While we perform any work, if we have the attitude that we are doing it for the omnipresent Lord, our work becomes worship, instead of being just an ordinary act. This change of attitude, which does not involve extra effort, becomes the mightiest purifying factor in getting rid of our repressions, fears, and obsessions. It is also the greatest driving force, because we now dedicate our work at the highest Altar — the Lord, the Source of Infinite Happiness. This attitude of working is known as karma yoga and is one of the greatest scientific methods of purification given out in the scriptures.

Swami Chinmayananda:

Fall in love with life, not with things and beings in your life. Be in love with living. Don't be satisfied with a superficial life of mere sense pleasures. Search for treasures hidden beneath the world of thoughts. Build for yourself a temple of peace which no man can take, no power can destroy. With life in harmony, find your joy in yourself exactly where you are now. If our inner nature can be arranged and continuously held in that arrangement so as to make us react to the world positively, then we have discovered the secret of living in peace with the world.

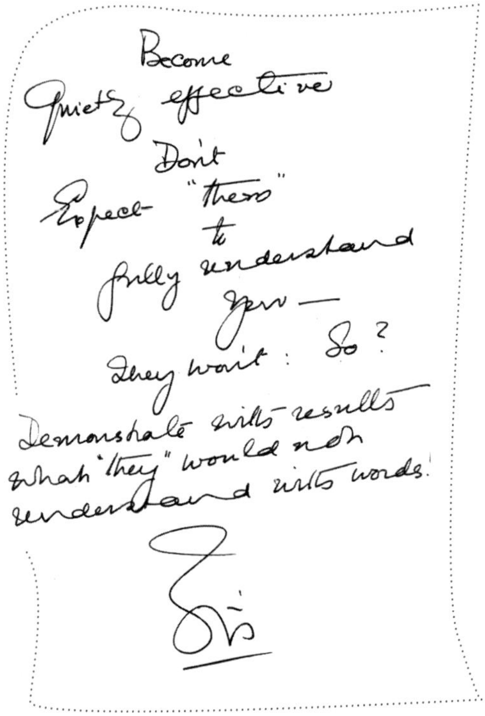
Become
Quietly effective
Don't
Expect "them"
to
fully understand
you —
They won't : So ?
Demonstrate with results
what "they" would not
understand with words!

Man must perform fully his entire obligatory duties in life. As long as an individual as a member of a society enjoys a social life, demanding protection and profit from the society, he has no right to abandon his obligatory duties. We do not live alone; we are gregarious; we live in a society. Therefore, we have not only duties to ourselves, but we have a widening field of duties — duties toward the family, relations, community, nation, and world. Let each man try to fulfill all his obligatory duties as best as he can in a spirit of unattachment, joy, and dedication. When we work with this attitude, we are released from our inhibitions, repressions, and other emotional entanglements. Mental hang-ups are swept away, and the individual gets reborn into a new life of alert vigilance, productive exertions, and blissful satisfactions.

A family, a brother, and so on, are pieces set up around you to give a definite, chosen experience, which alone will be conducive to your progress. Take what life has to give you as the Lord's gift, His prasāda. The Lord places us in the exact environment required for the exhaustion of our vāsanās. Don't ever dare question His wisdom. Be thankful for what you have. Stop craving for what you have not. Often we are tempted to run away from our given duties, saying, "I was mistakenly placed in this situation." But environments are not thrust upon us by blind fate without any rhyme or reason. To protest or weep against it is useless. Each should pursue his life in the field where the omniscient Lord has placed him, because He knows exactly what is needed for our inner unfoldment.

No doubt, let all young men seek success in life. Let them strive, struggle, and adventure forth. Let everyone earn as much as they can, save, give, and thus serve as many as possible, in their community and nation. Wealth in itself is innocent; philosophy is not against wealth. He should not leave his capacity to earn and produce, but leave only the thirst for creating wealth. 'Desire for wealth' is the relationship that the individual keeps subjectively with the objects of the world, which he believes can probably give him happiness. Thirst for it destroys our equanimity. Let him enjoy as much as it is his desserts — popularity, affection, consideration, and even reverence from others. But these are to be considered only as hobbies; the main occupation of life should be the art of self-purification, the craftsmanship of seeking perfection. The real achievement is to be gained in one's own personal inner contemplation.

The capacity to 'earn and save' should be taken in its widest scope, since wealth embraces in its meaning 'all things that can add to human happiness.' This power to 'earn and save' should include all powers, spiritual and secular, everywhere, at all levels in the soci ety — the capacity of the scientist, of the politician, of a teacher, of a speaker, of a manufacturer, of an artist, and so on. And never complain about the number of hours you have to put in to do a job, but how much of you was put into each hour of your daily work.

The path of action called karma yoga is a highly scientific way of life, which all of us can easily adopt when once we have understood its total implications. The world of objects and beings remaining the same, every one of us, in whatever condition we may be at present, can learn and slowly grow to unbelievable heights, gathering to ourselves a new stature, undreamed of by any one at any time. The theory is simple — so simple that it generally escapes our recognition. When any action is undertaken with ego and egocentric desires — 'I' and 'I want' attitude — that action leaves its impression as a vāsanā in us, prompting a repetition of the same action. Thus, one drinks with an attitude of "I am enjoying, I like it, I want to have it." Then you find him growing in his habit of drinking. An innocent village woman in the hospital takes an ounce of brandy daily for six weeks, and yet she does not develop the habit because she was taking it daily only for improving her health — as a medicine. A criminal mind becomes a professional murderer with each added manslaughter, while an army officer, though he has killed many, never becomes a murderer! He, in the battle, killed not for his own ego and ego satisfaction but in the defense of his country. This secret of vāsanā-exhaustion is called karma yoga. If we fix our vision high and act in a spirit of surrender and dedication, the mind gets purified and the vāsanās get automatically exhausted. Once these vāsanās, the storehouse of our repressions and suppressions, are exploded into noble activities, thereafter the bosom becomes calm and the resultant quiet mind is the field for intense thoughts and inspirations. While serving, the most important things are: 1) Keep Nārāyaṇa bhāva, that "I am serving the Lord." 2) Do not pause to question the possible fruits of the service. 3) Renounce the sense of doership, that "I am serving."

For the bhakta who has already surrendered himself and all his profits, losses, successes, failures — in short, everything — unto Him, anxiety cannot be there. But, so long as this great Reality is not apprehended, or such a great and all-consuming bhakti has not been gained, our worldly duties are not to be given up. It was on this principle that Lord Kṛṣṇa did not allow Arjuna to leave the field of his action. If, at this moment, you run away to the Himalayas for meditation, it will not do. First, win over the situation; then go to the Himalayas.

Live the vāsanās with which you have come here, not into which you have come. And when, in spite of your sincerity and full devotion to any work, it goes 'off,' consider it the will of Nārāyaṇa. This is for all times. Never take up any work when your inner one is not in it — when you cannot marshal into it all your devotion and sincerity. And, when you have thus worked and if the work did not succeed, leave it and move ahead, waiting for the next assignment. The failure will prove to be a direct tuition from above — a preparation. And when preparation meets opportunities, there is brilliant 'luck.' There is nothing like luck anywhere in this orderly cosmos.

Passive goodness is not the duty of a householder. When we are working in a field which is often threatened by dynamic evil, it is necessary that we must meet it with dynamic good. Passive Rāmachandraji (Rāma) lost his wife to the dynamic evil of Rāvaṇa. But when dynamic Rāma met equally dynamic Rāvaṇa, the ultimate end was the glory of the good. Therefore, if you think that you are being maligned by others and your rights have been overlooked, and that others are making use of your goodness, you must strike back and educate them that it is not worthwhile to be evil.

Letter to ***Swami Tejomayananda:*** I am thrilled to receive your note. May the Lord be ever with you. Surrender to Him and act for the welfare of all. Take the insults and praises all as His prasāda. May the work itself become your ardent field of sādhanā. With your kīrtanas [praising and celebrating through worship] and Vedānta pravacanas [sacred writings or spiritual discourse], try to lift the veil in others.

Letter to ***Sarla Birla:*** From the lifting of a kerchief to the decision-taking work at your office table, let all your work be done in a calm inner poise, with all sincerity and total attention. This is easy when we do it under the direct gaze of the Lord of the Universe who placed us where we are, who provides the outer opportunities and the inner abilities. All are His. Ours is the joy of doing His job as best as we know.

Letter to ***Ācārya Darshana Nanavaty*** *in 1977:* Darling Child! Grow up! Be a woman first. Then we shall think of spiritual expansions!! You are a baby now! Be balanced and learn to watch the procession of happenings marching along your life. SMILE.

Letter to ***Margaret Dukes:*** Until your father's sufferings have been forgiven and he merges into peace, your place is next to him. Get his permission and then come to India, or else it will be a waste, as you cannot but feel mentally disturbed that he was not happy when you left.

A doctor, who was also a wife and a mother, sought Swamiji's help on how to decide to which of the roles she should give prominence. That lady was ***Dr. T. Ganapathy****, who followed his advice, and from her efforts arose Chinmaya Mission Australia.*

Your problem is a typical example of a fundamental mistake multiplying into a chain of mistakes. The 'doctor' in you should not have married; the 'wife' in you should not have been a doctor! The duties of a 'wife' must necessarily collide into the duties of the 'doctor,' something like the married Mahātmā!! Now you must decide: are you essentially the wife and mother — or merely the doctor? Accept the important role as your duty, and the other one as an added chance for 'sevā,' for example, a wife who is also a good songster! Wifehood is the essential duty, the music in her — an added charm in her domestic life!

Similarly, I feel that you are essentially the wife and the mother. Your doctoral education and the experiences are no doubt your added charm. Practice medicine and serve the society wherever your husband is. Serve him and your daughter: I feel these are the main duties of the wife and the mother in you. The doctor must play the third place to the main part, the mother to the second part, and then the wife to the first part. This is for the ordinary woman. If you feel that the doctor in you had married and had the child, then the doctor is the main, and the wife and motherhood is the secondary; then what you are now doing is right. But the real 'dharmo-meter' (the deciding factor of what is right and wrong) is your own person. Are you happy… and undisturbed by the regrets–pangs?

Guarding one's country is one of the nobler fields of sevā, as one's vision expands from the personal, familial, and provincial ties to the national level.

***Col. Rakesh Sachdeva (Retired)*:** I wrote to Gurudev that I had declined a seat in IIT and joined the National Defense Academy instead, since I wanted to be an Army Officer. Promptly, I received a two-page handwritten letter from him, congratulating me on my getting where I wanted to be. He also advised that the aim of military service should not be to seek promotions but to serve the nation. When I met my father a few weeks later, I showed him Gurudev's letter, which read: "Blessed One! I am writing to you in between my sessions of meditation." The letter ended with the words, "To a real army man, character is his armor." Gurudev added, "Remember Him (the Lord) always, as you march in your line of duty, "Left, Right, Left, Right… Om Namaḥ Śivāya! Om Namaḥ Śivāya!" declaring, it was a soldier's duty to guard the sanctity of the Kailas peaks. To my father, Gurudev was God living on earth, and our father successfully inculcated the same reverence in our minds. My father's words were, "Eldest, with this letter, you have been initiated by Gurudev!" It was then that I grasped the full significance of this letter, which was to set my vision and mission in life, and my moral compass. It was written on Mahā Śivarātrī Day in 1966, the only holiday that Gurudev took in the whole year, when he spent the time in deep meditation.

Karma yoga gets devalued when performed for praise:

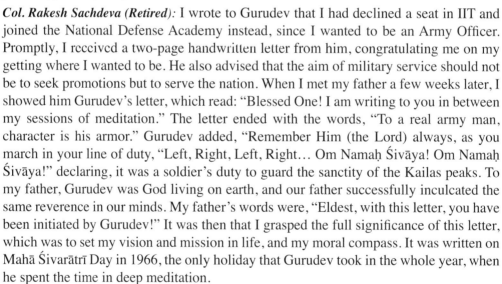

***Swami Shantananda*:** Gurudev was staying in a very nice and luxurious house of a doctor in Kerala. The hostess had beautifully decorated the house with verses from the *Gītā*. Gurudev had noticed the decoration on the first day itself but kept quiet. She thought that Gurudev would say something on the first day because she had made so much effort. On the second day and on the third day also, he did not say anything. She could no longer resist and said, "Swamiji, I have decorated the house with all these quotes from the *Gītā*." He said, "Amma, you spoiled it! Whatever you have done is karma yoga! (He was teaching *Gītā,* Chapter 3, during that yajña). See, your sevā is directly between you and the Lord. If you expected praise or applause from people, then it has no value. Now that you have done it, it is finished. I did not want you to lose your puṇya (merits) and that's why I did not make any comments, but you were so anxious."

It is natural to feel satisfaction and a sense of fulfillment for a work well done. Gurudev explains how not to feel self-important about it:

Ā cārya Gaurang Nanavaty: When Gurudev came to Houston, where I had started teaching Vedānta classes, I approached him with a concern: "Swamiji, when I teach, people praise and say that I am good. But I know that I am not able to totally live up to the teaching. How should I behave? Also, when everyone appreciates [my work], I feel good. I don't know if this is arrogance. All I know is that I am very grateful for everything from you." To that, Gurudev clarified: "It is natural to feel gaurava (a sense of achievement) when you do something good. But a false pride that you are better than others, you should not have that. A sense of satisfaction is bound to come when you do good work. Then, give credit to your Guru — 'You are doing through me.'"

Sometimes, the Guru suffers our service to him so that we can be purified!

Ashlesha Madhok: In 1991 in Sidhbari, Gurudev had some eye-related issues, and I thought I should do something to help with the symptoms. So every evening, I would go to his cottage with cold milk and cotton and ask him to do cool compresses to his eyes. He would do what I asked him to do for 5–10 minutes. I did that for about a week and felt good about the fact that this treatment was helping his symptoms. After I left Sidhbari, Isabel Taylor took the cold milk and cotton to him and he said, "I do not need this — that was for her!"

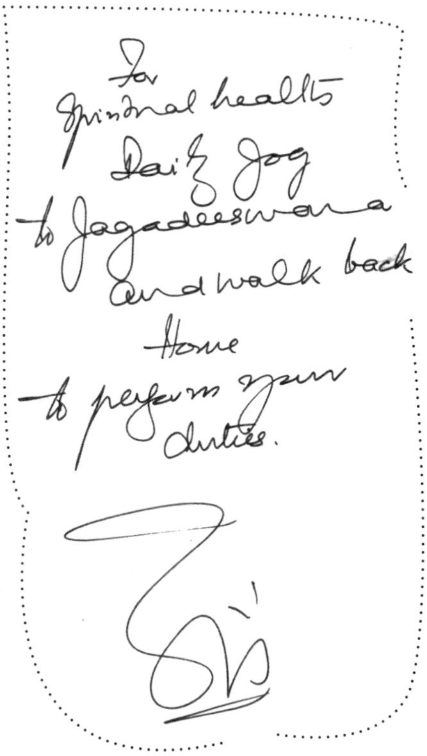

It is advisable to get married when the vāsanās are there, so as to avoid suppression:

Bina Sutarwala: Whenever I had the opportunity, I was traveling and serving Gurudev. As time passed, the moment of my marriage arrived. This was a hard step. I knew Shailesh, and so did Gurudev, but I was afraid I would change. "I would rather not get married, Swamiji. This life of service is what I want," I told Gurudev. In response, he said, "You must perform your own duty. When you do your duty without choice and unconditionally, you will gain Vedāntic poise and many more will benefit. Shailesh is a good partner and he loves me; together, do His work. Give it all to the Lord of the hills and mountains — Shailesh. This is your duty, and duty is determined by your identity."

Replacing "for me" with "for others" is karma yoga:

Prarthna Saran: Once a boastful industrialist was relating to Gurudev: "Swamiji, I do karma yoga everyday as I run a factory, and that gives employment to so many everyday." "Shut up!" said Gurudev, "the intention of your work is to earn money alone, employment to others is a by-product of your selfish action. That is NOT karma yoga."

Replacing "I do" with "He does" is karma yoga:

Rudite J. Emir: One time, when some of us asked him about projected programs the year after next, he said, "I don't want to cheat the Lord of what is His," reminding us that he was not the doer, but only a vehicle for the Divine, that the doer was God alone. Another time he wrote, "Learn to keep noble aspirations in your mind and wait and watch for His plans for you. Let Him finally decide. If He wants you to serve in-laws, they shall reach; if He wants you to study more of Vedānta, He will stop their arrival. Make Him the decision-making power in your life!"

CAUSE AND EFFECT

If we assume that God is neither unjust nor partial to some people, then the differences we see in the lives of people must be due to the Law of Karma. The Law of Karma is based on the scientific law of cause and effect. Every action has a reaction. The result of a good action is happiness, and the result of a bad action is sorrow. Ultimately, the doer of the action alone is the enjoyer or the sufferer. One's karma does not end with the action; it ends with the result. Twenty-five bad actions plus ten good actions will give thirty-five results. The good does not cancel the bad actions, but it helps one to face the results of the bad actions. Some actions, called prārabdha, are the results being experienced now. Our present vāsanās prompt future actions. In this way, the person who gives you the result is only a 'nimitta,' an instrument through whom you receive the results of your own actions. If we understand this, we will not hate anyone.

Swami Chinmayananda:

If we are to assume that life has started directly from God, then we will be forced to assume that the Creator, in his omnipotence and might, is a tyrant, and like any mortal king, dispenses his favors according to His whim and fancy, sometimes justly and often unjustly, always partial and inconsistent, he is not a God at whose feet a devotee can offer his heart of love in total surrender and devotion. And there is no religion in the world wherein we have the conception of a God who is cruel, partial, unjust, and mad in his lustful powers!

In a world which is a cosmos and not a chaos, 'fluke' cannot function. Fluke (coincidence/chance/luck) cannot happen in a scientific world. What we understand as fluke is our incapacity to understand the chain of causes.

Reincarnation is not a belief, but an assumption put forward based on the law of cause and effect. Religion must be supported by a philosophy that logically explains what we see and experience around us, and its relationship to the higher Reality. How else would you explain the differences and the injustices that you see in the world? Why is one man born a king and another a beggar? When the disparities in life do not arise from any visible cause, they must be the effect of some invisible past cause or causes. People do not come from nowhere, and at their death do not become mere nonexistent nothingness. Correct philosophical thinking guides man's intellect to the apprehension of a continuity from the past — through the present — to the endless

Life is not
What you THINK it is.
Life is
What you make of it.

future. The spirit remaining the same, it gets seemingly conditioned by different body-equipment, and comes to live through its self-ordained environments.

Indeed, there is no philosophical concept so tight in logic and so true in reason as the Law of Karma. If properly understood, the Law of Karma gives into our individual hands the privilege and the might to carve out our own destinies to be lived by in the days to come. With reference to the past, the present is a product, the unavoidable — destiny; with reference to the future, we are the inevitable cause — free will. The Law of Karma is based on the theory of cause and effect, but has often been misunderstood as the fatalistic law of destiny. Thirty-two feet per second is the law of gravity. Action and reaction are equal and opposite. Depending upon which is stronger, the head or the stone will break!

Man alone is given the freedom to act as he likes; and to the extent he disobeys the universal law of sacrifice, to that extent he suffers. When you live against the Law of Nature,

the Law
crushes
you
down!

You will always get what you deserve; you may not get what you desire. The Eternal Law provides each one of us with circumstances in life and occasions to enjoy or suffer strictly according to, and in continuation of, our past. Nothing happens in fits and starts. There are no accidents in the Eternal Law. Moment-to-moment life is progressive, continual, and logical. There is a strict mathematics about it all. This law is indeed an omnipotent power that rules, governs, controls, and directs all life everywhere at all time. Thought by thought, new channels are created, flowering seeds sown, weeds plucked out, and, in time, the jungle in our mind can be rendered into a fragrant garden. By self-effort, everything is possible. Man can, with the right understanding, guide destiny.

What you meet in life is prārabdha (destiny). How you meet it is puruṣārtha (free will). Prārabdha is determined by the matured vāsanās, which have started yielding their fruits. Therefore, your birth and your death, the quality of your

BMI (body–mind–intellect) and the situations created by the OET (objects–emotions–thoughts), are all ordered by the prārabdha. The vāsanās belong to the PFT (perceiver–feeler–thinker), the individuality, who did the karma in the past. Therefore, to the extent you rise above the ego, to that extent you are free from prārabdha. The water is always in the tap. But unless you open the tap, the water will not be available for you. The 'opening of the tap' is called puruṣārtha.

Man has been preparing, bit by bit, a blueprint of his life by his choice of action. The edifice of external environment and inner impulses in which he finds himself is of his own making, while his present choice is within the limitations of that edifice. What we will be — will be the product of what we do today. Regarding the future, we have got the freedom; regarding the present, we are limited by the past. Today, we are products of our entire past, plus 'what' and 'how' we have faced life during the last twenty-four hours.

Every good thought sent out rebounds a hundred times its force on the sender himself; so, too, bad thoughts. Let us, therefore, avoid sending out even a single bad thought.

All our activities are called karma. Karma is of three types. It is classified with reference to the past, present, and future. The total impressions gained by an individual through his activities and thoughts accumulated at the unconscious level of the mind are called sañcita, which means acquired. The large number of vāsanās within is all sañcita karma. Of them, a few become fructified and surge forth to express themselves. They are called prārabdha karma, that which has started yielding fruits. There are yet other vāsanās, those which are awaiting maturity. They are yet to become effective. Such vāsanās are called āgāmi, or yet to come. The sañcita, which are acquired in the past, and the āgāmi, which are yet to come — both are destroyed at the moment of Realization. They can no longer affect the individual because he has transcended his little identification and has experienced the Bliss beyond. The individuality, which is to be accused for the past karmas, is no more in that equipment. It has dissolved itself in the transcendental experience of the Infinitude. When the ego dies, all vāsanās become widows!

This body is the arrow, which has already started from the mother's womb and has been aimed at the tomb. From womb to tomb is its journey. In that flight, that arrow, having started its career, cannot be stopped by anybody. Once the thoughts have been wished and willed in a particular direction, they have to take their course and come to manifestation in that given body. The body has to go through the convulsions of enjoyments and sufferings. No one can stop this. Prārabdha karma is very strong, even for those who have known Reality. The āgāmi and the sañcita can end by the experience of the Higher, but prārabdha will end only when it has been lived through. Then, whether a person is a jñānī (spiritually knowledgeable) or an ajñānī (spiritually ignorant), he has to live through it. There is no escape. A jñānī may have a luxurious smile on his face since he knows that he is not the equipment. An ajñānī, unfortunately, will make a long face, for he will not have the strength to grin and bear his lot.

A question was expressed by ***Sharda Chawla*** *on behalf of a relative, whether well-meaning parents suffer on account of the misdeeds of their children or is it their own failure or their own prarabdha? Again, when one is unable to change a given situation in spite of years of sincere efforts, is it the person's failure? Is prārabdha all powerful?*

To which ***Swamiji*** *replied in a letter:* "... Self-effort can mold you but not others. We can wish our children well — but how they shape up is as they choose under the compulsions of their past. Pandavas, even after the attempts of Kṛṣṇa, had to fight and go through their tragic sorrows. Kṛṣṇa shared their trials. In such cases, we consider it all as kaniṣṭha prarabdha. [Kaniṣṭha literally means 'younger'; it is prārabdha that we experience indirectly through our relationship or contact with people; direct prārabdha is what we experience because of our own actions.]

Our karma will unfold, one way or another, as illustrated in the story of the man and his cow:

Bharati Sukhtankar: One day, when Swamji handed me a pair of cufflinks to pack, I asked him, "Swamiji, someone had given you a pair of cufflinks, small orchids dipped in gold. Do you still have them?" "Naah!" he said. "I must have given them to somebody. I will give away these, too. Learn to play with your prārabdha. I know the art — you still have to learn it! Remember the story of the man and his cow?" I remembered. There was a rich man, but an astrologer predicted that he would lose all his wealth and possessions, save one cow. That was his prārabdha. One by one, the man lost everything. One cow remained. The man reflected on the situation, untied the cow, and gave it to the first beggar he met. The man's neighbor saw this and felt sorry. "Poor man," he thought, "surely he deserves to have one cow." He untied one of his own cows and gifted it to the neighbor. So, the man had one cow again. The next morning, he took the cow to the village and gave it to a group of nomads. Now, another neighbor observed this, felt sorry, and brought him one of his own cows. Once more, he had one cow. The man continued this pattern of gifting. Soon he acquired the reputation of a 'gifter of cows.' More and more people gave cows to him. And because of his prārabdha, there was always one cow in his backyard!

Is there really a free will?

Swami Advayananda: Vedānta speaks of three types of destiny: weak, mediocre, and strong. Weak destiny is overcome by minimal self-effort, the mediocre can be conquered by strong self-effort, and strong destiny remains unconquered by any amount of self-effort. This philosophy of prārabdha and puruṣārtha was explained by Gurudev as the Karma Theory of Vedānta. It made a lot of sense, but in relation to the concept of Īśvara, God, I was confused. If destiny and self-effort govern an individual's life, how can Īśvara be seen as omnipotent? I started believing that there is no self-effort.

We, brahmacāris, were at Sidhbari attending Gurudev's Vivekacūḍāmaṇi Marathon Camp. I saw Gurudev sitting with just a handful of campers. I quietly took my handkerchief and put it on my left hand. Then I diffidently stated my question: "Does God know to which side of my hand — left or right — I am going to drop my handkerchief?" Gurudev replied firmly, "Of course, the Lord is sarvajña (omniscient)." I had expected this answer. "If so," I argued, "the Lord has already decided which side I am going to drop my handkerchief! Where is the question of my free will?" Gurudev vehemently disapproved, "No. No. You do have the free will to decide which side you want to drop your handkerchief." I contended, "If that were the case, then the Lord cannot know now where I am going to drop the handkerchief — to my left or right. He cannot be omniscient." This was a proverbial 'catch-22' situation!

I looked at him gravely. The ball was in his court! He lovingly smiled at me. I became receptive. He looked at me straight and asserted, "What you are now is a product of the past, and what you will be tomorrow will be the result of your present actions." He illustrated his answer with an example, "The river flows with a certain speed, say ten kilometers an hour. Hence, a boat afloat on the river will also travel with the same speed. Is it not? But if one needs to travel in a direction opposite to the flow, a motor will be required. The boat is you. The natural flow of the river is your prārabdha. If you do nothing, you will flow according to your prārabdha. But in you lies the capacity to change your destiny. Attach the motor of self-effort. With its help you can now travel even against the current. You are what you are today because of your past. But what you are tomorrow will be according to how you act in the present and what you do now." He paused. Then he cited the *Bhagavad-gītā*, "Uddhared ātmanā ātmānam — lift up yourself by yourself. Would Kṛṣṇa state thus if there was no free will? In you lies the strength to change your destiny."

It became clear to me that, as a seeker, I had to work hard and conquer the mind. But my question on self-effort versus God's omniscience remained unanswered! Those lucid eyes of his, packed with energy and dripping with tenderness, fell upon me. He appreciated my good reflection and said that I should study diligently and reflect deeply. He closed the discussion with a loud "Good!" I prostrated, got up, and left feeling strongly that though there is no free will, Gurudev did not wish me to believe so!

It has been almost twenty-five years since I had that discussion. As I reflect back, I see now his compassion and true guidance. Both these notions — (1) there is free will alone but no destiny, and (2) there is destiny alone but no free will — are erroneous. The fact is: it is the free will of today that fructifies to become the destiny of tomorrow. Hence, they are two sides of the same coin. Notwithstanding the above, it is not philosophically fallacious to hold that all is the Lord's will, and, ipso facto, there is no free will and destiny. Unless a seeker is mature and spiritually advanced, the teacher may not reveal this, for this type of cogitation could turn detrimental for the novice, who may turn idle.

The truth is this: Only a person who has given up his ego can rightly claim that there is no puruṣārtha and prārabdha. And he alone is a true Guru who knows what to teach, when to teach it, and, above all, to whom to teach what. That day, I felt that Pūjya Gurudev did not answer my question, because he knew what was good for me. Gurudev was the greatest teacher. I now understand that teaching is Love that has to be slowly revealed.

MEN OF LABOR, WORK, AND ACHIEVEMENT

Success and achievement depend on our attitude of mind. Activity expresses itself as labor, work, or achievement, depending on the attitude in which it is undertaken. The activity we don't like doing and about which we have no choice we call labor. Activity done out of compulsion and for personal gain we call work. Achievement happens when activity is undertaken with the attitude of dedication, excellence, enthusiasm, application, efficiency, and focus — and is underpinned by a philosophy of action, a vision. A vision is the powerful motivating factor that energizes us, keeps us on track, and guides us to make decisions that lead to achievement. The greater the vision, the greater is the achievement. The greater the achievement, the greater is the long-term impact on society, often for generations. People of achievement are leaders of society.

Swami Chinmayananda:

Life belongs to only him who is ready to pay its price. Life has its laws. Two plus two alone is four; four cannot be gained by adding anything else to two. Similarly, our life can be successful only when we prepare ourselves for great success.

Lord Kṛṣṇa's life is an example, an ideal, for man to change his attitude in life … how he should live and perform his duties.

Apart from intelligence and educational qualification, a successful man must have certain mental qualities such as concentration, will, consistency of purpose,

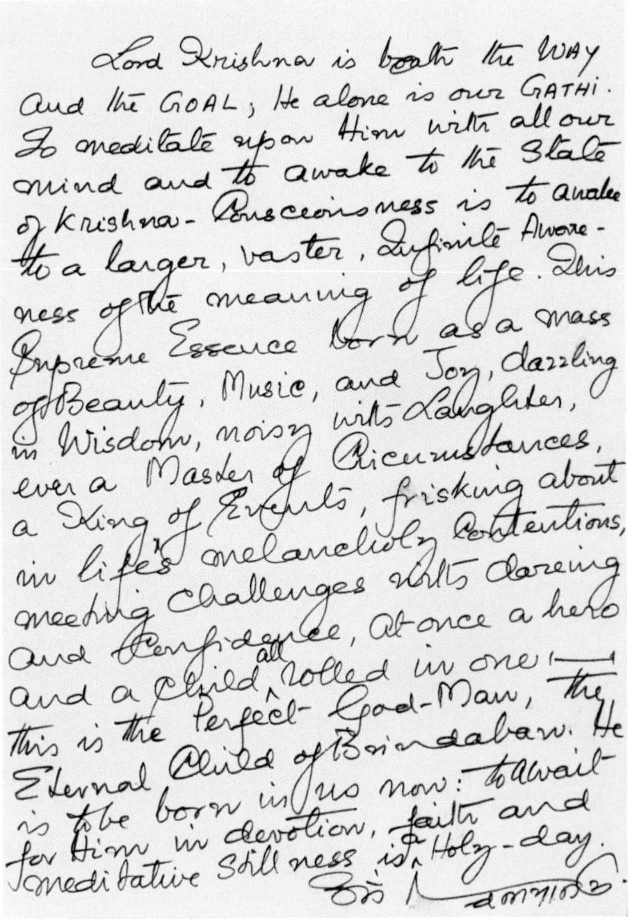
Lord Krishna is both the WAY
and the GOAL; He alone is our GATHI.
To meditate upon Him with all our
mind and to awake to the State
of Krishna-Consciousness is to awake
to a larger, vaster, Infinite Awareness of the meaning of life. This
Supreme Essence born as a mass
of Beauty, Music, and Joy, dazzling
in Wisdom, noisy with Laughter,
ever a Master of Circumstances,
a King of Events, frisking about
in life's melancholy Contentions,
meeting challenges with daring
and confidence, at once a hero
and a child all rolled in one! —
this is the Perfect God-Man, the
Eternal Child of Brindaban. He
is to be born in us now: to await
for Him in devotion, faith and
meditative stillness is a Holy-day.

determination, courage, devotion to an ideal, and cheerfulness. These will take time to grow, to blossom forth, and to fructify.

Everyone with knowledge exerts, sweats, and toils. But only a few succeed in life. They generally forget that the mind is the 'doer' in us, and the body is but our tool. Thoughts alone create, not mere activities. Activities gain potency from the thought power that feeds them. When the feeder is choked and dissipated, the executing power in external activities becomes feeble in strength and efficiency. Thoughts from a single-pointed mind must flow steadily in full aspiration and enthusiasm toward the determined goal, which the individual has chosen in order to assure spectacular success in all great undertakings.

Human beings are capable of a tremendous amount of effort. This is possible only when we are inspired; otherwise the ability remains dormant. The quality of an action depends upon the ideals, which guide and inspire an individual. A person with no ideals feels fatigued in his work. This fatigue is caused by the strain and stress, which we invite by craving for indulgence in sense objects and ceaseless expectation of the fruits of our actions. Our work is love made visible. A man of achievement does not work in the world for profit, nor for success or recognition, but from a feeling of self-fulfillment that he did the best he could. He discovers his joy in the precision and perfection of his work, and a silent stream of joy sings a secret song at all times in his heart. He does not care whether others recognize him or not. He is a master of circumstances, a ruler of his own generation. Faith is power; faith fulfills. This is the secret of achievement, whether the desire is for worldly things or for the fulfillment in spiritual life.

Let not fear of failure or fear of obstacles slow us down even a bit. Once we undertake a great and noble work, we are already set on the grand road leading to total Realization soon, in complete success. Spectacular successes were achieved in little courageous steps taken with self-confidence and faith in the nobility of the final goal chosen. Small efforts that were continuously and cheerfully put forth pyramid up to become the edifice that stands out as great work and noble achievements. Courage of conviction and tireless enthusiasm to continue we must have in plenty. Success is sure for the sincere seeker.

The real men of achievement are people who have the heroism to fuel more and more enthusiasm into their work when they face more and more difficulties. Enthusiasm is the very fuel of all great men. By the inexhaustible ardor for whatever they undertake, they generate an extraordinary drive for action. In spiritual self-improvement and in serving the nation in its cultural and spiritual aspects, the workers and the missionaries must discover in themselves the secret of invoking this trajectory force of true and flawless enthusiasm. When you do social work or selfless service, you have to do everything pertaining to it, as best as you can, because, only then, it is worship.

Cultivate *excellence*. Anybody can win if he is the sole entry. Unfortunately, in every field of endeavor there are many entries, and so to win, one has to cultivate excellence. The excellent man has a better chance to win than a slipshod, third-rate, careless idler. Efficiency is the capacity to bring proficiency into expression. Trifles make for perfection, but perfection itself is not a trifle.

The illiterate masses that listen to the thundering eloquence of the leaders on platforms may not often understand the full import of their ideals, but they appreciate the behavior and attitude of the leaders in society. Imitation is the greatest compliment you pay to another person. We try to imitate the ideal we try to reach. These millions copy the decorum set as a standard by the leaders, not by their words but by their actions. And we know these millions constitute the country. Thus, rebuilding of a society or a country can be achieved only through the integrity of character of its leaders. Time and tradition alone can build up the strength and beauty of society. A true leader should fall in line with the generations by him setting an example, and slowly and steadily he should guide his generation to act in the right direction. If only men in power and might, persons in position and status, were to be so straight in following the laws of dharma, then others, the lesser ones, would not have dared to disobey them at all.

Evolvers are creative thinkers, pioneers who enlarge our world, so that the average man, who is an adapter, can go forward. A generation of labor motivated by a philosophy of action will lead to real victory of society.

When an unscrupulous man comes to power in any country, we know what a menace he can be to society. Spiritual knowledge and its concomitant strength will be misplaced in an imperfect student, as he will make use of it for his own annihilation as well as the annihilation of the world.

Answering a query in a letter on the difference between aspiring for a goal and setting a goal, but not worrying about the results:
Whenever we undertake a project, there are two definite stages: (a) we plan, and (b) we execute. During planning, we collect all the data, bring out the entire knowledge of the past to play upon, and determine our strategy of how to meet the challenge and reach the goal that we have decided upon. In short, in the light of the past, we remold the present in order to reach out to a covetable goal in the future. This is the planning time. After the planning, once you enter into the field of execution, it is then that the *Gītā* tells you not to worry or grow anxious for the result. By so doing, you will be wasting all your mental energies in worrying over the future, which is really unknown to us. Surrendering to Him, go on doing His work and accept the result as His prasāda. With a goal to reach the top place in the school and get more than 95 percent, plan your work and start your studies. While studying, and even while appearing for the examination, refuse to worry whether you will reach the goal or not. If you start worrying, your mental energies get dissipated and actually you will bring into your field of work a weak, fatigued, incompetent mind that can never really help you in achieving. Surrender your efforts unto Him.

In Gurudev we saw all the qualities of a man of achievement, as observed by devotees:
Swami Tejomayananda:
Vision: When Pūjya Gurudev learned the scriptures from his Teacher, he thought about how he could pass on this man-making knowledge to all people of the nation and the entire world. This is called 'Thinking Big.' Swami Vivekananda used to spend restless nights in America thinking of the welfare of India and the world. That which is needed foremost from modern youth is right thinking, leading to a clear vision of life. We should

remove all the barriers of pettiness, and Think Big! Big things are achieved in the world, first by daring to conceive them in the mind. Man dared to think that he could fly like a bird and the first flying machine was invented. He dared to think that he could reach the moon — and lo — man landed there! Nothing is impossible for the one who thinks so. Our thoughts alone bind us and make us small, and thought alone can free us.

After Thinking Big through proper vision, one should then strive hard to act wisely. As Pūjya Gurudev said, "Plan out your work and work out your plan." Sometimes, the organization, which starts with a particular vision, ends up with a totally different one! For example, you might start an āśrama, but over time it could end up like a five-star hotel! ... The mission and the vision of the founder are lost. But if the followers keep to the vision and move forward in that direction, then there is expansion in the same direction as envisioned by the founder. Another example: When a train track changes, even a little, where the change occurs may seem miniscule, but later the course of the train ends up miles apart from the original! One might think that a little change of vision might not make a difference, but it can take you far apart.

Perseverance: In the early days, when Swamiji started his work, British rule had just come to an end. Many people were orthodox or in a confused state. But Swamiji's courage of conviction and fearlessness was unmatched. So many were opposed, but he did not become bitter; he just went on doing his work. If he felt that things were not right, he himself apologized. Swamiji used to say humorously that his Guru had asked him to continue the work only if five people were there on that first day. To his great luck, there were five people, including himself. It was the only Upaniṣad yajña of that time and lasted for 100 days. When people asked him why 100 days, he would jokingly say, "Because nobody else called me in those days. But after 100 days, they called." Thereafter, it became 70, 50, and then 20 days… the rest is history.

Dr. Apparao Mukkamala:

Vision: A less well-known trait of Gurudev was his skill and talent as the founder and head of Chinmaya Mission Worldwide. Once, I asked Gurudev, "What is the purpose of starting Chinmaya Mission?" His answer was revealing: "I did not start Chinmaya

Mission! All of you did it! It is not mine, it is yours." This shows his VISION. In modern-day management classes, we are taught that a chief executive has to be a visionary. The best startups are led by people who have identified a major pain point in the marketplace and understand how to address and fix it. Hindus all over the world had lost their grip on their scriptures. It is this that prompted Swamiji to create this Mission statement for Chinmaya Mission: "To give maximum happiness to the maximum number of people for the maximum time."

Administrative skills: In the late 1970s, a proposal was made to shift the publications division from California. We were at a loss as to who could undertake this work. Gurudev had the unique ability to identify the right people with the right talent to do the task at hand. A decision was made to move it to Pennsylvania, where Gurudev identified a devotee couple. To date, the Chinmaya Publications division is housed in Pennsylvania. Gurudev had the unique ability to delegate and then let the people do their work. He was the Master Administrator who built a dedicated and committed team of workers at each Mission center, identified proper resources, and kept track of it all.

Ability to execute: There were many obstacles for the projects that Chinmaya Mission has initiated. Gurudev would encourage the devotees to forge ahead and execute the decisions without any hesitation. One of the major centers in India faced some organizational problems and thought about shelving a project due to lack of funds. The letter came to Gurudev. His reply was very clear and direct, "A decision has been made, and now is the time to implement it. You hang onto 'Nārāyaṇa' and 'Lakṣmī' will follow." Swamiji had the unique ability to execute decisions without hesitation and achieve measurable milestones — against all odds. He was able to solve complex organizational issues skillfully and artfully.

Connector and communicator: Swamiji used to wake up at 4:00 in the morning and start writing replies to the letters that he had received the day before. Once I asked him, "Swamiji, why do you have to reply to all these letters by yourself? Why don't you let us reply to some on your behalf?" His answer was: "They will be very disappointed if they do not see a reply from the Swami!" Gurudev wanted to stay connected with his devotees and created a lasting relationship with them. Every devotee felt that he or she was the most important person in the Mission. Communication is of paramount importance for any chief executive to be successful. Each letter that Swamiji wrote had a message and advice. Blessed are those who have received these letters!

Passion and a kind heart: One of the devotees in an organizational position at Chinmaya Mission had become quite argumentative with Gurudev. I felt that we should relieve her and suggested it to Gurudev. His answer was: "No, let her continue. Her commitment to the Mission is real, but she has no diplomacy. This is because of the background that she was raised in. It is not her fault." A successful chief executive is smart, has a good heart and courage. Swamiji had all of these. The most important is to have a kind heart. Each and every one of us is a beneficiary of his infinite kindness.

Service above self: In August 1980, a decision was made that Gurudev should undergo open-heart surgery. We were all concerned about his health and the potential risk of surgery, but Gurudev was more concerned that he would have to cancel some of the scheduled yajñas. Swamiji put the organization before himself and anyone else. He was very clear that the expenses for the open-heart surgery should not be paid by Chinmaya Mission, but by devotees, if they so chose. I asked him if we could collect the funds through Chinmaya Mission to pay the hospital bills. His answer was straightforward: "No, I do not want Chinmaya Mission funds for my personal healthcare needs. You can pick another organization to channel the funds through."

Unconcerned with popularity: When Swamiji was in Flint in the late 1980s, trustees from a nearby center came to him to resolve a dispute. Gurudev suggested that some of them resign from the board as they could not get along, and so they did. He was never concerned about his popularity. He always said, "You can't please everyone all the time, but we should do what is good for the organization." Devotees who were not team players were let go. Swamiji did not hesitate to say no, did not hesitate to let someone go, and did not mind breaking a relationship if it was good for the organization. He used his authority effectively. The buck stopped with him. He took full responsibility for the actions taken.

Recognizing devotees' efforts: In 1980, when Gurudev was conducting a Gītā Jñāna Yajña in Flint, we came up with the idea to build a temple. Swamiji was fully supportive and immediately gave the name 'Paschima Kasi Śrī Viswanatha Temple.' He reviewed the temple plans, suggested changes, and gave details for landscaping. He said that we should build a study center, along with the temple, where Bala Vihar classes could be held. Swamiji always recognized and thanked his devotees, sevikās, and the members of his management team. He was consistent in recognizing people and timely in communicating his recognition, either verbally or through letters.

Resources: A successful chief executive uses the resources that are available to attain his vision and accomplish the mission. Swamiji had meager resources at his disposal when he started the Mission. It is not the resources, but how you use the resources that matters. Swamiji was best at that.

Devotees are at the core: I had the unique privilege of organizing one of the first family spiritual camps in Olivet, Michigan, in 1979. To my surprise, quite a few Christians and even some Muslims registered. Since I was new, I asked Swamiji if we should allow non-Hindus to attend the camp. His answer was: "Chinmaya Mission is not limited to serving just the Hindus." Each and every action of Swamiji was focused on his devotees. He said many times that he wanted every Hindu to be a better Hindu, every Christian to be a better Christian, every Muslim to be a better Muslim, and so on. Spreading the message of the scriptures to the masses was his core mission.

R. Krishnamoorthy:

Perfection: I had sent Gurudev a list of items to be brought from Chennai and Delhi to Sidhbari for the Hanumān Abhiṣeka Pūjā. The list was 150-odd items, including everything that one can imagine, like the red cloth for Āhuti, the size of the wicks, the oil, and so on. I got a reply "Well done — but you have forgotten matches!!!" — written from somewhere in the U.S.A. That was the perfectionist in him!

On teamwork and humility: Swamiji would emphasize the role of team effort and how to be a real leader. He said to me, "It may be that you are in charge of the function, but don't forget it is the result of the devoted work of many, who, despite your arrogance at times, ignored it and helped you to perform this." It touched the strings of my heart. I learned to be humble. Once I got letters, written by people, to Swamiji praising my work, and then another one complaining about it. He sent all of them to me and said "Open a file — call it bricks and flowers — and file these letters in that one file."

Confident people with a will to achieve will always be ready to 'bell the cat' and learn from it.

Swami Tejomayananda**:** Gurudev told us about an incident during Gurudev's law student days. Deliberations centered on interviewing the renowned and strict barrister, Tej Bahadur Sapru. Gurudev bravely volunteered to go. The busy barrister agreed for a brief interview. Gurudev gathered courage for one quick question: "What is the secret of success?" The barrister answered, "Work like a horse and live like a hermit." On hearing this, Gurudev immediately ran away! But he got the message right. For the rest of his life, he really did work like a horse and live like a hermit!

Mimi Robins *recalls an interesting conversation wherein Swamiji reveals what he would have become had he not become a Swami:*

On one occasion, while riding to the early morning Upaniṣad class at M.I.T., a young man, a Westerner, sitting in the back, asked Swamiji how he became a Swami. Swamiji chuckled and replied: "Becoming a Swami was a joke God played on me. I wanted to become a socialist prime minister who would usher Mother India into her rightful place in the modern world." Later, in India in November 1984, I was in a car with Swamiji en route to Uttarkashi in India, and Swamiji remarked: "Here in India the social workers think I am a Swami, but the Swamis think I am a social worker." While traveling with Swamiji in India, I saw projects, inspired by his vision, become a reality: schools, clinics, hospitals, āśramas, temples, hostels, housing for the elderly; the list was endless with new projects being brought to him for his approval wherever he went. Instead of becoming a socialist prime minister mired down in the world of politics, he became the inspired, inspiring spiritual prime minister, lifting thousands, maybe millions, into higher states of awareness, and committed himself to dedicated service to humankind, both in India and abroad. The Chinmaya Mission statement and goal — "To give maximum happiness to maximum people for the maximum time" — was a worthy goal for our spiritual prime minister.

THE GENTLE ART OF CARING

With every act of kindness, as we put others first, the mind gets purified. Eventually, through repeated kind acts, clarity will come to the mind and intellect, and inquiry into Truth will give reliable results. Sympathy with others shifts the focus from the small, ego-driven self. It helps to expand the mind to move nearer to Truth. It also brings positive results in the future. The lives of great men show us how kindheartedness can be practiced in many little ways.

Swami Chinmayananda:

The highest prayer in this world is *service,* the greatest devotion is loving the people around us, and the noblest character trait is divine compassion for all living creatures. Discover the joy of service by placing at His feet not your achievements but only the sense thereof. It costs you nothing, but brings everything. Surrender and serve.

To handle *yourself* in life, use your *head*; to handle *others*, use your *heart*. Compassion implies a readiness of the heart to flow out in love to bless others — that attitude of mind, which compels us to rush out of ourselves onto the altar of sacrifice only to save another — as Buddha did to save the serpent clan from the voracious vulture species. That is *compassion*.

Charity must flow from one's own abundance. Thus, the first requirement would be an effort to earn sufficiently in order that you may share it with those who have a need for that commodity which they do not have. Charity is an attempt wherein I try to expand and bring into the ambit of my life all others around me and grow to consider the other man's needs and requirements to be as important as my own personal needs.

The elder citizens' generation carved out for us our present, ill or well. We serve them in their old age when they are tired and fatigued, to sit back to rest and revive. A word of sincere sympathy, a look of love, a smile of true affection can give to the recipient much more than a heartless check.

Swamiji's caring nature was evident even from his days as a young sādhaka (spiritual student):

Mata Brahmjyoti *(a sannyāsi sadhak in Gangotri and Uttarkashi, doing sādhanā at the same time as Swamiji, but under a different Master):* When I first met Swami Chinmayananda at Gangotri, in the days when buses only went up to Dharasu, he was living on the other side of Ganga to where I was, near Swami Tapovan's kuṭiyā. His kuṭiyā was very small with just enough space to sit in. He had the aura of a great tapasvin (ascetic). He was kind to me and treated me like a younger sister. I prayed to Gangaji to bless him to become a great saint who would propagate the Vedic dharma. And he did!

Once he saw me stuck in Dharasu, unable to proceed as I was not well. He said that he had to go urgently that day but promised to send back someone to help me. When I said I would manage, he chided me saying, "Can't I do even this much for a 'fellow traveler' who lives near Swami Ramanandaji's kuṭiyā?" (Swami Ramanandaji was a revered saint in Gangotri at the time.) Sure enough, the next morning, he sent another brahmacārī, who helped me from Dharasu onward. In later years, he would often come to meet me and, once in Uttarkashi, I gave him a bowl of rice with a dal, which had a good 'tarka' of ghee. The person caring for him advised him not to eat it because of his diabetes. He ignored the advice, saying, "She is my little sister who gives me only amṛta (nectar), in whatever form!"

Swamiji honored acts motivated by love — even if it resulted in cold tea:

Christine Grimmer: While traveling with Gurudev in Manila, I noticed that Gurudev's cup of tea had gone cold. So I brought a fresh one and was about to remove the earlier cup, when he said, "You may give me whatever you like, but never take anything away from me." That instruction bewildered me for some time. Surely, it makes sense to replace a cup of cold tea with a hot one? Then I understood that another devotee had lovingly given that earlier cup. Swamiji honored every act of giving as precious. True love never takes. It only gives.

Though working twenty-two hours a day, Swamiji cared for his students and devotees like children:

Swami Siddhananda: Gurudev asked me to bring some books urgently to Nagpur. So I reached there and wanted to leave the next day. But he asked me to stay back for Śivarātrī. When Gurudev came out to go for the yajña, he sat in the front seat of the car while others filled the back seat, and there was no place for me. Then he asked me to come and sit next to him in the front. That was a memorable journey! Another time, after the open-heart surgery in the U.S.A., Mrs. Kamala Chanrai called Gurudev and asked, "Swamiji, how are you?" Immediately Gurudev replied, "I am fine, Amma; when they opened my heart, do you know what the doctors saw inside?" She asked eagerly, "What did they see, Swamiji?" "Amma, when they opened my heart, they saw you there!" The answer delighted the elderly devotee.

The potency of compassion and love:

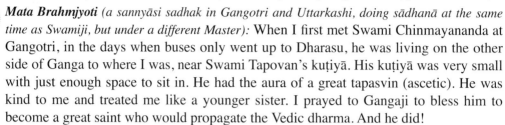

Swami Mitrananda: Gurudev was about to go out when he was informed that a young man, who had attempted suicide twice, was waiting outside, wanting to meet him. Gurudev asked him in and held him close to his chest and said, "If Einstein had done this, what would have happened to science?" See the brilliant connection — how he broke the ice! Then he said, "I have written a book *We Must*. Read that. Join the teenagers group (CHYK). Be in touch with the brahmacārī." The short conversation lasted only forty seconds. The man has changed and is now a committed worker of Chinmaya Mission.

Making light of a mistake to ease guilt:

Swami Shantananda: One time, I forgot my clothes, which I had washed and hung to dry. The host discovered that I had left my clothes behind and told Gurudev about it. When Gurudev arrived, he said, "Ha! I got your clothes."

Teaching devotees that they, too, have a responsibility toward their Teacher:

Ācārya Dr. Sadananda: When Sudheer Chaitanya (Swami Dheerananda now) first arrived in the U.S.A., he did not know how to cook. This fact so worried our president Nanik Lahori that he raised the question with Gurudev. Gurudev kept quiet. When I was passing by, he instructed me to cancel all his scheduled programs for the rest of the year! I looked at him with puzzlement, "Why, Swamiji?" He replied, "Because I have to stay back here to cook for your brahmacārī, as your president is very worried." I laughed and promised Gurudev that we would take care of the brahmacārī.

When you surrender to the Lord, he will definitely take care of everything for you:

Jyoti Madhavan: During Pūjya Gurudev's last camp in Washington, D.C., he told me a story. He said that when the grandfather of the household is alive, there is unity, harmony, and togetherness in the family. When he passes away, chaos and disharmony can potentially arise. It is up to the entire family to work together to preserve the grandfather's legacy. For myself personally, Gurudev had arranged and given instructions for me to get married to my dear husband Ravi Madhavan during the last camp in D.C. I was shocked when he told me about his wish for me to marry. I was worried that he might not let me travel with him as his nurse and secretary afterward. It turned out that Ravi, too, had gone to him with the idea to serve. Ravi was surprised by his suggestion to marry me. Shortly after this, Gurudev attained Mahāsamādhi. I feel that this plan had been his way of guiding me and taking care of me. My three loving children have grown up under the nurturing guidance of Chinmaya Mission.

Caring for nature:

Ācāryas Gaurang and Darshana Nanavaty: After a lunch at a restaurant, Gurudev took the cloth napkin with him when he went to wash his hands. I said, "But we have paper towels in the washroom." He remarked, "To dry my hands, why should I kill trees? If you are not careful, there may come a day when we don't have many trees. Don't destroy anything unnecessarily." He showed care in every action.

Christine Grimmer: I recall an evening bhikṣā in Gujarat, where the host had a beautiful garden with an enormous cage filled with hundreds of budgerigars. Lights were trained on the little birds to keep them active and chirping after dark — for the entertainment of visitors. "Turn the lights off," Swamiji said, chiding us gently. "They must be sleepy!" We all felt chastened and the host immediately turned off the lights. The little birds slowly stopped their chattering till it was very quiet. Suddenly, one or two gave out a couple of chirps. Swamiji smiled sweetly and said, "They must be finishing their sentences!" The tension was broken. We laughed — and cried!

Dietary laws take second place to the well-being of devotees and students:

Laju Chanrai: I had the honor and privilege of flying with Pūjya Gurudev to various parts of the globe. On one such trip to the Canary Islands, we were accompanied by my grandfather Papa Mulchand, my mother Kamla, Amma Nambiar, Laksmi Reddy, and Pushpa Rohira. During our return flight from Las Palmas to Lagos, we were served a vegetarian lunch as requested, but to my horror, it had been garnished with slices of boiled egg. To my great surprise and utmost relief, I observed Gurudev move the slices of egg to the side of his tray and commence to eat. All those in our party followed suit. After lunch, anticipating the turmoil in my mind, Gurudev said to me, "If I had refused to eat that meal, your old grandfather, mother, and Amma Nambiar, all of whom are diabetic, would have starved and been at great risk of a dangerous drop in their sugar levels, and the rest of you would have also starved on the long flight, so I chose to be practical and not make a fuss. If your mind and heart are clean, you will be untouched by the dirt around you." I learned from that episode the true meaning of a Guru's grace, love, and concern for his devotees.

You can only truly care if you have surrendered your ego, like Swamiji:

Cate Hallpike: Traveling with Gurudev made me realize that he was a living example of what I was searching for and wanted to know more about. He was there for every devotee to take from him what they needed and to share all their joys and concerns with him. He gave himself whole-heartedly to hundreds of thousands of people, continuously — never once did I see him turn away, or turn anyone away, even me! The girl who thought she was there by mistake — who saw herself as hoax and a pretender! He was ready to meet the needs of each and every devotee, at whatever level they approached him.

The compassion that blesses from great heights:

Swami Mitrananda: During a camp in Coimbatore, immediately after a meditation session, we, the members of the youth group, went and asked Gurudev if we could go and see a waterfall nearby. He just stayed silent without uttering a word. Much later I realized how silly it was of us to ask Gurudev, who was trying to lift us to the sublime through meditation, about visiting tourist sites. Even then, out of compassion, he tried to lift us up to the Highest, to inner silence. No wonder on another occasion when I asked him, "How is it up there?" he said, "It is very lonely on top!"

HAVE YOU MADE ANY NEW FRIENDS LATELY?

Friendship binds people together when they find they have things in common, things they like and appreciate. Another binding factor is the power of selfless love. Why do some people have many friends and others live a solitary life? The lives of great men show us how to extend a hand of friendship. People whose hearts were open became friends with Swamiji, and then turned into his lifelong devotees.

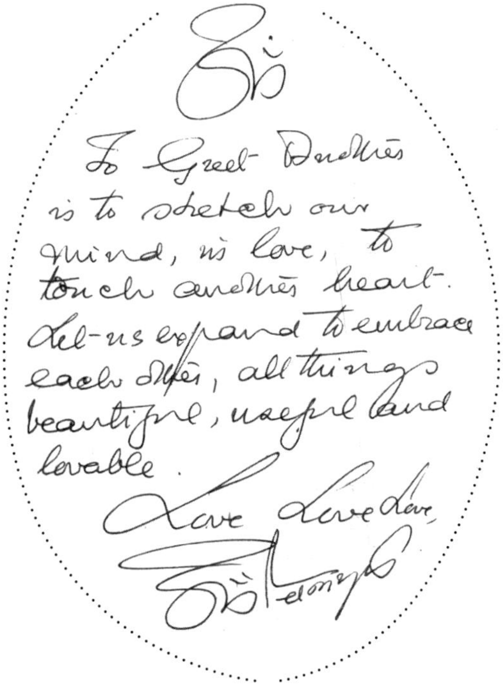

Swami Chinmayananda:

The recognition in another man of some aspect of you is the basis for all friendship and love. The animosity felt toward a stranger leaves us the moment we, in our conversations, recognize him as a man from our own country or district or town. Even if the other is a foreigner — yet, if he is recognized as one who had studied in your own college, he becomes a friend! A man may be a stranger — but when he is recognized as one pursuing your own profession or art, he becomes at once a pal to you. These are some instances wherein the recognition of at least a part of yourself in the other builds an immediate bridge between you and the other person.

He who comes to you with love and cheer, when all others have left you, is a true friend. Such a true friend is discovered not by searching outside for the right person to be a friend but by your growing to be the right person to deserve a friend. We cannot compel anyone to be a friend; we have to discover a friend. Some people complain, "Nobody loves me." You are alone in your heart. You unconsciously got locked in, and you cry out to others to open and release you. The door of your heart cannot be unlocked from outside. Nobody other than you can ever throw it open. Never sit and cry, "Nobody loves me!" Nobody will unless you start loving others.

Love is the greatest persuasive power we know of in life. Give love to get love. Be ever a spiritual giant, so that in your overflowing dynamism, unknown to yourself, scores of your friends become unconsciously reclaimed, mysteriously transformed, and divinely spiritualized! This is the greatest magic of all, the godly magic that discovers a God-man hiding behind every average man.

Friends are made by many acts and friends are often lost by a single thoughtless act. You must grow up to deserve a friend. To have friends, you must have friendliness in you; you must be selfless and loving, with deep concern for others, and then you will discover a friend.

It is not friendship that we seek in society; we demand a crowd to be always around us to escape from the shattering experience of loneliness.

Bathed in the rays of the shooting sun, the leafless tree invokes our sympathy and help. What has been all along its friend may now turn into a scorching enemy. Let it make some effort and bring forth the foliage, and the sun will continue to be its friend.

Advice to devotees on how to speak sweetly to people and how to treat guests:

Swamiji: You could have said the very same words in a sweeter way, and everyone would have appreciated and understood you. We must watch not only what we say but also how we say what we say.

*To **Neeru Mehta:*** If more people are coming to your home, you must thank your stars, for to serve the guests is one of the rare merits in life. They flock to you because they find a special cheer and the charm of your grace that revives them in their own inner confusions. You should never complain, but must be thankful to the Lord. No doubt you are justified in feeling the lack of privacy, but if you reorganize your programs of the day, the guests can be disciplined to expect that at certain times of the day, you will not be available to them. Thus, you can take time for your studies and for your prayers.

*To **Sneh Chakraburtty:*** You may be sad one day or angry or tired. But nothing is an excuse for you to behave badly to others. If you can't be sweet to others, always, then go to bed and don't come out!!

*To **Ācārya Vilasini Balakrishnan:*** Be sweet to all, but keep yourself free from attachments. Attach yourself only to Him.

Gurudev had a knack for making friends immediately because of the love he had for mankind:

Christine Grimmer: I wanted my sister Deb, a Christian, to meet Gurudev. At a yajña in Coimbatore, I took her to Gurudev's kuṭiyā (small hut). I expected Gurudev to greet her, ask polite questions, and wish her well. Instead he leaped up, embraced her in a bear hug, kissed her on the head, and said, "You listen to me with your heart, not your head like your sister!" Ouch! That advice still haunts me today as my struggle has been a protracted battle to let the heart win over the head. Recently, I asked my sister if she recalled that incident. "Are you kidding?" she replied indignantly. "Gurudev gave me my mantra then." This amazed me. Gurudev did not, as a rule, give mantras. She said, "He told me to chant 'Om Namaḥ Śivāya.' I chant it, and whenever I need help, it works."

One could learn from Swamiji how he showed care and understanding for all those who came to him, be they unwilling, confused, or in his presence by chance:

Cate Hallpike: My husband Michael had been communicating with Gurudev by 'snail mail' for two years about traveling with him on a six-month journey in India. Unable to make sense of the strict and very harsh Catholic education process I had endured since early childhood, I had abandoned my religion, and my faith was weak. I had doubts, was confused, angry, and full of guilt. Nothing had prepared me for my experience when we landed in India. Driving in and out of winding streets among thousands of people, animals, and various forms of transport, each with different sounds and smells — all of it shocked me. The driver's dashboard featured every imaginable god or goddess from all different religions — strange idols I had never seen, and even Jesus, Mary, and Joseph! "How could this be? How could one person honor more than one God?" This was my first big lesson directly from Gurudev — one so refreshing and so meaningful: "The very heart of all the great traditions and cultures of the world is the same. Seek what is the same." Gurudev's attitude was one of total acceptance and giving freely of himself from the word go. His stories made me laugh; his very presence commanded respect; his direction was sure; and his heart was pure. For the first four weeks, he knew how hard it was for me to adapt and acclimatize to so many changes. He rarely spoke directly to me, but watched me, just as he watched everyone. He found little, yet significant, ways to communicate his care and understanding. The first time he saw me in a cotton sari, he walked by pretending to be a lady dressed in all her finery, flipping his walking stick in the air like Charlie Chaplin. In response to my self-conscious nervousness, he laughed, "Life is a game — play it!" I recall that Gurudev laughed at me soon after my arrival. In a room crowded with people, he called out, "She has carried her cross all the way from Australia to India!" But he wasn't laughing at me — he was giving me an important first lesson, "Learn to laugh at it; don't take life so seriously. It is all the Lord's sport." Then he shouted, "There is no guilt! There is only Love. Isn't that what Jesus taught?"

Friends and devotees are made not by forcing a method of worship, but by tuning in at the level of vision and ideas:

Swami Siddhananda: A Christian boy attended the entire Vivekacūḍāmaṇi Camp at Sidhbari. At its conclusion, he met Gurudev and asked what he should do after going back. Gurudev said, "What is there to do other than what you do? Go back, continue your own tradition, and keep Lord Jesus' picture at your altar and contemplate what you studied here, and study more Vedānta. You need not convert your religion." Another time, a nun used to attend Gurudev's yajñas wherever possible. After a few years, she requested Gurudev to convert her to Hinduism. Gurudev advised her not to change her religion but to continue as a nun, preach at the same church, and conduct Vedānta Study Groups.

Swamiji had a knack for making friends with children:

Mimi Robins: Although my son Steven and I were blessed with many talents and gifts, we both suffered from lack of ear-tongue coordination and audio memory. When Steven heard and saw the name C-H-I-N-M-A-Y-A-N-A-N-D-A, he blinked in dismay. But his face brightened. He found a solution and announced: "I will call him Swami Chipmunk" (henceforth spelled 'Chipmonk'). When I told Swamiji, of his new name, he was delighted. Whenever Swamiji wrote to Steven, he ended his letters with "Love, love, love," signed "The Chipmonk."

Inquiring after little things or appreciation of others' acts keeps friendships warm:

Mimi Robins: At a camp in Massannetta, I sat on the floor of the living room and attached my flash to the camera, waiting to snap Gurudev as he came through the door. My flash greeted him. He, in turn, flashed me his brilliant smile of recognition and asked: "How is Robins?" referring to my husband. I replied that he was fine. Gurudev went on to inquire about my children, the cats, and even my husband's parrot!

Ācāryas Gaurang and Darshana Nanavaty: In a congested house, Gurudev, noticing the aesthetically decorated ārati plate, said, "How beautiful, who has done it?" He paused to appreciate the artwork of Margi Dhruv. Even in a crowd, Gurudev took the time to observe and appreciate.

Friends are made by many acts of love:

Swamini Umananda: Just before leaving India in 1984, I decided to write to Gurudev. I received a letter, which filled my heart with joy. His letter began with these words: "Joy! Joy! Joy! You are now in India! The joy hit me between my eyes!" In the envelope was a small card with a quote describing a true friend. Also, Swamiji invited me to come to Sidhbari. Immediately, I began to make plans. Analyzing my thoughts, it occurred to me that my attraction to Swamiji was not emotional. I did not see him as an ordinary human being. He seemed completely detached from things that generally fascinate human beings.

Swamiji's natural spontaneity of living as the Self attracted many people:

Daniela Purchase-Schwarz: Gurudev had first come to Switzerland in 1971. Dr. Dagmar Liechti-von Brasch, a Swiss medical doctor, who had traveled in India, brought him to her clinic (Bircher-Benner-Klinik) in Zurich to recuperate after his heart attack. Dr. Liechti asked a German couple, Mr. and Mrs. Kollin of the Indian-Association Zurich, who had lived and worked in India for many years, to keep the Swami company. They thought that the South Indian Swami would enjoy the company of Shiva Nataraja in a foreign country. As there was no temple available, they took him to the Museum Rietberg in Zurich (museum for the arts from Asia, Africa, America, and Oceania), where a beautiful statue of Śiva Nataraja is exhibited. During this encounter, Mr. and Mrs. Kollin revealed themselves as disciples of Śrī Atmananda Guru (1883–1959) of Trivandrum, Kerala. It was immediately obvious to them that this Swami Chinmayananda was out of the ordinary. They felt a presence about him, which they recognized from being with their own teacher. It warmed their hearts when the Swami exclaimed, "Śrī Atmananda Guru was one of our greatest!" It so happened that Gurudev wouldn't just rest and recuperate. He started giving talks, even at the hospital. Mr. and Mrs. Kollin brought along their young friends who were interested in Indian music and philosophy. Some local people, who looked back on a long spiritual life, got attracted, too. After Gurudev left, a Study Group was formed. Gurudev returned to Switzerland regularly, and every year a small group of sincere seekers gathered to listen to the talks on the *Bhagavad-gītā* and the Upaniṣads. As time went by, other disciples of Śrī Atmananda Guru, among them my uncle and aunt, gave it a try and went to the talks. So it happened that in 1977, at the age of twenty, together with my uncle and aunt, I went to listen to the *Bhagavad-gītā* lectures by Swami Chinmayananda. This encounter confirmed this for me: "With Thee is the fountain of life: In Thy light shall we see light" (Psalm 36:9), which had attracted me from childhood.

HOW TO CHOOSE A MATE

What is the real attraction between two human beings? What kind of love is uplifting and what kind makes one disturbed? What is the difference between lust and love? In a marriage, to live harmoniously as well as to love, partners need to understand each other's psychological makeup. But what is love? How do we know that we truly love?

Swami Chinmayananda:

No activity in human life is taken up with so much sincerity and elaborate preparation as is man's search for the joy of love, and yet, no enterprise of man fails so constantly, with such regularity, as his quest for love. He helplessly waits to receive love, and yet, everyone is always disappointed.

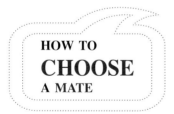

In the world today, lust is glorified as love, and based upon it, they hope to rebuild the world. All their attempts are therefore staggering with repeated failure; and curb-watchers, the growing youth of the world, are losing even their faith in love. The counterfeit is being circulated as legal tender and lust is lustily paraded in human affairs as love! This is a pernicious confusion.

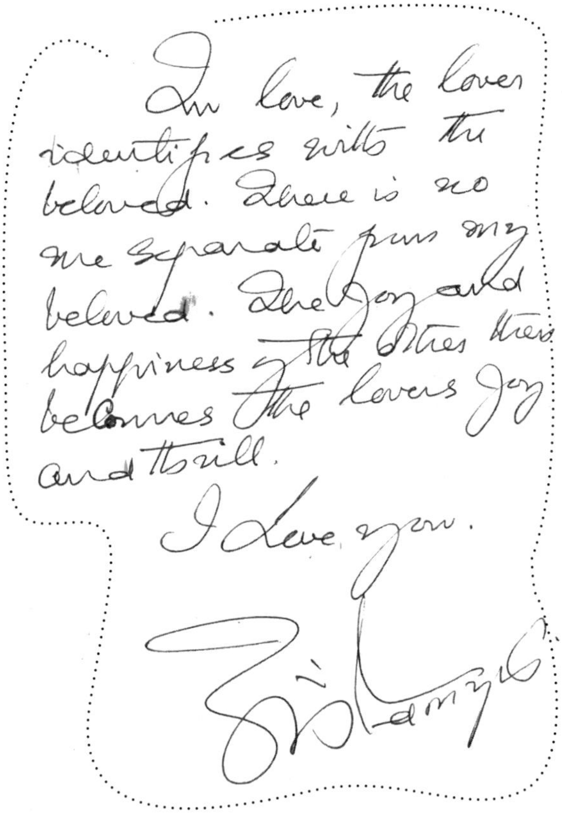

Love cannot be lust. In lust, there is abject dependence upon the physical object, and thus, in essence, there is in lust a spiritual subordination of one's personality to the enchantment of the object; while in love, the personality of the lover is turned up to the personality of the beloved. Love is thus experienced as a joyous life of brightness, of ecstasy, of light-hearted ease, while lust ends in exhausting fatigue. In love, there is an expansion in being, while in lust there is the suffocating squeeze of death, the throttling grip of the noose … a gasping slip into the dungeons of a tragic life. In lust, there is the sense of separateness, and naturally, it must endure all the consequent sufferings; in love, there is always the bliss of Oneness and the rewarding sense of fulfillment. Love creates and lust destroys the peace in the heart of man. Love is the victory of the Spirit; lust is the cry of the base flesh and the low mind. Love actually lives the joys; lust only seeks them. Love generates tranquility within; lust begets excitement all around. It is necessary to understand this difference of love with desire and love without desire. True love, in its purest expression, seeks no return. In the cheap illicit love based upon lust and passion, the highest gained is but an animal sense of gratification. Never can one discover in it any refreshing experience of satisfaction. The paramour approaches his ladylove only for the gratification of his passions. He is not interested in providing joy for her and to feel the greater sense of fulfillment in seeing her happiness. The secret lover demands and seeks only his own immediate happiness; it is always extremely selfish.

A lover can express his love only in the language of his ready sacrifices. Everywhere, we find that all lovers are always ready to make sacrifices, each for the sake of the other. In fact, the spirit of happy renunciation is the very heart of love. In love, the lover identifies with the beloved. There is no 'me' separate from 'my beloved.' The joy and happiness of the other then becomes the lover's joy and thrill. The love that leaves us with agitation in our mind is lower love. In true love, every action and sacrifice we make toward the object of our love reduces our egocentric desires and calms the agitations in your mind.

The more one knows the other, the more one comes to appreciate the other and, therefore, one's love for the other increases. Love deepens and expands with the completeness of one's knowledge of the beloved. To enjoy at the very joy given to his joyous beloved is the subtlest joy demanded by all true love.

The lower type of love is an escape from a person's sense of loneliness. Such an individual depends entirely upon other objects and beings for his existence: his home, work, money, friends, and relations. With these, he makes a prison for himself and ever willingly suffers in it. The higher kind of love is dynamic. The lover ennobles the beloved and, at the same time, retains his own individuality.

According to the Hindu śāstras, man and woman in wedlock must live, no doubt, in a spirit of togetherness, but the Ācāryas insist: "Let there be space between the two" — let there be no clinging attachment to each other, which is unhealthy for both. Marriage is not where two young people look into one another's eyes and sigh, but where they stand shoulder to shoulder having a great grand vision of a flaring future. Entering into married life does not hamper spiritual sādhanā. Only we have to be under self-discipline and slowly create a disciplined house where both you and your children can grow in spiritual beauty, wafting peace and cheer to all. Realization is possible in a gṛhastha (householder): The common factor that rules the Self-realization is one and the same, be he a sannyāsin or one belonging to any other of the three stages in life. It is only constant contemplation upon the universal Reality that takes us to Self-realization.

Is marriage essential?

***Question** asked by an Indian-American couple settled in the U.S.A.:* What is the meaning of marriage? What is the difference between two people (male and female) living together as man and wife or not, besides the legal aspect?

Swamiji: "Why should we marry? Your question is very valid in these mad days of crazy permissiveness. My dear, if the act of lust alone is the function for which a man and woman come together, all they perhaps need is but a soft grass meadow or a mattress. ... We must have a purpose. ... Marriage is essential. Unmarried living together is generally a lust-centered life; at the very first instance of clash, either of them may think of quitting the other. The innocent child, the by-product of your sweaty, perhaps drug-dimmed, carnal lust, gets neglected, perhaps thrown out on the wayside; to throw it away is equivalent to breaking your own limbs and throwing them away in a wayside ditch. After such an act, where can there be peace in your mind? Even if you keep the child, where is the joy in it? That very child when it grows, why should it respect you? How can it love you? You are not going to be young at all times ... when you need him the most, there comes the retribution. Your own acts of thoughtless excesses in your youth boomerang upon yourself. Is this living together with your chosen he-man for a few paltry moments of pleasure worth living, at the price that you have to pay for it? Is marriage necessary? To tell you the truth, I don't know, as I am unmarried myself."

Special words on the eve of marriage:

Bharati Sukhtankar: Ajit and I had gone to invite Swamiji to our wedding. He looked at the invitation card and joked, "My girl is getting married — she thrusts a knife in my heart; she gives me a card, and even twists the knife! Ooooh!" Then he said, "I will not be able to come in person, but on that day, when you become man and wife, my thoughts will be with you. And these are my special words for you — carry them in your heart. Marriage is serious business. It is not child's play. It comes with responsibilities. Putting it quite simply, it is a lot of give and take — more give than take." He continued, "That goes for both. Build your partnership on the firm foundation of friendship. Who is a friend? According to the śāstras, he who encourages you to perform noble deeds and leads you away from the path of unrighteousness; he who highlights your positive qualities and underplays your negative qualities, who rejoices in your good fortune and stands by you in times of adversity — he is a friend. Be each other's best friend. Okay. Friendship can only be between equals, where there is mutual love, warmth, and respect. No one is superior or inferior. Understand that husband and wife both have a role to play. Their roles are not interchangeable. A woman must not try to become a man and vice versa. There must be total loyalty, trust, and confidence in each other. No selfishness and petty ego issues here. Remember, the other must come first — always and every time .... Learn to cheerfully bear the pinpricks that your respective family members may give you from time to time. Learn to be patient with all. Learn to be tolerant and forgiving. Always keep in mind the noble duties of your gṛhasthāśrama (life of a householder).

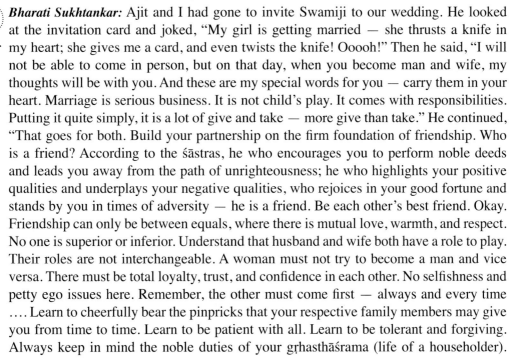

You are entering an important phase in your life. Use it for sevā — of the young and old in your family, in the community and society at large. Perform your religious and social duties diligently. Keep up your sādhanā. Always keep the Lord — and Truth — on your side. Don't turn away anyone from your doorstep. Feed whosoever comes to your house — human, animal, bird, or insect. The first dharma of a gṛhastha (householder) is to see that the atithi (guest) is fed, no matter what the time. What a chance you get to feed the Lord!"

All this Swamiji said slowly, with emphasis and deliberation. "There is no easy way out of difficulties. Face the challenges of life with maturity and dignity. Look at Sītā and Savitri — they were devoted to their husbands. Mind you, their husbands were equally devoted to them. That is why, my dears, these examples are held up to us as epitomes of not just good marriages, but great marriages. Successful marriages are based on mutual love and understanding. Lots of it. May yours be a truly successful marriage. One last word: Never go to sleep on a quarrel!" With that, he brought out a gold chain with a cameo pendant of Tapovan Maharaj and put it round my neck with the words, "What can I give you on this auspicious occasion, except my own Guru Maharaj?" My eyes were wet with tears. "Captain!" he addressed Ajit with a smart salute. "The Army is always in the front!" And through the forty-two years of our married life, through all our ups and downs, our hopes and aspirations, Swamiji has always been with us. That evening, the bride-to-be locked herself in a room and wrote down the words of the Master.

*Excerpts from Gurudev's letters to **Margaret Dukes** on how to keep a marriage going after it had broken down:*

When I first met Gurudev in 1975, my husband and I had just separated. At the time, we had two children, seven and ten years old. Gurudev asked about my life and I told him what had happened. I also told him I was a hatha yoga teacher. He immediately thundered, "How can you help anyone when you can't even help yourself?" After that devastating scolding, I went back home and reconciled with my husband. Gurudev's advice was to stay together at least until the youngest child was eighteen, and then we could reconsider. Through the ensuing years, Gurudev wrote the following letters, always emphasizing what a great sādhanā it was to create a happy, loving home:

January 1979: "I am glad that you have realized that children and husband are no handicap at all for a true yoginī [one who practices yoga]. In fact, to look after them, to keep the home for them in itself would become a part of the sādhanā if you know how to make use of it properly. Without attachment and sentimentality, serve them with love, and that is yoga. Feed your husband with the choicest and the best that he wants. He has lived a whole life as a non-vegetarian, so don't expect him to change all of a sudden. But you diligently stick to your vegetarian diet. A happy home — if you can create it, you must consider that you are a successful spiritual seeker."

November 1982: "You will do exactly as your husband wants. Realize that the Lord sends us messages through our dear and near ones. The environments often declare His wish. To swim in His grace, as He wills, is the best for each seeker. You will come for three days with your husband and return, as he wants. Yield!"

It all depends on how you look at it:

***Ācārya Vilasini Balakrishnan*:** To a housewife who said, "I'm a mere housewife," Gurudev replied, "You are the queen of the home!"

Nirmal Bharwani: One day as we were returning from a temple, Gurudev suddenly started saying, "A woman must be a wife, a mother, a mistress, a sister, and a friend to her husband. According to his mood and need, the wife must know which role to play…." I had been married for about fifteen years and everything seemed fine, but deep inside, I was trying to find my identity. And suddenly, like a breath of fresh air, this wonderful saint clarified the role of a woman and taught me the joy of living. I realized how important my dharma was as a wife and mother. In one of his informal talks, Gurudev said, "If a man goes astray in a marriage, the family will still be safe with the mother, but if the mother goes astray, then the whole family gets destroyed. The woman is the upholder of culture and will protect her children. Fathers may financially support the family, but the care and the love are mainly from the mother."

He would say, "A woman can do everything a man can do. Work and support a family, but a man can never do what the woman does — give birth. So a woman is definitely superior to the man; then why does she feel the need to prove her superiority? Father is the producer of the seed, and the woman is the mother of the world. You cannot separate them. They are part of the same whole."

For those who feel they have 'no time' to practice Vedānta:

Bharati Sukhtankar: A gṛhastha (householder) once asked Gurudev, "Swamiji, we are so busy with our day-to-day lives. Where is the time to practice Vedānta?" Swamiji smiled and said, "Really? No time to practice Vedānta? Do you need time to breathe, to love, to feel?" Then he thundered in his characteristic booming voice, "The right place and time are here and now!" Sometimes, people would complain to Gurudev that their spiritual progress was hampered because of non-cooperation from family members. "The whole point of Vedānta," Gurudev would explain patiently, "is to get there not only because of but also in spite of. Eknath's wife was kind and helpful and a partner in all his spiritual activities. Tukaram's wife was a sharp-tongued virago (shrew) who never missed a chance to rail at her husband. Both were saints of the highest spiritual stature. So don't blame the spouse. You can get there, with or without."

HELP YOUR CHILD TO WONDER

Our children are our future world. The responsibility for what that world will be belongs to parents, especially mothers. The role of the mother is central. In molding their children, mothers have the opportunity to positively influence the mothers and fathers of the future. It is crucial for us all to recognize the importance of the mothers' role and for women to embrace their responsibilities for the sake of all the children yet to be born.

Swami Chinmayananda:

One little child can change the entire history of the country. That is how all the great men of the past were made — a Śivaji, an Einstein, a Tagore, a Mahatma Gandhi. From childhood onward, some ideas were inculcated into them and all of them, invariably, declare in their autobiographies that for the greatness they achieved or for whatever good they were able to do, they were indebted to their mothers. It is always the mother at home who gives the values and ideals to the child, who molds the mental thinking of the child. The children of today are going to be the leaders of tomorrow. And we must supply them with a vision. But when the parents have neglected the child — look at the crooked dynamism of a Hitler, how ugly it became, and how through him the entire moral caliber of mankind has been brought down a few notches since the Second World War. One solitary individual with an unhappy childhood, the neglected child of a cobbler — how he brought about disaster in the world outside!

Only when a plant is young can it be trained to grow straight. A plant can be trained but not a tree. Once it becomes a tree, we can only trim the branches but not the trunk. Similarly, training of our children can only be done between the ages of six to twelve. Between the ages twelve to eighteen, it can also be done to an extent, but after eighteen, the 'tree' has become set, and one will have to go through fire in order to become hot and plastic enough to change. Once we have gone beyond the younger ages, it is not so easy to change our pattern of thoughts and our attitude to things and beings. So, early childhood is the time for training.

Mere talk about a 'value-based' educational system started around the country is not sufficient. We, the parents, must change. Children do not learn from books. These higher values cannot be imparted to the students by institutions, by a society or a community, or even by a committee. They imitate their parents. In Rāvaṇa's kingdom, every child wanted to strive to become as vulgar as Rāvaṇa! We have to mold our children to think, not in our pattern, which we have understood to be disastrous, but in a new pattern with a new inspiration and with a new vision in their minds.

It is said that Nārada Muni took the queen of Hiranyakaṣipu to Vaśiṣṭha's center, where she was allowed to listen, day and night, to the discourses of Vedānta. In this way, she was exposed to Vedāntic ideas from the seventh to the tenth month of her pregnancy, and thus the child within her was remolded, not outside, but in the mother's womb — a prenatal education. It is that child who became the great Prahlāda! Because of the prenatal spiritual training, that one solitary little child stood against the entire materialistic culture that was developing in the country at that time. He brought the country back again to the healthier and eternal values of the Upaniṣads. What is the prenatal education that mothers are giving their children today? Television, cinema, video, those stupid best-seller books! These are the ideals you are feeding the children, and when they come out as rākṣasas (demons) you say, "The children have gone astray! We don't understand what has happened to the world!" Let us have the square shoulders to accept that we are responsible for this terrible, monstrous age in which we are living at this moment.

Nowadays, between the father, the mother, and the child, there is no inter-relationship. Breastfeeding has stopped and that is the time when the mother intensively contemplates, looking into the eyes of the child, and they become intimate at the mental level. The infant also, while sucking, looks into the face of the mother. They feel extremely devoted to each other. But now that entire system is gone. We have to bring back the healthy system, which in our neglect, we have thrown away.

The father comes into the house like a storm in the evening, beaten out and wounded, angry at the world. Even if the father does sit down with the child for ten minutes, what will he talk about? Not the soft things of morality. He can only pump into the child the ideals of ambition, greatness, and success. It is the mother alone who imparts the soft values, who gives the ideals of charity, goodness, tenderness, affection, and forgiveness. She never imparts values by giving a discourse, but in her life, the mother demonstrates these ideals, and as the child sees them, the ideals become embedded in him. If the mothers have lost touch with the spiritual values of the country and the adults' lives have become loose and unethical, all the children's values also will be lowered down and they will want to escape through drinks and drugs. It is time that the ladies start learning the cultural values of the country — for the sake of the children and the future.

We are neglecting the children unconsciously. We have to take responsibility for molding and preparing them to face the world of tomorrow and to lead and guide the world of the future. Once you realize the responsibility, you will be handling the children more intelligently. We are not giving enough respect, reverence, true love, or affection to our children. Nature herself will guide every mother in how to train the children. Even animals and birds train their children properly! Youth are not 'careless' or 'useless' but are 'cared [for] less' and 'used less'! If everyone looks after and cares for their elders and little growing children, the society blooms happily and grows up vigorous and secure. But this is not done because of the indifference born out of our own dire and ugly selfishness. In our blind hunt for our personal happiness in society, we ignore and refuse this sacred duty. May Jagadīśvara bless us with greater chances of serving our children. This is true national wealth: to cultivate them is national rebuilding.

To have a reading session at home — where the father reads and all the children listen and discuss — I assure you there is no greater heaven upon earth.

Letter to ***Sneh Chakraburtty,*** *a Bala Vihar teacher and a mother:* I am thrilled to hear of my Bala Vihar children. Give them stories. Encourage them to tell the story back to you. Create small dramas: Dhruva, Prahlada, Kuchela Sudhama stories. Teach them to act.

Words of caution about pressuring children:

To ***H. P. Eshwar:*** Ayyappan should not be pressured. Over-pressured children tend to revolt. He is a brilliant student; therefore, leave him alone! Ordinary students must be hours at their desk, but brilliant students continuously revolve in their minds what they have heard and what they have studied. So, just because they are not going to the table and sitting there with a book in front, it doesn't mean they are neglecting their studies. Firmly tell your father and mother that Swamiji denies them the right to disturb the boy. And tell the boy I expect from him only the best results.

Explaining the difficult truths of life in a natural way:

In a letter to ***Rudite J. Emir:*** Collect your children around you, and in a beautiful mood, perhaps in the prayer room, show them a drooping, wilted flower, and explain to them that everything in the world has to die, but how we live and waft our fragrance everywhere while we are blooming is the important thing. Then take the example of their grandfather. Then repeat the flower. If these two ideas get fixed in the child's mind, she will have no occasion to weep at any death thereafter. Give them the brutal truth that what is born must die, and what is made must perish.

To ***Divakaran Namboodiri,*** *whose children had grown up:*
You have done more than what is needed of a mother to the children. Now release them to be free to grow in their own fashion. Take the props away; no more ironing jackets for them. They are great and really good ones. They will flourish and grow well, spreading shade all around them.

How easy it is to start a Bala Vihar and its purpose in imparting values to children:

Uma Jeyarasasingam: The year was 1981. I was a young mother of 8-year-old Gayathri. We had just moved from San Francisco to Los Altos, California. We were surrounded by Christian Caucasian neighbors, who regularly attended church every Sunday. Their children went to Sunday School there. One Sunday, my daughter was invited by a neighbor's child to attend the church's Sunday school with her. We had no objection. Gayathri started liking the school and wanted to attend every Sunday. After the 4th class, my husband and I began wondering about its influence on her young impressionable mind. Pūjya Gurudev's annual visit to the San Francisco Bay Area coincided with one of these weekends. I broached the topic and sought his help, "Swamiji, I am in a dilemma. Our daughter has been attending Sunday school at the local church for the last four weeks and seems to like it too. What am I to do?"

"You start one yourself, then," said Swamiji. "Start what?" "Your own Sunday School" was the prompt reply. "Like the one at the church?" I asked. "No, ours shall be called Bala Vihar," he replied. "It shall be a place where children can 'learn' through 'play.' They shall be taught Hindu Culture with games and stories." Then, he added, "Don't worry, I will train you on how to teach it to children." And He Did!

His step-by-step instructions for Bala Vihar began almost immediately. Swamiji also provided me with topics to be taught in each grade, from kindergarten to 12th grade. To this day, we follow the same syllabus in each of our three locations, San Jose, Fremont, and San Ramon. Teachers are residents of communities nearby. Classes are conducted on Saturdays and Sundays every week.

The Chinmaya Mission San Jose (CMSJ) Bala Vihar program had a modest beginning at the Los Altos Community Center in 1981, with 7–10 students of different ages. As Chinmaya Study Groups became popular in Fremont and San Ramon, demand for Bala Vihars also grew. Study Group members began volunteering as teachers. Once again, Gurudev's words, "Form Chinmaya Study Groups and take part in them wholeheartedly, and walls will form around you," were proven many times over at many places. The CMSJ Bala Vihar Program, initiated, nurtured, and sustained by Pūjya Gurudev, grew from 10 students in 1981 to 2,193 by 2013 and continues to grow till this day at all the above locations.

Bala Vihar classes accomplish what grandmothers used to do:

Nirmal Bharwani: The best thing that was introduced to me was Bala Vihar. When my children were in their teens, I insisted that whomever they wanted to marry would have to attend the classes. Today, my daughter and daughters-in-law run Bala Vihar classes and all my six grandchildren attend them. All Gurudev's grace!

Contending with the metaphysical at a young age is very laudable:

Christine Grimmer: On one occasion I recounted in a letter to Gurudev that, while discussing the all-pervading nature of God in Bala Vihar, a little child had asked, "Is God in my fingernail?" One child had seriously replied, "He must be." While the other children laughed, much discussion ensued. I had meant to share it as a humorous anecdote, but Gurudev wrote back that it was very significant and expressed delight that in our Bala Vihars, our children have the opportunity to flex their hearts and minds by grappling with the metaphysical at a very young age.

Gurudev understood what effect saints have on children.

Swami Advayananda: Gurudev requested me to bring my parents to meet him. When they arrived, he asked them, "Were there any saints in your family?" My father shook his head. Gurudev said: "He wants to join the Vedānta course. I have asked him to come after the twelfth standard. I want him. I hope I have the permission of both of you." They both gave their consent. I was in ecstasy. After that, whenever Gurudev met me, he would say, "Come after your twelfth immediately!" That is how I joined the āśrama.

A change of attitude turns a chore into a fulfillment:

Bharati Sukhtankar: Once, when I was straining under 'tiresome' chores, coping with a growing child and social pressures, I wrote to Gurudev, who replied: "You must consider that the Lord has given you two very special people to look after. Nobody else can take care of them, so He has appointed you. Whatever you do for them, do it as your worship unto Him; change your attitude. All the gopīs were gṛhasthas (householders) — they occupy top rank among the Lord's devotees. Be a gopī. Need I say more?"

WHERE DOES EDUCATION STOP?

The purpose of education is to create men and women of character and enterprise who can contribute effectively to a nation's well-being, prosperity, happiness, and world harmony. To make a nation great, team spirit, hard work, a noble goal, and an inspirational ideal are necessary. Of these, a noble goal is the most important. Without this, the other three might get channeled toward unhealthy or destructive ends. Therefore, cultural values are central to effective education. When educationalists fail to understand this crucial factor, and, in the name of secularism, remove moral science or scriptural teaching from the education system, the very purpose of education remains unrealized.

Swami Chinmayananda:

Education is nothing if it does not train our faculties to capture all our opportunities, to be useful to all others, and to be happy always in ourselves.

Mind-to-mind confrontation is the secret of education. What they call education today is a fraud. There is instruction and no teaching. Instruction does not constitute education; education is a subjective phenomenon kindled in the student and maintained by the teacher. Thus, we are in an era of instructors and not in the age of teachers. Even today, teachers are irresistibly respected — not instructors. Educators should transform the student into a person who has learned the art of self-control and gained an insight into the ugliness of his own mind: its strength and weakness. Education is the goal to be reached, and it is to be gained by one's own reflection. Colleges must give that new luster built on the mystic moments when mind confronts mind, and a student suddenly senses the power and richness of his own intellect.

The quality of your behavior will depend upon the respect you have for the association, the institution to which you belong — maybe caste, creed, religion, nation, or community. "I don't know my father, and I have no respect for my mother" — such an individual feels lonely in the world; he has no moral values [with which he can] compare whether what he is doing is morally right or wrong. Is it not true today that when we try to solve our problems, the question of morality never comes up? Look what a terrorist does to take what he considers to be his state — putting bombs in ordinary buses, and that, too, in other cities, not bothering as to who dies. Is this the solution that a perverted intellect can find? This is because the sense of belonging is not there.

Culture constitutes a storehouse of the pooled learning of a group. Culture comprises ways of thinking, believing, feeling, and acting that are common to a group of people. Cultures teach us what is 'real,' what to be sensitive to, what to believe, and how to learn and think. It trains and develops our tuning mechanism so that we tune certain things on and others out without ever being aware of it. We must learn to identify a shift in values as one of the objectives of cultural learning, so that a person cannot be said to have learned a second culture unless his values have changed.

Never can children's education be complete unless we impart in them a true appreciation of the eternal values of life. A real intellectual cannot keep quiet when he sees an injustice, and he acts without worrying about the consequences! Therefore, we must teach the children not only to have right values and convictions of their own but also the heroism to live up to them.

The youth of our country is experiencing today the need for an ideal that can supply to them a consistent motivation for self-sacrificing and dynamic action. It is natural for the youth to have the daring to plan, the irresistible urge to act, the enthusiasm to conceive, the energy to work, along with their shy impatience with all inefficiencies and ugly defects that they find in the world all around. Each one of these can release an avalanche of power and strength, energy and vitality, thought and action. To channelize these resources in the bosom of the heroic youth, they must be trained to study the problems of life and to evaluate each of them correctly. This calls for a special mental balance in each and an unerring intellectual self-application to arrive at potentially creative judgments and constructive conclusions. In the very midst of confusing situations, how does one train the mind and intellect to evaluate and judge situations? This knowhow is explained exhaustively in the *Bhagavad-gītā*. [Arjuna was] a proficient man; [but] due to his mental agitation, the great warrior in him becomes temporarily inefficient. Great achievements are earned not through proficiency alone, but achievements are the rewards of efficiency. Today, all around us we find in our country that, through education, we have stepped up the general proficiency in our youth. But their capacity to apply their knowledge in the field of their activity is definitely at a low ebb. Where gathered knowledge adds up to form proficiency, the ability to translate that knowledge into action at the appropriate field is called efficiency.

The truth of this paradox is experienced by every one of us in life. A doctor can be a drunkard although he has full knowledge of the adverse effects of alcohol, and yet he may come to die of cirrhosis of the liver! A lawyer who knows law may, under provocation, commit even a murder. That we know is not sufficient for us to live what we know. Intellectually, we may applaud and appreciate a certain moral value of life, but by the time it has to be expressed as action, we act as lowly as though we had no education at all. Strange is the enchantment of this paradox! Just because I can appreciate music or painting, it does not mean I can sing tunefully or produce a masterpiece! Knowledge is needed; but to express the knowledge, we need a lot of laborious training.

Disintegration is the first stage before a nation collapses. Whether it is the Moghul Empire or any other empire, when they were founded, they were all together, united, and integrated. After indulgence for some time, disintegration started, and that was the beginning of the end of that dynasty. At the same time, I cannot blame my youngsters for not having this love for the country or [for having] an awareness of what is happening around. They are the products of the education that we have been giving them. Even the attempts at changing the education system were all corrupt. The ministers never thought of our culture and how to tune up our children to it and keep them inspired by the very word 'Bhārat.' After centuries of condemning our country, we have come to a point where we have no respect for the nation and no sense of belonging to the nation.

Advice for school directors:

The result is good. But we must dissect and carefully examine if we can do still better. Congratulate that young principal for me, please. The adventure — a day's outing program — can do the children much good. Why not think of really first-class staff students, give a special coaching Saturday and Sunday, talent training, to bring them up to the rank level in the state, or even in India? The greatness of a vidyālaya (school) is not the large classrooms or the vast playgrounds. They all become great when the students work sincerely and grow up to be successful men and women of character, ability, dynamism in serving their Country, Community, and Culture.

A Chinmaya Vidyālaya director heard Swamiji say:

Don't you think that the television program of Rāmāyaṇa has changed the color of thinking in this country to a large extent? In Delhi, where I was just now, at that time on Sunday morning, there was not even any traffic on the road. Everyone was seeing Rāmāyaṇa! They didn't want to miss it. Why? In that old story, you see the greater and nobler values being demonstrated, which you are silently and expectantly hoping for in the youth of today. And you are charmed by it, because it belongs to the very genius of the country! So it is not so difficult to impart these ideas to the children. But we need workers — mainly girls. It is only the motherliness of the lady that can impart these things to growing children. All schools must start a program, a period during the week to give special training to the teachers in how they may, whenever possible in their classrooms, make the children understand that there is an Unseen Hand which molds the affairs of the entire universe. Why are you afraid to have such programs? Christian churches do it; Islam is doing it in their schools. How is it that the Hindus alone cannot do it? And, if the Hindus have no morality, India will have no morality, because in this country, 82 percent are Hindus.

Tips to teachers:

The teacher should be neither lofty nor authoritarian, but his [or her] enthusiasm in communicating a subject should command a natural respect. Even a dry subject can be taught effectively in some intellectually honest way to any child at any stage of development. A teacher should talk clearly, present relevant material logically, and convey enthusiasm. A teacher must be the most committed student in the classroom. In my lectures, I just try to make things clear to myself. I find I am learning things all the time. Be acutely aware of the expressions on the faces of the students. A puzzled look in anyone's eyes must make you stop short. Then re-explain, rebuild, redecorate, and refurnish the house of truth you have already built for others. Facts are mere raw materials for building relationships between the teacher and the taught. The real job of teaching is to weave a fabric of relationship with your ideas and to attach it to so many points of the student's life that it becomes part of him. The talks are the canopy of words spread from the mouth to the ears of the student: the actual transaction of truth takes place, under this auspicious roof of words, between the hearts of the teacher and the taught.

Advice to parents seeking guidance on how to bring up their two under-three-years-of-age children:

Do not ever misunderstand that children of that age are merely passive observers; how then are they able to learn a language? Is not everything new, fresh, and mysterious for them? In fact, child psychologists have concluded that children in that age group need more rest as well as more frequent feedings, because during those few years of early childhood, they have to be alert and learn much more than in their later life. The rate of absorption of knowledge and experiences in those early years is stupendous. Therefore, an atmosphere of religion and spiritual values around them is very important in molding and enhancing their mental life. Between the ages of three and five, your children can be introduced to stories of Christ and Kṛṣṇa, of Rāma and Buddha, and of Mohammed and Moses. These stories of the spiritual giants of the world, recounting their experiences, their trials, and their inner strength in overcoming temptations, as well as the positive experiences of joy that they gained, may all be passed on to your children with appropriate expressiveness. Let these stories be told now and then by the father also. Make it a point for the children to pray before their meals, not too elaborately, but for just a short moment. Whenever they ask questions about flowers, clouds, butterflies, or frogs, be alert enough to flavor your honest explanations with a hint about the play of God around us. Leave them with these small hints. Do not go into details. Allow a corner in your home for prayer: a quiet, private chapel or a simple altar. Let your children watch both of you praying to the Lord regularly. When the children have grown to be between the ages of eight and ten, at a fixed time for one-half hour every day, sit down with them and read them *The Gospel of Sri Ramakrishna*. I suggest this book because much is expressed in the innocent language of children. The endless stories and analogies can lead their minds on an independent journey to see for themselves a greater message for life and a larger value in life.

The following selection is excerpted from a letter that ***Swami Chinmayananda*** *wrote to a teacher who had approached him with a question:*

The doubt of your ninth-class student — "What good does your moralizing do for us in this present-day world of sin, deceit, and hypocrisy?" — is to be answered directly to his cousin, uncle, or father, who must have raised this doubt in him. Explain to the class: When we have a disease, we go to the doctor. When poverty is all around, we try to make people rich. When society is immoral, we need to teach our children moral values. When they grow up, they will help save, serve, and change society. What if the boy were in medical school and said, "What is the use? There are so many sick people! In spite of all the hospitals, the sick ones are only increasing in number — so let's not study medicine." If you want to save one who is drowning, you must know how to swim. To save society from its immoralities and vulgarities, our children must get ready today to change their fathers' vulgar world. This change is called a moral revolution. We are creating heroic revolutionaries to change the rhythm of our social behavior. As the demand — so the supply! Today the people want drinks, women, murder, fighting, nudity, and impropriety, so the movie theater screens depict them all. Therefore, spiritual education is the only remedy. You teachers have not yet realized what great work you are accomplishing. By changing the vision of life in the children, you are changing the mission of the entire community and its goals.

Letter to ***Shrichand Krishnani:*** Without teaching us the mechanism and the art of driving — we are taught the traffic rules! They are necessary — but can that knowledge make me a safe driver on the road? I wonder.

The impact of a Master:

Anil Sachdev: I had stood first in my class. That year, Gurudev patted me on the back and said, "First, always first, and first in all that you take up!" This appreciation from the Master himself at a young age was a source of great inspiration for me the rest of my life.

*N*ever can children's education be complete unless we impart in them a true appreciation of the eternal values of life.

STEP 3

HOW TO LIVE WITH INSPIRATION

This is verily the last birth for all true seekers. Strive! You are at the goalpost, at the tape held across the winning post.

-Swami Chinmayananda

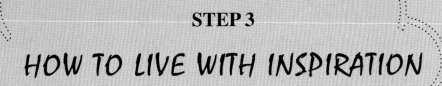

10

Dealing with Pressure

During the match between Ferrera and Edberg, Swamiji said, "It is not lack of experience here, but pressure." The next day he told Edberg, "You missed it! And it is not your Guru's fault. You were sleepy, and he withdrew his advice."

Swamiji often said that if the pressure of vāsanās is reduced, then meditation can be highly successful. We are tied down with a hundred different attachments to the world outside. Swamiji said, "It would be easier to pluck out one or two — but the whole lot? To free yourself totally from these entanglements, you have to axe them down! You have to dedicate your BMI (body–mind–intellect) totally to reach out for this state."

In the process, many times God or Guru showers grace (advice in the tennis analogy above). But if the pressure of vāsanās is too much, or the devotee is too busy, excited, agitated, or emotional to receive it, then the opportunity to benefit from the grace is deferred. But such grace never goes to waste. If the agitated mind is pacified, then it may receive the effect of grace later. At moments when the load on the mind is decreased, one can receive the blessing of God or Guru easily. The Guru can show the path and the method for going ahead, but one has to practice it oneself and become fit for receiving His grace.

HOW TO HAVE A **PEACEFUL** HEART

So long as the heart is agitated with disturbing thoughts, it does not find peace. Declutching or detaching from the frivolous things of life and holding on to the noble ones is the first step. Then a thorough overhauling is needed at the subconscious and unconscious levels to get suppressed matter out of the system. It is when this basic cleansing takes place and we find the mind reaching a state of equipoise that we can really start the journey of contemplation.

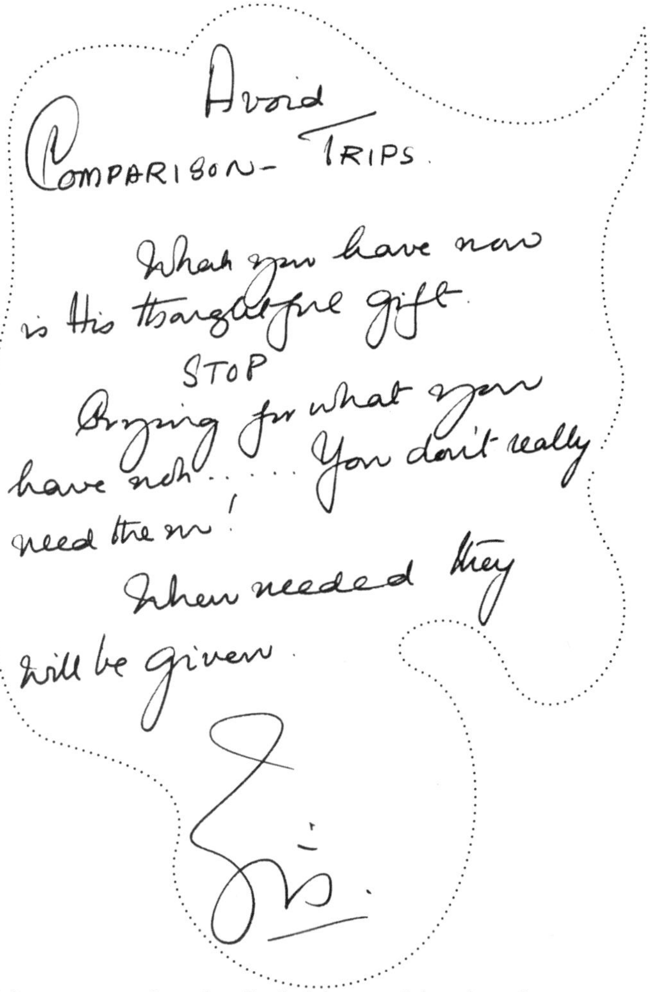
Avoid
COMPARISON-TRIPS.
What you have now
is His thoughtful gift.
STOP
Crying for what you
have not...... You don't really
need them!
When needed they
will be given.

Swami Chinmayananda:

The objects and beings cannot in themselves bring any storm into us. We receive all the shattering shocks in life — not only the tragic events but also the day-to-day pinpricks in life — only because we are making wrong contacts with the world around us. If our inward nature can be arranged and continuously held in that arrangement so as to make us react to the world positively, then we would have discovered the secret of living in peace with the world.

To be happy, one should act only as a trustee. They are rich who are content with what they have. Even a king is but a miserable pauper when he feels his vast kingdom is not enough for him. Against the besieging troops of uncertainties in life, man builds imaginary fortresses around him with money and wealth. Even a millionaire is found to be not happy because he wants more!

The seeker is struggling to recognize no enemy. But someone might come to him in idle gossip imputing that someone else had insulted the seeker. Watch now what happens! Even when the seeker sits for meditation, his mind starts planning how to get rid of his reported adversary or how to revenge him. All peace is emptied from the seeker's heart. Tranquility is the atmosphere of grace required for the blessed Self-communion to take place.

Love and hate both are conditional. Even hate has a condition; if the condition is removed, you don't hate anymore. When a person raises himself into greater ambits, his mind will no longer entertain agitations at the ordinary level of likes and dislikes. One who is striving to learn the art of meditation must slowly and carefully develop in himself an attitude of holding himself neutral in all perceptions of stimuli and in his responses to them. None of the happenings at the level of the mind can be of any serious consequence to a person who is trying to detach from the dualistic experiences and who has learned the art of drawing inspiration from something beyond.

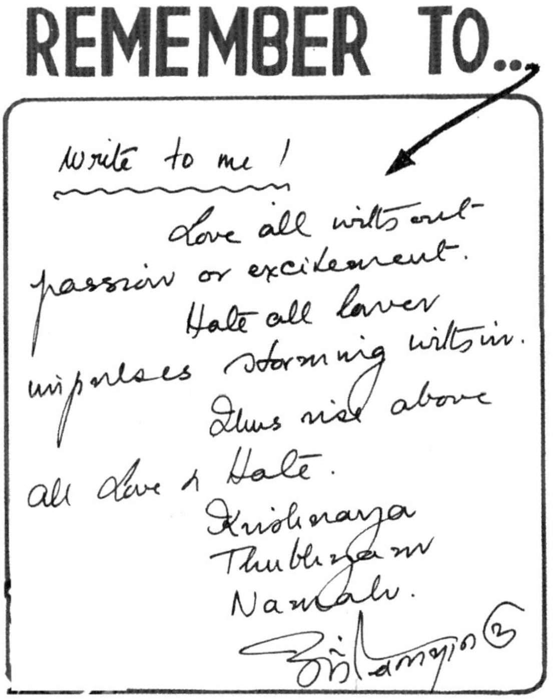
REMEMBER TO...
Write to me!
Love all without passion or excitement.
Hate all lower impulses storming within.
Thus rise above all love & Hate.

Accept whatever environment you get in life as His prasāda. Remove all anxiety. Revel in Nārāyaṇa smaraṇa (remembrance). The burdens of saṁsāra are all in our own subjective making. The disturbed mind has no power and feels helpless. When it surrenders to the Lord, it becomes quiet. Meet life as it reaches us. With or without the things our minds demand, our life can be a glorious joy, a brilliant success.

Your life will be blessed if you need nothing until you have it. Spirituality is not merely knowing what you want but also understanding what you don't need. In a life of vairāgya, there is a sense of self-sufficiency, a fabulous feeling of joy, compared with which the external world of objects is a petty, paltry, filthy nothing. Ordinarily, in the world, we are joyous when we acquire something. Here you gain the supreme joy of total withdrawal from every disturbance by giving up your hold on objects. This withdrawal is not the direct cause for realization of the supreme Infinite. It sets in motion a series of consequences which ultimately lead the seeker to Liberation.

In fact, it is very easy to give up the external objects. Just walk out. But if you have an attachment for them, wherever you may go, you will create a world of similar objects around you. To exhaust the vāsanā burden, the secret lies in karma yoga. Karma yoga is an attitude in action in which one fixes the vision high. An army officer's vision is for the nation, and in a spirit of self-surrender and dedication, the mind gets purified and the vāsanās get automatically exhausted.

First, sublimate your vāsanās, the innate tendencies that express themselves as desires in the intellect, as thoughts in the mind, and as actions at the body level. When thoughts are moving like the wind, the vāsanās are what guides them in a particular direction. Vāsanās are channels of thought-flow left in our personality by our past physical and mental actions. They come to play only when your thoughts are flowing about. The directions in which your thoughts tend to flow are called the vāsanās, or tendencies. When we are conscious of the pull of vāsanās and realize that some of them are dragging us into incompetence and into futile mental and physical dissipations, we call them 'mental hang-ups.' We struggle in vain against them, and, ultimately, in our weariness, we come to yield to them.

The human mind functions on three levels — the conscious, the subconscious, and the unconscious. Vāsanās are psychological tendencies — repressions and suppressions — buried in the unconscious layer of our personality, which is even beneath our subconscious layer. The conscious is the surface mind, containing thoughts we have fully realized. Unfinished thoughts, undigested experiences, mutilated ideas, crushed emotions, suffocated desires — thoughts that have met with conflict — sink into our personality and are held in suspension in the subconscious mind. The unconscious is constituted of impulses, instincts, and emotions that are unknown to us, but those come up and express themselves under certain stress of circumstances. The unconscious is equivalent to the causal body (called vāsanās in the terminology of Vedānta). Whenever the conscious mind is quiet, the subconscious has a chance to float up.

On all occasions of congregational prayers or ritualistic celebrations in the church, mosque, or temple, we conscientiously make our conscious minds quiet, allowing the subconscious mind to float up. We experience a greater lightness of heart, and the personality gets temporarily released from its constrictions. Manifestations of the subconscious on the platform of the conscious mind are generally experienced in dreams. In this sense, we can say that dreams are nature's exhaust pipes through which tensions and pressures created in the mind are released.

The 'causal' level of our personality — the unconscious depth-layer of our mind — is indicated as ignorance. The ignorance of the spiritual essence and its infinite glory and perfection in us is the cause for our sense of restlessness, loneliness, fear, and so on; therefore, the intellect desires for, the mind agitates with, and the sense-organs indulge in the world of sense-objects.

Vāsanās give direction to our actions and are three in number — sattva, rajas, and tamas — the pure, the agitated, and the dull. The tāmasic vāsanās can be removed by cultivating rājasic vāsanās, and rājasic vāsanās can be removed by cultivating sāttvic vāsanās. When the mind gets purer, even sāttvic vāsanās get exhausted, thus allowing the divine Self to shine forth vividly.

Each of our recognized negative tendencies is to be treated with its opposite noble virtue. This is called substitution. When the mind is full of the noble values of life, the mind gets ready for its leap into the Reality through contemplation. Contemplation fulfills itself in the higher State of Consciousness when the mind ceases to be and, therefore, even the noble vāsanās are sublimated. Introspection, detection, negation, and substitution — these constitute the preliminary processes in the purification of the seeker. Without this mellowing treatment, one is not fit for the strains of spiritual growth.

When an individual gains the supreme joy of full devotion to the Lord, he comes to live in a sense of utter fulfillment, and he has, therefore, no further desire for the things of the world. He has thereby come to live and experience a new order of existence; to him, the objects, emotions, and thoughts that constitute the only fields of relaxation and entertainment for us, are of no avail.

Excerpts from an interview with an American journalist on psychoanalysis:

Wadsworth: The modern religion that we have, particularly in Southern California, is psychoanalysis, and I am curious to know how you feel the *Gītā* fits in with psychoanalysis?

Swamiji: Psychoanalysis is at this moment very rudimentary, at the beginning stages. It is changing every day. Freud is no more in the picture. And today's man will not be there probably next month. Here, we are interested in mind as such, but you are trying to analyze thought with another thought. If we have no concept of the very basis or source from which thoughts originate, and when we have not got this fundamental idea — we are playing mind with mind. But when you think of analyzing the nature and structure of the mind and how to unfold the mind and go beyond the mind to the greater realm, this present psychoanalytical method and inclination so far gathered in Western countries, I don't think personally, will be of much help.

Wadsworth: You mention Freud. Do you see any difference in the findings of Carl Jung in his work on symbols and archetypes?

Swamiji: I know they are all beautiful, as far as they go at their level. But they don't have any altitude, just an expansion. Psychology in the West today is expanding. No vertical movement, but only a horizontal expansion. So at the level at which they are, they are winning new areas of knowledge, but it is, I think, even today, a horizontal movement.

Wadsworth: Just to carry on with Jung's work a little further. What is your opinion of his work on dreams? What do dreams represent, if anything?

Swamiji: Jung's point of view on dreams — I say it is a jigsaw puzzle, child's play. We, the Vedāntins, don't take dreams seriously. We take dreams only as serious as we consider any plane of consciousness. Long, long ago in the Upaniṣads, we find that all the three planes of consciousness have been analyzed, and they came to the conclusion that these three are the expression of a fourth one, the pure Consciousness. Now you are asking me about dream interpretations. These, according to the Indian philosophy, are only an expression of inner psychoses. Let us say the subconscious mind, for example, in throwing out the bits of undigested thoughts and ideas, is doing so in order to cleanse it and make it ready for tomorrow's experiences.

Wadsworth: There is one exception to this. I found Patanjali mentions in his Aphorisms that dreams of holy men are to be taken very seriously.

Swamiji: Any modern psychologist would immediately understand, if he were not prejudiced, that Patanjali supports what I said. What I said was that the subconscious mind, coming up to the conscious level, is called the dream. The subconscious mind contains thoughts that we have intensively thought and have not exhausted completely in the waking time, and these are suppressed to the subconscious. So, if I dreamed of holy land, holy places, holy things, then the teacher came and advised me of certain things or removed some doubts, and so on, it clearly shows that the student, the seeker, has been seriously thinking during the waking time of these things. Naturally it is a beautiful indication that the boy was not spending time on a film star or a girlfriend of his, or else he would have dreamed of them. If he has dreamed of spiritual values and ideas, it shows that he has been keeping his mind on the right track.

Letter to ***Jujhar Singh:*** Love breeds love. Violence echoes violence. This is the law.

Letter to a devotee who was getting affected by the unhappiness of family members:
Why are you worried about the family members? Do as best as you can, whatever you can, and if they are not satisfied or happy, forgive them for their trespasses in the understanding that it is their vāsanās that make them miserable. You can congratulate yourself that you did the best for them.

Letters to ***Ācāryas Gaurang and Darshana Nanavaty*** *in 1980:* Plunge yourself in study and reflection upon the nature of Nārāyaṇa, the Atman in you. Be good and cheerful. Watch the world and its play all around you from within; just WATCH. Don't ever react. The entire Upaniṣads and *Gītā* you shall find demonstrated and dramatized around… Be sincere. Ignore all you see and hear – inauspicious. Fix your gaze upon Him and act diligently. Progress comes in its own time… With ardent devotion hold on to His Feet, cheerfully play life and its ugly perversions and dance on to your own inner Goal of Peace and Joy!!

Letter to ***Sheila Sharma:*** Be happy. Happiness is a midway station between having too much and too little. In the sense of contentment, this is discovered.

Letter to ***Prof. Laksmi Reddy:*** Be noble and sweet in all your contacts, whatever be the environment you meet. This is our only freedom. That life is brilliant which has been lived fully, careless of the texture of happenings around. This "Balance" can come to us only when we have in our depths the firm devotion to the Lord, the Ideal. Without it, in the storms of life we get ourselves tossed about without an aim or a purpose, drifting rather than sailing toward a purposeful harbor.

Will change of time and place make a difference?
Swami Chidrupananda: I once asked Pūjya Gurudev, "In this scientific and technological age, there are many sorrows, whereas in the past, life was much more peaceful." Gurudev answered, "You are thinking that it is the age that is responsible for all the evils in the world. Even if I lift you all to the golden age of the past, do you think you all will be happy? No. It is man who creates the situation…"

Finding a deeper insight into psychology:
Ācārya Vilasini Balakrishnan*:* I was not a very likely candidate to be Gurudev's disciple, having been raised in the United States by a mother who was a psychologist and a father who was an attorney and who attended an Episcopal Church. In the 1970s, psychology was an up-and-coming profession that attracted many brilliant people who were creating

different therapeutic modalities, and I would hear about them at the dinner table. But perhaps this background primed me for appreciating Gurudev's teachings, as he truly had the most profound insights of a master psychologist and the deepest experience of divine Presence. Gurudev talked about a daily practice of "Introspect, detect, negate, substitute, and sublimate." I resonated immediately with the first four, as they perfectly encapsulate Western psychology. The last directive, "sublimate (the ego)" is what put Vedānta heads above all of psychology. 'Sublimate' contains the essence of Vedānta — how to detach from our ego and attach to the Higher.

To be happy, one should act only as a trustee.

11

Hit the Ball!

While watching some older Wimbledon finals games on the video, between Ivanisevic and Agassi, Swamiji said, "Ivanisevic does not know how to receive Agassi's ball." Again, "Ivanisevic is not good at receiving." At another time, "He does not have a sure stroke!" Swamiji continued to tick off one comment after another: "This boy is not ready to receive it!" — "In that chopping, he has no control, yet he chops. Once the concentration is gone, he will lose the game. He is uncertain in his cuttings. He is just purposelessly hitting." — "What would have been his condition if he knew beforehand that he wasn't going to win? One must have the faith that one will reach the goal; then only will the striving toward it be dynamic."

To go through life aimlessly, moving from one selfish activity to the next, reacting without discrimination and without following a noble goal or making a determined effort to find true happiness, is the "chopping" and "cutting" we do most of the time. Having heard the teachings, if one does not start regular sādhanā, which is essential for becoming established in this knowledge, one will have learned a philosophy without fulfilling its purpose of raising us to reach the goal. Also, the student will have neither the faith ("sure stroke") reinforced with understanding, which is essential for receiving the Guru's grace, nor the conviction that he will succeed, which would provide the dynamism to sustain the power of concentration necessary to make the most of opportunities for progress. This is true for all endeavors in either the sacred or the secular realm.

During moments when the mind gets very integrated, Swamiji advises us to be alert and focused; otherwise, the opportunity to forge ahead will be lost — "once the concentration is gone, he will lose the game!" It is at the point of mind-intellect integration that great progress takes place, because it is at this point that the Guru's grace can have a potent effect — just as Ivanisevic could have been ready to receive Agassi's ball had his mind been focused.

GET INVOLVED

Once the goal is clear in our mind and we have understood our purpose in life, it would be most unwise to procrastinate in our quest. We should diligently start living the way of life that we have understood to be the best for us. Just knowing about it will not move us an inch forward. To apply this understanding in our daily life takes years of practice. The know-how about application is captured in spiritual practice and religion. The scriptures are reports of and from Masters who have trodden the path before us. By following the scriptures we can advance more quickly in spirituality, as they contain the proven way to the Truth, the final awakening.

STOP

Living on a thin diet of miseries — come to the Geeta way of life

24-9-74

Swami Chinmayananda:

If the seeker is still doubtful as to the goal and the path, he is not yet fit for any intense practice. A seeker must know what is the goal, what are the values that are against achieving the goal, what are the values he must develop in himself, and what are the false traits present in him that must be made ineffective. We need to note modes of living conducive to these attempts at self-evolution, as they constitute the spiritual values. At the highest peak of divine life stand the mighty Temple of Meditation.

Religion is a great science, and it has a glorious utility in the world. We are not referring to the religion of ringing-the-bells. We are referring to that aspect of religion that helps us to discover in ourselves a new strength and vitality to face our challenges in life.

The only viable alternative for the world and the survival of its human race seems to be religion. Blind faith in religion is dangerous. Ignorance of religion is ungenerous. Neglect of religion is preposterous. Fanatic religion is as dangerous to the world as fanatic secularism.

Religion is a happy and intelligent blending of philosophy and ritual. If the two aspects are not synchronized properly, there can be no religion. Unfortunately, however, human beings commit the error of taking only the ritualistic aspect and calling it religion, and then attributing its decadence and failure to religion as a whole. True religion knows no failure, because ritualism here means far more than the mere physical performance of ceremonies. Ritual also includes all modes of practical religion, applicable to the mental and intellectual levels of our personality. It therefore includes rites, ceremonies, and duties practiced externally; devotion cultivated by the mind; and subtle discrimination and meditation undertaken by the intellect.

By religion is meant, in the larger sense of the term, rising above one's limited ego in dedication to a higher goal. Wherever one has an altar of dedication — that is called religion. The altar may be art, literature, politics, or one's own profession; whatever it is, it becomes a religion. Religion is a challenging call to dynamic living. Religion is a science of living which aims at individual perfection, and from it, to world perfection. It can only help those who are able to live exactly according to its instructions.

The program for a progress in yourself as an individual is called spirituality. It is, therefore, that no Teacher, however great he may be, can impart the subjective Knowledge to a student. All that the Teacher can supply is a clear vision of what is involved, a glimpse of the Goal to be achieved, and logical arguments to convince the student of the blessedness and perfection of both the Goal and the path.

It is absolutely necessary that the intellectual entity in a seeker must first of all discover a complete satisfaction about the aim and goal of philosophy as explained by the Teacher. If there are great doubts and misgivings about the reasoning of the Master, no student can feel completely inspired to follow sincerely and intensely the ardent path of Self-realization. Once convinced of an ideal, he makes honest attempts to live it. In the initial period of practice, the seeker is found to live this new life of his discovered ideal, only when he is not called upon to vigorously deny and contradict his own old ways of living. Whenever convenient — whenever the temptation is not strong enough to challenge his intellect, whenever he is not called upon to make any extraordinary sacrifice — at all such intervals, he lives his own convictions. The more he lives what he knows to be true and what he is devoted to, the more he experiences an ampler joy and fulfillment. Naturally, he is won over by the tremendous charm of the true way of life. Here begins his involvement with the ideal.

The last lap in evolution is left to you to choose. Crack the surrounding encrustment, hatch out of the egg of selfishness, and come out into the vaster ambit of your own real nature. This last lap is in your hands. Nature can do nothing. A totally convenient hour of our imagination may never come. In fact, waiting for the auspicious time is actually sinking into inertia and developing tamas. Start now! Waste not even a second, whatever be the condition. Now is the most auspicious time to start.

There is a duty toward yourself: to live in self-control, to eat and sleep properly, to exercise your body, to maintain a loving and peaceful attitude toward all, and to educate yourself more and more in your scriptural knowledge, so that you can serve well the people around you. Never give up self-study. Worship the Lord. Meditate regularly. Be a fanatic in performing your daily prayers. Never give it up, even for a day, whether you are traveling or are sick. This brings sweetness and a special insistence to the words in your speech that makes them fly directly into the head and heart of your listeners.

A Vedāntin who practices meditation intelligently reaches this Godhood here and now, and not after death somewhere. Perfection is not a post-mortem state. It is here and now. This is the birthright of every living man. The time limit of its achievement is only directly proportional to the amount of sincere effort and correct application put forth by the seeker. Regularity, sincerity, and right understanding are the three keystones in the Castle of Perfection. Remember: behind each one of you there stand a million who can, at their best, grace only the lower rungs of the ladder of evolution.

How much you have studied is not the question. How much you have moved toward it is what matters. It is not enough if you go through the *Gītā;* the *Gītā* must go through you! This inner revolution cannot be accomplished as a half-hearted hobby, but it can only be the result of a lifelong dedication and full-time endeavor. Even at the porch of death, don't stop the spiritual search.

Merely hearing Vedāntic discourses may give the listeners a vague concept of Vedānta, but will not make the listeners men of perfection unless they are ready to live as Vedāntins in life. In Vedāntic literature, we find an emphasis on the sincere companionship of great men. The mind grows in the direction in which it is engaged. When there is any revolutionary change in the religious ideologies and the philosophical concepts of a generation, the entire pattern of life in the society changes.

Letter to ***Swami Swaroopananda*** *when he joined the Vedānta course:* Study hard, and as your mind gets more and more absorbed in the study, its wanderings must necessarily cease. To the extent the mind has ceased its wanderings, congratulate yourself that you are progressing.

Letter to ***Erica Proelss:*** Amma, get out into 'That' from which you came to reach this movie house. Now start your study, reflect upon what you study, and contemplate; strive to reach the State of Meditation. Transform. Without the change in your moods and modes, no spiritual progress is possible. Be ready to change from a limited ego, victim of its limitations, to the supreme State of Perfection, divine and holy. Be cheerful and dynamic all the day round. The Lord is our guide: why worry?

'Wanting' to change helps to make it happen. Devotees recount:

Pranji Lodhia: On many occasions I have had the good fortune to drive Gurudev from the San Francisco airport to Krishnalaya for camps. Often, there were just the two of us in the car, and I would ramble on about all that was going on in my business and other matters. On one occasion, I asked, "Swamiji, I have been coming to lectures and camps for all these years. When will I change?" Gurudev paused for a moment, and then with a roar said, "Have you ever wondered what you would have been had you not attended?" In a few words he had made me aware of a very different perspective.

Swami Shantananda: Our entire Vedānta course batch of students had gone to Uttarkashi for a spiritual camp. I was kind of rājasic, quite hyper. There was one Swami who suggested that I ask Gurudev for a mantra. Gurudev did not give mantras. But Swamiji said, "Tell him that I told you." The next morning, I gathered some courage to ask Gurudev for a mantra. He looked at me and said, "Okay, tomorrow." The next day, Gurudev gave it to me, telling me to not forget it and to chant it every day. "It is your rope to climb the ladder," he said. I became busy with studies and work and did not use the mantra. After the course, I went to Hrishikesh to study Sanskrit. I told Gurudev, "Now I am using the mantra and chanting it regularly." He replied, "Good. Now, even if you leave it, the mantra won't leave you."

One need not keep waiting for someone to tell us to serve:

Col. Ajit Sukhtankar: Once Gurudev asked me what I was doing after office hours. "Nothing in particular, Swamiji," I said. "Please give me some work. Any work. I'll do it." Swamiji looked at me gravely and said, "When I started out from Uttarkashi, I did not ask anyone, 'What should I do?' I saw what was the need of the hour and I started off. You, too: look around you; see what needs to be done. Then go ahead and do it."

TWO WINGS OF A BIRD

The various ways in which people worship God comprise the religions of the world. A religion is a spiritual philosophy put into practice. Sincere worship of God through any religion is equally valid. Within any religion itself, there may be many paths that cater to different temperaments. Hinduism describes the three most common paths: a life of service while dedicating all activities to God, called karma yoga; the path of devotional love toward God, called bhakti yoga; and the path of intellectual discrimination and inquiry, called jñāna yoga. Love for God develops when we try to know who or what God is. When the mind reduces its burden of vāsanās through the process of service and becomes lighter, it is able to develop the two wings of devotion and intellectual appreciation. It is not possible to fly with just one wing. Along with trying to know God, or the Reality, one must cultivate love for God. It is not only that a jñānī comes to know the Self, but the Lord promises in the *Bhagavad-gītā* that He will also give the Knowledge of the Self to the devotee who surrenders completely at the lotus feet of the Lord.

Swami Chinmayananda:

The divine pronoun 'That' indicates all concepts of God, and it includes the manifest and the unmanifest, the immanent and the transcendent: both are concepts of God — with form and without form. It is in vain to waste one's time considering which God to worship. Worship Him in any form. It is the sincerity of devotion that matters.

The method to be followed in contemplation of a deity or an idol like Śrī Rāma, Kṛṣṇa, Hanumān, Gaṇeśa, Śiva, Viṣṇu, Buddha, or Jesus is that you must remember him as though he is just behind you, looking over your shoulders, watching over what you are doing, guiding you and leading you from morning to evening — that is saguṇa upāsana (worship of the manifest). His qualities come automatically to the mind and, in due course, you find that your values have changed. For example you cannot think of Mahatma Gandhi without the idea of nonviolence arising in your mind. Buddha brings into your mind peace and tranquility. On the other hand, when you think of Hitler your mind will be tainted by his cruelty and atrocious crimes.

Contemplation is not an intellectual comprehension or an emotional appreciation. It rests on the two, like the two wings of a bird. Upon both the wings, like an eagle, it soars high. A bird cannot fly with one wing. Both wings are of equal importance. Both must be equal in length and strength. Your intellectualism must be sweetened with devotion; your heartfelt emotions must be reinforced with knowledge. The head and the heart must merge together, to let the mind glide into the higher climes of subtler realms of consciousness.

The path by which you can realize the Truth is not merely dry intellectualism. If dry intellectualism could realize Truth then all philosophy professors would be already realized. The other type, or path, is of mere emotionalism. Mere emotion cannot take you there. The mind needs a form on which to fix it itself in devotion to the Lord. It is unavoidable. Thereby, through contemplation, pierce through that form with the intellect and see what that form represents. Thus, knowledge and devotion are the methods and techniques by which the understanding of the Lord's nature and devotion for the Lord are enhanced. Neither of them, by itself, is capable of realizing the Truth, because it is beyond the mind and the intellect. But where the mind and the intellect merge, the instrument so forged is called the 'heart' in all scriptural literature.

You may do years of sādhanā and meditation, but unless the mind and intellect get integrated, it will only be mechanical. The mind should want to execute the ideas of the intellect. The paths of devotion, action, and knowledge are to be practiced in synthesis, although you may take one or the other of them as your main path according to your temperament. Since the paths for changing the quality, quantity, and direction of thoughts are so intrinsically interrelated, the accomplishment of one is at once the fulfillment of the other two.

Let love lead you through life's rough and stony maze — to teach you through the minutes, the hours, and the days. There is so much to learn, so much to realize. Let love be the way and the goal, the means and the end. Love is a link that connects, a force that attracts, a fascination that seizes, and a clasp that grasps. Therefore, when one establishes himself in the relationship of devotion with the Divine, he steps up into a realm of his own, having his own enchantments and personal experiences. All dedicated acts of love, when they generate devotion and drive the loving mind toward the Lord of Love, are all effective practices of bhakti.

Bhakti and jñāna are not two different things. Both of them are one and the same experience. They appear to be different due to the difference in the seat of their manifestation. Bhakti is the attitude of the heart, and jñāna is the attitude of the intellect in a person toward his Creator. No bhakta can be a true one unless he be a Vedāntin; and no Vedāntin is perfect unless he be a lover of the Lord.

Identification is the measuring rod of love. When identification is complete, love is fulfilled.

That which indicates a subtler Truth with its gross form is an idol. All ancient Hindu Vedic gods are but functional names of the One Supreme Power. The story of Kṛṣṇa is the story of the infinite Reality imprisoned in matter. Kṛṣṇa is not a historical figure; He is the perpetual Truth. He does not belong to the past. He is of the ever-immediate moment. History is the chronological order of things that happen in life. He is beyond chronology. History is happening in time. History is played out in Him just as the waves play in the ocean. Rooted in this wisdom, Kṛṣṇa is the most perfect Man of Realization. The Lord Himself, playing in the world, is Kṛṣṇa, the Infinite.

Question sent in a letter by a Westerner who had heard Swamiji's talks in Toronto:

Q. You have stated that bhakti yoga, karma yoga, and jñāna yoga are essential in purifying the BMI. As a brain-heavy Westerner, I find it very difficult to surrender myself in devotion and prayer. When you mention that Vedānta is nothing without prayer and devotion, I became troubled, Swamiji.

Swamiji: I can fully appreciate your situation as nobody else can, because I myself was a man of no faith — even worse, I was a positive atheist. I did not reach the āśrama to live there or to renounce life. With my camera hanging from my shoulder and my scratch-pad and pencil ready in my pocket, I visited the āśramas just to gather ideas, to criticize them, and to discover how the Masters in monasteries keep up this bluff called religion, with an impossible God and an unnecessary devotion to Him. I think I went there on Friday, thinking that on Monday I would return... that Monday has not yet come! That is why I say I sympathize with you completely. Love increases with understanding and knowledge. First, I see a girl and feel attracted toward her, perhaps because of her shape, the color of her hair, the placing of the eyes, the grace of her movements. Thereafter, I meet her, I talk to her, I cultivate her friendship, and through these contacts, I come to know her more and more. Then I marry... perhaps beget a few children. Both anxious parents work hard and watch over the children's growth and education. They grow up. We become grandparents. By now, my love for her becomes total, inasmuch as I know her through and through. Knowledge increases love. Therefore, inquire, investigate, reflect, and watch for His unseen hand that constantly works in and through all of our experiences. Thus, the more and more we know of the nature of Reality, our devotion for It increases ... devotion shall come into your bosom as an end product of all your spiritual studies. With Prem and Om, Thy own Self.

***Question** from a Postal Course student:* What is the role of rituals in religion? Are they to be discouraged?

Swamiji: The rituals are objective dramatization of the subjective art of self-perfection. Such ceremonies and attractive display of rhythm and beauty cannot be eliminated from human life. Historically, it is true that whenever ritualism is removed, and churches, mosques, and temples are closed down, they get replaced by military parades, nightclubs and their excesses, racecourse crowds, boxing galleries, and so on. Let the public decide what they want. I would prefer my countrymen to have religious rituals entertain them rather than the more dangerous and immoral alternatives available.

Q: Since God is all-pervading, why should you go to a temple or house of God to pray?

Swamiji: You know that the essence in the cow is in her milk, and this is pervading her entire vital body. Yet, if I want to milk the cow, I cannot get it by squeezing her horns or her tail; we must go to her udder. God, the Lord, is all-pervading, but to invoke Him, we need the altar. THINK. In a democracy, the government of a country is present at every point within the frontiers of that nation. Yet, when I want to invoke the government for a permit or for help, I must reach the capital, approach the right departmental head, and invoke the government's protection or patronage. THINK. My girl is in her place. Her picture is in my pocket. The picture is not she; but the picture helps me to be with her in thought. The world is not a map, but a world map is useful for those who travel round the world.

*Letter to **Anjali Singh:*** Love is the power behind the most powerful philosophy, and if love is in your heart, guard it well, cultivate it well, enlarge its scope, and spread it all around you. This is the most effective fortress around you. You are precious; guard yourself well — not by guns or artilleries of powerful objective knowledges. Wrap your heart in love tender, in affection sweet, in cheerful brilliance, and meet the world. You have all the philosophy you need — all the spirituality for liberation. Cultivate love.

How many types of meditations are there?

Swami Swaroopananda: The youth of Hong Kong were invited to meet Gurudev. This is the first chance I had to be in his close presence. The Study Group coordinator broke the silence by repeatedly insisting that we should ask questions. Gurudev interrupted and silenced him: "When the mind is quiet there are no questions. In the presence of the Master, the mind becomes silent." Finally, after some time, I asked, "Swamiji, is there one type of meditation or many types?" Gurudev bent forward, looked me straight into my eyes, and said, "How many types of medications are there? As many diseases, that many medications … as many diseased minds, that many meditations!" He went on to explain humorously, "Some will say look at the fly, wings and all; now look at its fat body, see it intensively; and now see that small rolling face attached to that body.

Look at its eyes staring at you, then its lips only, and then its smile.... Your mind is silent! Now don't ask me my method of meditation; I will confuse you further." He then saw the drive of my question. He roared: "All great Masters have expounded the same truth in different manners; it is these unintelligent followers who disgrace their Masters and create confusions." My heart whispered within: the one who so universally accepts many Masters is indeed my Master. My search had ended.

That evening, all of us CHYKs were so inspired that we went to The Peak, a high point in Hong Kong on top of a hill, to meditate; we were so lost in contemplation that it got late in returning home. Hell broke loose at night! The elders had worried and one complained to Gurudev. Gurudev was leaving the next morning, and when we went to see him off at the airport, he gave us a loving hug with the advice, "You don't have to go to the Peak to meditate. In meditation, reach the peak."

God-symbolism is an art in Hinduism. Deep philosophical truths are expressed through idols, sculpture, dance, and music:

Leela Nambiar: This is how Gurudev explained Kṛṣṇa to me in a letter: "Blue is the color of the Infinite, and whatever is immeasurable can appear to the mortal eye only as blue; thus, a cloudless summer sky is blue to us because the endless distances of space is interpreted by the physical eye as blue in color. The yellow represents the earth. Anything that is buried in the earth gathers a yellowish hue, and in fire, earth (mud, silica) grows yellowish. Thus, Śrī Nārāyaṇa represents the infinite, immeasurable, all-pervading Reality (blue color) clothed in earth — earthy matter (yellow color), meaning Śrī Nārāyaṇa is the Infinite clothed in matter; He is the Infinite expressed through a form."

But what he showed to me, a bhakta, was this: In 1966, Gurudev was in our house at Chennai. During the talk, Gurudev suddenly got ill and was advised to rest, and so he extended his stay for one week. During this time, devotees would gather at our home in the evenings to either sing for him or have spiritual discussions with him. On one such evening, Gurudev asked me to bring the idol of Lord Kṛṣṇa and place it next to him. Then, he asked me to bring my best sari and place it on the table on which the Lord's idol was kept. As the devotees waited for Gurudev to speak, I suddenly saw that the idol was moving. I looked closer to ensure I wasn't dreaming, but there he was, this jewel of Yadukula, flute in hand, dancing away, as if to some ethereal tune! I was wonderstruck. I looked around to see if anyone else was seeing what I was seeing, but the devotees did not seem to have witnessed this visual prasāda. I looked at Gurudev and saw him looking at me. A few minutes later, Gurudev said, "Hmm... enough, enough..." and the dancing Lord Kṛṣṇa stood still, as I sat stunned among the large group of devotees gathered around. To this day, I still try to understand Gurudev's intention for this vision. However, in my heart and soul, I was filled with an unshakeable devotion to Lord Kṛṣṇa and was convinced that a great Mahātmā can infuse life even in an inert idol.

Love Love Love!

THE THINKING CAP

Service, devotion, prayer, and meditation help to quiet the mind. However, unless this calming of the mind is reinforced with intellectual discrimination and unless the meditator knows what the goal is and what is to be rejected, meditation efforts will lead to a wayward, floundering exploration leading to a volcanic eruption of the suppressed mind. Two things take place with discriminative reflection as guided by the scriptures: the nature of the Self begins to become clearer; and by the power of the logic innate in the scriptures, our beliefs are transformed into conviction. We learn to make the distinction between the Real and the unreal, between Truth and falsehood. We slowly come to reject those false identities to which we are glued and learn to be what we really are.

Swami Chinmayananda:

Life looked at through distorted equipment naturally gives a distorted vision. Life's beauty depends upon the beauty of the philosophy upon which the life is built. If the foundations are false, the edifice, however strongly built, will prove to be in no way better than a castle built out of cards.

Vedānta contains the cream of all human experiences. The declarations of the ṛṣis have been formulated after close observations of the outer and inner lives of man — not at a given period of history but through generations of teachers and disciples. Such a great wealth of knowledge cannot be the personal property of either an individual, or a community, or a nation. Vedānta, the science of life, is the common wealth of man, and every full-grown man who has started asking questions upon the logic of creation, the goal of life, the state of perfection, and so on, has a right of free access to it, irrespective of his caste, creed, nationality, age, or stage in life. When, through discrimination, we are intellectually convinced of the fallacy of our way of thinking, detachment is the fructification of that discrimination.

Suppression of mind is not a process of raising it into the perfection of Godhood. It will erupt as a volcano, if it erupts. Mind is to be held back from its self-destroying imaginations through a diligent process of discrimination. Uncontrolled by the intellect, the mind should not be brought forcibly to a sudden and jerky standstill. Mental elimination should come about as a result of intellectual conviction and discrimination. A mind controlled by a purified intellect alone can take us to the greater realms of spiritual perfection. Many seekers feel themselves ruined after years of meditation when they come to feel that there is no progress in them. The difficulty is that they try all along to control the mind with force, and ultimately they succeed in suppressing the mind and not in sublimating the mind.

The process of Self-realization followed by the Vedāntins to purify the mind is through controlling it by the intellect. The devotee controls the mind by the mind; the hatha yogi gains his mental control through prāṇāyāma (breath regulation), but in the case of the Vedāntin, he controls his mind by the higher instrument, the intellect. Discrimination is the subtle motive force by which the Vedāntin controls and regulates his mind.

Listening is the first step in the ascent to the Divine. The strategy of the veiling power of tamas, or inertia, is met and defeated by the Vedāntic practice of listening called śravaṇa. The second stage is reflection called manana. Here the agitations of the mind get controlled and a person gains a fair control over his senses. In order to develop the required subtlety of intellect and discover in it the necessary amount of balance and vigor, the intellect still must undergo a certain type of pre-vicāra (insight, reflection) training, and this is available in japa.

There are two types of seekers: some reach the halls of Vedānta in sheer intellectual curiosity, while others come with real spiritual hunger. The former type takes up a laborious course of study. The more they study, the more arrogant and vainglorious they become about their bookish knowledge and their capacity to argue and decry, condemn and substantiate, quote and establish, and refute and assert the various points of view expressed in the sacred texts. They, too, are seekers, but they unwittingly enter into a jungle of mere words and miss the subtle, deeper imports and sacred suggestions contained in the ṛṣi declarations. Due to the lack of sādhanā, the very knowledge, which would have freed them from their personality entanglements, gets them tragically encrusted with a new type of vanity, the laughable vanity of wisdom, which is more dangerous than the pitiable arrogance of ignorance.

According to Vedāntic Masters, direct hearing from the teacher or indirect reading alone is not sufficient. What you have heard (or read) is to be reflected on independently, alone, away from the Teacher, with all the books closed. By this process, the ideas, which were in the book, become your own. Having understood the scriptures thus in depth, our Teachers want us not to stop at pure intellectual understanding, but to strive to bring it into our own direct experience. In listening and in reading, mental participation is necessary. In reflection, you must be mentally involved with the ideas, and in contemplation, you must try to get yourself committed to the ideas digested and assimilated earlier.

Manana and dhyāna (reflection and meditation) prepare the mind for a single-pointed application by bringing it to the state of least agitation. This is the condition of the mind and intellect fit for vicāra, the highest spiritual sādhanā known to man. This is exhaustively indicated only in Vedānta. Constant vicāra upon the meaning of Vedāntic truths leads one to true Knowledge. Vicāra is a term that has no corresponding word in English. Words like thinking, contemplating, reasoning, analyzing, and so on, do not fully express the meaning of the technique of vicāra. Vicāra comprises all these in synthesis, along with certain essential mental and intellectual discipline. With a mind and intellect trained and made steady, a seeker rips open the Upaniṣad declarations, one by one, and comes to experience the implications and the deeper suggestiveness of each mantra. This process is called vicāra. During moments of meditation when we strive hard to experience the meaning of Upaniṣadic mantras, we are in the realm of vicāra. Through vicāra our misunderstandings about ourselves, which are the expressions of our ignorance, are removed; and when ignorance is banished, knowledge shines forth. The power to do vicāra is the very fuel, which helps the spiritual vehicle to maintain its motion. The fire arising from a constant discrimination between the Real and the unreal, between the Self and the non-Self, between Spirit and matter, is fanned into a blazing brilliance through steady vicāra in which all the effects of ignorance are burned down. When ego ends, we realize our real nature to be intrinsically Divine, eternally free and of the nature of absolute Bliss.

The halls of learning where the scriptural texts are taught need no gatekeeper: the unworthy will automatically move away from the very atmosphere of such a sacred and divine study.

Some powerful Vedāntic reflections by Swami Chinmayananda:

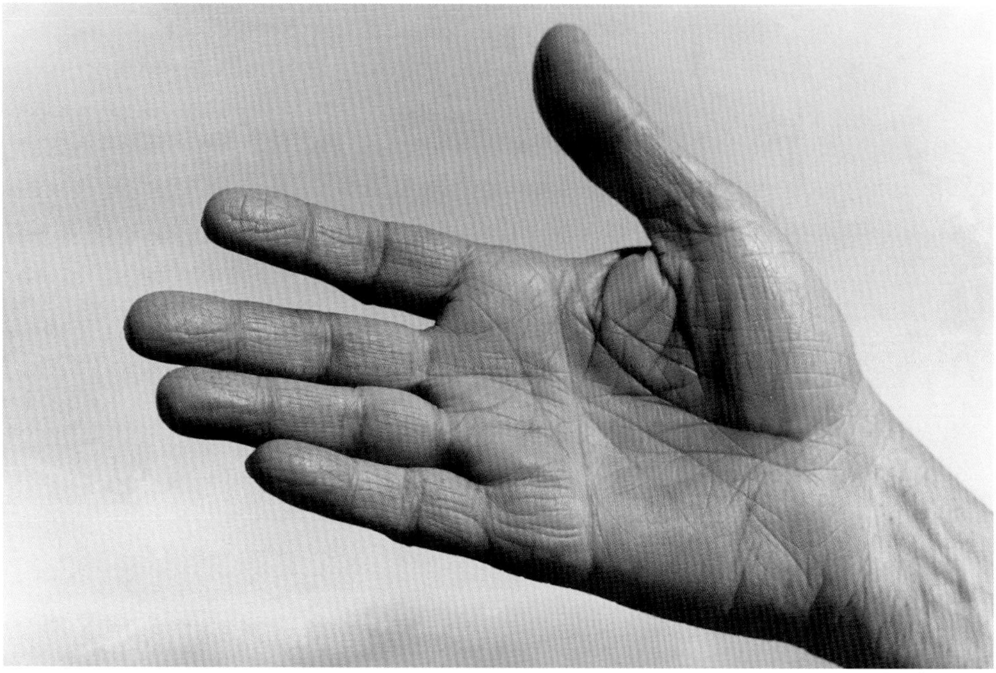

When you see the area of the palm of the hand, you see the palm plus the light that is illumining it. When you remove the palm, what remains is light, which you cannot perceive, but you intuitively know it is there. Each thought is shining in the Light of Consciousness. If you can subtract and reject the object from any thought in you, you can reach for that State of Consciousness in which the thought shines. Each one has to do it himself. Nobody can do it for another. You have to acquire this ability to extract Consciousness from thoughts by practicing it in yourself and coming to experience the deathless and changeless Experience beyond time. If you are able to do this, your life is fulfilled.

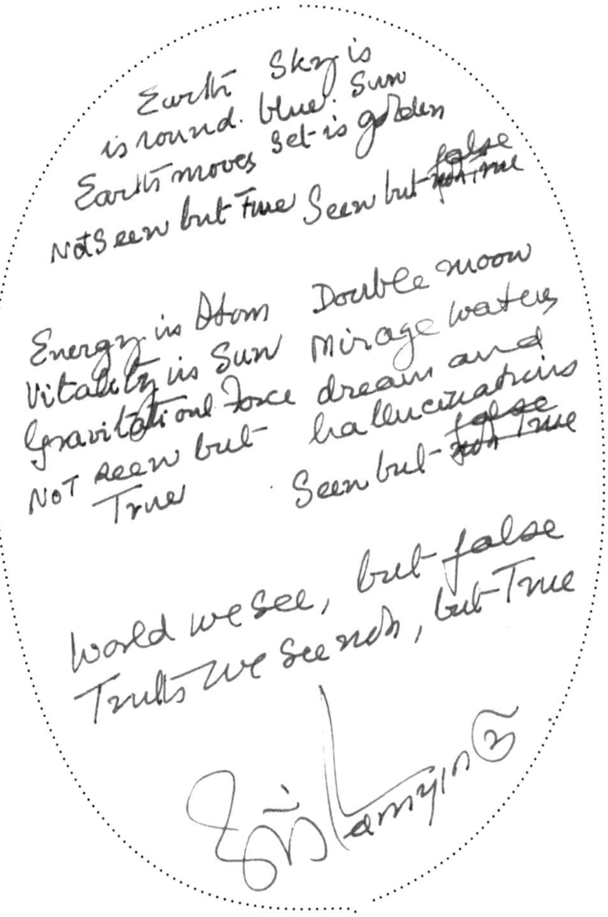

Earth is round, earth moves, not seen, but true. Sky is blue, sunset is golden, seen, but false. Energy in the atom, vitality in the sun, gravitational force, not seen, but true. Double moon, mirage waters, dreams and hallucinations, seen, but false. World we see, but not true. Truth we see not, but true.

'Relationless relationship' is the only relation between the Real and the unreal, between the True and the false. It is never possible that one who has seen the rope as a rope will ever have the fear and sorrow of a snakebite. But in the gathering darkness of dusk, a traveler mistakes an innocent rope to be a snake. The serpent delusion is created in the mind of the traveler because of his ignorance of the rope–reality.

Time and space are really the concepts of the mind and intellect. Distances are measured in space between two relative points; and time is measured as 'the interval between any two successive experiences.' Then the interval between these two different experiences is called the measurement of time. Every experience is entertained by the mind in terms of its thoughts. Thus, the interval between thoughts is the unit-measurement of time. If there is no other experience-B, then time ceases; at experience-A, time is zero! In the seeker who has transcended his mind, there can be no thoughts, and, therefore, the concepts of both time and space cannot be in him when he is abiding beyond his mind in the Self. In time, the mind entertains the illusory ideas of the past, present, and future. In the Self, these illusions can have no valid existence. For one who has thus transcended the concepts of both time and space, the very idea of eternity has no meaning, because the very concept of eternity is: 'nonstop-time.'

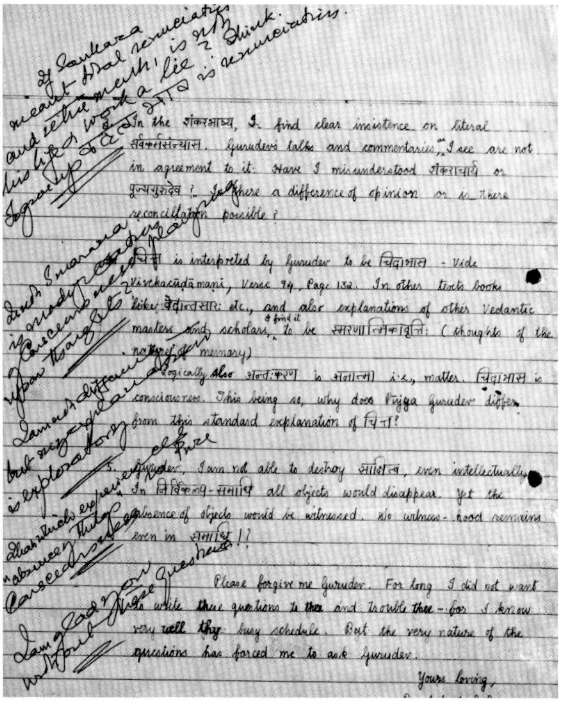

In the शंकरभाष्य, I find clear insistence on literal सर्वकर्मसंन्यास. Gurudev's talks and commentaries, I see are not in agreement to it. Have I misunderstood शंकराचार्य or पूज्यगुरुदेव? Is there a difference of opinion or is there reconciliation possible?

... is interpreted by Gurudev to be चिदाभास - Vide Vivekacūḍāmaṇi, Verse 94, Page 132. In other texts books like वेदान्तसार: etc., and also explanations of other Vedantic masters and scholars, I find it to be स्मरणात्मिकावृत्ति: (thoughts of the nature of memory)

Logically also अन्तःकरण is अनात्मा i.e., matter. चिदाभास is consciousness. This being so, why does Pujya Gurudev differ from this standard explanation of चित्त?

5. Gurudev, I am not able to destroy साक्षित्व, even intellectually. In निर्विकल्प-समाधि all objects would disappear. Yet the absence of objects would be witnessed. So witness-hood remains even in समाधि!?

Please forgive me Gurudev. For long I did not want to write these questions to thee and trouble thee - for I know very well thy busy schedule. But the very nature of the questions has forced me to ask Gurudev.

Yours loving,

A reply to Swami Advayananda's letter

Some say that this world cannot be unreal. Try and jump into the river in your dream. You will drown. Only on waking up, you will realize it is fallacious. A man dreams that he is a destitute in a jungle, famished and looking for safety and shelter. A hungry lion pursues him relentlessly. He runs to save himself and jumps into the Ganges, and the touch of the cold water wakes him up. The dreamer in the man, forgetting his own real identity, became the destitute of his dream. The moment he woke up, he understood that he had never been famished and that he was never in a jungle and that the lion was nothing but a creation of his own mind. In the ignorance of our real Nature, we start identifying with our egocentric concepts, such as: "I am the body," "I am the mind," and "I am the intellect" — and thereafter, the conditions of the body, mind, and intellect, in my stupidity, become my conditions. To end this ignorance is to gain the Wisdom of Reality. To rediscover our Self is to invite into our life the cognition of a greater intellect and a divine Consciousness.

The impact of the Lesson Course[3] — extracts from a letter to a student:

When you finish the course, you will get a glimpse of the possibilities that are lying dormant in yourself. No intelligent man can live satisfied with a lesser life than he is capable of. All qualifications for gaining the subjective experience of knowledge will be added to you by the time the twenty-four lessons are over. Thereafter, we shall pursue a serious study of the entire scriptures in a very organized manner. Continue your Lesson Courses.

---

3 Foundation Vedānta Course introduces the student to Vedānta:http://chinfo.org/chinfo_courses/foundation/. Advanced Vedānta Course gives a thorough understanding of the concepts of Vedānta through the Prakaraṇa Granthas — http://chinfo.org/chinfo_courses/advanced/ and the Bhagavad-gītā Course teaches the application of Vedāntic knowledge in daily life http://www.chinfo.org/courses/bhagavadgita/

Independent thinking and a questioning mind are most helpful in Vedānta sādhanā:

Swami Tejomayananda: What are the striking features of Gurudev's life? First was his spirit of independent thinking. As a child, whether he observed a pūjā, went to school/college for education, or participated in the national movement, he always had an inquiring mind. He would say: "Don't believe anything just because I am saying it," and add, "The longer the beard, the greater the suspicion!" He always underlined: "Think! Think! Only when it rings in your mind can you accept it." Second, he kept questioning — as a student and as a journalist. And in his Vedāntic quest, it was his questioning that took him such a long way. There are people who go on questioning and arguing, but his questioning was actually the path of inquiry to find the Truth.

When there is a thirst in the heart to know, the opportunity comes in the form of the environment or a Guru:

Anil Choudhary: When I started my CHYK journey, I got an opportunity to read books like: *I Love You, Self-Unfoldment, A Trek through Uttarakhand, and Kindle Life,* all by Pūjya Gurudev Swami Chinmayananda. All these books were very inspiring, but somehow, I felt the need to know and read even more about Hinduism and spirituality. After coming to Delhi for my post-graduate study, I came to know that there are books on the Upaniṣads and the *Bhagavad-gītā* on which Swami Chinmayananda had given commentaries. I used to wonder if it could even be possible for me to get the time to read these books while simultaneously performing my worldly duties. Then, in 1993, I got a call from the CEO of Central Chinmaya Mission Trust, requesting me to join CCMT in their Computer Department. My prayers had been heard and answered, and I was in the storehouse of Knowledge.

Ācārya Vilasini Balakrishnan: In 1978, I had returned to the States after finishing the Vedānta course. I wrote to Swamiji about my struggle with meditation in my new environment outside of the āśrama. He wrote a handwritten reply: "You are not able to meditate only because your mind and intellect have not become meditation-worthy. Through loving selfless work and through living life centered on devotion to the Lord, recognize everything as His plan for us. Through daily study and steady meditation, we can make the mind more fit for deeper and deeper meditation."

Anjali Singh: Most religions have one holy book to which they adhere. Swamiji would say that we have a library of them! However, Swamiji made it simple to choose one when he wrote the following in my *Vivekacūḍāmaṇi* book:

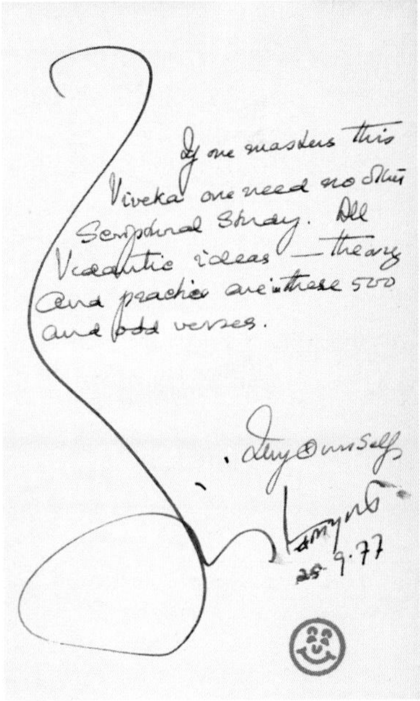

STEP 4

HOW TO LIVE IN CONTEMPLATION

*T*he roar of Truth is not heard in the scriptures, nor listened to in the Teacher's words; it is not in the song of the birds, nor in the thunder of the skies; it is to be heard within our own bosom in the utter silence of the quietened mind. This deafening silence is the roar of the Truth Divine.

-Swami Chinmayananda

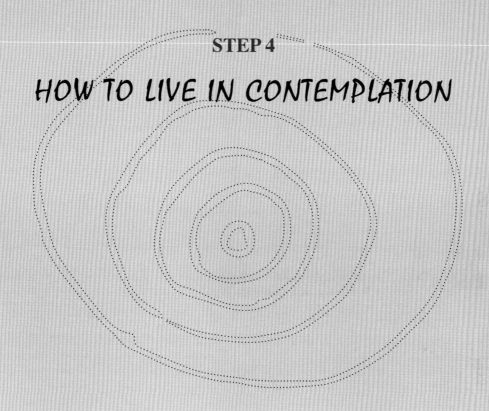

12

Deciding the Pace

On the third day of the French Open in 1993, devotees were gathered around Swamiji as he watched the match on television. There was a movement in his frail body, and the devotees thought that perhaps some strength had returned to him. He raised his head and said to one of them, "Which is your 'horse'?" She replied, "Bruguera! And yours?" "Courier!" said Swamiji. "The odds [of losing] are higher with a newcomer, whereas with an old hand like Courier, they are much lower."

This was Swamiji's warning for novice meditators. Swamiji always advised that a newcomer to spirituality, like Bruguera was to international professional tennis, should not jump into deep meditation immediately, expecting to reach the goal without setbacks on this inner journey. The process of meditation accelerates spiritual progress, but the seeker may find the resulting psychological changes perplexing, unless the mind has been prepared for them. This preparation is done through dedicated action, devotion, reflection on the teachings, and making an attempt to apply them in one's life. Therefore, the "odds are higher" against an inexperienced student to reach the state of samādhi, because the preparatory spiritual steps have not been taken — though it is not impossible!

Swamiji's last camp in India — a large youth camp held in Sidhbari at the end of May 1993 — left him physically weak with little energy. After the camp, doctors advised him to take complete rest. All his talks were canceled until June 9, when he had to go abroad. Swamiji was seventy-seven years old. He had seven to twenty missing heartbeats per minute and was living with only 22 percent heart function.

As instructed by doctors, he would watch the French Open while reclining in his chair, without speaking. On the third day of this regimen, when Swamiji asked about the 'horse,' it was thrilling to know that he had regained enough strength to resume his teaching of Vedānta through tennis.

TREASURES OF MEDITATION

Contemplation is popularly known as meditation. However, contemplation is an action, an attempt, or a process to bring the mind from disarrayed thoughts about the world and one's body to one stream of thoughts about Brahman. This leads to meditation, which is a state arrived at in which there is no activity of body, mind, or intellect. The 'doing' of meditation is the first part, and the 'arrival' of the mind at a state of absorption, called samādhi, is the achievement. Just as mind and body consciousness dominates if we are always thinking, "I am the body and mind," similarly, for God-consciousness to prevail, we have to substitute the usual thoughts with the thought "I am Brahman." This, in turn, puts an end to the contrary notions of "I am the body and mind," deep within at the causal level of our psyche. When, by the constant practice of the thought "I am Brahman," the mind becomes subtle, it soon ceases to be at samādhi, and Brahman alone remains. This abidance as the supreme Brahman is true meditation. All else are the means for this meditation and are termed 'contemplation.'

Swami Chinmayananda:

True meditation can fashion out of any ordinary person an incomparable genius.

The science of Vedānta advises the treatment of meditation to make a genius out of an ordinary man. Meditation becomes a true education, a secret preparation to face the world of unsteady circumstances and evanescent glories, and achieve the impossible. The stories of the great sages of the world all tell us that they grew to their brilliant statures through their practice of meditation. Ultimately, they became immortal people of wisdom. Meditation is the final gateway that leads to the discovery of the Supreme within.

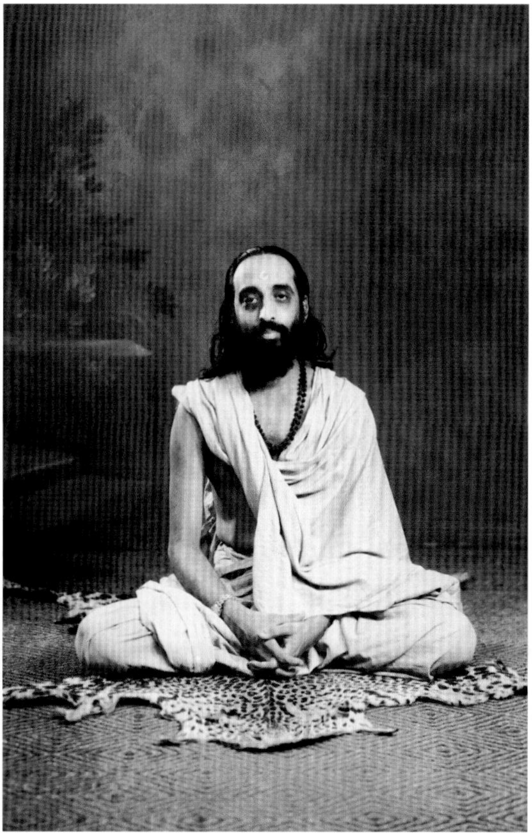

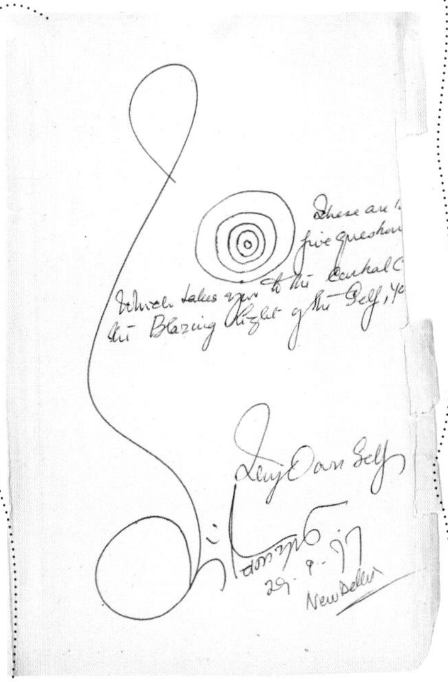

These are five questions that take you to the central core of the blazing light, You!

Contact with a Guru and the constant study of the scriptures are factors that can guarantee success. The Guru, for the purposes of meditation, is the one who has guided you to detect and experience your divinity. He need not be a priest or a monk; he can be a friend, a leader in society, or an insignificant person in your neighborhood. He who has, through his life and work, unveiled a greater vision, provided you with a thirst to aspire or kindled in you a greater hunger to live and face your problems courageously — he is your Guru. The teacher may be a book, it may be a passing statement, and it may be an experience in life itself. The teacher is the one whose remembrance helps you to be a critic of yourself. He is a guide who, at all moments of moral and ethical compromises, rises up somewhere in your memory to warn you not to fall prey to temptations, and lends you the courage to come away from the fascination of the moment and walk heroically the rugged path of righteousness.

One who is striving to learn the art of meditation must slowly and carefully develop in himself an attitude of holding himself neutral in all receptions of stimuli and in his responses to them. A man of reflection does not identify with these. They may go on at the physical level because of the prārabdha of the body, but he is not involved in them. He is otherwise busy.

The student in the seat of contemplation is trying to reverse the direction of his mind's attention in search of that mysterious mighty power called Life, which enlivens the mind and the body. This spring of Consciousness, which is the One Life everywhere, manifesting Itself through our minds and bodies, is the goal of the entire attention of the contemplative student. Just as behind the Iron Curtain was Russia, behind the Bamboo Curtain was China, behind the Sugar Curtain was Cuba, so, too, behind the Thought Curtain is the pure State of Consciousness.

In our daily contact with the world of plurality, things happen in such a hurry and quick succession that the mind is not able to digest many of our encounters properly. Undigested thoughts, ideas, expressions, and experiences sink into the mind and load the subconscious mind. They don't get a chance to come out and dance because the conscious mind is so vigorously engaged in gathering new experiences. When you sleep, the conscious mind is quiet. It is at such times that nature brings out much of the subconscious mind in the form of dreams. By this, the subconscious becomes relatively empty, and, consequently, the conscious mind becomes efficient to deal with matters the following day.

The following quotes include invaluable advice on posture, mental attitude, and intellectual focus, along with thought exercises to harness the mind for entering a contemplative state. The pieces of advice below have been arranged in the order of advancement; hence, the advice to a novice may differ from that to a seasoned meditator:

Basics common to all:

A bent or strained vertebral column interferes with the functioning of the nervous system and helps to disintegrate feelings and thoughts. If the body is kept erect, with the vertebral column perpendicular to the base, it will be in equilibrium, with its center of gravity contained in the base.

Experienced Masters advise that the meditator next relax the body in the erect position. We are always straining and stiffening thousands of muscles, keeping ourselves stiff. It is rare that we achieve complete relaxation. Relaxation of the muscles revitalizes the cells. Wondrous cures for even incurable diseases can be achieved if we know the knack of consciously relaxing the particular limb or organ that needs rejuvenation. Relaxation before meditation is effected through a process called thought massage, by which the meditator, with closed eyes, sends his thoughts consciously down his body, mentally relaxing and massaging every muscle in every limb.

How to Begin:

Let the mind run, and whatever the thoughts, don't try to classify or label them as good or bad or worry about them; just ignore them. Consider that they are a military march passing by, and you, the officer, are taking the salute; or that you are sitting near a river and the waters are flowing by. Don't jump into the river — just watch. When you watch the play of the mind with indifference, and you yourself are not involved, you are no more — as though pedaling the mind like a bicycle. The bicycle itself has no movement; you are the one that gives the movement to it. When you stop pedaling, it loses its momentum until the cycle falls away from you.

Remember one thing: that when the mind is running riotously, you should not run with it; you stay put. You hold onto the feet of the Lord, for that is when we need Him. It takes time to learn the art of staying detached when the mind produces its thoughts. At that time, for your steadiness, you must have something to hold onto. And that may be your personal God, or deity, or the feet of the Guru. This creative altar provided for the mind to hold onto, is called the point of contemplation. Worship is a means of purifying the instruments of the mind and intellect for the higher purpose of deep and intense meditation.

Preparation — Japa and Mantras:

One evening, you were sitting under a tree on a mount. Down below, in the spreading valley, stood a temple. As the dusk deepened and the darkness started covering the edifice, suddenly the priest switched on the lights, and the House of God stood shining in its own light. Soon you started hearing songful chants accompanied by striking cymbals — the ārati was being performed at the sanctum. You could not see what they were doing, but you could hear their chanting wafting to reach you. You were not in the temple. You were under the tree seeing the temple and hearing the chanting. Since you were seeing, you were the seer; since you were hearing, you were the hearer. The seer and the hearer are something other than what is seen and what is heard. Similarly, in your contemplation seat, you are seeing your body resting without any movement, like the temple. You are hearing your mind chanting the mantra. You are the seer of the body and the hearer of the chanting of the mind. Your relationship with the body and the mind is exactly like your relationship with the distant temple and the chanting when you were sitting under the tree. You were then something other than the temple, and you were certainly something other than the chanting and the chanters. Stand apart and be alert, supervising that the body is not moving and the mind is steadily and continuously chanting. Slowly realize then that you have a positive existence apart from the body and the mind. You are the subject, and the body and mind are the objects of your awareness. The mind and its entire thought-play are all only objects of your awareness.

Just as we give children a set of very attractive, colorful toys, we give our mind a command to chant a specific mantra of our choice. The mantra brings to the mind a form, a color, a smell, a taste, and a touch. This mantra is given to the mind to play with. Each student chooses a mantra that is very dear to him: it can be the holy name of Śiva, Viṣṇu, Jesus, Allah, or Buddha. The concept of God is needed for a seeker to tune up his mind and intellect and to point them at a single, elevating, inspiring, and meaningful altar. The intellect appreciates Reality as represented in the altar of God, and the mind flows toward Him in supreme love.

Japa, if properly done, can bring about a sustained single-pointedness more efficiently than all the hasty methods of meditation. Mantras are exercises in meditation. With each mantra, lift your mind to the suggestion and blast it in silence where it merges with the Bliss–Self. As I recite a mantra — "I am Śiva" — the meaning of its shine in my consciousness is called meditation.

Every mantra has a presiding deity. The belief is that when one chants a mantra, he or she should keep in mind the form of that deity. Then, just as someone who responds upon being called by his name, the deity of the mantra is invoked by the chanting. It is also the belief that only after chanting a mantra for a hundred thousand times can we hope to see any benign influence of the japa practice.

Of all the mantras, the most powerful and significant one is the single syllable incantation called 'Om.' Without Om, no sacred chant has power. Om is the symbol of the Infinite. Om represents the Self, which is the supreme, nondual Reality. The Self is known in four states, namely, the waking state, the dream state, the deep-sleep state, and the 'fourth' state called the Turīya. All these states are represented in the three sounds of aum (A U M) and the silence that follows and surrounds the syllable. The sound A represents the waking state; the sound U represents the dream state; and the sound M represents the deep-sleep state. Memory is impossible unless the 'rememberer' and the experiencer are one and the same individual. In all three planes, there must necessarily be a single common factor that is the witness of all the happenings in the three planes. There must be some entity within us who is present in the waking world, who illumines the dream, and who is a distant observer in the deep-sleep world — but who is not conditioned by any of these three realms. This entity, conceived as the fourth state (Turīya), is the Real, the Changeless, the intelligent Principle.

Instead of now concentrating your entire attention in making the mind chant Om and listening to the sound of Om, as though rising from the heart or the mind or even from a point farther down, your next attempt will be in a different direction altogether. Continue chanting Om as sincerely as ever before, but you will no longer strive to note the source of its rising. Now you will watch the Om-vibration rising from the depth of yourself, growing and merging to an ever-increasing peace and joy. Let this atmosphere of Om-vibrations grow and expand into the uncharted extensions of the Absolute. Get yourself reduced to nothingness in the ever-growing atmosphere of the Om-substance. Contemplation is neither necessary nor valid once the individual has merged into the pure Self and directly lives the State Divine.

The Om symbol is not only an idol representing the absolute Reality, but it also represents the relative reality. The worshiper or the meditator can meditate upon it as the Supreme or as the relative. And through deep and long meditation when the meditator comes to discover a personal identity with the very thing the symbol stands for, he gains the realm of his identification. "As you think so you become" is the eternal principle of all religions. If a meditator has become one with the meditated, and if, to him, the symbol is a representation of the Total Mind, he gains the state of existence available in the world of the Creator. If, on the other hand, the symbol represents the supreme Reality, he comes to gain, in stages, a greater inner purification, a deeper power of concentration, and, through long ponderings upon the nature of the Self, he gains in the end an identity that 'ayam aham asmi,' meaning, 'This I am.' Unless he establishes his contact with God, no divinity can flow into the seeker. Can you pluck a jasmine from J.A.S.M.I.N.E? Words can never reach the Reality. You have pronounced the name 'Om'; now go and seek the 'thing' so named!

Leave the idols alone. Turn inward — reach the silence. Burst into it and scale the heights to arrive at the depths of That which is all these. Taste it and be silent in the within. When full, there shall be no blabbering — no words…

Meet me *There.*

Practice — the Great Silence:

The entire steadiness that you need is only for about two minutes, and you are the master! Experimental psychologists have proved that no dream can stay more than one-and-a-half to two minutes. It is in those minutes that you watch years of drama. Similarly, for those two minutes when you can stay in meditation consciously, the mind will bring up all suppressions, loves, fear, attachment, affection, vanities, and all the psychological ulcers that you have created in yourself. All these will come up, but you stand apart: "They all belong to the not-Self; whereas, I am searching the Self. I have nothing to do with the past, I am not anxious about the future; even the present I have surrendered unto you O Lord!"

Expose the vāsanās to the inner silence of contemplation. You don't have to live them out. Mountains of vāsanās can be ended this way. When a seeker or student sits down for meditation, the mind generally plays or acts riotously. Early students feel despair at this mad frenzy of activity of the mind and they stand aghast. They consider it is impossible to control such a mind and persuade it into the moods of meditation — this is natural. You should congratulate yourself that your mind is bringing out all these immoral, moral, good, or bad thoughts. Here we are conscientiously making our conscious minds quiet and allowing the subconscious mind to float up. After this purging, we experience a greater lightness of heart. Eighty percent of the meditators stop meditating because they are worked up about the quality of their thoughts; but understand that it is all the vomit of the mind. The texture of your thoughts depends on the thoughts that you have entertained in the previous twenty-four hours. With meditation, you are giving yourself a free psychiatric treatment.

The mind is inert. The Consciousness of the Self is the power from which the mind draws its strength to act and function. Withdraw your grace from the mind. The mind is the devil that has invoked you and received your own blessings, and it is now threatening to annihilate you! Learn to destroy him quickly. A seeker must intelligently assume a get-tough stance with the mind. When a meditator stands thus as an alert witness, watching the self-exhausting excesses of his own mind, he will notice how the tempo of his mind's drunken revelry slowly quietens down. As you thus proceed, even as little as in six months' time, your entire mind will start to feel transformed and will become hungry to reach the goal. Inexplicably, God becomes your main concern; the world's charms retreat and get misted away from your perceptual concern.

The mind is powerful. Its power is generated by the flow of thoughts. Anything moving in rapid succession gathers power and strength like the flow of water that creates hydroelectric power. The rapidity with which the thoughts move, like the film moving in a projector, creates the concrete world of plurality. The world, which has been created by the thought-flow, has as much reality as the pictures on the screen or the patterns of a glowing point. If the thoughts are expelled from the mind and ultimately crushed out of existence, the pluralistic phenomena vanish to reveal the presence of pure Consciousness.

Observe the mind stuff without the objects that it shapes itself into. Then see the content of the mind stuff. Consciousness then sees the reflected consciousness. It is like seeing yourself in the mirror. Even though it is an object, its perception is of the subject.

Seek the unborn Mind, the Mind before it was born. Trace everything back to its source. The entire world is a projection of the mind. Trace it back to its source — the unborn Mind. It comes out from It, it folds back into It, just as a dream folds back into the waker. Seek the Mind that is above the mind, below the mind, behind the mind, the Father of the mind and the Mother of the mind. Reject everything else. You have to leave everything, because everything else is the mind's interpretation; whatever comes in front of you is the mind's projection. In seeking the Father of the mind, you can say, "I am the son of the Father." The

Father and the son are one; the dreamer and the waker are one. The dreamer has to disappear to become the waker. What you are seeking is inside your mind, in the core of your mind. When you have finished your seeking, sit down in your seat of contemplation and search for that center in you whose circumference is nowhere and whose center is everywhere. You know it is with you; it is you, the unborn Mind. Leave off everything else, all other forms of contemplation. At that time, don't even ask, "Who am I?" or say, "The mind was never born," or "Consciousness is unborn." Seek the unborn Mind, which is beyond even consciousness, because consciousness has a bit of the mind in it. If you can keep yourself in that for six months, you will enter samādhi! Other than the unborn Mind, you can equally follow any other good pointers out of thousands of gems that are strung along our scriptural literature. All of them have equal validity. None of the scriptural pointers is the Truth, but all of them are guiding pointers to that peaceful State.

Don't lose heart:

Again, even after full preparedness, some may find themselves stagnated for long periods. Such stagnation is essentially a sign that the meditator is getting entangled with his own subtle attachments, with the outer world of objects, and with his own inner world of emotions and thoughts. When the mind is loaded with its own inhibitions, it cannot enter into the subtle layers of the higher Consciousness. Success in spiritual unfoldment comes only when we are regular. By exercising once a week, you cannot improve your body. If you eat once a week, it is not nourishment enough. It must be regularly done, every day, at a specific time. Never give it up even for a day, whether you are traveling or are sick. When concentration is developed, all sādhanā is almost at an end. You must continue your practice until you achieve the realization of the flameless Light of Consciousness.

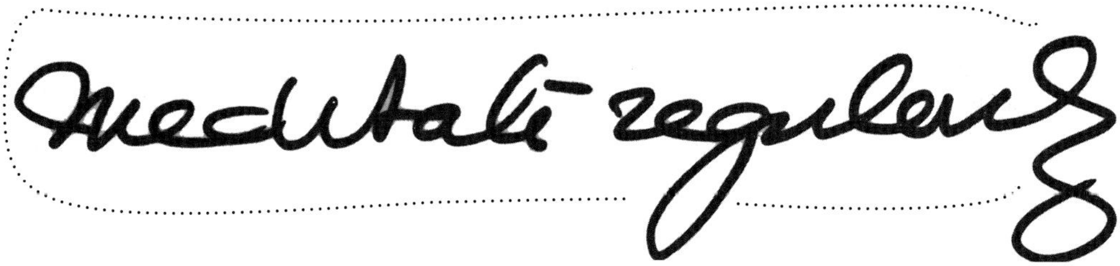

When you reach the thoughtless state, hold on to it as long as you comfortably can. In that silence, there is no flow of thoughts; when thoughts do not exist, there can be no discrimination; and when discrimination is absent, the intellect has no existence, since the intellect itself is a faculty of discrimination. When both the equipment of mind and intellect are transcended, the individual merges into the infinite Reality.

Letter to ***Dr. Kambham Suhasini*** *when she asked:* "Although I feel guilty that I have enough help at home, I am not meditating regularly..." Swamiji answered: "You have everything a girl can ask for and if you miss study and meditation even for a day, it will be surely inexcusable."

How the mind gets easily distracted:

Prarthna Saran: Inspired by Gurudev's pre-dawn meditation classes in Sidhbari, we scrambled quickly to Satsang Hall, some keener than others to move ahead quickly. One such enthusiast was my husband Naresh. One afternoon, as he was 'meditating,' the tea bell rang invitingly. I tiptoed into the room and quietly picked up my glass and spoon so as not to disturb the 'meditator.' Then I heard his voice saying, "Get a glass for me, too." This was narrated to Gurudev in the evening. Oh! His laughter was such a delight to watch. He used this example in his talks later to show how easily the mind slips into habitual channels of distraction to reach out to sense objects.

Not necessary to make contemplation so complicated:

Anjali Singh: In Khatmandu, in 1990, I asked Swamiji, "When I concentrate my mind on the Self, it becomes an object of my concentration. Then I quickly shift my attention from the object (the Self) and shift it to me, the subject (the Self), but it again becomes an object. So a part of the mind is the object, and a part of the mind is the instrument, the thinker…" Swamiji interrupted me and supplied the correct word, "Intellect!" I agreed: "Yes, the intellect. But 'I,' the Consciousness that looks at both of these, keeps getting pushed back from subject to object like rotating in a cycle wheel, leading to 'regress ad infinitum' and not to the Self!" Swamiji grimaced at the use of academic words. Then he looked into my eyes, and since I was sincere, his tone changed and he said very gently, "You are right. It will lead to that, because it can never become an object. But there is no other way to do it. Still, one should go on attempting this, and in this attempt, one wakes up suddenly! That which is sparkling in you as your life is the Substratum of the whole universe."

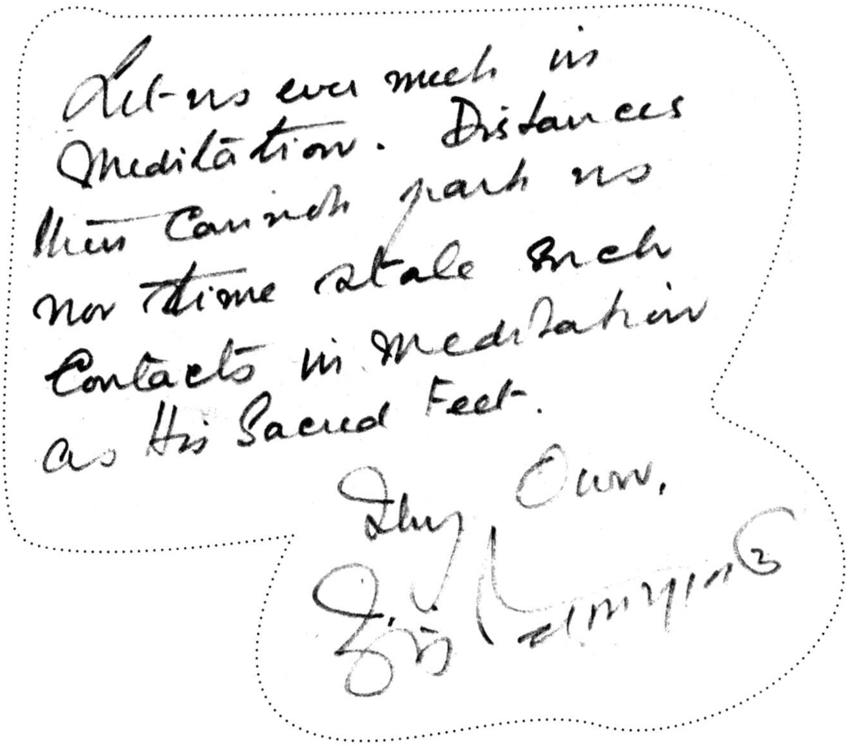
Let us ever meet in Meditation. Distances then cannot part us nor time stale such contacts in meditation as His Sacred Feet.
Thy Own,

13

The Hidden Power in People

Swamiji was watching a match between Stefan Edberg and John McEnroe. During a tiebreak, a question came up: "Whom are you backing?" "Edberg," replied Swamiji. "No doubt, his (McEnroe's) strokes are beautiful, but he does not have the energy — and at night?" When McEnroe caught up from 1–4 to 5–6, the odds seemed to have changed. A devotee exclaimed, "He could win!" Swamiji replied, "Yes, it is almost equal. It could even become 7–5. Nobody can tell who will win. Not even He. Even the coach can't tell when it will happen. It can happen in a moment."

When Swamiji refers to 'energy,' he does not mean the energy of the muscles, but an energy that gives us the patience, determination, dynamic concentration, and the staying power to achieve our goal — whatever the goal. This subtle kind of energy is created by the joint partnership of the mind and the intellect. When the emotional aspect is in agreement with the thinking aspect and the clash between them has gone, the dissipation ends and a new kind of energy is created.

The reference to 'night' made by Swamiji means that when the body or mind is tired or sluggish, the mind is less alert. At such a time, any attempt toward excellence will be compromised.

The best shot at higher achievements — whether spiritual or secular — is to work with a quiet, alert mind. Such a mind is more inspired and more creative than an agitated or sluggish mind. Great works of art, scientific discoveries, and so on, can also issue from such a mind. And if one directs the power of such a mind toward Self-realization — that goal can also be reached.

HOW TO INCREASE YOUR ENERGY

When the vāsanā pressure is reduced, the mind gets a momentum of its own. A dynamism gets generated within, without any help from the world of pills. If we understand how energy gets wasted and how it gets generated and apply this understanding in our life, we would be taking a major step forward in our spiritual and secular life. This energy must be used for creative purposes; otherwise, it could either get spent in indulgences or be wasted on other unproductive activities such as worrying!

Swami Chinmayananda:

Man wastes his whole life's energies in the acquisition of things not yet with him, and in the preservation of what has been acquired already. Mental energy is wasted also through regrets of the past, anxieties for the future, and excitements of the present. Anxiety leaks away energy; inspiration conserves it. From morning to evening, we search for happiness through wealth, position, name, woman, property, house, furniture, and more. The secret vein of energy that runs in every one of us is struck, not through pills and elixirs but through dedicated actions. Selfish actions drain our energy. Actions dedicated unto the feet of the Lord, or unto any higher cause, generate energy and stir up enthusiasm in man.

Operate from strength. This inner strength comes from —
Sincere study,
Regular Abhyas,
Firm Conviction,
Missionary Zeal,
&
Deep Devotion to what you undertake to achieve.

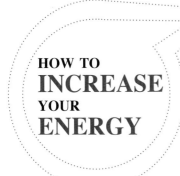

Two forces from within distract men from pursuing their ideal: unawareness and concern for worldly things. It is generally observed that when a man is fired with enthusiasm to dedicate himself to an ideal, the less intelligent and unenthusiastic people around him try to dissuade him. If he yields to this pressure, his enthusiasm will ebb away; consequently, his efforts will weaken miserably. While at work, if he allows his mind to slip into unawareness and inadvertence, his efficiency suffers.

Disparity between thought and words creates in the mind a habit to entertain self-cancelation of thoughts. This impoverishes the individual's mental strength, willpower, and determinative dynamism. Such an exhausted mental character is too weak thereafter to make any progress in life's pilgrimage. Without truthfulness, we develop a split personality. Where there are two personalities, the mind diverges itself in distraction, and any existing integration is lost. Then the mental saṅkalpa-śakti (power of willing) is lost. A spiritual seeker without will power will be a hapless victim of his own mental passions and intellectual confusions.

Sense-gratifications bring but more and more fatigue at all levels in the sensuous man and never a deep consoling satisfaction. Dissatisfied, the individual's intellect plans yet another desire, and the body sweats and toils again to seek and fulfill it — only to discover the same disconcerting sense of emptiness filling his heart and a painful weight of dissatisfaction crushing him in the end! Sooner or later, if intelligent, one realizes that all the wealth acquired, all objects of pleasures procured, all relationships maintained, name and fame gained, work done, and achievements accomplished — none of them have any relevance to the inner, actual peace and joy lived. The entire life then seems an empty struggle, a futile exertion, and a meaningless mission. A fatigued mind cannot reach and maintain high altitudes of meditation; and without the mystic vitality, poise in meditation will be totally absent.

Every disturbance and lack of concentration takes energy from consciousness to run away. Nothing can move without expenditure of energy. Thoughts fly: this flow of thoughts is the mind. With every thought that sparks out from us, a wee bit of our mental energy is spent. When thousands of thoughts stream forth from an individual's bosom every moment, such an agitated, disturbed man's mind soon becomes exhausted and fatigued. How can such a weak, and so sick a mind function efficiently in life? Only when you are acting with ego can you get upset emotionally, exhausted physically, and confused intellectually!

Overeating saps vitality, ruins health, and, in the end, kills. Food is also called a great universal medicine. In right doses, it blesses; in excessive doses, it kills. When indulgence is reduced, the mental energy, which would have otherwise been spent in indulgence, is conserved.

Meditation, by its own mysterious logic, generates in us a powerful energy, which can be used for reinforcing moral and ethical living. The mind has tremendous dynamism. Its energies are stupendous. Ordinarily, its energies are spent completely by its profitless wanderings. When all possible wanderings are blocked, the energies of the mind, which would have otherwise been spent, are conserved. The conserved energy multiplies itself, and thus an irresistible column of mental force is damned up within. The human will, however strong it may be, cannot hold this energy beyond a certain level. The very creative force of the mind shatters the will and runs out madly into the sensuous world. Such an outburst of mental vitality brings about the fall of a man of self-control.

The river waters held in a dam must find a useful outlet or else it will overflow the dam, or even pull down the dam. But if the waters of the dam are guided in the right channels, they can irrigate miles of fields around. Similarly, mental energies cannot be held idle, because the source of vitality is a perennial living one. The technique of meditation would have been incomplete if it had explained only the self-control aspect of it without intelligently directing the conserved energies to an altar. Continuous and regular practice done for a long time can add up in imperceptible accumulation to become a great magazine of power, which can, all of a sudden, rocket the mind of a seeker to surprising heights of brilliant meditation. This is the Lord's grace in full manifestation.

The more one gets integrated in the mind, the more dynamic becomes one's intellect. The purified mind-intellect equipment gains a greater efficiency and a greater power of flight. Vision increases the power of speech, and the inspired speech makes vision more penetrating. The greater the heights from which we look around, the wider is the prospect that unrolls under our gaze. With the mind thus cleansed of passions, one must meditate upon the Reality. If the mind is withdrawn from its present preoccupations, it becomes empty — and nature abhors a vacuum. When the mind is withdrawn from the objects of its entertainment, it gathers in itself an infinite momentum, a new vein of dynamic energy to apply in self-created fields of self-perfection. And if it cannot discover these, it is sure to dissipate itself again into a different set of objects.

To manage your life, the higher values and ethical virtues are necessary so that your reaction to the outside world does not dissipate your energy. Through spiritual living, the negative vāsanās of lust and ego are replaced by love and selflessness. Such a mind, surcharged with its own attentiveness, with all of its energies well conserved without dissipating in the world of OET (objects–emotions–thoughts), is the pure inner equipment ready to spring forth on the path of contemplation.

Through study and reflection our understanding becomes clearer; and in contemplation, when we start reaching subtler states of growing joys, we gather a new strength in our determination to pursue the path. If a seeker has not discovered this strength, he will not have the stamina to stay steady in his moments of higher contemplation.

Spiritual energy welling up to nurture and nourish the fatigued morale in a well-integrated personality is called fortitude.

Letter to ***Swami Tejomayananda:*** Whenever you feel tired or soiled with fatigue, run to Sandeepany and rest there; revive at the feet of Jagadīśvara, and go back to serve.

A vision in life generates the energy and enthusiasm to work. Devotees recount:

Manisha Khemlani: I reflected on what was it that inspired me. The answer was simple — it was Pūjya Gurudev, his Vision, and his Mission. Vedānta itself was one of the greatest sources of inspiration. I finally found that my hobby and pastime had become my fulltime passion and love. In such a situation, exhaustion, fatigue, and so on, do not count. One never feels like one is doing a job. It is twenty-four hours of pure joy and bliss. No longer did I have to think about how to spend my four weeks of leave [vacation] from work. Now work and 'leave' were all one! Amazingly delightful!

Mimi Robins: During the later years, with serious heart ailments, Gurudev was brought in a wheelchair to the door of the auditorium, where he stood tall, walked to the platform, seated himself, and commenced his talk. A couple of times during the camp, an Indian doctor approached me with awe and concern: "If Gurudev was my patient, he would be in intensive care." It seemed that Gurudev's will and spirit were the master, animating his body to fulfill his mission of imparting Truth, beauty, and wisdom. After the talks, Gurudev would return to his cabin, recline in a large, lazy-boy chair, and watch the Wimbledon tournament tennis matches on tape. Now and again, he would comment, "Good shot!" as he enjoyed the game.

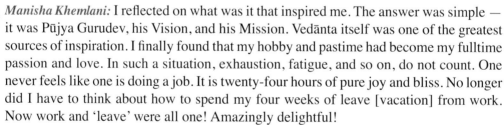

Ācārya Vilasini Balakrishnan: Swamiji was prescribed several medications for his heart disease and diabetes, and these had to be given a few times a day. He was least bothered about taking them, and we soon realized that someone would have to give him his pills and insulin injections or he would not take them. After evening dinner, he held out his hand to take the pills, and I would give them to him as he swallowed them one by one. One evening, a young boy from the bhikṣā host's family was looking wide-eyed at him. Swamiji said, "See these pills? They are keeping me alive!" To a doctor, he commented, "See, doctor, my life depends on these tiny pills!" He was quite humored by the thought that such tiny pills were supposedly giving the gift of life.

When energy gets generated, we must not get excited but be alert for the blessings of God:

Anjali Singh: In Sidhbari in 1992, before going to my room, when I went to prostrate to Swamiji while he was watching tennis, he said, "It was a good session." I informed him that the Lord Kṛṣṇa videos had arrived. He said, "When you have been good, Kṛṣṇa will come, and don't get worked up when He is coming. It is Kṛṣṇa who is coming. Hush up your mind and listen. Don't tell me that there is nothing to hear. Be alert!"

HOW TO THINK CREATIVELY

Whenever one has an important piece of work at hand — give a speech, be interviewed, write or paint — or one is in the midst of a scientific discovery or facing a demanding situation, the most valuable advice given by Vedānta is to still the mind for a while. This freeing up of the mind can effectively be done in a session of deep meditation, when we try to be in contact with our innermost Self. The inspiration that wells up from within helps us to do the work in a more inspired way.

Swami Chinmayananda:

The science of Vedānta advises the treatment of meditation to make a genius out of an ordinary man. When the mind is quiet, greater are the flights of intellectual apprehension. Great ideas are conceived only by the alert mind held steady in meditative poise of unbroken concentration and dynamic vigilance.

Out of purity and silence come words of power.

A genius at work is he who has established a perfect identity of his own mind and intellect with the work at hand. The best can come out of an orator or a painter or a sculptor or a musician or a writer only when he forgets himself and gets lost in the work at hand. A painter will beg at your feet to enjoy his creation, a musician will make you miss your train, a writer will make you read volumes of manuscript, and an Archimedes will forget his own nakedness and run along the roads of the city crying "Eureka!" These are instances when man rises for a fraction of a moment from his low identifications and gets a glimpse of the minutest ray from the knowledge of the Absolute. Creative art is at its best when the limited ego makes an exit in its entirety.

Artists get veiled glimpses of beauty like through a muslin cloth. The intensity of mental disturbance will determine the clarity of the Vision Divine. When an individual has discovered new energy within, has learned the art of stopping the dissipation, has learned the art of fixing the entire energy to the piece of work at hand, a great joy called 'the joy of the artisan' starts welling up in the mind.

Sāttvika is the creative pause of the mind before it launches out into a burst of creative thoughts and actions. It is full of inspiration and meditative poise. The three guṇas — sattva, rajas, and tamas — are the three attitudes with which the mind functions. Sattva is perfect purity and luminosity. Under sāttvic influence, the mind is steady, reflecting ever faithfully the Consciousness, the Self. Under the influence of sattva, the mind is in an inspired and creative mood; it is actually intelligent and capable of taking the longest flights into the realms of wisdom. On all such occasions of vast knowing and deep understanding and right choice, the inner equipment is under the influence of sattva.

It is very well known that in all activities, inspired work gathers to itself a texture of divine perfection, which cannot be imitated or oft repeated. Whenever an individual is at his best, his masterpiece is always accepted by all as a work of inspiration. Thus, da Vinci could not repeat for a second time and copy on another piece of canvas the enigmatic smile of his Mona Lisa. Keats's pen could no more recapture for a second time the song of the nightingale in its flight. Beethoven could never again beat out of his faithful piano a second "Moonlight Sonata." Lord Kṛṣṇa Himself, when requested by Arjuna after the war to repeat the *Gītā,* admitted His inability to do so!!

Inspiration is not an accidental and mysterious happening over which the mortal has no control at all. A balanced life — wherein we live as unaffected witnesses of even our own mind and intellect — is the realm of self-forgetfulness, where instead of becoming inefficient, our profession gathers the scintillating glow of a new dawn. This extra aura in any achievement is that which raises an ordinary success to an inspired achievement. A perfect man has learned the art of living in utter inspiration all the time, since inspiration comes in moments of self-forgetfulness.

Let us try to see the world, as it was some millions of years ago. At the time of its early transformation, we know life on this planet was dominated by two great factors. On the one hand, there was a vast turbulence — volcanoes, huge and terrifying, vomiting their lava from inexhaustible fires in the earth's core. On the other hand, there was the miniscule evidence of protoplasm — microscopic, invisible to the naked eye, fragile, quiet, yet vital — lying along the water's edge. Where would you have placed your faith — in the turbulent volcanoes or in the quiet, microscopic dots of throbbing protoplasm? We know now what emerged from this fragile matter: life, spirit, artists, scientists, saints, and prophets.

Swamiji outlined four ages of Perception, Observation, Inquiry, and Contemplation:

Age of Perception: In the scheme of evolution from animal to man, various levels of subtle growth were experienced. In the beginning, the human being was in a state of mere perception. He perceived things around him and reacted instinctively, because his intellect had not yet evolved. In this Age of Perception, humankind, in its childhood stage, felt happy when perceptions were harmonious with the mental moods. In fear and confusion, the man of this age escaped to safety, prompted by his inherent instinct for self-preservation.

Age of Observation: Later, man's intellectual capacities developed, and his perceptions began to be supported by his intellect. Intelligent perception is called observation. He started questioning his perceptions: Why? How? When? Where? But since man's intellect was still crude, his analysis could not go very far, and all that he gathered was only superstition, not knowledge.

Age of Inquiry: In time, the intellect became more assertive and gained a sharpness that was not even suspected in the earlier stages of evolution. Thus, superstitions were thrown over, and man sauntered into the Age of Inquiry and Investigation; he initiated the Era of Science. Man's vision of the world changed as he moved from the Age of Perception through the Age of Observation into the Age of Inquiry. Today, we stand on the summit of science. We laugh at the crude past with its confusions and wrong notions. Historically it is true that the man-of-observation was not appreciated by the man-of-perception. The evolved one was condemned and laughed at. History also tells us how the first systematic observers of the world who initiated the Age of Science were persecuted by the powerful men of the Age of Superstition. Today, in the Scientific Age, the prophetic seers and philosophers, the evolved men of a future age, stand condemned by the men-of-inquiry and investigation. Thus, if today the great scientists of the world fail to realize the glory of true religion, it is not altogether inexplicable. They conquer outer space, they may occupy Mars or the moon, but they will not understand the vision of religious masters and philosophers, because these men of inner knowledge and spirituality have a more evolved intellect than the scientists.

Age of Contemplation: The fourth stage of development of the human intellect is the Age of Contemplation. Just as every child has a dormant sex impulse waiting to manifest itself when biological growth is complete, so, too, the power of contemplation is waiting to become manifest. All scriptures are words of wisdom given by people of contemplation to students who have cultivated this subtle evolutionary perfection. Meditation is the process by which the seeker develops his dormant faculty of contemplation. Once you come to the seat of meditation, you will realize that they are actually self-evolving processes that are at once scientific and spiritually effective. As you read, you are a person-of-inquiry; when you sit down for meditation, you become a person-of-contemplation. And is not our world silently moving from the Age of Inquiry and Science into the Age of Contemplation and Meditation? Your father and grandmothers may not have even heard of these terms, while, in your times, contemplation and meditation have become popular, and many like you have started contemplative practice.

Letter to ***Padma Jaisinghani:*** There are endless potentialities in each one of us. We doubt, we hesitate, we fear — all due to ego. Surrender the ego — invoke Him — let Him express Himself.

Letter to ***Hemalata Rajan:*** Various institutions may be striving, apparently speaking differently, [giving] different emphasis on different aspects of the entire theme. Try to see the uniformity and universality in them all. This is creative thinking. Detachment is the secret of living life with inspiration, at all times and in all circumstances.

Letter to ***Sheila Sharma:*** Meditation sharpens all faculties. Your writings, also, you will find inspiring in polish and depth as you meditate more and more.

The "Aha" moment, a moment of sudden inspiration:

Swami Tejomayananda: Gurudev was inspired watching the flow of Mother Ganga as he sat on a rock at its bank. It was as though Mother Ganga were speaking to him:

"How I flow from here down to the plains — nourishing and nurturing all; in the same way, this jñāna-gaṅgā also must flow." He received blessings from both Swami Tapovanji and Swami Sivanandaji and embarked on his journey to spread this knowledge.

Rudite J. Emir: Gurudev often portrayed for us, in words, a moment of scintillating creativity, an "Aha!" moment, a moment of sudden inspiration and insight. He said that creative people experience such moments — when the mind has forgotten the past and the future and the bearer of the mind has forgotten himself or herself and has become a conduit for an energy beyond the personal self: "In that moment of creativity — that creative pause — great works of art are born," he said.

Anjali Singh: In the presence of Swamiji, sometimes the mind would automatically surrender to the Divine. It is in such a frame of mind that all creativity is generated. This moment is what the Guru can give as prasāda. What took us months of sādhanā, he would accomplish in a moment.

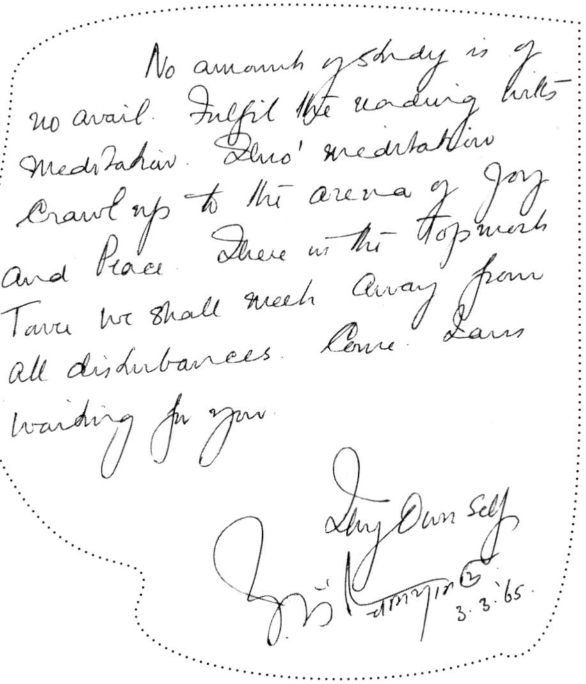

No amount of study is of no avail. Fulfil the reading with meditation. Thro' meditation crawl up to the arena of Joy and Peace. There in the topmost Tara we shall meet away from all disturbances. Come. I am waiting for you.

Thy Own Self

3.3.65

14

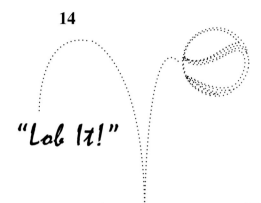

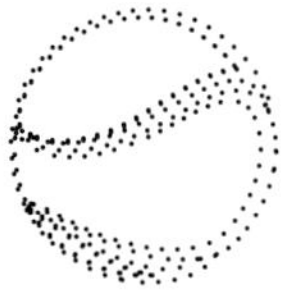

"Lob It!"

When Swamiji thought that the player needed to go to a higher level of play, he advised him, "Lob it!" It was not clear what he meant. So, a devotee asked, "What exactly does 'lob it' mean in terms of tennis?" He answered, "Lobbing is when you hit a ball high in the air, but it falls near the net. The opponent gets the impression that it is going to fall further back, but it falls near the net. The ball must not be too slow in coming down, otherwise the opponent will move to it. The other person is taken off guard and left behind, while the ball comes back near to you. 'Lob it' is to hit the ball high into outer space, but it does not go out; it comes and lands within the lines of the court, into your own Self!"

Swamiji had once said, "Your mind has always been debilitated, thinking, 'I and my family, my desires; if my family is not happy, I am unhappy' — this is how you have lived for so long, millions of years in your evolution. Now a new vision and a whole new world have to be opened up." The new vision he was referring to is Vāsudeva Kutumbakam — the whole world is my family.

At a higher level — the whole world is my Self. This expansion of the mind to include the whole universe is what Swamiji meant when he said, "Lob it!" and, "Hit the ball high into outer space." Just like the trick of the lob, the trick of expanding the mind to embrace Infinity actually brings us closer to our own Self.[4]

4 Swamiji advised "Lob it" on another occasion, as well. Please see the section "Forget the Scoreboard."

INSIGHT: THE GREATEST LEGACY

The paths to God are many, experiences are many, but the ultimate Vision is one. All paths are there only to suit different temperaments. They are like paths climbing from different directions to reach the highest peak on a mountain range. After reaching the heights, one still has to enter the Temple and 'see' the Truth, which is like the 'Vision' gained through the sacred Knowledge of Oneness imparted by a Guru. Such enlightened Masters, when they guide others, the insight that they have shared becomes a legacy. When they share their insight via the medium of language, it expresses itself at the intellectual or emotional level, which is then understood or interpreted by the recipients according to their capacity and personality that is characterized with different intellectual and emotional temperaments, affected also by the influences of the era. The varied explanations of the nature of Reality are also the result of the epistemological means that they hold valid — the very means of knowledge that each Teacher had used in his or her own ascent — means such as perception, inference, proofs through examples and/or the words of saints. And if some happen to not be climbing the same 'hill,' then the experiences may be different, depending on the hill. That alone is true Vision or insight of the highest Truth which remains intact, uncontradicted and changeless, in all three states of consciousness — waking, dream, and sleep; and in all periods of time — past, present, and future. If the God-experience, or Vision of Reality, gets 'lost' in any state or time, it is then not the ultimate Insight or 'Experience.' The word 'Experience' is to be understood as a revelation and not a state of the mind.

Swami Chinmayananda:

Christ called saints "the Word made flesh." The Lord and the Word are one and the same: "I and My Father are one" (John 10:30). "The Word was with God, and the Word was God" (John 1:1). "And the Word was made flesh and lived among us" (John 1:1a). Christ: "Believe Me, I am in the Father, and the Father in Me" (John 14:11). He repeats: "The Father is in Me, and I in Him." (John 10:38).

The eternal Truth finally experienced by all the saints during samādhi is the same. The routes may be different, the explanation of the experience given by the seers may differ, and yet the place or destination is the same. In philosophy, terms like real and unreal, truth and falsehood are used to express some special import. That which exists in all the periods of time in the past, present, and future, ever without any change, is called the Real. And that which did not, and will not remain the same, but is seemingly available for our present experience, is called the unreal.

The final peak of success aimed at by a mind in meditation is its own merger into the great Silence — into pure Consciousness, which is the matrix behind the entire subtle world of subjective thoughts and emotions and the gross realm of objective things and beings. The conscious thoughts, in their enlivened vitality, give us the apparent illusion of individuality, known popularly as the ego. Self-rediscovery is the art of unveiling the Spirit by drawing asunder the veils of matter that now cover It. The ṛṣis of yore accomplished this consummation and lived in fulfillment of the life's goal. The whole world of thinkers and students gapes in amazement and wonder as it delves into the bosom of our scriptures, the achievement of these Masters being so unbelievably beyond the wildest imagination of their minds.

"Know thyself" is the final call of philosophy, but like the doctor who merely diagnoses the case and prescribes the cure, it leaves you exactly where you are — a little wiser perhaps, but certainly not a trifle better. So, religion has to step in and dispense the prescription. If the doctor is good, the prescription will be good; if the philosophy is good, the religion also will be good and effective.

Just as in sports like tennis where special tips are given for better performance, so also there are tips in meditation given out by a teacher, which come from his own experience. The investigators, our great ṛṣis, or sages, found that the subtlest of the subtle, the Principle, or Truth, resides within us, a divine Spark enveloped as it were by the grosser coatings of matter, the grossest being the physical body. All plurality is only an appearance, like a rope mistaken for a snake. Appearance is time-bound. The God-principle is beyond time.

You, as an infant that crawled on the floor, are completely different from you that you are now, and the old man that you would perhaps become. Physically, mentally, and intellectually, you have changed. No cell in you is the same as it was when you were young; no emotion in you is the same. Even your intellectual conceptions have changed. So who is the real you? How dare you call yourself by the same name you had in infancy when not a thing about you is the same? Yet, despite this very logical discretion, none of you can have any doubt that you are the same person that you were twenty years ago. Hence, the real you is away from all this, and it is the bedrock on which all these changes take place; and this entity is the Ātman, or the very Self in you.

On attaining anything other than the Ātman, the mind still seeks gati (progress). What you understand about Brahman with the mind and intellect is Brahman with form — and not formless Brahman. The unconditioned Brahman is never understood; you just 'become' it when the mind ends. What is ever changing can never be the absolute Truth. And change can be perceived only with reference to something that is changeless; it can be perceived only on a substratum that is changeless. We perceive the river flowing only because the bedrock beneath it is absolutely firm; the observer also is not floating on the river. If the riverbed were also moving, and if the observer, too, is floating down the river, then the movement of the river would not have been experienced. The moving film can only be perceived when it is projected upon a changeless screen. Hence, all change has to have underlying bedrock of Reality; and the experience of the change must be, in essence, because of the Changeless.

You are you because of the Infinite functioning through the total vāsanās. When you remove your equipment, there is neither a world for you nor a concept of God. Then alone will you come to understand that jīva and Īśvara are one and the same. In order to realize that one is Brahman, the Reality, the intellect must be prepared by the study of the scriptures as well as by independent thinking and reflection. This divine Spark of Life, the spiritual center — called the Ātman in Vedānta — is considered to have been enveloped by the various layers of matter of varying degrees of grossness. The outermost shell, the grossest, is the body; and we, almost all through our conscious existence, go about conceiving ourselves to be only this body. Very rarely, a few of us may be aware of the existence of our mental and intellectual personalities and, indeed, probably none of us is even remotely conscious of the Vital Center of all life and the Bliss in us.

Bring your mind to Me with devotion and love through a personal God; it is unavoidable. Thereby, through contemplation at My altar, pierce the idol with the intellect to see what the idol represents, and come to experience My real nature, which is beyond the mind and intellect.

To realize "I am this Truth" (tad aham asmi) is [to realize] the supreme state of identification with the divine Truth; and this is true bhakti, or devotion. The Reality is ever present with you, expressing as 'I, I, I.' You are not the thoughts. You are the Awareness that knows the thoughts. That power within each of us — that is the seer behind our eyes, the listener behind our ears, the smeller behind the nose, the taster in the tongue, and the feeler in the skin — is the Soul of man, the Ātman, the Self.

Vedānta is the highest achievement of man's wisdom. Let the whole world come. We have but the same song to sing, the one truth to declare: that man is God and not the devil that he plays! When we say, "Man is God," we do not mean that the size of man is the size of God, or that the shape of man is the shape of God, or that the imperfections of man are the imperfections of God. We only mean that in man there is a Godly essence. Man is subject to birth, God is unborn; man is limited, God is unlimited; man is a perishable being, God is imperishable; man is mortal, God is immortal. Remove all these qualities. Then what remains is pure Consciousness. Just as in the example, "That Devadatta is this man," and also in the declaration "tat tvam asi" (That thou art!) — when the contradictory conditionings are removed, what remains is the same infinite Self.

The definition of Truth is summed up thus in the greatest of testimonies in any scriptural teaching: The *advice* by the teacher: "tat tvam asi" (That thou art!); the *moment of direct experience:* "ayam ātma brahma" (this Ātman is Brahman!); *the roar in the declaration*: "aham brahmāsmi" (I am Brahman!). Wise men — having understood the One Essence in both man and God — say that the essential core in God is the essential core in man. Thus, hundreds of great declarations indicate and glorify the great oneness of Brahman and Ātman.

If the Infinite pervades the finite, what exactly is the relationship between the two? Has the Infinite produced the finite? Has the Infinite Itself become the finite? Has the Infinite modified Itself into the finite? Do they have a father-son relationship? Or do they have a master-servant relationship? All these are found in dualistic philosophies. But the philosophy of Advaita Vedānta, non-dualism, cannot accept anyone of them, as the Supreme is one imperishable, indivisible Self. Relationless relationship is the only relation between the Real and the unreal, between the True and the false, between the infinite Lord and the finite world. A statement to jolt and prod one toward the moment of intuition and illumination is a satori; the paradox in the statement jolts and prods one into a contemplative flight. The supreme Self is indicated as the very soul and cause of the pluralistic world. The expressions are so couched that they play as the delayed satori of Zen Buddhism. Some of the statements in the scriptures have the same effect upon meditators where they realize the significance of the pronouncements. "All beings exist in Me, but I do not dwell in them." The ocean can say, "The waves are in me, but I, the ocean, am not in them." The world of beings exists in the

Self, but the tragedies and sorrows of the beings do not affect the blissful Self. The waker in me is never, ever really affected by the most explosive experience of the dreamer. The relationship between the false and the Real is the relationship between the fickle breeze and the infinite space.

The fulfillment of devotion is a state of experience, at which level bhakti and Vedānta are not different from each other. In the same way, the physicist says that the world of matter is all the play of the positive and the negative electric charges. The biologist claims it is nothing but evolution. The astronomers and astrologers call this the dance play of the planets. According to the geologists, the sun is the only essence here below, for they say a portion of it fell down, cooled off, and became the earth. This is the nature of all arguments. Each aspect is right, but the separate investigations, while arriving at partial truths, do not express the totality of Truth. It is like the five blind people who each felt the elephant and got the knowledge of the great animal. Each one was right, but all of them were wrong. The one who found the leg to be like a pillar was right, and he who proclaimed the rough skin of the elephant's huge side to be a fortress was also correct. Each was perfectly right according to his personal investigation and limited experience. But since they were blind, none of the conclusions were correct. They could not see the whole; they could describe only what they investigated and experienced in their incomplete attempts.

A Postal Lesson Course student asks, "Where is consciousness under anesthesia?"

Swamiji: "Where was the consciousness, Swamiji, when they were doing all sorts of things to my body and I knew nothing?" — is your question. Please read it again and again and more with special emphasis on the last three words!! You were conscious!! You were conscious of 'nothingness.' "I KNEW *nothing*." "No-thing I knew which they were doing." When the mind was dozed off, the consciousness was clutched off from the *body-world* and the *mind-world*, and, therefore, their pains were not known to you — hence, not conscious of it all. The absence of everything you KNEW. But you were; Consciousness was there. The fumes of chloroform dozed off only the mind–intellect, and what was available for them of the world outside was zero.

Is solipsism the answer?

Prarthna Saran: It was one of those beautiful nights in Sidhbari when we had Gurudev all to ourselves after dinner. That night, I told Gurudev in a lighthearted conversation, "Swamiji, you have told us that the world exists in the mind alone! So, I exist in Anjali's mind and she in mine. So now, Anjali's bright idea is that only one of us should work hard toward Realization — if she realizes, then I will automatically realize!" Gurudev had a good laugh at this foolish piece of conversation. With a twinkle in his eye, he looked at me and said, "My dear, if you are depending on Anjali to realize, then good luck to you!" The dig was on us both.

One must constantly 'live' the vision that inspires us:

Swamini Vimalananda: A child had a birthday during a camp in Sidhbari. Gurudev made a big fanfare of the birthday and wished her a happy birthday and hugged the child and made her very happy. The next day it was my birthday and I went and prostrated to Gurudev. Somebody mentioned to him that it was my birthday. Gurudev said to me: "You are unborn! And don't let even your parents ever convince you that you were ever born!"

Do all philosophies lead one to the final Truth?

Anita Thapan: "So many great saints," I sighed. Gurudev had always appreciated and encouraged us to read the writings of different saints, so the discussion was on that. "All of them saying the same thing in so many different ways," said another lady. "But all are not equally great, are they? Guruji (referring the question to Swami Tejomayananda), would you say that the view is always the same from the top of the mountain?" "Depends on which mountain it is!" came the prompt reply, plunging us into silence and reflection.

DYNAMISM OF TOGETHERNESS

If God is absolute and infinite as the sages of all religions declare, then by definition He must be the Substratum of this entire universe. To say that God does not exist in a particular place or object would be to limit God's infinitude and all-pervasiveness. If we have the conviction that He is the Support of all, then He has to exist in all as the divine Spark of Existence and Consciousness and the Bliss of feeling complete. Our goal is to expand the mind and aim to see His underlying presence in everything — to see the whole world in the medium of God.

Swami Chinmayananda:

Nārāyaṇa, the infinite Truth, is the very essence and support of the entire universe. Nārāyaṇa is the throne at which all righteousness takes its refuge. Without reference to Him and His glory, righteousness has no meaning, just as the law books of a country are empty pages when a government falls. Nārāyaṇa in the many is standing around; Nārāyaṇa in one is within.

The universe is a cosmos and not a chaos. There exists a mental affinity, a scientific law, a rhythm of mental relationship in which the entire living world is held together — in one web of love. To assume differences in the world is to belie this great oneness in life. Learn that you are one thread in a fabric. You go over some and under some; you can't remain on top always. One thread needs the gloriously intricate weave support of the other threads to enable it to form that great fabric whose noble task is to clothe the world's nakedness. Everyone has a precise place in the scheme of created things. Each one has an importance and none is to be despised. There is no redundancy in the Lord's creation, not even a single blade of grass is unnecessarily created. Your neighbor's job and his attitudes are all different from you, just as your leg is different from your hand. Yet, are they both not yours? Nobody can afford to hate himself. Even when a part of the body is ulcerated and gives endless pain and the doctor may advise an amputation, yet man hesitates. If you understand this idea, then you will see the whole universe as one mighty expression of the divine Spark of Existence.

Most educated people love humanity; it is the next-door neighbor that they hate and detest. Unfold your within and discover therein an accommodation even for the cruel, for the desperate, for the wily. They need your love and help more than others. Run to them always with all love, extreme humility, full devotion, and complete sincerity. They are delirious; they may kick you back. With more love, nurse them: they need all your tender and patient love.

Love is the heart of religions, the theme of all classical works of art and literature, the song of all devotees. Scientists know only what love does — not what love is. Love can indeed empty our asylums, perhaps all our prisons, maybe all our hospitals. People suffer in life due to lack of love. Love is to human hearts what the sun is to flowers! Pure love breaks all bonds. It pulls down all barriers. It annihilates all differentiations. It flows perennially toward the entire creation, even as the sun shines equally upon all. This love is indeed God — the universal God. It is a potent remedy to destroy the disease of hatred. He who has pure love in his heart wins the hearts of all. A sense of isolation is the cause for all social disturbances, international tensions, and individual revolts. Fanatic secularism is as dangerous to the world as fanatic religion. Hatred can come only when we see the thing hated as something other than us. Tolerance is the only test of civilization. Love is the solvent of all problems. To give love is freedom, to demand love is slavery. Some of us love only if we are loved in return, like a commercial transaction. Very few are rich in love. How can they love when they have none in themselves? Service of others is the expression of love in one's heart. Love is a consistent passion to give, not a meek persistent hope to receive. Love is not love if it does not serve and sacrifice. The day you take up the policy of giving love instead of demanding it, that day you will have rewritten your entire future destiny.

Surrender to the world of His plan; know and be joyous that you have been made an instrument in this great work, and take life as a sportsman. Be content with what you have and try to be a giver in life rather than a taker. Everything in nature gives, never takes. The sun, the rain, the spring, and the rivers work in a rhythm of giving. The sun gives light and energy. The moon, the flowers, the birds — they all give. The trees give, the rivers give, the earth gives, the stars give. Why then must we be anxious only to take, to amass, to gather, to hoard? To expand oneself in spiritual vision and experience the totality as one's own Self is sarvātma-bhāva, the recognition of the universe as the Self. At present, our personality is extremely egocentric. We fail to recognize or to identify with our country or state or community or even beyond our own terrible attachments to our body and possessions. In fact, beyond these attachments, we have no other personality. From this self-centered, extremely limited, supremely circumscribed, frog-in-the-well experience, we have to grow, expand, and gain the vision of 'the entire Universe-as-the-Self in us.'

To experience "there is nothing other than the Self" is true Knowledge. To experience that the meditator himself is Divine in his core, but thereafter not to recognize that Divinity everywhere around him, is only a partial knowledge, and, at best, a fanciful imagination. A man of full Realization instinctively becomes a lover of the whole universe. Living as he does in this intimate understanding of Oneness, he cannot but love others as his very own Self.

Expand to realize that "All is the Self." Try to find accommodation for everyone in your compassion and in your love for the world around you. Recognize that all things are Nārāyaṇa Himself, His various divine forms. As such, they are all the moving temples of the Lord. Therefore, the Lord alone exists. Ultimately, when you come to experience that "The Self in me is the Self everywhere," then alone, there is total liberation from the bondage of the mortal. There is nothing superior to this experience of the Oneness in everything; this is the highest experience. Identification is the measuring rod of love.

God sleeps in stones, breathes in plants, dreams in animals, and is awake in man.

Seek Him in the smile of your friends, in the glow of angry eyes, in the throb of love, in the storms of passion. Everywhere it is His glow that is gleaming through different emotions, thoughts, and actions. Seek Him in the thrill of the dawn, in the sadness of the dusk, in the embrace of rains, in the hustling storms, in the murmuring breeze, in green pastures, in the blue lotus, in the saṅgama (confluence) of the graceful Ganges and the restless Jamuna. He is everywhere — in everything — not with mortal legs and hands, but in His Presence as the divine joy Infinite. You are in Him — you are but He alone.

Swamiji showed how to 'live' the attitude that 'The Self is All':

Ācāryas Gaurang and Darshana Nanavaty: He signed his letters with, "Love, Love, Love!" He lived that love in its many-splendored dimensions, and continues to mesmerize seekers of all ages through time, then and now.

Ācārya Vilasini Balakrishnan: Nalini Browning, the first CMW Secretary, asked once, "Swamiji, is it tiring for you to have people around all the time?" This was in 1980 after his heart bypass surgery, and, literally, at least one or two people were in his room round the clock for weeks. His hosts even slept on the floor at night in case he needed any assistance. Swamiji put Nalini's question to rest immediately. He exclaimed, "Do you ever get tired of your own arm? You may get tired of your clothing and change it, but your own arm? How can I get tired of you all?"

Understanding the true import of the all-pervading nature of God expands the mind:

Som Oberoi: In one of the earlier trips to Kuwait, Gurudev brought a beautiful idol of Lord Kṛṣṇa for the Mandir in Kuwait. Someone said, "Swamiji, you brought Kṛṣṇa to Kuwait!" Swamiji, quipped, "Did I bring Kṛṣṇa to Kuwait? Can one bring Him where He is not? He is all-pervasive like space, immovable, motionless Reality, eternal, far and wide." It is He who brought me to Kuwait." On another occasion, someone who was videotaping Gurudev said to a devotee who had come in front of the camera, "Vishnuji, you are covering everyone." Gurudev remarked "What a realization! Finally, he can see only Viṣṇu everywhere!"

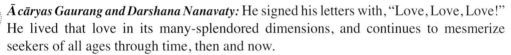

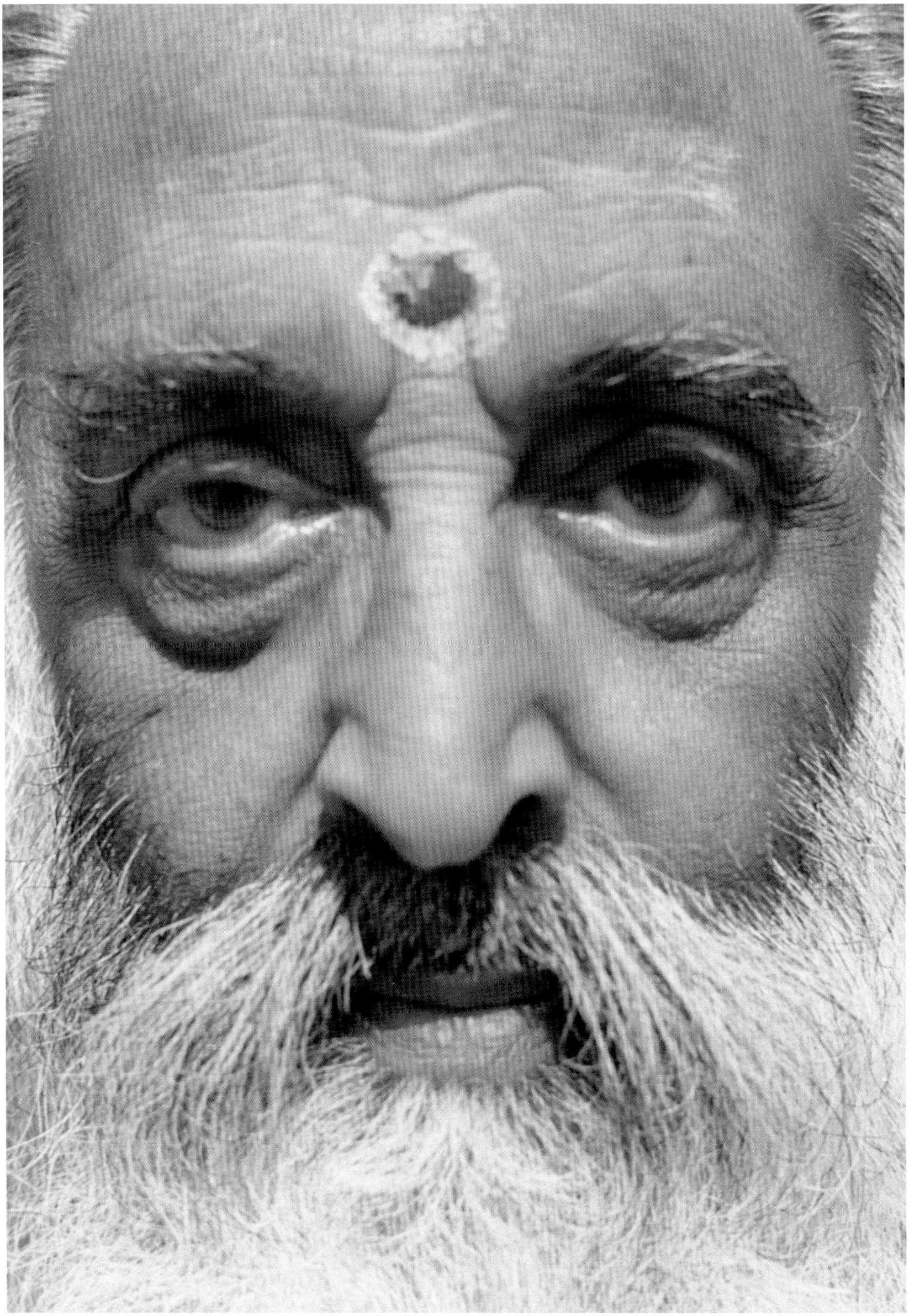

STEP 5

HOW TO LIVE AS A WITNESS

The statement (in *Kaṭha Upaniṣad 1.3.14*) that the path is as risky as the knife's edge is made by the scripture only to emphasize the importance in strictly following the path under all conditions and circumstances. This should not in any sense of the term be misconstrued that the path is impossibly difficult; nothing of that sort is intended to a true seeker. Jesus Christ also expressed a similar idea when the Lord said: "Strive to enter in at the straight gate, for narrow is the gate and straight is the way that leads to Life, and few be they who find it." (Matthew 7:13–14)

-Swami Chinmayananda

15

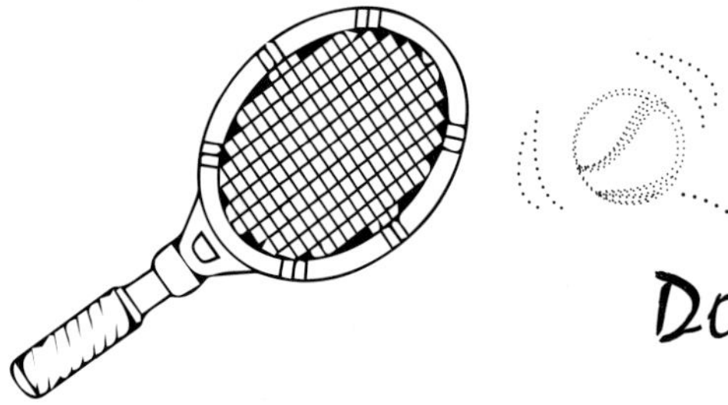

Double Fault

In a match between McEnroe and Wheaton, Swamiji said, "He is always putting it into the net." Then he said, "Double fault!" He keeps hitting into the net, never over it!" At another point, Swamiji remarked, "He tried for an ace but it landed in the net!"

Swamiji was seemingly commenting on the tennis match, but was actually talking about hurdles in meditation. He was subtly indicating how, despite effort, impediments like agitations or sleep may keep coming in meditation ("double fault"). Meditators may try for "an ace," but land "in the net."

When devotees heard this, many felt the need to make an extra effort to focus and aim at total peace in meditation. But this could not be sustained. Swamiji used another tennis conversation, on another day, to address the problem of how to sustain the quietude in meditation. We will be looking at that later in this book.

THE FLARE-UP

When the mind becomes purified, the potential for Self-realization is at hand. However, hordes of vāsanās may now make an upsurge to the surface from where they were buried in the unconscious, because the quietened mind has space for them to emerge. This vikṣepa must be faced before the vāsanās disappear from the psyche forever. The reason they were buried in the first place is that we lacked the spiritual stamina to confront them. They surface in many forms — agitations and desires, a feeling of having a million thoughts per minute, depression, a draining of energy, a feeling of not being able to face the world, a sense of great fear, not seeing a way out, or a feeling of extreme helplessness. If we avoid facing them, they remain buried within. To be rid of them forever, we should neither try to overanalyze them nor run away. The only remedy is to witness them as they emerge, resist engaging with them, and calmly allow them to disappear.

Swami Chinmayananda:

When the fiery touch of the Lord's grace descends upon His devotees, it is invariably felt by the seekers more as an avalanche than as a refreshing shower of divine Mercy. When a flame dies, it first flares up and then dies.

The divine path leading the pilgrim to the Temple of Truth is not always even; it contains many a steep ascent. It wends through dangerous gorges, dark tunnels, fearful jungles, and precipitous steeps. To control the mind and to move steadily on, away from the fields of perceptions and thoughts and to ascend the tranquil peaks of the infinite Consciousness, is no pleasant travel.

The path of spiritual unfoldment is reserved for the wise heroes and not for simple-minded foolish cowards. Let not those who are practicing meditation ever feel aghast at what they have to accomplish. Nothing in the world is permanent; the disturbing factors also cannot remain permanently with you.

When seekers enter the spiritual field and courageously start their honest efforts at hastening the fulfillment of their evolution, a great, divine Power comes to help them at every turn. Even a mountain can be slowly, slowly reduced to powder; even a rocky hillock can be blasted by repeatedly shooting arrows at it — that is the glory of continuous practice. Even an ignorant one can gain wisdom. This is the unfailing reward of steady, daily practice, sincerely undertaken for a long, continuous period of time.

Deep-seated urges and inclinations (vāsanās) have to be thrown up from the unconscious to the level of the conscious mind. They may play for a while in us and then they will depart, never to return — if we have developed the necessary stamina and discovered sufficient courage to stand apart from them as a disinterested witness during their threatening uprising. Such explosions are unavoidable in any seeker on the march. Not to identify yourself with the rising tide of thoughts but to remain as a witness of them all is a definite stage in the efforts at meditation.

Vāsanās are exhausted and bondages loosened in our constant and deliberate attempts at meditation. The more intense the meditation, the faster the vāsanās get ablaze.

In the rainy season, the clouds are all driven away in a moment, and yet, the next moment we may find the sky cloudy again. The breeze that removed the existing clouds brings, in its next windy dash, a hoard of new ones. The sun shines brightly at one moment, and the next moment it is hidden again behind the newly gathered clouds. So, too, the mind is at one moment steady in prayerful meditation, but the next moment, there is a gush of thoughts which, dashing the brilliant poise of the mind-at-meditation, makes it full of agitations. Generally, you feel more distracted when you come out of the pūjā room than when you went in. All this is the devastating play of the ego. Therefore, beware! Be a man. Today determines the tomorrows. Even at the porch of death, don't stop the spiritual search. Conquer the ego and continue with the alert vigilance of a successful conqueror. Never think that the ego has left you permanently. It must have only receded into the background — it can come up again if you slacken your diligence.

Many a time the pilgrim feels waves of passion, gushes of despair, storms of despondency, and cyclones of hopelessness rocking his courage and shattering his sincerity. To pursue the path in spite of these benumbing influences, the pilgrim must be a great hero who has a private exchequer of inspiration and confidence from which to draw. He must indeed have an unlimited exchequer of power and strength. This exchequer of infinite strength is called faith.

The Self, the Lord, is the very source of joy to the devotee, and to live away from Him becomes to him a tragic bereavement; on such occasions, he experiences a deep anguish. To a true devotee such moments of forgetfulness of the Lord are moments of despair, when he feels himself like a fish out of water. He can find again his peace and life, his balance and movement, only when he reaches back into the tranquil waters of the devotion in his own heart. In this rediscovery of devotion in one's own Self, some may find worship and others may find singing His glories a method. Yet, for another, steady contemplation upon the Self in himself is the quickest way to rediscover his at-one-ment with the Lord of his heart. Rest in Him who is ever the same in your heart, and watch the parade of events in the stream of time.

Swamiji tailored advice in spiritual practice to each devotee and his or her needs:

Letter to ***Vinita Asrani:*** I learn from your letter that there have been disturbances in your sādhanā. This is natural. As we proceed, the old vāsanās have to rise up in the mind and then disappear. At such moments, remember the Lord's name. In japa, hold on to your inner balance and just keep on watching the procession of these moods without identifying with them. When such moods come, sādhaks are advised to go to the nearest temple, go around the parikramā, remembering the Lord's name.

Letter to ***Madhuri Jhala:*** Surrender to the Lord is the greatest remedy for depression. Expect nothing. Be satisfied with what He gives. Where can there be depression?

Anjali Singh: During the last two years of Swamiji's illness, I asked Swamiji for advice on how to deal with depression, which came in bouts every now and then. He said, "When depression comes, don't identify with it. Treat it as Nārāyaṇa standing before you. And, similarly, when bliss comes, if Nārāyaṇa is standing before you, will you run away? You will do namaskāra to Him! When He has given his darśana, He will disappear." I said that this curiously happens after a good meditation session! He replied, "Sometimes, deep meditation stirs up the unconscious and makes things come up which you are not aware of. Once you have decided to live a spiritual life, then have the faith that you are on the path. No fall is a fall, because the vāsanās have to come out every now and then. You should, in fact, congratulate yourself when vulgar thoughts are thrown up!" Then I asked if I should do japa? He replied, "Why do you want to take the long route and do japa? The shortcut is to say, 'They are in Me. I am not in them.'"

The pause between two flare-ups of vāsanās, though it gives a respite, does not decrease the pain of sorrow:

Anjali Singh: In Sidhbari, Swamiji was watching the scene on television in the Bhāgavata Purāṇa in which Kamsa temporarily gives back the baby girl that he was going to kill, only to take it back from the mother Devaki. Swamiji remarked, "In drama, the pathos increases when Kamsa gives the child back; she becomes very happy, and then he takes it away, and the sorrow is doubled." Then again, when the log fire flared up as the embers were being extinguished, Swamiji said, giving hope, "When a flame dies, it first flares up and then dies!"

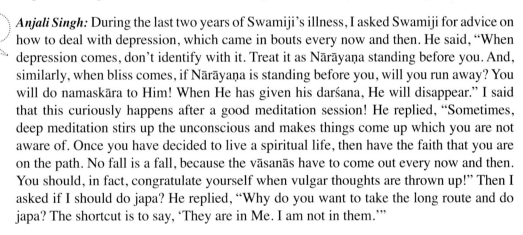

THE SLEEPY TRANCE

When the mind is not agitated and, yet, has not found God, or realized the Self, and is therefore not yet reveling in Self-realization, then what will it do when it becomes quiet in meditation? It goes off to sleep! The mind is quiet, but it is still in ignorance, so it slips into an enjoyable state of trance-like sleep, or stupor, called 'laya.' This is a hurdle in moving forward in a seeker's quest for Realization of the Self. Realization is a state of dynamic Consciousness and Bliss, and not the passive joy of a sleepy mind. What can ensue is a seesaw between agitations (vikṣepa) on the one hand and laya, or sleep, on the other. Both are obstructions to progress. The determined meditator has to dexterously balance the seesaw while remaining in the center and thus conquer both agitations and sleep.

Swami Chinmayananda:

One of the most difficult and tragic obstacles into which the mind unconsciously dips during its meditation is what is technically called laya (sleep or stupor). When the mind during meditation has been withdrawn from its fields of objects and the pacified mind is again, through concentration, made single-pointed, it is apt to fall into an abyss of ignorance called 'sleep' or 'oblivion.' It is not necessarily of the type of sleep that we generally get. It is, indeed, an experience highly captivating in its joyous contents. It is sometimes indicated by the unscientific terminology of 'trance.' A quiet mind has an enchanting bliss which is most enjoyable. In this state of trance, some write poetry, some come out with the highest philosophy, and some dance. This trance is called laya. Trance is indulged in by the weakness of the mind. At such moments, the advice is that we should awaken the mind and make it once again active. One could do prāṇāyāma (breath control) exercises. Breathe out and hold the breath! When we have conquered this weakness by repeated self-application, we reach a stage when the mind would no longer, of its own accord, slip into this stupor.

At this stage, the obstacle is that the mind so awakened, when applied in a single-pointed concentration, cannot easily revel there, but on its own accord wanders away, either into its memories of joys experienced *before*, or with the joys it is experiencing *now,* or into the labyrinth of sense satisfactions to be fulfilled in the *future*. The mind gets disturbed by the desire and thirst to enjoy the things of the world. In this condition of mental agitation, we can educate the mind and get over its false values and thus, from the helm of true meditation, when the mind is brought under control with discrimination, the state of sublimation is not like the dull inert experience in stupor or sleep. In sleep, certainly the mind is not active, and yet, it is only an impotent state wherein the mind with all its impressions is only being drowned in ignorance. But when the mind is consciously and intelligently purified, then the mind is sublimated, and what remains is not *knowledge of the ignorance* but a *knowledge of the Knowledge*. It is not a negative existence *remembered* as happiness, but a positive dynamic being *experienced* as Bliss.

You have to get yourself out of both obstacles — of agitation and of trance. The attraction for the joys of 'spiritual sleep,' or laya, is as much ruinous as desire for a true pursuer on the Path of Self-realization. The meditator cannot progress any more in his conquest so long as he is a victim of either the laya or the endless desire-agitation. In laya, or trance — wake him up; in vikṣepa (agitation) — turn the mind to the Goal and say, "Kṛṣṇa! Kṛṣṇa!" Don't say "I am an Advaitin." When you are going up the mountain, it is very helpful to have a staff. You are taking the staff. The staff is not taking you. But it is of help, and you have to remove the obstruction with His help, even though you have to carry the staff up the climb. But it takes you there.

Knowing when to aim for samādhi:

Ācārya Vilasini Balakrishnan: I found Gurudev often making subtle adjustments in our practices. When I was video-shooting his talks and satsaṅgas from 1981 to 1984, a beautiful Sahasranāma Pūjā was being performed in Gurudev's presence. I turned the camera on and put all my attention on recording. But Gurudev said, "No need to film this. Keep your attention on the pūjā." This put me in a deep state of samādhi. Then another time, I thought I would follow this advice again. I turned on the camera and left it to record, and then fell into a deep silence, forgetting all about the camera. Gurudev got my attention and said sternly, "Don't go into samādhi now — film the pūjā!" I could see his message: to flow with whatever is called for in life, detached from all of it! He was always trying to lead us deeper within!

Advice not to indulge 'laya':

***Anjali Singh*:** I asked Swamiji whether vāsanās also get exhausted in sleep as they did in the dream state. He said, "In sleep, how can vāsanā kṣaya take place? In deep sleep, the mind is not destroyed; it just ducks under. It exists. It is not dead. When you wake up, you get the mind that you slept with. A controlled mind in meditation gets overwhelmed by apprehension, not the non-apprehension of sleep. That state is Brahman, the absolute Reality of pure apprehension. The dark beauty (Kṛṣṇa) is always hiding behind the thoughts." Then I asked, "What should one do when one experiences joy in meditation?" He said, "One should stand apart and observe this joyous state of mind; then it does not bind one. Don't allow yourself to go into laya. In your case, you should get up from your seat of meditation!!"

THE DARK NIGHT

Even though the vāsanās may flare up as vikṣepa and the seeker may overcome them through discrimination and detachment, yet the vāsanās of many lives that are very subtle in nature still lie unmanifest in the unconscious. If they were to manifest themselves, they would become vikṣepa — but they do not, for they are subtle. It is these vāsanās that now prevent the meditator from progressing forward. These vāsanās are like'darkness' that is a subtle kind of dirt, termed 'kṣaya.' Because of these hidden vāsanās, one feels stagnant in the pursuit. It seems as though a dark wall or a dark cloud has blocked one's progress. A feeling of complete hopelessness could then overpower the seeker. All one can do is be forewarned that this condition is unavoidable, that it will be there for some time. Be strengthened by the knowledge that transcending it is the final stage to freedom. How is one to progress in the face of this obstacle? One should stay firm and not give up practicing contemplation even though it seems not to help. By the power of meditation, these subtle vāsanās also get destroyed. A high quality of patience is required, which will help to keep steadfast on the path of sādhanā. The dark night is usually more intense for those on the path of devotion rather than those following the Vedāntic path, as the latter have done reflection (mananam) and created detachment through discrimination and inquiry.

Swami Chinmayananda:

The periods for a sincere seeker during his spiritual life are the moments before the final divine experience. The pathetic anguish felt by him on the path is called 'the dark night of the soul.' This stage of extreme helplessness, complete disappointment, total dejection, and utter despair — though unavoidable — can be minimized if the seeker, on his meditation flight to the transcendental, is well equipped and fully trained for this supreme, subjective adventure. It is the unprepared student who falls into unproductive, progress-halting ruts of thought, and gets torn in the rising storms within him.

When we have conquered the weakness of sleep or stupor by repeated self-application, we reach a stage when the mind no longer slips into this stupor nor wanders into wrong channels of thought. When both these have been overcome, the seeker must understand and be forewarned that his mind is a decoction of sensuous vāsanās, and at any time it can pull him down. It has its negative impressions, potential and subconscious, which are lying dormant and must come up, at least once, before they get dried away in the fire of enlightened and discriminating meditation. The animalistic tendencies gathered by him during his beginningless births are in the subconscious zone lying dormant now — which at any moment may start their revolt against the discipline and bring down, with a blast of despair, the dream of success in the spiritual aspirant. This warning is a great help, as the student thereafter can have no despair in his spiritual pursuit. These subconscious animal traits in his mind, now lying in a dormant condition, are called the kṣaya of the mind.

It is always darkest before dawn. At the doorway to Truth, the frail seeker must tremble with a growing gloom of dejection within. The recognition of the futility of conscious effort in the last moments of seeking should bring about a sad weariness and overwhelming sense of melancholy in the seekers. Many have reached this point and have, in utter despair, turned back. We can reach only the frontiers of the finite but must hesitate, in growing fear, to plunge into the unknown. Ardent devotion steadily and continuously flowing toward the infinite Self, the Lord, is the secret method of drawing upon the reservoir of a nameless courage and determination, which alone can help the seeker at this stage of meditation. To invoke the Lord at this point is the sacred tip, a secret charm, which can discover for us light in our darkness, hope amid our fears, and strength in our weakness. The Lord is the mighty benevolent Power that shall guide us out of our confusions and despairs, fears and sorrows, into the infinite Glory. To invoke Him is the only solace for a meditator in despair.

In a cave there is darkness, though outside there is plenty of light during daytime. The darkness in the cave could not have come from anywhere else: it arose from the cave. Thus, the darkness born out of the cave thereafter veils the cave and gives us the fear and the dread of imaginary phantoms within the cave and drains away our courage to enter it. In the *cave of the heart*, arising out of itself, are the darkness of egoism and lust, selfishness and arrogance, and the ideas of doership and enjoyership. And these breed many a horrid phantom of thoughtless imaginations. The poor individual stands limited by his own dreams, persecuted by his own fears, strangled by his own desires! The inherent psychological fear-complex is one of the most difficult obstacles to cross over on the way to Self-realization. When the clouds move away, when the light penetrates into the cave, when the misconceptions of Reality are driven out by the rediscovery of our real Nature, all fears are set at rest, all miseries end, and the Bliss of Perfection is rediscovered.

Life is a pilgrimage of the alone to the Alone, all alone ... it is a subjective unfoldment.

Swamiji's advice in a letter to a devotee on how to deal with depression and why it had come:

Every time you get the sense of depression, your letter itself confesses that it is a reaction to a terrible sense of attachment. So you generate the poison in yourself, and you get poisoned. Learn to surrender it all to Him. Your mind is your own enemy. In the last two years, the shocks received are the shocks that affected you. All others around you in the world are there, each one to fulfill his or her own past.

Letter to ***A. Balakrishnan:*** May the exploding New Year bring you more and more out of the dreary darkness into full, bright, blazing light of the endless grace and blessings. Come out of this dreary darkness. Regular meditation -- and cheerful spirit of surrender unto Him.

Letter to ***Vinita Asrani:*** Even when it comes, you have the Brahmāstra (weapon) to destroy it: "They are in Me, I am not in them."

Symbolism of the churning of the ocean:

Swami Shantananda: The practice of meditation can be very frustrating. The story of the churning of the ocean, symbolically, is meditation. The gods and demons are the positive and negative forces; the mind is the ocean; you are churning with the rope of the ego. The ego pushes this side, and then it pulls that side. The mantra is the rod. As you churn, what comes out is poison. This poison is nothing but our impurities. Before meditation, you are a nice person; after meditation, you become a different person — you are irritated because negativities are coming out. It takes time. You become worse for a while and you want to give it up. But you should congratulate yourself. Gurudev says that under an ordinary light, you don't see dirt; but if you increase the voltage, every little bit of dirt shows up. Similarly, in meditation, we increase the voltage and we see dirt very clearly, because sensitivity increases. Don't try to analyze what is happening; you won't able to handle it. Learn to unload; then all good things come.

Consciousness is a unique Light that illumines both light and darkness with the same felicity:

Anjali Singh: Mrs. Shakuntala Bindra, a devotee, complained that she could not see Swamiji's face, as the floodlight on Hanumānji was shining in her eyes. Swamiji said, "When enlightenment comes, Kṛṣṇa becomes formless in the dark!" He likened the Rāma-tulsī (with bright green leaves) and the Śyāma-tulsī (with dark green leaves) growing near the Hanumānji idol to light and darkness, saying, "The dark beauty, Kṛṣṇa, is always hiding behind the thoughts. When you reach there, He will be surrounded by light and you will have to see the darkness, Kṛṣṇa, through the light — then He is That which is beyond both light and darkness."

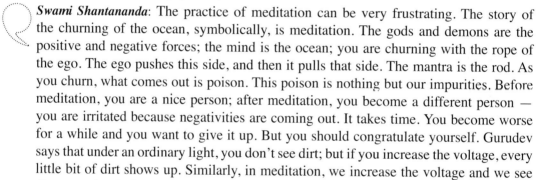

He is That which is beyond both light and darkness.

THE NARROW PATH

When most hurdles have been crossed, a few subtle points still need to be addressed by the seeker. Though humility, surrender, and commitment are virtues that have already been cultivated, at this level, they assume a key role in preparing the seeker for the last leap. Perhaps that is why the *Kaṭha Upaniṣad* says that the path is "as narrow as the edge of a razor." It is not that it is impossibly difficult, but the Upaniṣad makes this statement to alert the seeker to implicitly follow all the instructions and precautions given by the Guru. The Guru constantly points out all traces of inadequacies in his student, so that he may not fall from the heights which he has scaled. When total surrender of the ego has not yet taken place, the student may have the subtle vanity that "I am spiritual." This indicates that love for God has not yet reached a pristine texture and that it has not yet taken firm root. Only traces of ego are left at this stage: The presumptuousness that a seeker had in his 'prosperous' days will have left him, his mind having been thinned out through an outpouring of vāsanās. All the traces of vanity — the identification with the not-Self — have to be surrendered to the Lord, the Self, including the vanity of being special to the Guru, jealousies among the seekers, and the pride of scriptural knowledge. A day comes when you surrender to God completely, and this invokes His grace, which pushes the seeker to the Beyond.

ON THE PREREQUISITE OF HUMILITY:
Swami Chinmayananda:

When man is able to temporarily overcome his baser tendencies, he develops an ego that he did it, forgetting that it was Nārāyaṇa's grace that made it happen.

When the seeker has awakened his mind from its stupor and has led its course diligently, then that student may all of a sudden come to entertain a very highly optimistic opinion about himself and his mind, and thus jump into a hasty conclusion that he has conquered the mind and has smooth sailing toward perfection. This is all due to the play of the vāsanās and the ego-sense. Even though you have ended the ego, along with its roots, the vāsanās again can revive and rise up to tyrannize you. If you allow your mind this freedom, then the play of the ego-sense will start again. Therefore, beware!

When one has, to an extent, overcome the baser arrogance, then the sāttvic ego also becomes a bondage in life. The very vanity that he is a spiritual seeker or that he has spiritual experiences crystallizes his ego-sense, and so he cannot enter into the total State of Absolute Bliss. One notices dirt in other people and gives importance to one's own virtues. When this state of non-purity — the "I am sāttvic" idea — is attained, do not entertain that thought. Drop it and get free of non-purity. This is the condition of absolute purity, the thoughtless sāttvic state of dynamic Consciousness. Humility is a strange thing — the moment you think you have got it, you have lost it!

The vanities of family, lineage, name, form, and order in life, and so on, belong to the body, which is perishable and rotten. The vanities of doership and enjoyership belong to the subtle body, which is always changing. Renounce these vanities and experience the nature of unbroken Bliss, which is the eternal Self.

When, with such development, regular meditation is observed, the remnants of the ego are dissolved and the individual experiences Godhood. But the last trace of individuality, or the I-ness, still remains. This State of Realization is called savikalpa samādhi. The culmination of evolution, however, is the state of nirvikalpa samādhi, when the I-ness, or the feeling of individuality itself, merges with the infinite Experience, and what remains thereafter is the one, all-pervading, supreme Reality.

The taunting words of the Master are tipped with sharp ridicule in order to really wound the student's vanity, if he is not already fully established in the pure, immutable Self. Water flows only from a higher level to a lower level; so, too, it is with the flow of Knowledge. Unless we have the meekness and spirit to surrender, Knowledge cannot reach us.

The Guru will always warn the student either in advance or just afterward when he sees that pride has arisen as a result of attention given or a gift given by the Guru.

Neeru Mehta: On the spiritual path, there are bitter pills to swallow, though they always have a sweet aftertaste of joy. Many times, Swamiji would keep me at a distance but soothe me from within. If the devotee's ego puffed up at some attention shown by him, he would start ignoring that person completely to deflate her ego. I once said to him, "You just kill the person, Swamiji," to which he replied, "I destroy, to rebuild!"

Sheela Kirpalani: It is said that the spiritual path is like a razor's edge. Only years later did I realize that whenever I was caught up in my own small self, Gurudev would efficiently push some button that would make me react. Acting innocently, Gurudev would then ask me what was wrong (knowing exactly what it was!). Once, I told him in no uncertain terms that I was not going to be insulted anymore. Gurudev nodded his head and said, "But you are not your ego." Instantly, I realized that whatever Gurudev said or did was for the sole purpose of demonstrating how this profound teaching could be practically applied to life.

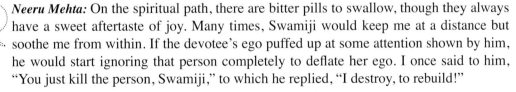

Anjali Singh: In Vishakapatnam, in March 1993, whenever Swamiji would go in for lunch, he would make a funny face at us who would be waiting in the lobby. It was like a ritual, and we loved it. One day, before he entered his room, he looked back and said to me, "Wait, I have something special for you!" His host, Mr. Mittal, who escorted him inside, came out of the room after a minute or so carrying a huge envelope in his hands for me. When I opened the envelope, there was a colorful card with a beautiful peacock on it. My smile broadened. But when I opened up the card, I saw that Swamiji had written in bold, in his most dynamic handwriting: "Your vanity has no legs to stand up!"

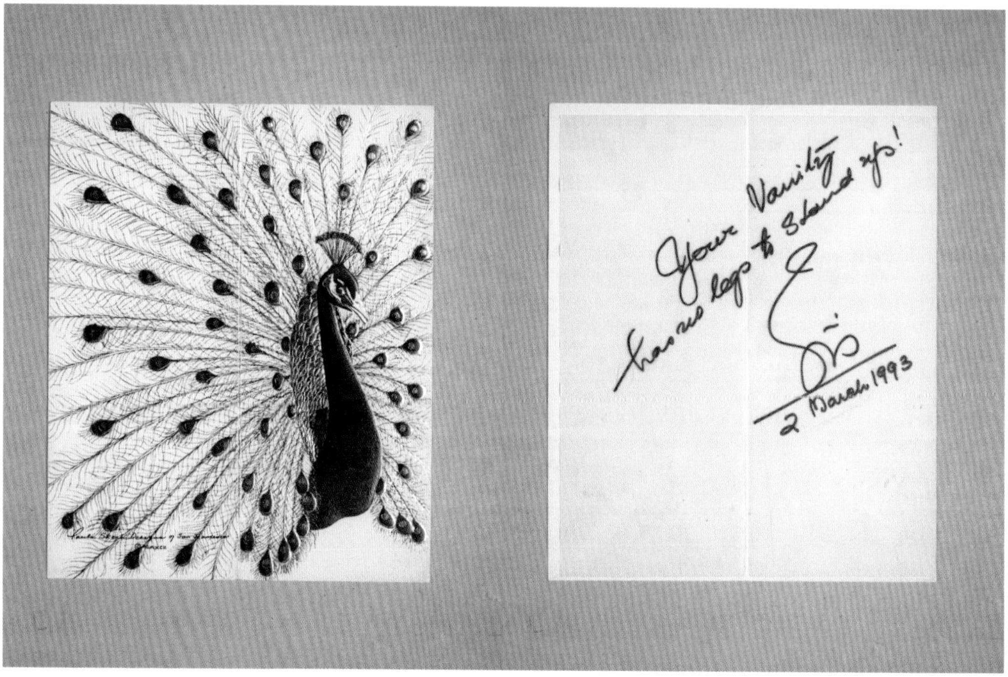

Ācāryas Gaurang and Darshana Nanavaty: During the Vancouver yajña, after his discourse, Gurudev saw us going back to the hotel. He was on his way to his dinner bhikṣā and asked us to go along with him. We hesitatingly pointed out that we were not invited. Brushing it aside, he said, "You come as my guest. Where I go, you go, too." So, later when we, as new devotees, were inspired to go see Gurudev in L.A., we felt like a million bucks! We felt we were very special to Gurudev. During the satsaṅga, Swamiji could certainly read my 'dirty' mind, which said proudly, "I am very special." So, quite suddenly, Gurudev said, "Gaurang, go get my bags," in a tone similar to one addressing a porter. After the satsaṅga, Darshana and I went to our room and discussed this, "The way Swamiji is treating us, maybe he doesn't want us here." So, we were trying to see how to leave while trying to save face. But, he knew it all. Next morning, Gurudev called us and said, "Come with me," as we all left for his early morning talk. Before we knew it, we were melting in his hands. He made us feel so good that we forgot about leaving. He had put us in our place to show that, just because the teacher loved us, we should not take the teacher for granted. Again, a teaching through that thoughtful action — when Gurudev knew and loved you, he never waited; he taught again and again!

Swamiji lived the humility that he taught:

K. C. Patnaik: The Managing Director of Rourkela Steel Plant was to inaugurate the Gītā Jñāna Yajña by Pūjya Gurudev Swami Chinmayananda. But since his secretary forgot to remind him, the Managing Director (M.D.) did not arrive. Later, the M.D. rebuked his staff for not alerting him in time. The next day, the M.D. slipped in his bathroom and injured his hand. When Pūjya Gurudev heard about it, he visited him at his bungalow to inquire about his welfare. The M.D. was deeply touched by the gesture. That day, Pūjya Gurudev's spontaneous gesture of humility and compassion taught me the importance of being a good human being.

THE FINAL SURRENDER
Swami Chinmayananda:

The disturbed mind has no power and feels helpless. When it surrenders to the Lord, it becomes quiet. Desireless mind alone can be silenced effectively. Enter into this experience of dynamic dynamism. Namaskāra means to surrender. When the prostration is complete, there we awake ourselves to the experience of the Infinite. When you get ready to execute His will, the shackles snap! The bolts open! The doors of the prison slide outward, leaving you free to walk out!

Whatever you do, O Lord! Who am I to quarrel with Thee? Does a picture ever quarrel with the painter?

Give away the last penny and ten pennies must and will come. He, the Protector of all, has to replenish the pocket of his devotee, only the giver must have absolute faith and indomitable courage. This is at once the great secret of renunciation.

When this ego is surrendered, the supreme Consciousness explodes into awareness, and all the sense of limitations experienced earlier by the seeker are lifted off his mind in one great heave. In fact, the Supreme is the State of Fearlessness, and yet the dualists are afraid of surrendering themselves completely and ending their ego-sense and thus allowing a total sovereignty for the Supreme even upon himself. In the higher climbs of meditation, the student is jerked out of his equipoise, merely because of his fear to lose his last lingering hold of attachment with his sense of individuality! This inherent psychological fear-complex is one of the most difficult obstacles to cross over on the way to Self-realization. The ability to maintain inner equipoise is gained because of the continuous experience of the higher plane of Consciousness. This is considered as a sure test for the Man of Realization. Life stories of all the saints and sages of the world bring out this common, salient feature in all of them — their ability to keep an undisturbed mental tranquility in spite of the most disturbing environments around them.

Death is your final procession — in which you are absent! Thus, when the ego is surrendered at the altar of the Self, then Realization of the Bliss of Brahman is at hand. Die to Live! You will never understand It. Learn to go and stand under It. That is all. Reach there! What you are now attempting is objective science. Not an iota of this can be smuggled into That. You have to die to relive as Brahman. The ego has to die! The dreamer must die to realize the waker. Death is only the death of false vanities and the delusive ego-sense. When the little 'I' dies, what remains is the Godly and all-pervading, spiritual 'I.'

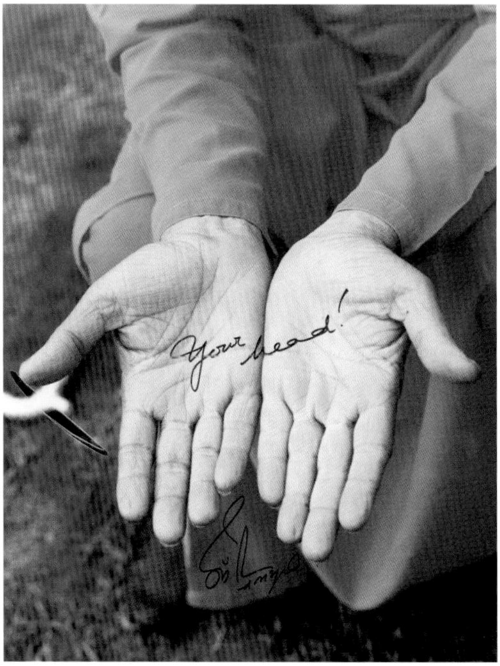

The last leap into That is rather difficult. In this last moment, there will be fear. To move into a new dimension, there is a hesitation; it is fearful. You are attached to what you are used to. Whether he is a yogi or a bhakta, the last leap is fearful. Fear is only in the state of plurality. The devotees insist upon the eternal existence of both, the individual ego and the total Self. According to them, they want to enjoy the vision of the Supreme as an object independent from themselves. This is their only method of expressing an inward fear, which they entertain about totally surrendering their egocentric personality. This fear can be quietened by the Vedāntic method of discrimination by the intellect.

In letters to ***Anjali Singh:***

HANDS UP:
SURRENDER TO SURVIVE!!!

When I listen to the cadence of Baby Kṛṣṇa screaming His heart away through His tiny reed, I listen only to a single word that tumbles out of His breath again and again. And this sacred word is "give." In order to add melody and charm to His Divine Song, He often raises the pitch in three stages when the enchanting notes roll up to merge into an infinite Silence. Innocently, it always starts with just a suggestion: "Give." Then in His inordinate enthusiasm, the song gathers a mellifluous dynamism when it warbles: "Give Away." And, lastly, in a tumbling peroration of deafening intensity the song thunders: "Give Up!!" The sound dies away into an overwhelming Silence where I experience nothing but the sweetness inherent in the smile of my infinite Child Divine. Without giving, nothing can be added on to us. To give up is our job; adding on to us the divine glory is His. This dichotomy ends in the zenith of His melody, when all are given up. What is left is only an eloquent Silence of the true Being.

An example of total surrender:

Swami Tejomayananda: I was with him when he was asked, "You are building so many āśramas. What will happen to them and all the work after your departure?" His answer was simple: "I felt like doing this work, and I did it for the Lord. After this, if," and he pointed to me and many people, "they want to continue, then they will continue." In an organization, changes constantly happen. After Gurudev's Mahāsamādhi, so many people left, and many people thought the Mission would break down. But Gurudev had said that the Mission came as God's will, and it will stay as long as God wills, and it will also go only when God wills. This is total surrender. To the world, Gurudev appeared as a man of knowledge, action, and wisdom. But deep within was that very special quality of surrender and devotion. "Nārāyaṇa … Nārāyaṇa … Nārāyaṇa …" was his constant chant with which all his actions were dedicated. He was always in tune with his Guru and the Lord.

Surrendering to His will is the ultimate secret. Devotees recount:

Christine Grimmer: Surrender is deeply interconnected with faith and devotion. In various ways, Gurudev helped us to understand that surrender to the Guru is practice for surrender to God. It's not easy, especially for those among us who have a healthy self-confidence (read here: ego) and conviction that we can and should work everything out, including spiritual inquiry, with our head. Gurudev has shown me in so many ways that there is, in fact, very little that I can 'work out' or get right at all.

Uma Shergill: I was hesitant to go for just two days to Bengaluru with Pūjya Gurudev to a Mahātmas' conference, "What if I am not allowed into the conference?" "If it is an open meeting, then you come inside; if not, then you stay outside!" said Gurudev. It turned out to be a closed-door meeting and I was not allowed to go in! When there were no tickets for the return flight to Mumbai, Gurudev said: "Doesn't matter. Send her back to Delhi. She can go back tomorrow!" I felt angry. I thought, "What was the point in asking me to come?" Later, I was told that an economy ticket to Mumbai was available. But Gurudev was in business class; I would not even get to sit next to him! Next morning, I went early to the airport. While I was waiting at the counter, Gurudev arrived, waved at me, and sailed through security. This annoyed me even more. Finally, the counter opened and there was one seat available right next to Gurudev's seat in business class! I went through security and found Gurudev leaning against a pillar with his arms folded. He said: "So much agitation! So much agitation for two days! If I have asked you to come here, did you think I would leave you behind?" It was a jolt of lightning! Since that day, I never questioned him. I just did what he told me to do. On that day, I learned complete surrender. It was a life-changing incident.

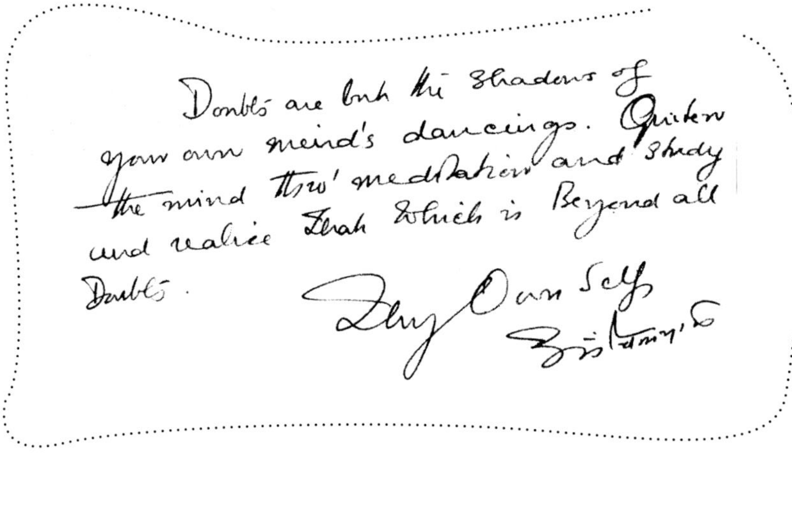
Doubts are but the shadows of your own mind's dancings. Quieten the mind thro' meditation and study and realise that which is Beyond all Doubts.

Thy Own Self
Chinmaya

16

Maintain the Tempo

Swamiji said, "Maybe Bruguera cannot maintain the tempo for two days. Then he needs a rest!" His next remark was, "Sheldon is also like that. His serves are good but the strokes are casual. If they happen, it's wonderful!" Later, when Swamiji was not watching any tennis, he made a remark about a tennis player "being ready to hit the ball, when it comes, with the racket with both hands. But if there is no time to hit it with both hands, then even with one hand, because it is possible to miss it, as the ball is so fast. Come on! You are losing time. It is only for one day. Hit the ball!"

When extraneous thoughts, other than the goal, are excluded from the mind — an integrated energy is generated. But it is difficult to "maintain the tempo." Therefore, when the energy is there, the Guru's advice is to remain very vigilant, ready to receive the Guru's grace "hitting the ball, when it comes, with the racket with both hands." These are moments when we can be awakened, or at least get 'glimpses' of the higher Reality. The glimpses come in quick flashes "the ball is so fast." We have to simply be vigilant – be "ready to hit the ball."

THE WAFTING FRAGRANCE

The mind never remains in one state; it is either in ascent or descent. This is normal as one practices contemplation. When the mind becomes integrated after long practice, then the bliss within, which is the reflection of the true nature of the Self, begins to be experienced like a wafting fragrance. This is savikalpa samādhi making its first tentative entry! Then a meditator gets convinced that all his problems are gone forever. However, because visits of the 'gleam of God' enchant the mind so fully, the withdrawals are felt with keener sorrow. One feels like a fish out of water when the whiff of bliss gets covered again. In the earlier stage of 'vāsanā purging,' the oscillation is between turbulence felt in the mind and feeling normal. Here, it moves up one level; now it is the oscillation between feeling blissful and feeling normal! However, the normal feels worse than the earlier turbulence because one has tasted a bliss that one had never imagined before and the contrast is felt more keenly. The striking thing about certain statements of the scriptures — for example, 'Yoga comes and goes' — applies at every level. Even the quality of bliss takes a different form in vividness and purity as one's mind gets more integrated and advances to the next level of sādhanā.

Swami Chinmayananda:

If concentration were that easy, meditation would be an everyday event, and all of us would rise to a supremely higher state overnight. It is indeed rare for us to be able to keep up the tempo of concentration. But you can get it by continued untiring effort. It could very well be a lifetime project … so, don't despair, and never give up.

When the outer world of sense-objects is conquered, the mind of the meditator tries to entangle him in pleasant, heavenly, and subtle sense-experiences. These experiences arise from the 'subtle elements' and are delusions of the meditator's own mind.

If the study of the *Gītā* gives the scholarly student an intellectual and objective picture of the goal and the path, a few drops of the Ganges sipped from the hollow of his palm give to the ardent devotee the flicker of a joyous vision of the distant goal. To him, the harbor is no more too far away because he has seen the flashes from the lighthouse! And yet, he is still in the open sea of life, buffeted by the stormy waves of sorrows around him. But he has hopes; he is now confident. The harbor is not far and he makes a dash toward it.

That state is called yoga when there are no more vagaries of the mind. This yoking of the attention with the Higher has got both a high tide and a low tide. Even for the Mahāpuruṣas (great Spirits) in the Himalayas, who are doing this full time, even for them, every day is not a Sunday.

Yoga comes and goes. When yoga comes you enjoy it, and if it goes, it is because some vāsanā in you has emerged out. It has to exhaust itself. Because of that disturbance from within, the mind does not quiet itself. Thus, yoga — the integration of your personality, the continuity of attention to the Higher, the yoking of your attention away from objects, emotions, and thoughts to Nārāyaṇa — is never steady. On certain days it is wonderful, and on certain days it is vulgar. People get frightened or despair and run away. It is not your mistake. Some vāsanā that was already in the mind has come out. The days that it is not all right, you must congratulate yourself, because your meditation has become effective: it is bringing the dirt and the filth, which was down below in the mind, to the surface. It is quite natural; so do not get perturbed by it.

Whenever the mind is quietened, a ray of the infinite Bliss comes out.

Each time the understanding happens, but because the mind has not been purified, it gets covered again with ignorance. So one should not feel dejected at such times. When the real understanding happens, the mind will disappear altogether and there will be no fall.

Seek Him in yourself. In the hushed silence of inspired joy, in the roaring laughter of silent meditation, in the motionless dance of ecstasy, in the freezing heat of tapas — He whispers His deafening message: "I am you – you are Me."

Letter to ***Dr. Kambham Suhasini:*** Joy will break when mind gets agitated. You, as a Vedāntic student, should never get involved in these moods of your mind. Don't identify with the mind when it is in a dirty mood. At such times lift your mind from its morass by remembering Him who is ever a mass of purity. "They are in me, I am not in them."

Letter to ***Premila Modi:*** A taste for those inspired moments is good. But so long as you crave for it, you can only be away from it. End the craving and be quiet: you are in It. It is the One that illumines the craving; It is the subject 'you,' and craving is the object 'that.' Be in yourself! Everything springs from you!!

Letter to ***Dr. Thangamma Ganapathy:*** In flashes, the Truth is revealed to the sevaks. The experience of the tranquil is never gained in a sudden introduction. Like deep friendship, it can be cultivated from mere acquaintance through extended contact and a sort of mutual appreciation. The experience that you report is a very good sign. And when one constantly gets oneself established in that inward experience and yet works in the world outside, it is most important for others, but an entertaining hobby for you. Continue the sādhanā of study, japa, and meditation as you are now doing. I shall certainly be watching your progress. Don't strain or struggle. Highest concentration comes when there is a total relaxation at the mental level. Refuse to get worried over any actions in the outer world and see the result in meditation. Surrender yourself only to the Lord within, meaning — dissolve your individuality in the total acceptance and self-identification with the Center within.

The first appearances of samādhi *do not stay for long:*

Mimi Robins: My last and most intense experience of Gurudev occurred in 1993 at the last camp. Swamiji had just returned to his room. He settled into a comfortable reclining chair to watch tapes of tennis matches. His eyes intensely followed the play on the court. His body was limp and relaxed, appearing to be like a garment laid out on the chair. I sat on the floor and was soon engulfed in a silence with a peace beyond understanding — a stillness flowing with particles of light that cast no shadows and with pure, undivided love. It was a State of Being I had never before experienced. It was a blessing. Although it did not last, it was a very real State of Being.

Parvathy Raman: I wrote to Gurudev that, in the bustle of the marketplace in Kangra, I could not retain the divine vision. And meditation, too, had its ups and downs. He replied, "Every day is not a Sunday .... In yoga, there is ever a high and low tide. You must have somehow mentally got wounded — any desire not fulfilled, ego got crushed, vanity wounded, expectation not fulfilled — something. Never mind. Surrender to Him, 'They are in Me, I am not in them.' Thus, stay in sākṣi bhāva (witness in a State of Being). Pray. Repeat His names. Read the inspiring portions of the Upaniṣads. Have satsaṅga with Dr. Akhilam (later Swamini Nishthananda). Surrender and come out of this rut. The mind, once back on the rails, will easily jog to the levels where it was before."

The allegorical appearance and disappearance of bliss and how to handle it:

Anjali Singh: The three of us — Swamiji, another lady devotee, and I — were returning in a car from a visit to the Meenakshi Temple near Houston, Texas, on the eve of its inauguration in 1982, when the sky turned inky with dark clouds. Then, an exhilarating network of lightning lit up the entire sky. It would flash on and off for a long time, as if Meenakshi Devi were presenting a special sound and light show for Swamiji, with Indra Devatā throwing in a thunderbolt! Swamiji, sitting in front, was a silent witness to this grand spectacle. However, the lady on my right had her eyes shut tight and was chanting the Mahāmṛtyuṃjaya mantra for safety! I couldn't help interrupting Swamiji's profound silence, as I wanted him to look at her! He turned back and said comfortingly, "The lightning that you see does not have your name on it! The lightning that strikes you, you will never see."

ENCHANTMENT OF JOY

Swamiji helped his students through very subtle adjustments. He took us to silence but then warned against becoming attached to that state, which is still a state of mind. Here, the only sādhanā to be done is not to enjoy the bliss as an object but just to witness it — the same with visions and lights one may see. For that reason, rasāsvāda (reveling in the Bliss of Peace) is also considered as a hurdle in meditation. Without this important tip given by those who have trodden the path, one might continue to remain at the individual perceiver–feeler–thinker (PFT) level as a 'feeler' of joy; whereas, if one is a witness to it, one is witnessing it as Consciousness. One is then not the PFT but the witnessing Consciousness. One's identification stays with Consciousness rather than with the mind, which alone is the feeler or enjoyer of bliss.

Swami Chinmayananda:

When the seeker has transcended or crossed the obstacles of stupor, agitation, and submental impressions, he will thereby reach a state of intellectual equanimity (samādhi), which is a very enjoyable experience, indeed. In fact, it would have the flavor of a transcendental bliss. The seeker should not be a victim of the self-deception in considering that his experience is the Bliss Absolute. It has only, in fact, a counterfeit look of the Real.

In meditation the bliss that you experience is not you; it is His. The bliss is His; He just lets you taste it. The consciousness that you experience is not you. Both bliss and consciousness are His. He lets you have a taste. But thereafter, don't stay there, thinking that that is all or that you have reached. Know that they are His and wait for Him. The Reality can never become an object of your experience. From here, it is not for you to experience Him. When He wants, He will come and lift you up. Wait there for Him.

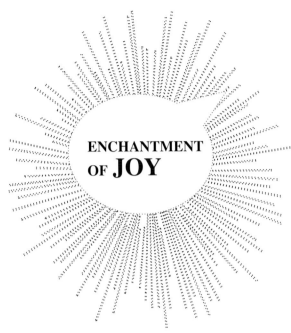

It is the experience of every one of us that the happiness yielded by the world-of-objects is also shot with the poison of sorrow. The mental peace or tranquility that we experience within is much more perfect; and once we get under the intoxicating charm of tranquility during meditation, it is very difficult for us to stand apart from it and still rise above and come to experience the Self. Hence, we are warned that if we be true seekers, we should not come to indulge in and enjoy the bliss, tranquility, or poise which may come to us while we are practicing meditation. Even at that moment of transcendental peace and joy, we must have the sufficient intellectual poise and detachment to stand apart from it and seek again the Illuminator of that inner peace. Renounce and reject all experiences in the plane of duality, until you reach the egoless 'I'-ness of eternal experience.

When the gross world of sense-objects is conquered, and a seeker successfully reaches a certain point of self-discipline, his meditation appears to become rewarding. He starts experiencing some strange things — only some of a million varieties of possibility — such as enthralling visions, fascinating sounds, pleasant smells, melting touches, and delicious tastes. He may experience enveloping darkness, expanding rings of effulgence, a flood of blinding light with or without clouds or melodious music. The mind of the meditator tries to entangle him in such pleasant, heavenly, and enchanting, subtle sense-experiences. These experiences arise from the 'subtle elements' and are delusions of the meditator's own mind. Any experiences that we may get are delusory projections of the dying mind, however satisfying and gloriously divine they may seem to be. They are to be rejected, denied, and destroyed. Visions in meditation are enjoyable, no doubt, but they are obstacles. Reject them; go forward. Don't hesitate to enter the innermost.

A great influx of joy is experienced by a mind in meditation. This joy is a million times more powerful than the world's paltry joys, which are in themselves difficult to leave, so one gets stuck in enjoying them. This is called rasāsvāda. Such a person has not annihilated the mind totally. Do not get caught up in that joy. When that joy comes, you remain detached: "I am the perceiver; I am not the object, the joy." Even at that time, do not stop your effort.

We must reject them all and rise above them. On the peak of purity dwells the infinite Self, the one eternal Substratum for all the illusory world perceptions and experiences. In order to arrive there and awaken to our own true Nature Divine, we have to leave all other perceptions and end our participation in the world of plurality. Unless we leave this plane of existence, the Higher cannot be gained. Nothing of 'this' can ever be successfully smuggled across the frontiers into 'That.' The State of Self-hood is unique; it transcends all the experiences of the lower plane.

In the stage called nidhidyāsana (abidance in the Supreme), the contemplation flights are higher and a person's intensity of concentration is more pointed and firm. A seeker slowly comes to manifest a certain amount of divinity and godliness at this stage.

At this stage, if a seeker is steady in his sādhanā and can still maintain his divine urge to know and to become, if he is passionate enough to reject and renounce even the powers and joys of Godhood, he, during the highest flights of his deepest meditation, wafts even beyond the yonder summits of sattva, and becomes sāttvatita, or one who has transcended even the gods. He experiences in himself the supreme Truth and becomes That. Having reached Om and merging in Om, he becomes Om.

Should one speak of one's experiences in meditation?

Anjali Singh: One of the people who had stayed back after the camp in Sidhbari in 1993 was Naresh Saran. He began to tell Swamiji some of the experiences he was having in meditation. Swamiji put a finger to his lips, indicating that they should not be spoken of in public. "It happens. It is nothing great to get so excited about!" he said. Later, I asked Swamiji why he advised Naresh not to talk of it to people. Swamiji said, "Not that you can't, but sometimes it happens that when you tell someone who might even be very close to you, and the person doubts and makes fun of you, your meditation will get disturbed."

Many devotees have reported parting gifts of grace:

Prarthna Saran: To get Gurudev for days on end, entirely to a handful of us, was his generous parting gift to us. He actually suggested to Naresh and me that we not go back home until he was resting at Sidhbari! While he watched tennis, we all sat around; it was a mind-negating experience, if at all I can call it an 'experience'! While my hands were active in the sevā of massaging his feet, my mind was continuously in silent japa. Totally stilled, my mind reached a no-thought zone. No thought, not even of the others sitting around, not even of my own body, remained. It was a 'peace that passeth all understanding.' I was in a homogenous limitless mass of nebulous bliss that totally engulfed me — silent, timeless, formless, limitless, unsurpassed. Lending words to the silent communion, Gurudev wrote to me after leaving India for the last time on the 18th of June 1993, "When hearts melt and fuse, communication becomes redundant."

17

Psychologically Set

Swamiji was watching Jim Courier play in the French Open 1993 on television. Referring to Courier, Swamiji said, "Now he can win because he is psychologically set correctly!" Till now, Sergi Bruguera had been Swamiji's 'horse' in the tournament.

Swamiji, by saying "psychologically set," was referring to seekers who have practiced karma yoga, purified their minds, and have achieved mental equipoise. The seeker is then psychologically set to enter the arena of deep meditation.

Swamiji would sometimes say, "You have to be born in Kerala to realize Brahman." We would think he is being partial to his home state, Kerala. But Swamiji was a creative thinker. He would use different terminologies with different people. In *Hymn to Badrinath,* he likened 'Badri' to the State of Realization, and the 'land of Kerala' to the launching pad. Psychologically set refers to that state of mind indicated by the 'land of Kerala,' the take-off stage to Realization. This is a peaceful and joyful state, a kind of plateau before the final take off, where the dire problems related to the mind have lessened and one has crossed over the hurdles of meditation. One has to just be vigilant not to fall back into the world and to wait for the Lord.

In 1993, during his last camp in Sidhbari, Swamiji explained how to take the napping ego by surprise and take off. He said, "If I say, 'Let us contemplate, stop thinking! Go beyond!' Contemplate on what? The unborn Mind. Your mind — unborn! Only after birth can the mind tickle you. Just before your mind is born, there is no mind. You cannot experience it, no doubt. But you have been set in a certain direction. That which is indestructible, permanent, immutable, upon which change is playing about, dancing about — contemplate on that higher Reality, exclusively! Withdraw the mind from the hungers and thirsts and turn it toward God!" Swamiji said, "Having thus set the student on the path and having equipped the pilgrim with the necessary knowledge, the teacher in the *Muṇḍaka Upaniṣad* says to the seeker: 'Godspeed. Good luck en route. May you go pleasantly beyond the kingdom of darkness into the Light of all lights, by whose Light alone all other lights are ever lit up.'"

THE SPRINGBOARD

When the Guru has seen the student through the most difficult period and is confident that the student is on the right track, he lets him experiment on his own, while watching him from behind, to find the Truth in his seat of meditation. Even this is quite a high state to achieve, and many are content to stay in it. It is a state of utter peace within, and, in its deeper moments, it holds a peace that passeth all understanding. Sometimes the experience is that of the remnants of the mind having gone to the depth of a soundless ocean. This is still the savikalpa samādhi state. As one practices samādhi more and more, its texture deepens. This is the plateau to which all religions, paths, and sects take a seeker, and this is almost all the way (so to say, about 95 percent) of the spiritual journey. However, this experience is still at the mental and intellectual level. This is the next to the prefinal experience before Self-realization; its translation into concepts is varied. When a seeker reaches this plateau, it is here that Truth is conceptually envisioned as either 'nothingness' or 'sat-cit-ānanda' or 'matter and Spirit' or 'God in every form' or 'no forms, only God.' There are many who reach the state of savikalpa samādhi, or the experience of Godhood, but they cannot always remain in It, since it is not the final State, which is the only one that remains un-negated and un-contradicted in 'time,' 'place,' or 'state,' as It supports these as well. It is the science of Vedānta that takes a seeker to the realization that "I am the Self," where all duality is totally negated, even the duality that I am separate from God. In truth, God, Brahman, or the final Reality is absolute, and the Nature of Absoluteness does not allow anything to limit Its absoluteness. The final lap of the journey (so to say, the remaining 5 percent) is accomplished by sheer grace, which is ever present as the blessing of the Lord or the Guru.

Swami Chinmayananda:

Equipoise is a state of mental equilibrium that comes when one has unshakeable intellectual foundations and the mental capacity to soar to the highest pinnacles of a greater vision.

The steadiness of our mind and the acuteness of our intellect are not accidental happenings but are the products of continued and conscious living of the Life Divine.

The tranquil mind, rendered temporarily peaceful as a result of spiritual practices, is the 'pad' from which the meditation must rocket up into the higher, infinite Consciousness. Only in the realization of the Self can complete transcendence be achieved.

The God State of Consciousness is not something you can experience through the mind, because the mind can only experience that which has form or quality. But what are we searching for? Consciousness! All experiences of the mind are shining in the Light of Consciousness.

Reject all hairy men if you are looking for a bald-headed short man. Reject everything of the mind when looking for the Self, the unborn mind. You know what is decaying; try to know what is God, the undecaying. You know what change is; now turn your attention to the Permanent, the Changeless. When you want It exclusively, and It alone, It happens. It is not an exaggeration; like sleep happens, and when you want it and it alone, sleep sucks you in.

Reject all experiences; seek the Consciousness that illumines the boundless 'light' and limitless 'bliss.' Reject light and bliss; seek the Subject. Never strain. Never demand. Just meditate. Be in meditation, expecting nothing, wanting nothing, desiring nothing.

"On the basis that all the five sheaths are delusions, when I negate them, I find a state of sheer non-entity, a total absence of everything, an empty void," cries out the disciple. This is the despair of the intellect when spiritual ideas are merely thought of by it. This is where the Nihilists reached and cried out that the experience of total annihilation and complete negation of everything is the Reality. They insisted that pure non-existence is the ultimate Truth. And yet, the teacher said, "What remains, is to be known by the wise man." The disciple questions here, "When there is a total negation of everything, then, at the end, I find only a void remaining. I find naught therein. What then is to be known by the wise man?" The teacher answers, "Behind the naught is the Knower knowing the nothingness! When all the five sheaths have been negated, what remains?" "Nothing" says the disciple. "But who is knowing that there is nothing?" asks the teacher. "I," answers the disciple. "Who is this 'I'?" asks the teacher. It is this 'I' factor, the Subject, which the teacher is trying to indicate.

The negation of everything (the state of void, or nothingness) is not the Reality. Behind the 'naught' is the Knower knowing the nothingness. When I say something is not, it doesn't mean negation of the something. When I say there is something, it also does not mean I am affirming the something. These are only my own intellectual estimation of things. The Self illumines both these intellectual conclusions equally. This Self is not bound by the logic of the intellect — It is ever the spiritual Fact.

Negation is a dangerous process; overemphasized, without guidance, and without precise knowledge of its implications, it might lead a hasty student into a state of 'dark nothingness' or 'utter non-existence.' This was the tragedy arrived at by a serious school of Buddhist Nihilists.

To contradict the idea that 'Nothingness is truth' and to indicate that there IS a positive, vitally dynamic, immutable and eternal Truth behind the seeming world, it is said that the only truth is the Nameless, the one Light of Consciousness. All other things experienced are delusory superimpositions upon the great Substratum. Just as the dream experiences are, in fact, lived through by the dreamer but have no reality of their own, so, too, the plurality exists only as long as the Infinite is not experienced.

Suppose I remove this book from the top of the table and ask you, "What is there?" … Your answer will certainly be, "Nothing." Now, supposing I point out not only the book but also the table upon which the book is lying, and after bringing the table that carries the book to your attention, if I remove the book and repeat the same question, you will implicitly, effortlessly, and naturally cry out, "That is a table." When you are aware of the table and the book, and then negate the book, the presence of the table is felt. But if your attention is only on the book, you are not taking into consideration the table that supports the book, and then when the book is removed (negated), even while looking at the table, you will experience and cry out, "There is nothing." Vedānta avoids this practical difficulty. First, the superimposition of names and forms upon the Truth was described; and then the world of names and forms, superimposed upon Brahman, is negated totally, and Brahman is indicated as the positive, eternal Reality.

When you see the all-pervading Consciousness and Bliss, remember, the carrot has still to be scraped! After the negation of the false, realization is complete only when we come to live the vital Truth in Itself. Negation of the ghost should be immediately followed by the assertion of the positive existence of the post.

Go deeper and deeper. Forget the body and the very act of meditation, and seek… seek within for the Light that illumines the seat of all our consciousness, the well of life in us. When concentration is developed, all sādhanā is almost at an end.

The path of meditation is difficult — not so much for the meditator to practice as for the teacher to describe and initiate an ardent student into it. There are more chances for the student to misunderstand the lay of the path. But once the idea is clear and he is set on the path, guidance thereafter becomes unnecessary, for he will be steadily progressing onward on a royal path, cut ever so very straight to the Palace of Truth.

Having thus set the student on the path and having equipped the pilgrim with all knowledge, the teacher in the Upaniṣad says to the seeker: "Godspeed. Good luck en route. May you go pleasantly beyond the 'kingdom of darkness' into the Light of lights, by whose Light alone, all other lights are ever lit up."

*Letter to **A. Balakrishnan:*** This is spiritual dawn! This inner glow in satisfaction in study, reflection, and meditation is the first burst of light peeping out at the eastern sky, long, long before the sunrise. That is That! Sincerely continue. Smile away at the imperfections of the fools around us. Rise above their clamor and noisy blabberings, and live in your own inner understanding.

***Swami Tejomayananda,** amid a conversation on how long the journey would be from Uttarkashi to Jaipur, commented:* "Do you know which the longest journey is? … The longest journey is from yourself to your Self!"

A quiet mind is still a mind:

Anjali Singh: In 1993 on a train journey from Hyderabad to Vishakapatnam, Swamiji said, "You are seeking the unborn Mind but what you are looking at is a quiet mind. Your attention is still on the mind. The moon shines in the bucket and you feel happy looking at it. When you can look up at the original, why do you want to look at the reflection? The reflection can get shattered when the water is disturbed. No reflection of the moon can be the true moon. A quiet mind is still a mind. The moon that you see in the bucket is still a reflection. It is not the moon."

No sincere student should expect any immediate reward. This practice has to be continued ceaselessly for a long period of time:

Swami Mitrananda: In 1988, as a Yuva Kendra member, I was attending Gurudev's Vivekacūḍāmaṇi Marathon Camp in Sidhbari. On one of the days at the camp, I asked Gurudev, "Swamiji how can I get your pādukās (sandals) to worship?" He looked at me and said, "It's very difficult!" and walked away. I kept quiet, not knowing how to respond to Gurudev's words. I was confused and was wondering if it was a 'yes' or a 'no.' Will I get them or not? On the same afternoon, Gurudev sent word for me through Shivaramji. I ran to his kuṭiyā with a slim hope that Gurudev may give his pādukās to me. But there, I found an elderly devotee, Narayan Kutty, sitting at Gurudev's feet. When he saw me, Gurudev pointed to a new pair of pādukās that he was wearing and said, "This is for you, but Narayan Kutty Amma will keep them. Whenever you want to pray, go to her house and pray. The pādukās are for you only after her." I was thrilled with joy and nodded in agreement. He laughed loudly and added, "Now, don't be in a hurry to get them!" Once again, I did not know how to respond, and all I could mutter was, "Yes, Swamiji! Yes, Swamiji." I knew Narayan Kutty Amma, a senior citizen, for a long time, as she lived on the street that was next to my home. She lived alone. There was nobody else to take care of her. We have to appreciate Gurudev's love and compassion for her. He made sure I would visit her often, and if she needed anything, I would do those small errands and be of some service to her. Many times I would bring her to Mission programs and drop her back home. This continued until I went to the Sandeepany Sadhanalaya. Even later, as an Ācārya, on important occasions and before undertaking new projects, I would visit Amma and offer my salutations to the pādukās, and Gurudev's words would remind me that I should not be in a hurry to get them. Narayan Kutty Amma had told me very many times, "Gurudev gave these pādukās for you only and told me to keep them for you. I am only a caretaker." In the year 2013, Narayan Kutty Amma had become weak and very frail. Three months before she passed away, she came to the Chinmaya Heritage Centre in Chennai with a lot of effort and emotion to hand over the pādukās to Guruji and narrated the whole story to him. Guruji placed the pādukās on my head. When I walked with them to my room, I remembered and understood what Gurudev meant when he said, "It's very difficult." I knew I was not in a hurry, but waited twenty-five years for them! Through this episode of the pādukās, Gurudev taught me to love and be detached at the same time. I also learned that I cannot reach HIM; all I can do is only wait for HIM to reach me. Those pādukās are now placed in the 'Call of the Rishi,' an exhibition of Gurudev's life and mission in Chennai.

Invoking God's help:

Anjali Singh: Swamiji had to leave Sidhbari in 1992 for a few days, traveling via Delhi to Germany for a meeting. In the train, I got a chance to tell him that no 'Bt' (my nickname for 'breakthrough,' or an exceptionally rare and good meditation) was happening. He quoted from *Vivekacūḍāmaṇi,* "Man eva manuṣyanāman kāraṇam bandha mokṣyoho," meaning, "The mind alone is the cause of both bondage and liberation." He added that some mental block was there. He advised, "A very important thing to 'say' before meditation, not (actually) 'say,' but have the attitude, 'O Lord! You have brought me this far — now, also, You take me further.'"

KNOW THE MOMENT

When a seeker has been practicing Self-inquiry for some time, his mind becomes poised and integrated. Whether it is through devotion, inquiry, meditation, or the Guru's grace, he starts having glimpses of the higher Self. He might feel a sudden expansion of space, a 'bigness' embracing the whole world — the 'here.' He might also feel the eternity of time in the present moment — the 'now.' Or he may sense the blissful shimmering of Consciousness in all things. These are moments that take one forward by leaps and bounds. When these moments happen, one should just remain in the awareness of one's identity with the Divine. It is important to recognize that the true 'experience' of the Self cannot be objectified. There are many sincere people who have come to this point and not gained entry to the Beyond, because they did not have 'knowledge' of the true nature of Reality.

Swami Chinmayananda:

When the mind stands thus in utter nakedness, it is the no-mind. And that is the auspicious moment of illumination.

All spiritual practices in all religions of the world are techniques — either emotional, intellectual, or physical — which aim at bringing about at least one solitary moment of perfect mental poise. Such a moment of poise is a moment of perfect mental illumination, the auspicious hour of Self-rediscovery and fulfillment of the reunion.

When the student is ready to receive the divine message, a casual instruction from the teacher is more than sufficient to set the student on the flight to the State of Pure Consciousness.

Contemplation ends when we reach the 'state-of-meditation.' To hold ourselves steady in that poise in the sacred moment when we glide into a higher State of Consciousness — call it Self-realization or Revelation of God, call it by whatever name you like — you are there in a new dimension of Consciousness. "IT happens," the scriptures assert.

To a true student, revelation of the Self comes instantaneously during his intense listening in rapt attention.

The sacred moment is not long and enduring in the first few instances of experiencing. Those moments come in flashes, so quick and sudden, that a meditator, unless he is extremely sensitive and extraordinarily alert in his sharpened awareness, will miss these moments of illumination. Once you find the moment, stay there for as long as you can.

When a meditator's mind has thus become hushed into a relatively quiet attitude, his meditation gathers an extra flight and efficiency. His mind is filled with the cool content of peace, and an unearthly joy spreads and dances in his heart. This state of expansion within, which invokes an unusual quality of inner joy and thrill, leaving behind for some time a subjective sense of holiness and contentment, is the first experience that assures the student of a richer reward awaiting him at the end of his journey. Once the student experiences this joy, he will never more become irregular in his meditation. All other external obstructions get rejected and ignored. Nothing can any longer entice the seeker away from his regular meditation sessions.

If you can catch a moment in time when the heart is touched, but the mind is not in pain or shock but is quietly expectant, it can do wonders for you. Actually, even a shock in life can take you very far spiritually, because a shock also causes a momentary quietude. But few people have the nerve or the guts to make a getaway through the gateway of that pause. The pain of the situation keeps the mind in confusion and self-pity.

Your goal is to make your identity with the ego disappear into the vision of the eternal Self. Be — just BE. This will move you to ecstasy by giving you a gleam of the Spirit that shines through the heart of all things. It will be but a cloudy vision at first and the early visions will disappear, each in resplendent, quick succession. Let them go and then reappear. Each glimpse revives, rejuvenates, resurrects. Thereafter, the meditator's personality totally changes, and, in the end, it comes to shine with an unearthly poise and serenity.

The vital moments of silence that we reach in meditation are eternal islands of Truth among endless billows of life's activities, temptations, struggles, and desires. We are not accustomed to this inner silence. We are like foreigners, self-exiled from our own real nature of peace and serenity. We do not know how to delve into this silent, vibrant existence and translate it into a way of living at once divine and omnipotent. When we are completely and totally in that state of silence, we are in the realm of Truth. This state, in which I am now in contemplation, is Me. A new vision, an awakening comes. It is not something I am 'experiencing.' In fact, there is nothing more for a human being to achieve. In that moment of silence — if we can consciously gain entrance into the message of its vitality and come to live its full glory — we would be living the very destiny of Godhood. Unfortunately, for many of us, when we reach there, we don't know it for what it is and fail to understand our experience: that it is, indeed, the experience of the Supreme, the Eternal.

'Experience' without knowledge is incomplete:

I meet a man in a public park and fall into a long and pleasant chat with him. That individual may be the very one whom I have been eager to meet for a long time; yet, unless I have the knowledge that the man whom I have been talking to in the park is the same individual I have been searching for, I will not, in that experience of accidental meeting, gain the real satisfaction. Similarly, though in that silent moment in meditation we may be experiencing the absolute Self within us, we do not feel the consummate satisfaction of the experience because we do not know: "This is That."

With Knowledge, this silent experience starts to give us the joy that it actually contains. It is in this sense that the scriptures declare that liberation can never be had without Knowledge. It then becomes our duty to charge our mind with the exact identity and nature of this 'zero point,' which otherwise may be misunderstood as a void. Once we understand that this vital moment is pregnant with potentialities, we will come to experience, more and more, the real nature of the Self, which is Brahman, the all Self. With this idea in mind, when you have reached that silent moment in your meditation, before entertaining any other thought, either chant or bring to mind any of the following verses, losing yourself fully in the meaning. Written by the famed Vedāntin Śaṅkarācārya, these verses are known as "The Song of Supreme Knowledge" (Brahma Jñānāvalī): "Unattached, unattached, unattached am I, again and again…"

Though it is so difficult to attain, we must never stop trying. This may be the last lap in our race to Perfection; this may be our last birth. We don't know when it is coming — it may come by evening! Because we do not know the exact moment when the favorable conditions will get established, we are thus unaware when the grace of the Lord will baptize us to bestow upon us this experience Divine! So, we must put forth our consistent, fullest effort. And if we are putting forth our best efforts, our faith in it shall increase. The promise of the ṛṣis is, "One with faith gains the Highest."

Inspired moments of wisdom are possible in rare moments of life — during study or when listening to a Master, and at similar instances. At such moments, an individual gets a glimmer of the higher possibility of the greater Consciousness. But rare indeed is the man who is completely established in his identity with the Higher. Such men who are established in the higher Consciousness are called sthitaprajña — 'rooted in Consciousness.'

Once the mind has started seeing things as they are — the immutable Reality is glimpsed by that mind. When this experience becomes more and more established in one, that individual becomes a God-realized saint, liberated-in-life.

Each time the understanding happens, but because the mind has not been purified, it gets covered again with ignorance. So one should not feel dejected at such times. When the real understanding happens, the mind will disappear altogether and there will be no fall.

*In a letter to **Śrī Trivedi:*** When japa takes you to a point of supreme inner Peace, the japa has done its best, has taken you to its destination. Learn to remain unperturbed at that point steadily. There it should happen!!

Missed the moment? Who knows whether an upadeśa or blessing bides its time in the atmosphere till one is ready to receive it? It is like an arrow that has been shot in the air, charged with the immense power of transformation that must, one day, find its target — the heart!

***Swami Chidrupananda*:** Once, out of the blue and totally unexpected, I received a letter from Gurudev. It was neither a reply to a question nor an acknowledgement to any letter, but the message was loud and clear. I had just returned from Sidhbari after attending the Mahā Śivarātri celebration in 1992. Gurudev said, "The Lord lives in the depths of our hearts. He is neither sat (gross), asat (subtle), or sat–asat, or the cause of sat–asat (vāsanās). He alone is. Nothing else. Seek Him and know it as your own essential nature." I was very happy to see the letter and its message. A thought flashed in my mind for a moment: how nice it would be if I was ready to receive it, but I was not. I missed it, I felt. It was a postal upadeśa given out of his compassion and love.

THE BLISS OF SAMĀDHI

Swamiji seemed to enjoy nothing more than seeing his students reach a state of inner stillness and peace. He had said that he is waiting at the doorway to the eternal Divine, waiting for us all to come with him. He would encourage people to stay in that state of attunement. His very presence would take people into that deep peace called 'samādhi' in Vedānta. Sustained contemplation eventually turns into samādhi, or absorption, or the state of meditation. The mind finds its depth in a single thought, "I am Brahman." Savikalpa samādhi is contemplation's final shape — a very advanced form of contemplation, full of joy. There is only a thin veil therein between the jīvātma (individual soul) and Selfhood. In savikalpa samādhi, while there are minor ups and downs of the mind, the downs are just gentle waves. The experience of bliss becomes most powerful now that the mind is attenuated and most of the subconscious wrong impressions have been cleansed. In contemplation (nididhyāsana), the seeker puts in effort to maintain the thought "I am Brahman," whereas in savikalpa samādhi, this thought flows effortlessly, thereby becoming yet subtler. The seeker should understand that savikalpa samādhi is not the culmination; hence, he should continue to deepen his practice of samādhi. The very abidance in savikalpa samādhi leads one to the thoughtless nirvikalpa samādhi. How? The thought "I am Brahman" of the savikalpa samādhi puts an end to ignorance. Also, being a thought and therefore being a part of ignorance, it also comes to an end when ignorance ends. Nirvikalpa samādhi thus opens the doorway for the Illumination (vijñāna, or Knowledge realized through experience) by actualizing the knowledge (jñāna) that one has gained through listening (śravaṇa), reflection (manana) and contemplation (nididhyāsana). In nirvikalpa samādhi, one does not just know Brahman, but one is Brahman.

Swami Chinmayananda:

To stay, as I am, is the present. This condition is samādhi — śama (calmness) + dhi (buddhi, or intellect) = no flux. The thought takes place because of vāsanās, (latent tendencies). When the last thought has ended, and a new thought is not yet born, then what am I? Pure, objectless awareness — objectless awareness of pure Consciousness is the present. When I am in the present, there are no thought waves. Since there are no thought waves in the body, mind, or intellect, naturally, there are no objects, emotions, and thoughts either. The entire world thus appears to have dissolved and rolled into me.

In the steady movement of contemplation, you will enter an atmosphere of pure bliss. This floods forth and drowns you in bliss (ānanda), or the revelry of the bliss experience. Just as in an undisturbed lake the heavens are reflected honestly, so is this state of samādhi, a state where there is no more any contact with the outer objects, a state where you are well settled in the Ātman. There you experience that supreme State from which nothing has ever come.

Samādhi is of two kinds, with thoughts, savikalpa, and with no thoughts, nirvikalpa. The former is popularly known as the state of contemplation, and the latter is called the state of meditation. In the state of contemplation, savikalpa, the contemplator has an awareness of the subject-object relationship, technically called the triputi, the triad. When the subject and object are merged into one awesome state of infinite Existence, that state is called total absorption, nirvikalpa.

Before the final experience of Oneness, "He am I," there is a lower state of realization that "I behold Thy glorious form" wherein the ego still remains experiencing a divine exaltation. This stage is called savikalpa samādhi. This precedes the final stage of the total end of the ego when the seeker rediscovers himself to be the sought — the supreme Self. The culmination of evolution, however, is the state of nirvikalpa samādhi, when the I-ness, or the feeling of individuality itself, merges with the infinite Experience, and what remains thereafter is the one, all-pervading, supreme Reality.

To such an individual, the phenomenal world of plurality itself becomes an experience of the divine Presence. They call it savikalpa samādhi, the state wherein the intellect is capable of apprehending only one Reality — the Reality that he has courted so long, wooed so diligently, and won so completely. It may be the aham-brahmasmi-vṛtti. It may be the soham-hamsa-vṛtti, or it may be Śivoham, Kṛṣṇa, Nārāyaṇa-mayam-jagat, or Christ-mayam-jagat. It can be any one of these according to the attitude (bhāvana) of the seeker and his cultural background. This is the last but one stage, and thereafter this 'I,' recognizing the pluralistic, phenomenal world, dissolves and sublimates into the Infinite (the Nārāyaṇa-vṛtti). In the beginning, 'I,' an entity, a seeker, am separate, and Nārāyaṇa, the goal, the altar of my devotion, is separate from me. To the pure devotee, now there is only 'I' and 'Nārāyaṇa' — the Lover and the Beloved. This is the last stage of dvaita — of a dualistic experience. When 'I' am also liquidated, nothing remains except advaita alone: the Self, Śrī Nārāyaṇa alone, the one infinite Love.

Kṛṣṇa never danced. He was standing, playing the flute, and it was they (the gopīs) who danced. The movements were only in the circumference and not in the center. Kṛṣṇa is the motionless Center in the midst of all movement, the Changeless in the midst of all change, the Immutable in the midst of all mutation. And this is called samādhi, where the intellect is not moving. What philosophy talks about has been picturized [in rāsa-līlā] for the average man to understand. He, by whose mere Presence all activities can take place, is Śrī Kṛṣṇa. Kṛṣṇa would say, "I was in a different level of Consciousness," where He was not even conscious of anything! It is beautifully brought out in that picture, which when expressed in drab, dreary, and naked words, is called philosophy. The same philosophy, when it is poetized and explained, becomes a piece of unforgettable art. So, when you sit down in your seat of meditation, don't complain about the body and its activities. Don't curb anything. Understand that all these activities are taking place only because of Myself … I am this Presence; I am not the activity. Thus, when you withdraw your attention from the BMI (body, mind, and intellect) and be your Self, this attempt to rise into that level of Consciousness is called contemplation …. So don't sit down [in contemplation] and say: "He by whose presence, my body, mind, and intellect are functioning at this moment." Instead say: "I am that Spring of Consciousness, that Spark of Existence, the Light of lights!" Thus assert and learn to wake up to that State.

***Query** from a Postal Course student:* Is samādhi the same as Realization? Is samādhi recognized as being qualitatively different from nirvikalpa and savikalpa? Is this difference only for those who live in duality, or is it different for the experiencer, too?

Swamiji: Samādhi is the condition of the intellect without ripples of thoughts rising when it [the intellect] disappears into the infinite Itself. As when in our waking state we merge toward the deep sleep state, we can conceive many different degrees of sleep (as 20 percent or 80 percent asleep), so, too, can the ego as it gets melted into the experience beyond. The teachers describe two states of samādhi, which declare two degrees of the Experience Divine. When the ego is completely merged (as in deep sleep), there is no 'I' separate from the Self. That is, before Ganga becomes the sea, there is an area of about ten miles which we call as Gangasagar. In this area, the salty taste has already started pervading the Ganges. Yet, it is a river, and only when it reaches the eastern coast of India does it merge totally to become the Bay of Bengal. Think.

*O*f all the mantras, the most powerful and significant one
is the single syllable incantation called 'Om.'
Without Om, no sacred chant has power.
Om is the symbol of the Infinite.

STEP 6

HOW TO LIVE IN SURRENDER

*T*he surrender of the ego is the unveiling of the Divine in oneself, and the degree to which the Divine is manifest, to that degree the individual raises himself in his potency to face life and to remain equanimous in all circumstances.

-Swami Chinmayananda

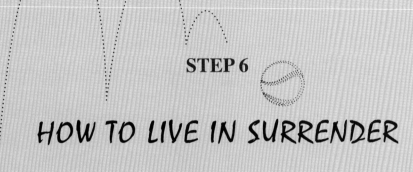

18

"Advantage, Bruguera!"

On June 6, 1993, the French Open had entered the men's final between Jim Courier of the U.S.A. and Sergi Bruguera of Spain. In the first set, when the players had won two games each, a devotee who was backing Courier said, "They are equal at this point. So it won't be unfair if I switch back to backing Bruguera? I want a daring newcomer to get a chance to win. Courier has won major titles before, so my sympathy has gone back to Bruguera! I think he can make it!" Swamiji asked, "You want to change horses?" The devotee replied, "Yes!" Swamiji said, "Nobody changes horses set by set. It is all five rounds that count." Then he conceded, "All right, even now, if you want to change — CHANGE!" The devotee had first backed Bruguera, then changed to Courier, and now was switching to Bruguera again. Swamiji continued, "Don't try to ride on two horses. You will burst into pieces!" As the match progressed and Bruguera began to take the offensive and seemed to have the upper hand, Swamiji said, "If he falls from that high position, he could become psychologically shattered!"

Bruguera was a newcomer in the finals of the French Open. Courier was a seasoned grand slam player. Bruguera represents the enthusiastic seeker, full of devotion, faith and sincerity, who has not gone through the process of study and reflection in a regular way, but wants to go into intense meditation. Courier represents the seeker who has advanced through listening to and reflecting on the teaching and has steadily climbed to higher levels in meditation.

Both players had reached very high levels of concentration because of their individual strengths. Swamiji had warned the seeker earlier that backing Bruguera meant greater risk (odds are higher of losing with a newcomer). However, he was allowing the seeker to back Bruguera, that is, allowing him to pursue deep meditation but warning him not to "change horses" (give up half way) once the final ascent to win had begun.

Swamiji was warning the seeker that if he were to change the decision, "change horses," again and stop the attempt midway, when the flight to higher realms through deeply focused meditation had begun, it might have psychological repercussions. Either this final flight to the Self be delayed to a later time after due preparation (through listening, reflection, and contemplation), or else the seeker must use all his grit and heroism to see it through. The path of deep meditation is difficult only if one has not prepared for it. One needs a climbing kit. The most important items in the kit are faith in the goal and the Guru, and love for God. If these are present, no problem exists that cannot be surmounted. Realized men and women are the guides who can tell us how to reach the ultimate Goal. Therefore, faith in them is necessary. If a living Sat-Guru is there to guide us, we are the most fortunate ones on this earth even when we are not fully prepared to take the leap.

FEARLESS CHOICE

The ascent to the Divine can only happen if we have been making choices that lead us there. This is especially important in the higher stages when the mind has become concentrated. For example, great artists, whose minds are very concentrated, are the nearest to God-realization, but often miss out on it, because they do not direct their artistic energy to God. They do not know what to do with the excessive creativity and often end up directing it merely to outward temptations. Swamiji says, "Generally, we are apt to take an eloquent or deep-thinking philosopher as an ideal person — but, in fact, he may not be an ideal human being. The mystical experience of the transcendental is a thing apart. A mere poet knows not the theme, and a Man of Realization has no medium to express himself. A poet-philosopher alone can handle this art." Is the excellence of man directed at gaining God or limited to gaining a position in the world? By our attitude and direction, we express our choice. A fitting example is the attitude of the musician Tansen, who sang only for an Emperor, and Tansen's Guru, Haridas who sang for God. The former gained a political eminence in the cultural and musical world of the time, whereas his Guru's voice was accredited to be the greater and diviner voice. If a person really wants to attain Self-realization, it is definitely possible for him. However, it is only a few who really want it, and, hence, the rarity.

Swami Chinmayananda:

A child cries: "I hid, but my friend ran to his house and never tried to play with me." God says the same thing: "I hide, but no one wants to seek Me!"

Whether Godhood is an ascent of man to the highest pinnacle of his revolutionizing possibility, or God's descent into man when His divine touch of grace divinizes the individual devotee — in their different arguments, each is pointing to one and the same Truth. In fact, whether the river reaches the ocean or the ocean receives the river, the effect is the same. Truth remains uncontradicted. In both cases — the river reaching the ocean or the ocean receiving the river — the river in its final stage loses its separate qualities and merges to become one with the ocean.

Perfection is not a post-mortem state. It is here and now. This is the birthright of every living human. The time limit of its achievement is only directly proportional to the amount of sincere effort and correct application put forth by the seeker. Regularity, sincerity, and right understanding are the three keystones in the Castle of Perfection.

Self-realization is not an impossibility. Rather, to realize the Godhood that now lies dormant in each one of us is the heritage of mankind. This embodied existence as man is fulfilled only with this superb achievement. If the student has the necessary mental tranquility and the intellectual purity to fly to the heights indicated, if he has the courage to take the plunge, it is impossible for such a student to ever fail to 'understand' this great state.

Liberation is so unique that it will not suffer even an iota of any other mental preoccupation. It must be everything… or nothing. If it is sought with a total mind, it is gained forever. The price to be paid for the experience of the Reality is a total renunciation of the entire range of all desires. For those devotees who have such a constant devotion, the Lord of Badri Himself (God) unveils His infinite glory as the very Self in their own faithful bosom.

Preach Vedānta wherever you will; the fittest alone will hear its message.

Friends, from the above, you should not conclude that, if it is so rare and difficult, none of us would ever succeed. Why not? Are you not the rare few who are regularly attending the Jñāna Yajña? On this globe of ours, in these days of irresponsible and licentious breeding, seething millions are being roasted in sorrow and salted with tears to the devil's own taste! Indeed, are you not then the very few who are listening to this science of life?

The chance to hear is rare. Even when heard, a student who can digest those subtle ideas is rarer. Then to find a Master efficient enough to initiate a student is rarest. Even if a student is lucky enough to have the blessings of all the above three, only the luckiest one comes to experience Godhood in this very birth. But you have no right to be pessimistic. Remember: behind each one of you, there stand a million who can grace only the lower rungs of the ladder of evolution. It is but a mere question of choice. If you cannot be optimistic, you may take it from Chinmaya: You are a fit student, and with a little self-effort you shall reach, in this very birth, the supreme Godly achievement. You have to leave everything for a few moments and turn your entire attention to It.

Many people have reached There. It is not a rare thing for those who have been able to leave three things — attachment, fear, and anger. As much time as it takes to master any profession in life, that much time it takes to master this, if one exclusively wants It, and It alone. When exclusively you want it — and it alone — It happens. This is not an exaggeration. Divine law does not entitle everyone to everything. To attach ourselves to the Divine is to detach ourselves from the un-Divine. To walk into light is to walk out of darkness.

The seeker who chooses the experience of the Self gains it. This choosing is accomplished and declared through our ardent devotion and single-pointed meditation. The consistency, sincerity, and enthusiasm with which a drunkard craves for his drinks, or a lusty man pines for his secret love, or a miser dotes upon his wealth, would be the right measure of the type of unbroken ardency and love a true seeker must have for the Self. The ardency and sincerity of our love is never a secret from the Lord, who is the pure Consciousness in us. It is not possible that we were devoted to Him, but He was not noticing it; for He is the very Consciousness in us, knowing everything at all times.

Letter to ***Dr. Kambham Suhasini:*** "When will this be?" What a question! "When you choose to be" is the scriptural answer — yame-vaiṣa vṛṇute tena labhyaḥ. Both the *Kaṭho* and *Muṇḍaka Upaniṣads* repeat this answer.

Signed in ***Shakuntala Bindra's*** Kaṭha Upaniṣad *book:* Come out of the moodiness and fears, which are the expressions of ignorance, the very realm of death. Invoke the sleeping Nachiketas in you and cry to the world: "You keep your song and dances; we want Thy own Self."

The kind of commitment required:

Daniela Purchase-Schwarz: There is not much of a Hindu Diaspora in Switzerland. Out of a population of 8.3 million people, only 0.5 percent are Hindus. Hence, the group in Switzerland remained small. It is remarkable though that out of such a small group would come seven students attending one of the Sandeepany Vedānta institutes for spiritual studies. The Zurich Study Group of the early years has maintained its momentum. Dr. Aviva Keller, a former Mumbai-Sandeepany student (1981–1983) was, as per Gurudev's instructions, leading it for the last good thirty years.

Swamiji occasionally sent a barb to challenge our sentimental attitude toward liberation:

Anjali Singh: Swamiji was sitting in his kuṭiyā in Sidhbari having satsaṅga with about twenty people. One lady said, "Swamiji, you can do anything. Why don't you bless me? Put your hand on my head and give me mukti (liberation)?" Swamiji straightened himself in his chair in which he was relaxing and said, "You want mukti? I can give mukti!" Everybody looked very alert. "How many of you want mukti?" he asked. Voices of all came up in a chorus of affirmation. He said in a very measured voice, "I can give you all mukti right now, here! But you will die! You will all die, but you will get mukti. How many of you are ready to give your heads right here and now? I will give you mukti! Put up your hands!" Only one person raised the hand. He looked at the devotee and said lovingly, "I know what you want!" Then he looked at the others and said, "Mukti is available, but there are no takers!" Nobody realized that the head he was referring to was the ego and the death he was referring to was the death of the ego into the expansion of the Self!

THE VIGIL

The path of contemplation on the Formless is rather severe. For the majority of seekers to deal with a conceptual topic is rather difficult to manage, even though this path is the straight one and therefore the shortest. Having made the choice to take the straight Vedāntic path to Realization and raise the tempo of meditation, the seeker at this stage has to be careful not to let the mind get distracted by worldly things. The seeker has spent his whole life in the pursuit of sense-objects and chasing the vagaries of the mind. After Realization, he shall have the freedom to roam where he likes. This is the short interim period when a seeker is required to withdraw from the field of action, and hence, if necessary, he has to retire to a solitary place for a while. At this stage, the mind has become highly integrated, and a little diversion can make it accelerate down the hill like a rubber ball. This advice is not to frighten the seeker, but to warn him to be vigilant and alert. Out of fear, one should not give up the goal to climb the path, because a sincere seeker, even if he falls, will land in the Lord's lap, from where he can climb up again when ready.

Swami Chinmayananda:

In Vedānta sādhanā, there are no other by lanes; it is one grand road; it is the shortest, and it shoots like an arrow straight to the goal. The progress in this path is directly proportional to the fuel supplied in terms of sincerity, self-application, and discriminative intelligence.

Sometimes a seeker may all of a sudden come to entertain a very highly optimistic opinion about himself and his mind, and thus jump into a hasty conclusion that he has conquered the mind and has a smooth sailing toward Perfection. Śaṅkara warns us in *Vivekacūḍāmaṇi:* "Even though you have ended the ego along with its roots, the vāsanās can again revive and rise up to tyrannize over you. If you allow your mind this freedom, then the play of the ego-sense will start again. Therefore, beware!"

It is much better to stay on the ground if you don't have the courage to go up; because, if you can't hold on, you will fall! So have faith and courage in yourself.

There is no greater tragedy that can happen in life than Self-forgetfulness, which comes when you have lost your sense of holiness. Forgetfulness of the holiness in you is the death of the spiritual man in you. Scriptures warn that it is easy even for a highly developed student to get lost in the midst of his successes, if he becomes careless for a moment, as it can lead to a great fall.

There is always a continuous pull of the mind and the senses upon the devotee to bring him down into his old habit of living a life of the sense-enjoyments, prompted entirely by his ego and egocentric desires. To live in obedience to the dictates of the śāstras is a mode of life wherein the devotee becomes completely inured against all such chances of a relapse of his old mental disease and the consequent false evaluations of life. He who ignores the injunctions of the śāstras and follows the urges of desires can neither attain perfection, nor happiness, nor the supreme State. These sādhanās are not to be given up in the advanced stage as some of the modern spiritual teachers do now. The total annihilation of ignorance of the Self is ensured only through the sādhanās of the most intense and highest order.

If you do not have the heroism to lift your personality to the ethereal heights of spirituality, away from the false values you have lived before, then do not start this climb. If you stay on the terra firma and fall, the fall will be little, but having started this great, grand pilgrimage to your own home, don't allow yourself to fall. Either you don't start on the mountainous path, or, if you start, then don't lose hold or let go for even a moment's inadvertence. Even if your thoughts run away a little, you can fall right down like a rubber ball.

Many a slip can take place even in the highest stage. Even when a meditator has successfully detached his mind from almost all objects and is steadily striving to lift it into steady contemplation, we often find that he suddenly becomes dispirited, dejected, and even diabolically belligerent with the spiritual path. He experiences a slip — a painful fall. Thereafter, very few have been found to have the guts to get up and walk the path again all by themselves. To realize, through one's own self-introspection, what the causes were in oneself for the fall, is to rediscover the required energy to get up and start moving on the path again. The reason for the fall, of even wise men, is falling away from their attention from their Goal Divine. If the attention is diverted, even a little, the mind tends to become extrovert.

Vigilance is the price you pay to maintain your wisdom. Indeed, this way of life needs diligent effort and consistent self-discipline. Having got the equipment necessary and the powers required to fight against the animalism in him, if an evolved man is not able to grow into his fuller stature of divine mastery over his own lower nature, he is, indeed, laying waste a golden chance, a precious opportunity, a divine occasion to reach the Highest. This achievement, the real fulfillment of life's journey, is within the scope of every mortal.

Letter to ***Pravin Gandhi:*** Be alert. At any moment, the old vāsanās may rise up. Turn to the Light in you. Then you are safe. From there, watch and see the tamas of the ego-trips in others around you.

Letter to ***Madhuri Jhala:*** This is true of everyone — vigilance is the price we pay to live a joyous life of perfection. Be careless — and we slip immediately.

Guru's grace can push us there, but our vāsanās may pull us down:

Ācārya Vilasini Balakrishnan: Gurudev would warn us, "I can give you a tourist visa to Brahma-loka [world or heaven of Brahma], but you need to earn the 'green card' and citizenship yourself! Otherwise, you will find yourself right back in saṁsāra very soon!"

In deeper stages of contemplation, the need for solitude will express itself naturally:

Anjali Singh: During a satsaṅga in Sidhbari out in the open courtyard, Swamiji was in a deep enigmatic mood talking about detachment in that slurry voice which signals that one wants to have nothing to do with interaction with the world. This was during the discussion on the verses on 'vairāgya' at the Vivekacūḍāmaṇi Camp in 1992. Then he went one step higher while talking about detachment and made a profound statement, "But, when the real vairāgya comes, you will leave everything — home, children, Guru, and go into the mountains to be alone for a while." When Swamiji said these words, a Spanish boy, who had been attending a couple of camps in Sidhbari along with his friend, seemed to have taken his words to heart and decided to leave that very day, not knowing whether or not he was ready for this kind of vairāgya. He hitchhiked to Mumbai to catch a plane to Spain and went off to the mountains there, never to be heard of by any of us again!

LEAP OF FAITH

The last leap, from the known to the Beyond, is accomplished with faith. The instruments of the senses, mind, and intellect do not have the ability to transport a seeker there. This faith is not a blind faith, but a faith which is guided by an ideal and a higher vision, which has been reinforced with study and understanding, just as a scientist has faith in the discovery/theory he pursues till it is proven. All knowledge can be understood with the intellect, but to 'experience' the Truth, all known instruments have to be left behind because the seer of Truth is the Self, which is beyond these instruments. We are not able to see our own eyes with a telescope! It just is not possible! In the same way it is illogical to say that Truth, the Self, can be known by the senses, mind, or intellect, as the Self is the very source of our seeing. Our identity with the body, mind, and intellect is so strong that we are afraid to leave them and make the last leap, soaring on the wings of faith to our Self-hood!

Swami Chinmayananda:

There is the authority of the Upaniṣads, wherein the great, mighty Masters, who have reached the Citadel of Truth, have declared from its balcony, "asti, asti, asti — there is, there is, there is!" Have faith in yourself and in the Goal, and put forth the effort in what you believe. As you go ahead, it will get confirmed. God never created you to fail in life.

If, in case a seeker lacks śraddhā (faith) it is not worthwhile for him to continue his pilgrimage. At the level of experience, language falters, stumbles, and lags behind. This last leap is done by śraddhā. That you have to accept what I am saying is not the meaning of śraddhā. Śraddhā is the ability in the human intellect to educate itself and grasp the higher meaning. We drop the contrary ideas by grasping the higher ideas of the Guru and the śāstras. Try to grasp the new dimension of Knowledge. Give up the lower ideas you had before. This self-upliftment in you is called śraddhā. It is a supreme infatuation with the goal you are pursuing. Faith indeed is that secret power in the human mind to hold on to what he intellectually believes but has not yet come to experience (see) in his life. One of the greatest definitions of 'faith' has been given to us by St. Augustine when he says: "Faith is to believe what you do not see, and the reward of this faith is to see what you believe."

Where the scripture stammers to express her thought, faith in a playful glide takes us there. Faith has the power to enter into sacred realms where even the subtlest logic of the Upaniṣadic declarations falters in exhaustion. To such altitude, faith secretly inspires the heart, and with Ariel-like gusto, rockets us up, right into the Absolute. The heights of transcendence to which faith can take us can only be compared with the depth of understanding to which, again, faith alone can take us.

When the boat has reached the other shore, you will not carry the boat on your head, but will jump out of the boat and walk the few steps to the temple. How can we go beyond the intellect with the intellect? The only way I can make you understand is that you consider the pole vaulter, using the pole to clear the ten-foot height. The sportsman advances with the pole, and, at the appropriate time, anchors the pole in the pit and hoists himself up with the help of the pole. At the point when he is crossing the bar, he has to let go of the pole, glide over the bar, and drop down onto the sandpit. Similarly, we reflect with the intellect, and a time comes when the intellect drops by itself, leaving the contemplator in the new dimension of consciousness.

Who is that man who will look through the telescope and say, "I am the telescope!" Who is that man who will look through the eyes and say, "I am the eyes!" Eyes are something I use to see objects. I am different from the objects and the instrument. I am the pure Consciousness that illumines all the objects through the instruments of the body, mind, and intellect.

But when it comes to the actual intuitive experience of Divinity at that sacred moment when the seeker, detaching himself from the body, mind, and intellect, stands hesitating on the lingering frills of a closing intellect — in that dark hour of thrilled emptiness and blissful nothingness, when breathless stands the meditator in an awe-inspiring realm of experience, which is neither the familiar land of thoughts and desires nor the satisfying all-full Brahman — at that gloomy hour of the mystic death, at the darkly lit-up lounge in the Palace of Death, indeed, faith alone, nothing but faith alone, can be our friend, our guide, our comforter, our inspirer.

Listening and obedience to the Guru have their own reward. Don't miss out!!!

Swami Siddhananda: After serving as the resident Ācārya of Chennai, I heard from the local committee member that I was supposed to take up an assignment at Adi Sankara Nilayam. I was unaware that Gurudev had decided this, and I was a bit upset. Gurudev asked me to come to Sidhbari to meet him. I immediately took the train to Sidhbari. When I met Gurudev, he was busy giving instructions. I waited. After some time, he saw me and hugged me. Then he asked, "Are you angry with me?" I said "No, Gurudev." The next day, I went to his room requesting to go back to Chennai, but he repeatedly asked me to stay. However, because of the large crowd at the Vivekacūḍāmaṇi Camp, I decided to return. I did not understand why he was insisting on my staying back. Unable to persuade me, he said, "Ok then, you go." I came to know later that I had lost the golden opportunity to get my sannyāsa dīkṣā from him, and that he had everything ready for the function. Apparently, he never told anyone prior to giving them sannyāsa. It was always a surprise. With this incident, I learned the lesson to never disobey one's Guru.

Can one hold a different viewpoint from that of the Guru?

Anjali Singh: I asked Swamiji in Uttarkashi in 1984, if it was wrong to disagree with one's Guru. I did not agree with him on some of his views on the socio-political scenario of that time. He replied that it was all right if one disagreed with him on intellectual matters, but it was not all right to disagree on spiritual matters. His thought-provoking reasoning was: "If you disagree with the Guru in spiritual matters, then when the time comes for him to say, 'tat tvam asi' (That thou art) to you, you will not understand it!"

Can faith in the Guru be misplaced?

Swami Advayananda: During a camp at Sidhbari, a lady from overseas asked Gurudev quietly, "I have got a doubt! What if this whole thing that you are talking of is a lie? The Guru tells the student; the student has faith, and tells it to his student, and so on. What if this — generation after generation of lies — just gets built up on faith?" Gurudev looked at her compassionately and said, "Don't you think I love you? Why would I tell you a lie? Look at me and look at the people around. Is there no difference? Yes, you are definitely different. There is a something which is not anywhere else. That is because of this Brahman." She was convinced.

Swamiji had suggested a marriage take place between Jyoti Barucha and Ravi Madhavan, both of whom were his devotees; however, they did not know each other and were living in different cities. Before it could happen, Swamiji attained Mahāsamādhi in 1993. Their decision to marry is a testament of great faith:

Jyoti Madhavan: Faith is having total confidence or trust in something or someone. I continually get reaffirmations that keep my faith strong. Whenever I think that something is going wrong, it always ends up turning out for the best. Just as Gurudev had told me, "God is ever present and keeps a watchful and protective eye on all." For me, God and Gurudev are the same. "Gurudev was the mask that God wore." When the time came for me to marry Ravi Madhavan, we decided that it was not necessary for us to meet. We saw each other for the first time on our wedding day. In today's times, this is a bit unheard of. But I had faith that all would be fine, and this was Gurudev's way of making sure I would be all right after He was no longer with us in the physical plane.

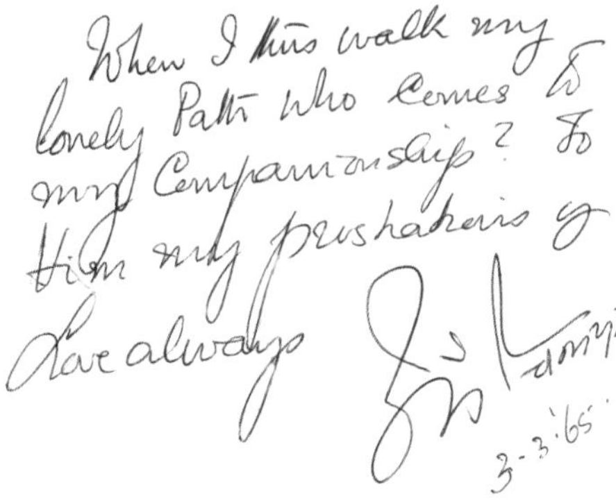

THE TRACKLESS PATH

In this higher climb, which is traversed by so few, logic and reason have fulfilled their role in bringing the seeker up to a certain point. From thereon, the two guides are only faith and intuition. Faith gives the courage to make the leap. This leap is sustained in full momentum by the power of intuition, which is a unique instrument that arises from the debris of the intellect that was once clouded by the ego. When the ego is surrendered, the subtle force that stands up to take its place is intuition. This intuition is like the rocket assembly that sheds itself upon the countdown to the Supreme.

Swami Chinmayananda:

We are told that the Einsteinian theory is, today, fully understood by only half a dozen people in the whole world. Only a highly developed and specialized intellect can grasp the subtle imports of the theory. Higher still, the Ātman is subtler than the subtlest thought-possibility of the intellect, because It transcends the intellect itself. Hence, with the gross instruments of knowledge, one cannot apprehend It. Then what is the instrument in whose focal length the subtle Truth is brought for our recognition and experience?

The only method by which a seeker can realize his Self is through the faculty of intuition. With a certain discipline of the outer senses, we control the mind; the mind generates a certain power, now latent in us, called intuition. And only with this wisdom-eye can we experience the Truth. Intuition is not to be created afresh. It is there within us, lying dormant in our intellect. The intellect resides in the *cave of the heart*, and from its glorious seat of activities, controls the workings of the mind. When the mind is silent, the intellect gains an inner peace. An intellect itself, thus in complete peace, dies away or disappears. Like the mythological bird Phoenix, which, singing its death-song, falls down to die in a mass of fire and then resurrects — the mind, out of its own ashes, rises up to a new faculty and potency called intuition. It is with this intuition that a seeker comes to realize his Self. Intuition is nothing but 'the capacity to know the Knowledge.' And knowing the Self is but the Self becoming aware of Itself. Thus, a successful meditator, meditating long upon the nature of Truth, in the sacred spirit of his practices, comes to gain an intimate subjective experience of Godhood. As we continue analyzing the value of things and thinking of the statements of the scriptures, we develop this nature. This power of apprehension, arising out of a combination of all our faculties, is called intuition.

Language has lost its integrity when trying to express emotion, and in expressing intellectual concepts, it has actually been broken up into fragments-formulae. And, in trying to express the Infinite, it fails totally. Therefore, the great ṛṣis use the language of negation. The land of Truth lies extended beyond the frontiers of the intellect and the mind. The intellect can investigate only the presence of things; Consciousness can illumine their absence as well.

So long as you are dreaming, as a dreamer you will never be able to appreciate and understand the state of waking. It is only on awakening that you realize that you are the waker, who has nothing to do with the dreamer-condition and its stupid dream world. We do not know how to instruct others about the Self. It is different from what is known, the entire objective phenomenal world, and it is beyond what is unknown, the negative unknown idea. It is clear that a positive illuminating factor illumines the negative idea "I don't know." I cannot explain the Truth to you, which is lived through intuition. The only way [for the Guru] to tell about It is through the traditional knowledge — repeated, endorsed, and given out to their respective disciples. They are the reports left for our guidance by those who successfully walked the path earlier.

When the thoughts have become subtle in the hushed moments of deep meditation, the mind is tuned up for the higher transcendental Experience Divine. It can be known only by the best among men who have perfectly purified intellects. Those who have lifted the veiling and reduced the agitations in the mind are said to have a purified intellect. This is the stage when the vāsanās have been reduced, when the desire for sense-objects no more agitates the intellect. The intellect that has stopped wandering into the fields of sense-gratification, such an intellect is capable of understanding this great Brahman.

Q: If someone reaches the highest State of Reality from which no one wishes to return, how can he ever communicate the existence of this State to our world?

Swamiji: True. True. Very, very true! In your question, you have unconsciously stumbled onto a serious fact. The State Divine, in all Its transcendental splendor, cannot be ever communicated to anyone. All that the teacher tries through his explanations is to give an illusory satisfaction to all your illusory doubts. Alas, illusion can be ended only by yet another illusion!! When we take medicine for our illness, the medicine administered cannot give us health, but it can destroy the causes for the illness, and after this job, the medicine itself gets eliminated through the excretory system. The natural condition of the human body is health.

Why is it a 'trackless path'?

Anjali Singh: During the three months' stay in Sidhbari in 1992, I would often write a question in a letter to Swamiji and give it to Shivramji, his attendant, who would place it on his desk. "If I make an effort at concentration, it seems at the time that it is working and one feels one is going forward. But of late I have tried another way, that is, not to make an effort, but to just wait in a vigilant, conscious way. While I am doing that, it seems

that nothing is happening while I am at it, but when I get up from meditation, I feel good afterward, as if more progress was made than by effort. What should I do, make an effort or not make an effort? If I don't make an effort, maybe I am not doing sādhanā." I waited for a few days but did not get a reply. Nor did Swamiji refer to this question in any way whenever I met him. On the third day, the answer came in the meditation session. I went excitedly to Swamiji while he was at breakfast and asked him whether he had received my letter and he nodded. So I said, "Well, you don't have to reply now, because today I got my answer!" He seemed very happy and said, "I had asked Swami Tapovanji Maharaj the same question, and he also did not reply to me. I also got my answer from within. That is why I did not say anything to you because I knew you would, too. You see, from here onward, it is a trackless path. Each person's experience is different. If I tell you it should be like this, and it does not happen that way, then you will be after me! Sometimes it works in one way and sometimes in another. Sometimes certain experiences happen, and if I tell you this is how it happens and it doesn't, you will keep waiting for it to happen and not move forward." Breakthroughs or glimpses happen this way because we enter an arena where logic can no longer guide us. That is why it is said that It is beyond the intellect.

19

Forget the Scoreboard

Swamiji said, "As a newcomer, he (Bruguera) will be nervous to play against a top player, but being a Spaniard, he has no such hesitation!" When Bruguera seemed to be doing well, a devotee said, "My 'horse' is serving for the set!" Swamiji then gave this advice: "He needs to get all extraneous things out of the way, forget the moment, the crowds, the scoreboard and concentrate on the game." Bruguera won the set by 6–4!

The spiritual aspirant who lacks experience in meditation will be nervous to attempt the higher climbs. His lack of experience and consequent nervousness are no doubt a drawback. But if he has an inner conviction that it is possible to achieve a breakthrough, this will definitely give him a sure chance of succeeding.

"Forgetting the scoreboard" or "Lob it," which Swamiji had advised earlier to mean embracing humanity, is to expand the mind into Infinity. Swamiji had said at one point, "One has to expand the mind into embracing Infinity. Take the ego off guard and leave it behind, with the thought 'I am Brahman' or 'I am That!' and try to just be. Brahman may appear to be very far, but indeed It is very near. When one tries to expand the 'I' into an unbroken, one-thought flow, the attempt to do so makes the 'I' turn around and land into its own true Self. Time is not in terms of centuries but in terms of millions of years. The world of matter is floating on the principle of time. In that vastness you try to recognize, 'Where am I now?' In that vastness the ego disappears."

In order to get to this subtle single-pointedness, being in a quiet place or a temporary retreat is very helpful, though not essential. Swamiji said, "You have to leave everything for a few moments and turn your entire attention, so that there may not be any obstacles on your path." He added, "One can have this peace and quietude at home, also, but one lets the worries and attachments to children take over, and they tend to shatter the quietude."

UNBROKEN MELODY

To begin with, the awareness of the thought "I am Brahman" has the distinction of containing the subject, 'I' the knower-ego, and the object consisting of the thought of "I am Brahman," and the relationship of knowing that exists between the subject and the object. When one contemplates by holding onto an unbroken flow of the thought "I am Brahman" for a long and sufficient duration of time, the mind becomes the potent thought form "I am Brahman," termed the 'akhaṇḍākāra-vṛtti' or the 'expansive thought.' The akhaṇḍākāra-vṛtti is also known as 'brahmākāra-vṛtti,' for the mind expands into the 'bigness' of the one, infinite Brahman in its attempt to end the division of the subject-object relationship. In this single-pointedness of the mind, the subject, the knower-ego 'I,' puts one foot forward onto the 'throne of God,' as it were. With the mind's expansion, the ego feels as if it has reached the State of Godhood. This is savikalpa samādhi at its best! In the continuous practice of reaching the State of Godhood, a point comes where both feet end up in Divinity, wherein even the brahmākāra-vṛtti ceases and there is no more any distinction between the individual ego and Brahman. The ego surrenders itself into the absoluteness of God and is swallowed up by Godhood. Negation of the not-Self and asserting one's nature to be Brahman are to be practiced simultaneously to break the contrary thought-habit of duality. It is also to be noted that the contemplation, consisting of maintaining the unbroken thought current of "I am Brahman" is different from japa, the repetition of a mantra, as contemplation has its roots in understanding.

Swami Chinmayananda:

Standing in front of a mirror and seeing your reflection — what do you exactly understand? If, for example, your reflection showed that it badly needs a shaving, would you then start shaving the 'reflection' in the mirror, or would you do it on your own face? Seeing the reflection, we do not actually come to know so much the reflection as, through it, we come to understand the source of the reflection, our own face. Similarly, when the mind and the intellect have been transcended in the last moments of the white heat of meditation, the individual ego, peeping over its own limitations, as it were, comes face to face with the eternal Self; and when, thus, the highly evolved ego comes to reflect the Light of the Eternal Knowledge, the reflection merges itself in a process of knowledge to become one with the Self.

As vāsanās get roasted in the 'heat' of contemplation, the mind becomes more and more pure — quiet, alert, and vigilant. The contemplation becomes deeper and steadier. There comes a time at the end of vāsanās that thoughts cease, the jīva (ego) gets released from this imaginary trap, and rediscovers its identity with the pure Consciousness. This is vidyā (knowledge) — the path of contemplation upon the nature of the Self. Vidyā alone is the last leap of the seeker into the Self-divine. At one stage, the meditator becomes the meditated. Man steps onto the throne of God! To give up meditation through meditation is the highest meditation! There is no greater meditation than the meditation-less meditation.

"I am Brahman" is considered as one of the Great Declarations (mahāvākyas) in the Vedas. This is the roar of experience of the student. To come to maintain this awareness constantly in the mind is the zero hour when the egocentric entity awakes from its long sleep of ignorance into the dawn of realization and inner experience of its own Infinitude. Such a student is asked to maintain an exclusive, unbroken thought current, that "I am Brahman." This is the last stage of self-effort in the ultimate realization of the Infinite. This is to be maintained and practiced continuously for a long period of time.

The objects of the world are not merely objects but objects in a medium of Brahman, objects playing in an Ocean of Brahman. Meditation consists in identifying not with the object but with Brahman, in which the object is playing through the vṛtti "I am Brahman." The firsthand subjective experience of Brahman comes when the seeker ends the vṛtti that he is Brahman and lives as Brahman Itself.

We may ask: Are we not again creating a thought during our contemplation? Instead of thinking thoughts about the world of objects, are we not merely substituting them with thoughts of the Self? Will not golden chains bind us as efficiently as iron shackles? When a mind gets fully engaged in the practice indicated, the quiet mind, uncluttered with thoughts of the world of objects, expands to embrace the concept of the infinite Self, the sole Substratum of the entire perceived world of experiences. In this thought of the infinite Self, thought is no more a thought: the thought-wave becomes a wave with no amplitude, and therefore becomes a no-thought wave. Thus, when one arrives at the Self, thoughts cease to be thoughts. The individuality merges into the Vision of the Reality. Just as the medicine taken by the sick corrects the disturbance in the physical system and then all by itself gets eliminated from the system, so, too, the brahmākāra-vṛtti, the thought "Brahman am I," ends all by itself when the seeker arrives at the Realization of the Self. "This merger is possible" is the daring assertion of all Vedāntic seers.

The knowledge of the identity of Brahman–Ātman, when intensified by long reflection, destroys the ignorance, just as medicine administered cures disease and itself gets eliminated. Constant practice is emphasized, because over a period of lives in the past, many vāsanās got accumulated, and we have to overcome them. Also, we have to eliminate all our attachment and identification with our body, mind, and intellect equipment.

With the right thought in the intellect, the wrong thought is removed. Here again, you are replacing one thought with another thought, but even this limited knowledge removes the false assumption that the not-Self is the Self. The constant contemplation in oneself: "I am Brahman, not a saṁsārī" is an unavoidable practice for one who is walking the Path of Knowledge. This constant thought-current, maintained unbroken, is called akhaṇḍā-ātma-vṛtti. Perfection is not gained by irregular attempts, however sincere and ardent the attempts may be. To one who is following this path strictly and diligently, the poet–seer guarantees that his mind will get merged into the silence of this thoughtless state, nirvikalpa.

The subject that knows the thought procession is the Consciousness. The brahmākāra-vṛtti idea should be kept alive during the entire period of our waking state. This, too, is a thought. The understanding arising out of this thought is also a limited knowledge (vṛtti-jñānam). But with this right thought (sad-vṛtti) in the intellect, the wrong thought (asad-vṛtti), is removed. When thus you practice on, ere long, the feeling "I am the body, mind, and intellect" is destroyed. Here again, you are replacing one thought with another thought. But even this limited knowledge (vṛtti-jñānam) removes the false assumption that the not-Self is the Self, an-ātmani-ātma-mati.

In this process, the ego is trying to disconnect itself from the world of objects, including the body, mind, and intellect, until at last it gets dissolved to become nothing but the Self. Thus, in Vedānta, there is a dual process to be undertaken with equal diligence at one and the same time in order to fulfill the condition that the ṛṣis have prescribed for Self-realization. Not only is it sufficient for an individual seeker to meditate upon the supreme Reality and Its nature, but he must also deliberately learn to disconnect his mind from its chains, warped out of the sense-objects. On the one end, there is the process of negation of the not-Self, which is efficiently partnered by an equally powerful process of assertion of the eternal qualities of the Self. Both processes are to be undertaken simultaneously with equal insistence.

'Thought' upon the Self is not, in fact, a 'thought.' A thought must necessarily have an object. The thought of the Self is a 'thought' on the Subject; therefore, it has no object. Objectless-thought is not a thought. And yet, for the last withering stage of mind, contemplation upon the Self is an unavoidable staff — helping the seeker along the last few steps to the threshold of Reality. When the sense of doership and enjoyership is completely eradicated, the ego disappears into the Vision of the Self. The meditator merges in the meditated — the river has reached the ocean — to be the ocean, no more can the river remain separate.

Just as a salt doll immersed in a salt solution gets completely dissolved and becomes one with the salt solution, losing its identity, the seeker developing in himself the vṛtti that he is Brahman, gives up the vṛtti itself, melting himself into Brahman. That total merger into Brahman is called samādhi.

The love (for God) in a seeker is like the unbroken flow of a river, like the constant stream of oil flowing from one pot to another, in which there is no break. Unbroken and continuous — his mind becomes a constant flow toward OM, the Reality, rather than toward the objects, emotions, and thoughts. This stream of love never leaves him; never is it dragged down from its heights, attracted either by the pleasures of the earth or of the heavens. Such love, continuously flowing toward the Reality, is rare. In most cases it is not a constant flow — only a drop here and there, broken throughout the day by our sense of identity with our body, mind, and intellect and other baser ideas and anxieties.

Is meditation absolutely essential for Self-realization?

Swami Advayananda: In 1988 at Sidhbari, listening to Gurudev's lectures on *Vivekacūḍāmaṇi,* it became evident that the doorway to Self-realization was meditation — by far the most important spiritual discipline to be undertaken by a spiritual seeker intent on Liberation. The example given was of the worm (pupa), which by steadfast and single-pointed meditation transforms itself into the wasp. At the 1989 Cochin International Camp, Gurudev was teaching *Kaṭhopaniṣad* in which Nachiketas requests from Yama, his Guru, the knowledge of the supreme Reality. Here, unlike *Vivekacūḍāmaṇi,* there was not much talk of meditation or samādhi (absorption). The focus was on the dispassion and purity of Nachiketas and the crystal-clear wisdom he gained because of his mental preparation. Indeed, meditation and its practice were not put on the pedestal. The difference was palpable and I was perplexed! I asked Gurudev, "Is meditation a must for Self-realization?" He answered in one line: "If you are a Nachiketas, it is not!" The answer was cryptic, and it took many years to decipher the full measure of Gurudev's reply.

The *Bṛhadāraṇyaka-upaniṣad* declares: "The Self ought to be realized — should be heard of, reflected on, and meditated upon." In this statement, we find the clear delineation of the means to Realization: (1) śravaṇa, (2) manana, and (3) nididhyāsana. The principle behind meditation is this: A habit is overcome by its opposite habit. The habit of "I am the limited individual" is broken by its opposite "I am the supreme Reality," but the actual dissolution of the 'knot' can happen only if "I am the supreme Reality" thought transmutes itself into a habit. The continuous, constant, and conscious meditation on this thought slowly generates a vāsanā, that of one's real nature being Brahman, which breaks the 'knot,' the contrary notion of oneself being the limited individual. Thereafter, one ever abides as the supreme Brahman — this is the dawn of Knowledge. Hence, meditation is a must; mere śravaṇa and manana, even though they are vital steps, are insufficient by themselves to grant Liberation — therefore, the unmistakable emphasis on meditation by *Vivekacūḍāmaṇi*. But why is this emphasis not seen in *Kaṭhopaniṣad?* When the mind is already very pure and alert due to discrimination and dispassion, it is able to quickly glide into Knowledge. For such a pure mind, clarity immediately dawns after listening to the Guru's teaching. Naciketas was such a fit aspirant. Hence, Gurudev's answer, "If you are a Naciketas, it is not!" And for sure, I was not a Nachiketas.

"*I* am Brahman" is considered as one of the
Great Declarations (mahāvākyas) in the Vedas.

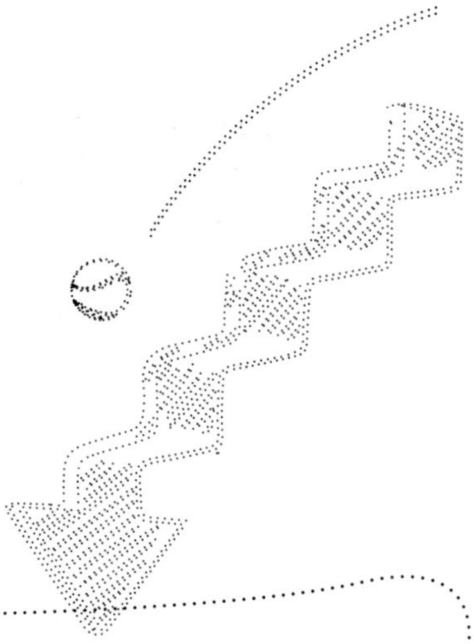

20

Watch Your Step

> When Bruguera began to lose his service game in the second set, Swamiji said, "We congratulate him. This is the second round and he is only a baby. 'Billi' hai abhi [He is only a kitten as yet]! In two years' time, he can throw Courier off the court! But he will have to be careful." Someone asked, "Careful — even after he wins?" Swamiji nodded. The devotee continued, "Is it because even after he wins the tournament, he needs to go on to win all four majors — the Grand Slam?" Swamiji nodded again. Then another question popped up, "Has he to be 'careful' for a year?" Swamiji grimaced indicating a "No." "Two years?" Swamiji replied, "Two years is more than sufficient! And then he will be safe." "One-and-a-quarter to half?" Swamiji nodded a "Yes." Meanwhile, Bruguera lost the set badly — at 2–6! Swamiji said, "Bruguera is still a 'billi' [young]. Even if he loses, it will be very creditable."

A meditator makes repeated attempts to achieve a breakthrough in his meditation. In case the meditator does not succeed right away, he still deserves credit for trying because these repeated attempts will add to the push he needs to get to the top. He still has to continue making attempts because that is the only way. He should not give up.

In case the meditator achieves the breakthrough, meaning — quietens the mind into samādhi (wins the tournament), it will still take some time to get fully established in the Higher (achieve the Grand Slam). He has to keep bringing the mind to a breakthrough point again and again till all his coverings are removed and he gets firmly rooted in It. Then he can start feeling safe and not fear a fall from the State of Bliss. He becomes a jīvanmukta — liberated while living.

ERE LONG

This section is to be read after the 'Mystic Revelation' as it addresses the means for getting established in the Self after the experience of nirvikalpa samādhi. But the sequence of Swamiji's tennis conversations was such that this portion was discussed before the final match of the French Open, winning which was symbolic of attaining nirvikalpa samādhi. With the experience of nirvikalpa samādhi, the contrary notion of oneself being the body, mind, and intellect comes to an end, and one starts getting established in the ultimate Knowledge. One has to practice reaching the nirvikalpa state again and again, which now comes easily since the knack of it is now known. However, Swamiji warned that a seeker must be extra careful during this period and not divert his mind to other things, since single-pointedness is very necessary in the practice of nirvikalpa samādhi. He even suggested that one go into the mountains to be alone. This staying alone is only for the purpose of getting established in that stage. In savikalpa samādhi, the thought "I am Brahman" exists, as also the triad of the seer-seen-seeing, but in nirvikalpa samādhi, the thought "I am Brahman" effortlessly ceases in the final Illumination.

Swami Chinmayananda:

Great teachers have the ability of talking at once to two different levels of students in one and the same breath. The ordinary student takes it as a method of upāsana and the realized student understands a deeper message of instructions and direction as how he should live in the world outside after his realization. The student has realized the source of infinite Bliss within himself. These moments of experience are generally limited and broken. Until he gets himself established in this experience, there will be for him moments of disturbances when he will be pushed out of that plane of God-experience to the consciousness of his egocentric existence. At such moments, the chances are that he will look upon the world of plurality as inauspicious, wretched, and pain-ridden and as a delusion.

On realizing his own divine Nature, he may, by a relative estimate, come to regard his own brother creatures of the world as something undivine, as something to escape from. In order to avoid this mistaken notion and the consequent estimate of the world as undivine, he must consider the world outside also with as much reverence and divinity as he considers his own experienced Self. He must realize that the world of names and forms experienced by the Experiencer (the Ātman) and the world are one and the same. The world without is as divine as the world within. To experience that the meditator himself is Divine in his core, but not to recognize the same divinity there afterwards everywhere around him, is only a partial knowledge — at best, a fanciful imagination. The waker cannot experience that he has awakened and still insist that his dream-wife and dream-children are living in the world of his dream; on his awakening, the world projected by the dreamer is entirely scrapped. This total experience of the all-full Supreme, where there is no distinction at all, this state of at-one-ment with the Lord, is called true Wisdom, complete Realization. Learn to meet Him in the quietude of your mind as well as in His expression in the world outside.

Truth, the Self, lies beyond the intellect, and It illumines constantly the very intellectual experiences themselves. So, to declare "I have understood" is not the final realization of Consciousness by which I have recognized the idea "I have understood." The student is advised to continue his investigations. The moment we comprehend a thing, it is always through the instruments of our comprehension and understanding. They, being limited, cannot but fail in grasping the whole. The language of intuition alone can soar into the realms of pure Consciousness.

In order to end his false identifications with the conditionings, a wise student must constantly practice nirvikalpa samādhi. He must try to bring the mind completely and absolutely to silence once or twice a day. The rest of the time, even while experiencing the various phenomena of the outer world, he should cultivate the habit of turning his mind into inner quietude. This is the 'practice of samādhi' — samādhi niṣṭha (established in quietude). The unmanifested vāsanās are destroyed in the practice of samādhi. The entire sañcita karma, which has been accumulated in millions of our past lives, is destroyed when we experience samādhi. When all the vāsanās and their consequent bondages are annihilated through the practice of constant meditation, the seeker, seeking himself, ends in the total exhaustion of his entire karma. At this stage, what is the experience? Is it an empty zero? When the PFT, the causal-body, and the vāsanās have ended, what can remain? At that time, you will have a clear, subjective experience of your own Self. That experience requires no special effort. Nothing need be done for it — either to reach it or to preserve it in us.

Except those who have become steadfast in the experience of nirvikalpa samādhi, even great learned and wise men cannot end their ego suddenly. Nirvikalpa samādhi is the State of Mindlessness, where all thoughts have been consciously eliminated and blissfully transcended. At this stage, merger with the Reality becomes complete. When the ego goes deeper and deeper into contemplation upon the purpose of existence, it totally disappears to become the Consciousness. This State of Final Beatitude is never as such expressed in any śāstra — only the last stage of the human effort, called the practice of samādhi, is indicated. The final experience is not gained by anyone. It is there already with all of us. Practice of samādhi only lifts the veil and reveals what was, is, and shall ever be: the eternal nature of the Infinite: "That Thou Art" roars the teacher in the *Chāndogya Upaniṣad*.

Many fail to get established in this grand State of Consciousness, though it may be admitted that many seekers do get some exotic glimpses of this blissful State. What cheats them of their Self-abidance? Why this tragedy in the life of some seekers? Effortlessness is the essence of a Man of Perfection. He is a master idler in the eyes of the men of the world. In the Self, there is no universe of plurality. Hence, the seeker must learn to forget all the memories of illusory objects experienced in the past. This alone is the way. Where the meditator forgets the body, mind, and intellect and his world of objects, emotions, and thoughts, the perceiver-ego in him ends, and this is the point wherein the ego disappears into the Vision of Reality.

When you get established in Truth, live uninvolved in the things that are happening around. If you participate actively in the happenings around you, you will again tumble down into agitations. Therefore, remain in the world; let the thoughts in you dance about, but never, never get involved with them.

The meditative man who withdraws from the world of ignorance, seeking to live the joys of the Self, would naturally become unfit for worldly success during his sādhanā period, because a seeker becomes mute, inert, and passive. You have to leave everything for a few moments and turn your entire attention so that there would not be any obstacles on your path. When one can, at his will, command such equipoise of his mind that he can experience the infinite Joy, which is his nature, there is no sādhanā for him thereafter.

A hundred other Masters with the infinite experience of the Divine might be living now or might have died, unknown in the secret caves of the Himālayās. The world and the children of the present generation do not raise even a single thought of gratitude for their divine expression of Reality. On the other hand, a Vyāsa or a Vālmīki, a Yājñavalkya or a Vashishta, a Ramana Maharṣi or a Ramakrishna, or a Vivekananda, a Guru Gobind Singh, or a Rama Tirtha, a Ramanuja or an Aurobindo — they are even now remembered with grateful adorations. They realized and recognized the Divine not only in themselves but in the entire world of objects. In their perfect wisdom, they had no fears of any fall at any time into the delusory net of misunderstandings or physical appetites.

A doll made of salt, tied to a string, and dipped into the ocean will not come back when pulled up to report the depth. The doll gets melted into the very form of the ocean. The salt doll was the ocean; it was born from the ocean. But it had for a time an identity of its own and a form. But once having reached the 'bosom' of its own nature and remained there for a time, it became the very ocean that it eternally was.

Letter to ***Erica Proels:*** Wherever we are, let us be in that Peace Center, utterly blissful, from where we realize that the forms and names are my own ripples!! Even with eyes open, see in and through the names and forms the steady Consciousness playing in joy. Purest mind is Brahman!!

Getting established in Truth:
Anjali Singh: During a break in watching the game of tennis, one devotee's son brought a polished pair of slippers and exchanged them for Swamiji's old ones. Swamiji saw him doing this and said, "Shoes of the Vedāntic Master should always be kept shining, so that when the devotee prostrates, what will he see there? Himself!" This was his way of saying that the devotee should repeat the attempts at meditation until the veil of ignorance about his identity is removed and he recognizes Himself.

Experience gets more vivid and prolonged till one is firmly established in the Ultimate.
Anjali Singh: During a satsaṅga in Sidhbari during the Vivekacūḍāmaṇi Camp in 1992, Swamiji said, "When Realization happens, you should be alone in the mountains for at least a month. If you can't go for a month, then go at least for three days to get established in it." We don't know whether he was speaking to anyone in particular. The following words were also said by Swamiji as part of the above satsaṅga: "When you are nearing the Palace, you see huge lampposts on the way. At first, they are far apart, and as you get nearer the Palace, the distance between the lampposts gets less and less. They are not the Palace, but they are the guiding lights to the Palace to tell you that you are nearing it. So, also, you get intimations, glimpses on the way to the Palace of Truth."

21

Championship Point

When Bruguera began putting the ball into the net, Swamiji said, "He should have crossed the line by now. So near it!" On another point, Bruguera rushed to the net and again hit the ball too hard, missing the chance of delivering a drop shot. Swamiji repeated, "He was so near it! He could have just stepped over!" "Really? Was he really that close?" asked the devotee. Swamiji explained, "He is too energetic! All he has to do is to hold the racket and let the ball go gently over the net." Bruguera lost the fourth set 3–6.

When meditation gets highly intense, it might feel like there is no forward movement. It seems to fall short of a breakthrough. No matter how much one tries, the result appears to be the same: one meets with a bottleneck. Earlier, when meditation had not reached this tempo, Swamiji would instruct the tennis player to "Hit the ball" — meaning to make an extra effort to get a taste of bliss in meditation. But now, at a higher stage, he asks the tennis player to just gently "hold the racket," and not make an effort to hit the ball, because the ball, with the force of the opponent's momentum, will on its own go back over the net as a drop shot since it is already so near the net. He advises the player not to be "too energetic." This is very important advice. In the last stages of meditation, one has to 'just be' and not try 'to become.' The rest will happen on its own.

DON'T BE AFRAID TO DO NOTHING

In the last sacred hour before the final divine experience of Self-hood, the kind of integration required for the launch can only be sustained through correctly following the Guru's instructions. The integration consists of an amalgam of patience, determination, courage, self-confidence, spiritual energy, fortitude, and a single-pointed, effortless eye on the goal. This is to be sustained until one gets pushed into the mystic revelation of nirvikalpa samādhi. The attempt at deep meditation is to be made when we have all the tools of fortitude, or spiritual energy, at our disposal. It is only when we are fully alert that we can be ready to receive the grace of God or the Guru. All the energy that was going out into the world becomes available to the meditator. The energy and dynamism generated by meditation can lead us toward the goal one has chosen. No kind of mental excitement should be allowed to hijack the final process. While the seeker recognizes that he is in a special state, though it is supposed to be 'effortless' because the 'speed' at which he progresses spiritually is like the graceful, majestic launch of a satellite into space, he must not get diverted or excited before its culmination. When this beautiful balance is achieved, one must be careful not to disturb it in any way or leave it unfinished, because to come to this point in life is no small achievement.

Swami Chinmayananda:

Now the Sage is giving, as it were, that last kick to the student, who is attached to his pursuit in the path of meditation. The very act of meditation nourishes the ego in the student and compels him to maintain a sense of meaningless distinction between himself — the meditator — and the Truth that is being meditated upon. Meditation and other spiritual practices are not necessary for high-level students. The various practices of devotion to the Lord — service to the society, study of the scriptures, reflection upon the truths, and even meditation — are all means to awaken us from the dreams of the ego and realize our true Nature. To students of higher meditation, this warning is appropriate and very necessary. Early seekers should not get confused.

In contemplation you reach a state called meditation. In meditation, contemplation also ends. From meditation to the Divine is a free transport. You have to just wait there, and when the condition is complete, it leads to a totally new direction, a new dimension of consciousness. It is a State to which you must surrender, just as you surrender to sleep and allow it to overwhelm you and suck you in. From here, it is not for you to experience Him. When He wants, He will come and lift you up.

As the student enters the higher states of meditation to the portal of Liberation, the Teacher wants the student to give up all these limited goals of life, which, of course, had their initial blessings to contribute in helping the student to the present state of his awakening. But in the last lap of the journey, he cannot accomplish the great leap, unless he gets tired of all his mental preoccupations with the ideas and values which were certainly valid in earlier levels of his ego-consciousness. In this great flight across the frontiers of the limited, the meditator is not allowed to smuggle anything through the barriers of Consciousness. Even the noblest aspirations have to be renounced. All mantras and prayers, all devotions and yoga, all meditations, and even the anxiety to realize the Truth are not allowed to be smuggled into the supreme State of Consciousness.

For a spiritual seeker, fortitude is a must. Fortitude is consistency of purpose, an ability to face all challenges that come to you. In spite of all obstacles, you steadily move in the direction that you have mapped out. When He wants, He will come and lift you up. When the ghost is no more nodding at us, when it is no more agitating us, that is the sacred hour of the dawn of the knowledge of the post. When the mind is neither ducking behind the veil of ignorance nor getting into its death dance of agitations, that is the hour when the mind is no more a mind, since we know that the mind is nothing but the flow of thoughts. Where the mind has thus committed hara-kiri (ritual suicide), that very space or spot of all our attention or cognition experiences or reveals the very Self.

When the aspirant has thus won over the vikṣepa and the kṣaya, he is the one knocking at the doors of Reality. "Knock and thou shalt enter," is the promise of the Lord. And while you are knocking, you must have poise and patience to wait at the door until it is opened. This idea is indicated by the statement that when the mind has attained the state of equilibrium, then "don't disturb it again." In the white heat of meditation, when the mind is neither sleeping nor agitated, when it is in that transcendental experience of the voiceless dynamic void, to disturb it is the greatest sin that a mortal can commit against his Self. Do not disturb that mind that has settled down. Don't even say, "My Guru has blessed me, my mind is quiet." Don't translate the experience — just stay in it. Stay in the resulting tranquil state of meditation as long as you can; stay undisturbed. Don't disturb that state by initiating new thought-channels. Just remain in it, quietly tuned up to receive rather than to remember and translate the experience.

"I meditate" is perhaps the last lingering thought in almost all the seekers in higher meditation. At the moment of the Vision of the Self, the seeker experiences not the Ātman but the Brahman. At the moment of Self-realization, the seeker is not only aware of his individual Self but is also at once fully conscious of the all-pervading Reality termed as Brahman.

During meditation, one should not in the least strain oneself; this is so vividly brought out by the analogy of 'drawing out the pith from the reed.' The reed itself is the most delicate of plants, and its stalk is more so; and to draw out this flimsy and subtle pith from its outer envelopments, constituted of the stalks of the leaves themselves, is a delicate act that needs a softness of touch, a measured and practiced application of force, and a subtle silky deftness in handling the entire process!

If you create the necessary conditions in the mind, and if the conditions are fulfilled, you will be sucked into that State of Supreme Consciousness beyond time. A desireless mind alone can be silenced effectively. Enter into this experience of dynamic dynamism. At that moment, all effort — all experiencing — is no more the seeker's responsibility. He, Himself, helps us to see Him and ultimately reveals Himself in the highest experience of God-realization.

Just Be! Try! Just Be! Don't Be-come. But, just Be. When this 'Be-ness' comes out to express itself as you, that is the becoming. Stop it and just Be. That is the State of the Highest Love, because Love is identification — total surrender. Because you have totally identified with It, you have fully surrendered to Him — you have completely become one with It. Therefore — just Be.

Signed for ***Bebe (Nanki Singh):*** *Letter to* ***Anjali Singh:***

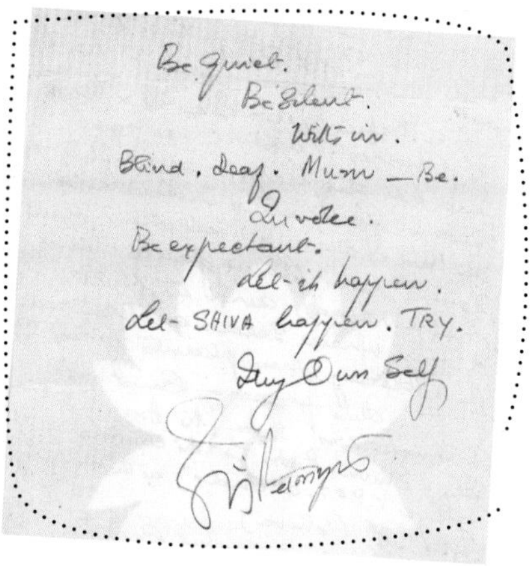

Be quiet.
Be silent within.
Blind, deaf, mum — Be.
Invoke.
Be expectant.
Let it happen.
Let SHIVA happen.
TRY.

What are you searching there? — the unborn Mind! When it was not born, what was it? That is called the God-state of Consciousness. Undeserving children, when they hear this, will say, "Swamiji said nothing!" At the level at which we are now talking, there is no experience. The word 'experience' is borrowed from the world. It must be removed. 'I,' the experiencer, and 'That,' the experienced, all that is gone. It is just Being.

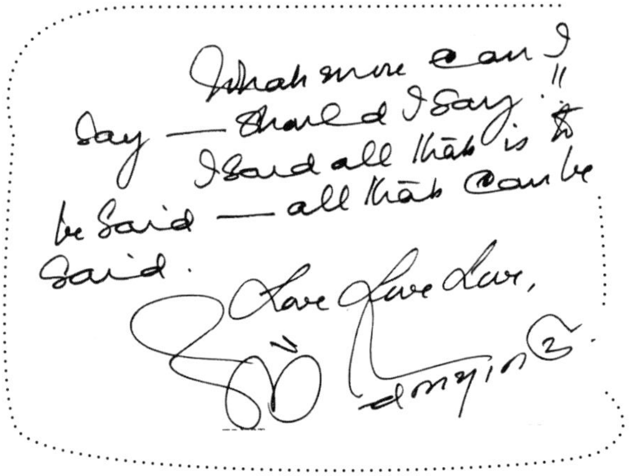

This is not an expression of the Teacher's despair but an open confession that language is utterly incompetent to communicate this knowledge. The intellect of the listener is not the vessel to receive what the Teacher wants to give. The student has to transcend his individuality, and come to be awake to the State of Pure Consciousness, all by himself. For those who have purified their inner-equipment, what has been said so far is more than sufficient. And to others, any amount of such discussions will not bring even a glimmer of understanding.

How does the final thought end?

Swami Advayananda: How does this last thought, the Brahmākāra-vṛtti, end? The answer is: It ends by its inherent strength. Gurudev would explain this with the example of sleep: The thought "I wish to sleep" is, due to other thoughts, initially weak. But slowly it gathers strength, and pushes away all other thoughts that are detrimental to sleep, thereby becoming a flow of one single thought, "I wish to sleep." This final thought, by the power of its own steam, ends, leaving but the thoughtless state of blissful deep sleep. In the same way, the Brahmākāra-vṛtti, too, ceases once it becomes a strong single flow. Such a state of thoughtlessness, which is without the last fragment of thought, the Brahmākāra-vṛtti, is termed 'nirvikalpa samādhi.' This is the state of immense benediction. Herein the ego finally perishes. This is the 'mystic death of the ego,' as Gurudev terms it: 'mystic' because the ego is not there to watch its death and feel how it feels to be without it. Gurudev famously said, "Meditation is a noun, not a verb!" Verily, this thoughtless state of nirvikalpa samādhi is not something which is done. It just is… is… is…. Gurudev reserved the word 'meditation' only for this nirvikalpa samādhi and differentiated nididhyāsana and savikalpa samādhi from this unique state by collectively calling them 'contemplation.'

Blending ungrammatical English with silent pauses to express what is difficult to explain:

Swami Advayananda: Language can communicate very poorly the nature and the process of the final mystic Experience. Still, Gurudev, an exceptional architect of English, could design, construct, mold, and recast the language at will when it came to communicating the lofty Experience and giving a glimpse of It. The Upaniṣad voices the Experience thus: "Wherein speech recedes, along with the mind, without even entering into its portals." While explaining how a seeker glides into the experience of samādhi, Gurudev would often express the final culminating moment thus: "In the white heat of meditation, when the last thought has been thoughted, and no more new thought is thoughting," … he would then give a long, profound pause — cease talking, be still, soar into that sacred Silence, thus giving all of us a glimpse of That — and then alone complete the rest of the sentence: "then is the mystic death of the ego, where the individual ego disappears into the sacred Vision of the transcendental Reality."

Even great beauty in the outer world cannot surpass the silence within:

Anjali Singh: One evening during the Vivekacūḍāmaṇi Camp in Sidhbari, we were sitting for satsaṅga when I asked Swamiji to look up at the beautiful full moon. The clouds around it made the moon look exquisitely magnificent. He said, "I know. I have seen it. Why are you making me extroverted? I am the Light that illumines these lights!"

Explaining the 'white heat' of meditation:

Swami Advayananda: Once the initial obstacles such as agitation (vikṣepa), sleep (laya), and so on are overcome, the vigor of this absorption (samādhi) grows by the moment, so to say at jet-speed, and becomes quite intense. This stage has been metaphorically described by Gurudev as the white heat of meditation. Just as a furnace turns really white hot, freeing the metal of its contaminants, so, too, staying in the furnace of meditation, one emerges cleansed, having given up all contrary notions and thoughts. Gurudev, in the context of samādhi, would often speak of the vāsanās being roasted therein — meaning they become ineffective thereafter, causing no bondage for the aspirant.

Anjali Singh: Swamiji would not sign my *Aṣṭāvakra Gītā* book for many years. Once, when I insisted, he did sign it, but with a warning because the teaching in it is meant to be followed when the mind has experienced oneness. Many unprepared scholars whose minds have not yet become quiet, stop meditating after studying such texts, which is meant only for advanced seekers.

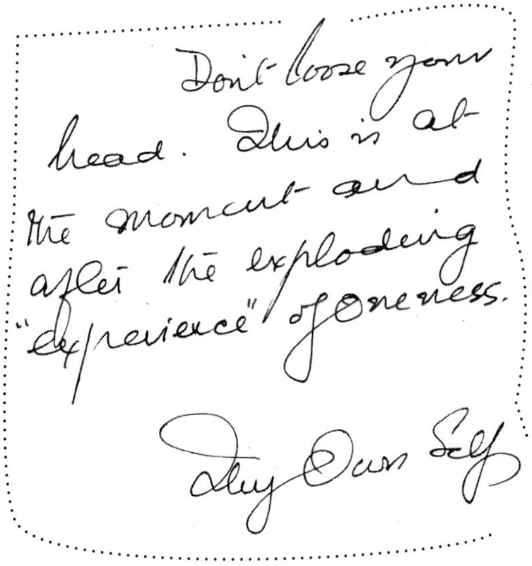
Don't loose your head. This is at the moment and after the exploding "experience" of oneness.
Thy Own Self

WINDFALL OF GRACE

The grace of God, and of the Guru who represents Him, is always there equally for all human beings without distinction of class, creed, color, race, or religion. It is the seeker's faith, born of love and inspired by a conviction that acts like a magnet, which draws the grace upon him. The love that invokes the grace factor can be for God or for the Guru who is established in God and is thus His embodiment. Ultimately, it all rests on the grace factor. One's love of God and the Guru, and the Guru's instruction of tat tvam asi (That thou art) is the final conduit to Realization.

Swami Chinmayananda:

A true seeker should feel a burning impatience, almost amounting to despair, about not knowing how to realize. Even though he knows the path, still realization of Truth lies just beyond the grasp of human effort. No doubt, through right living and right thinking, we can walk up to the royal chambers of the infinite Truth, but the last lap of the journey is a sudden windfall of grace Divine. The more we reflect upon the assertions of the realized sages, the more we are convinced that the final success is not in our hands to order.

Even an ignorant one can gain wisdom. This is the unfailing reward of steady, daily practice, sincerely undertaken for a long, continuous period of time. And one who is sincerely putting forth the right effort is assured of help from an unknown power, God's unfailing grace. Regardless of the efforts, one who strives to rest his thoughts steadily in the supreme Self, him the Lord blesses.

It is an endless controversy among the beginners of spiritual efforts — whether divine Grace will help them, or whether the entire path is built up by one's own independent, deliberately planned-out self-effort. Through self-effort, when the mind of the seeker is purified, the grace Divine shall rush in to flood his life with light and joy. In all religions the prophets make this point clear. The self-effort — "ask," "seek," "knock" — are the first, and, of course, grace Divine follows — "it shall be given to you," "you shall find," and "it shall be opened." The distribution of grace is not controlled by the Guru but depends upon the capacity of the recipient. To the extent the heart is open for the inflow of the Higher, to that extent we are under the grace of the Lord.

In Hinduism, the Guru's grace itself is God's grace, since the Guru is none other than Nārāyaṇa Himself expressing as Parameśvara (supreme God) to help the disciple. Guru's grace, scriptures' grace, and God's grace can positively reach to remold you only when Self-grace rains upon you from your own within. Then only you become the salt of the earth. It is said that a small bird once laid its eggs on the beach. During the high tides, the waters came up to drown the eggs. The bird, upon its return to the beach, saw its eggs taken away by the ocean. The bird decided, however, to see that the ocean was dried up and the eggs regained. It took a blade of grass and started emptying the ocean with it. At that moment, Garuḍa (eagle-like deity), who was going along the heavens, saw how one of its own species was so diligently pursuing such a heroic action and decided to help it. The ocean got frightened by the wrath of Garuḍa and came up to yield the eggs back to the bird. The story is often used to point out that, however difficult may be the attainment of Self-perfection, if an individual devotee consistently and with faith pursues the path, the Lord's grace would come, just as the king of birds did, to complete the seeker's great mission in life.

The assurance of the Guru's grace to the seeker who puts in the required effort:

Swami Chidrupananda: Like scores of his devotees and disciples, I often wondered at Gurudev's perseverance in whatever he did. Gurudev said in his talks, "Chinmaya sees to it that you realize the Truth." Gurudev declared that he would never leave anyone in the middle of the path. What an assurance! This I call the grace of the Master.

Up to what point does one have to make an effort, after which the Lord's grace take over?

Anjali Singh: One morning in Sidhbari, I asked Swamiji, "You said that we should make our minds quiet and 'the Lord will suck us in.' I keep trying to quieten the mind but nothing ever happens. What is the exact point at which I must make the effort to reach, after which it is the Lord's turn to do the rest? Give me an indication as to where I have to take it up to?" Swamiji kept quiet and did not answer. Then in the evening he gave me a copy of the new edition of his book *Meditation and Life*. He had written something on the front blank page. It was the answer to my question. He wrote:

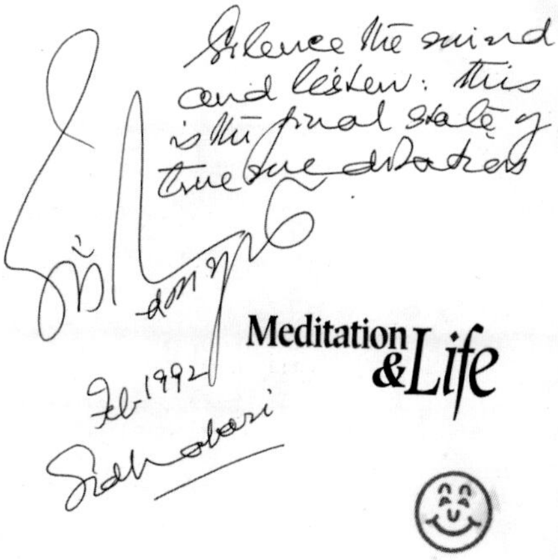

Grace is invoked by self-effort, sincerity, and love. Devotees recount:

Ācārya Sharada Kumar: The last day of the Vivekacūḍāmaṇi Camp in 1992 was the cūḍāmaṇi — crown jewel — for me! Filled with delightful emotions at being given the unique opportunity of chanting all the verses of *Vivekacūḍāmaṇi* for the first and only time, I was crying and ran straight to him. He hugged me. I felt I was floating on air! He wrapped a new mundu (a part of the two-piece Kerala sarī) around me and said, "The joy of finishing!" I have no recollection of what happened for the next ten minutes. I was walking around dazed, not knowing who was talking to me or what they were saying. It took me fifteen to twenty minutes to get back my orientation. Is this what they call "Brahma-sparśa (the touch of God)?"

Swami Chidrupananda: One afternoon, Pūjya Gurudev was unwell and was being given fomentation. I did not have the courage to see my Master suffering physically. But, Gurudev's face was glowing. He said, "You are looking at me as though I am finished." As he was looking at me, the power in the room went off. After some minutes, the power came back. Gurudev was still staring at me. He said, "When the electricity was there, I was there. When the electricity had gone, I was there. When the electricity has come back, I am there. I am That changeless Brahman." His roar mesmerized me. The entire scene is unforgettable. It was a great experience.

Ācārya Vilasini Balakrishnan: During one visit to the Sandeepany course in Mumbai, Gurudev was giving morning talks at Bharatiya Vidya Bhavan. The brahmacārīs were not attending these talks. However, eager to listen to him, I went to Gurudev for permission to attend. Swamiji looked very stern and replied, "I doubt there is room in the car for you." He was right: both cars were already full. On the third day, I was told that there was space in Gurudev's car. I quickly got in. Gurudev entered, turned, saw me, and said severely, "You haven't attended the earlier talks on *Vivekacūḍāmaṇi,* so get out and give your seat to someone for whom it will be more useful!" I exited, melting onto the pavement, and watched his car speed out. I nursed my wounds, fought my ego, stitched my pride back together, and made a determination: "I will read *Vivekacūḍāmaṇi* that day and approach Gurudev." The next morning, I quietly entered Gurudev's kuṭiyā at 4:00 A.M. He looked quizzically at me. I again requested permission. Swamiji hesitated, and replied, "Well, as I said yesterday, the classes may not be useful for you as you have missed the previous yajña on *Vivekacūḍāmaṇi...*" I interjected, "But I've been reading the book!" Swamiji looked even more surprised and said, "Well, I'm not sure there is room in the cars...." Even though there was no room, I was exalted that I had received permission from the Master to attend! Just then Pavitraji came and declared, "We are going by bus and train, right now. If we are lucky, we'll reach in time!" As there were no rickshaws, we walked a mile to the bus stop, took a bus to Andheri, and caught a train downtown. There we were, at Bharatiya Vidya Bhavan — only ten minutes late! Pavitraji and I entered the back of the hall. Swamiji was in the midst of his lecture. On

Pavitraji's insistence, I crept quietly down the central aisle and sat on an empty seat in the third row. Gurudev was speaking and staring right at me. He bored into my eyes for what seemed an eternity. Later, during the talk, he asked a rhetorical question of the audience. I shook my head in reply. Again he looked at me, and in front of thousands said, "Well, at least one person is listening to me." The next few mornings, magically there was room in a car for me! A week later, I went for darśana to Gurudev's office, trying to hide in the back, yet wanting to be in his presence. Then at one point, he caught my eye, and I smiled very awkwardly. He declared loudly, "When you meet your Guru, jump on behind him as though he were on a motorcycle, and hang on tight, but never let him know you are there!" This advice was timely and just perfect for me. I was so relieved that I had passed his test and would be able to learn from him.

When a student is ready, the Lord's grace transforms instantly:

Ananta Narayana (Uncle Mani): One of the most unforgettable days of my life was in 1970 when Gurudev came to hear that I was leading a Study Group on the *Vālmīki Rāmāyaṇa*. He asked, "What are you doing in the evening?' "Nothing!" "You are going to speak at Jagadeeshwara Temple!" Since Gurudev had told many people to come, a huge crowd had assembled there. To top it all off, he made me sit on the Vyasa Peeth while he sat on a chair at the side. My anxiety knew no bounds. I became so tense that my mind became blank! The *Vālmīki Rāmāyaṇa* is a vast book of 24,000 stanzas. I thought, "Where should I begin? What should I highlight? What shall I speak on?" Then, very much like an electric current passing through my body, came grace from the Guru; words emerged that summed up the core of the *Rāmāyaṇa* in the next one hour! The essence of my talk was that every Upaniṣad starts with a question. When a seeker asks a question, the Guru imparts the Teaching. In the Rāmāyaṇa, also, Vālmīki asked Nārada a question, and the Rāmāyaṇa was the answer. The repetition of the name Rāma had transformed the robber Vālmīki, so he asked the question "Who is this Rāma?" The answer, in a nutshell, consists of three points. One, the Rāmāyaṇa is the essence of the Upaniṣads; two, it presents an ideal way of living by highlighting virtues to be practiced in life; and, three, those virtues are personified in the role model of Śrī Rāma. At the end of the talk, Gurudev took from his neck a golden chain with rudrākṣa beads and put it around mine, thereby inaugurating a series of talks on the Rāmāyaṇa that I have been holding for decades — all over the world. Ever since then, my experience has been this: "His grace and blessings flow through us to the world around us."

22

Game, Set, Match, and Title

One devotee watching the game cried out the score, "Love All!" Swamiji replied, "Zero All! This is param Vedānta!" When it came to the final set and final game, the match was neck and neck. Courier had been the champion in 1991 and 1992; and now for the first time since 1975 at Roland Garros, a Spaniard had the chance to win the French Open! Ultimately, Bruguera had what it took to dethrone Courier! When Bruguera won it, the devotee 'betting' on Bruguera also won her 'game' with Swamiji.

In the match, Courier was a gracious loser and was waiting at the net with a smile to shake hands and congratulate Bruguera. Swamiji was also a smiling 'loser.' When the devotee entered Swamiji's room the next morning, he called out from afar, "Kalyani! Come on in!" This title was even better than having won the French Open! He had called her by a Kerala[5] name! Continuing the game, she prostrated at his feet and said, "Bruguera is mine!" — meaning that her morning meditation had been the most wonderful! With an expression designed to bring the devotee to alert attention, Swamiji replied, "Yes, Bruguera can be yours now. You are free!"

It is not often that an inexperienced meditator is able to successfully take the last leap. Usually, it is the 'Couriers' (the seasoned meditators) who win in the finals. But a seeker with deep love for God or the Guru can also make it with the help of the Guru's grace. God Himself undertakes to give the Knowledge of the Self to such a sincere seeker.

---

5 See explanation in "Psychologically Set" (page 234).

This Knowledge falsifies ("Zero All") the outer world as well as all distinctions within the mind. But it can also take a little time to get fully established in this Truth. It is like a river that has entered the sea, but its water still tastes sweet for some distance — until it gets fully assimilated with the salty ocean. That is what "Bruguera can be yours now" means. All that is required is to practice samādhi again and again (perhaps the five rounds that Swamiji had indicated earlier) — to be fully established in it. This is when Zero All is Love All — as one sees only the Self in others and everywhere.

THE MYSTIC REVELATION

When the meditator merges with the meditated and no distinction remains, not even the awareness of the thought "I am Brahman" as an object of meditation, then the subject-object relationship becomes one homogenous mass of Consciousness, the state of nirvikalpa samādhi. This nirvikalpa samādhi is the doorway to Illumination. Though this is the State of Godhood, or Brahman, the 'mind' returns when a person emerges from nirvikalpa samādhi. No doubt, the individuality that returns has been falsified and millions of karmas have been roasted in the conflagration of the Knowledge of Pure Consciousness. The scriptures advise one to practice entering and remaining in this state again and again, which now comes easily, as one now knows the knack. Ere long, one remains ever spontaneously established in the Self.

Swami Chinmayananda:

In contemplation, the mind rises above the inner and outer worlds of plurality and arrives at a unique State of Consciousness where the Self alone is. It is a state wherein all the mental and intellectual fluctuations have disappeared; therefore, the mind–intellect (dhī) has become thoughtless, totally undisturbed (śama). In this samādhi state, thoughts cease, the mind–intellect withers away, and the Consciousness that was caught in the web of thoughts gets released totally from all its encumbrances. In this total State of Liberation, one recognizes neither an outer world of names and forms nor an inner world of emotions and thoughts. The individual and his world of plurality merge to disappear in the experience of the Substratum, the Self.

There where thoughts retire and disappear slowly; where the mind and intellect are held at conscious attention through dedicated efforts at yoga; where the mind has ended and you are not pushed into a dark abyss of sleep; where the Self recognizes the Self, just as a waker recognizes a waker; wherein you discover total peace, no more a whiff of desire wanting something more to be complete; where infinite happiness is experienced, not where the intellect can apprehend [anything] — at the same time up to the maximum height it goes by the help of the mind and intellect, till, like a helium balloon, it bursts and helium joins space.

When the meditator keeps his mind undisturbed in the roaring silence within, in the white heat of meditation his mind gets purified, like a piece of iron in the smithy furnace. There it ends itself, just as a balloon goes higher and higher, blasts itself in the rarified atmosphere of higher altitudes and drops down, merging the balloon-space with the space outside. Similarly, the mind, too, at the pinnacle of meditation, shatters itself, drops the ego down, and merges with the Supreme. Just as the space in the balloon automatically merges with the space outside when the balloon has exploded, so, too, the finite mind, when ended, attains with ease "the infinite Bliss arising out of its contact with Brahman."

When the intellect is thus merged in the witness, it gets quietly hushed up until the last thought is thoughted and the witness can no longer be a witness. A witness is one who is witnessing something. When the last thought has ended, there is no object for the witness to watch and, therefore, the 'witness-hood' of the witness ends. Thus, the witness entity, the ego, merges with the pure, infinite Consciousness. Like a flame going upward and not wavering — you have 'reached' God! At that time, Truth gets revealed.

At the moment of Self-realization, when awareness coils upon itself, the subject alone exists. Without an object, there is no meaning for the term 'subject'; hence, the doubt arises: what is the object for the absolute Subject to illumine? The object is nothing other than Brahman, meaning that, at the moment of recognition of the subject by the subject, there is no object other than the subject for the subject to observe. At that time, who realizes the Truth? The unborn is realized by the unborn. Ātman 'sees' Ātman. Consciousness becomes conscious by Itself. All words are incapable of describing It. It is the 'thing' to be known. You have reached your destination — the All-knower. All knowledge is shining in this Light of Consciousness. Though the experience may be very momentary, in the final living moment of Truth-consciousness — God-consciousness — the experience of Truth is not within himself only but also all around and about him. At the Vision of Truth, nothing else remains as known or unknown but That! Nondual, One-without-a-second, Truth alone is, and "That I am" is the God experience!

Thus, the meditator, meditating upon the Infinite in the final fulfillment of meditation, comes to 'become' and thus experience an intimate subjective State of Pure Consciousness: "I am the Infinite." This is a State of Pure Being, of the Pure Self. In supreme devotion, a devotee experiences that 'I,' the devotee, is no more; and the entire universe, including the devotee, is nothing but He, the Lord. No more is he a victim of the world of plurality, nor is he thereafter ever afraid of the flux of matter. Within and without, he is the Lord of his vehicles [instruments] and the objects of his experience. This is the last stage of the pilgrimage, the termination of all effort, the fulfillment of all seeking, and the end of all evolution, the Goal Divine. When the seeker's mind melts in the warmth of his single-pointed love for God, the sublime fusion of the finite with the Infinite takes place.

When this identification with the higher Self is complete, then there is no more any sense of separation between the seeker–devotee and his Love. He melts to become his love for his Love. Of this great Truth — when it is experienced in the totally purified mind and heart — the best that we can say of this Love at its climax is that it is without any properties, with none of its usual attributes. There is not even a shred of desire that ever comes to muddy it. It is moment-to-moment intoxicating the individual without any break — unconditioned, ceaseless. It, in its joyous flow, devastates all other ideas or actions!

In the condition of nirvikalpa samādhi alone can this great Reality be apprehended with total certainty; you apprehend the Truth when all the ripples and waves in your mind have ended. When the meditator becomes the meditated, man steps onto the throne of God! With this experience of nirvikalpa samādhi, the personality becomes free from all its encrustations. Till this experience, one will function in the field of time and space with the body–mind–intellect and continue to experience constant change. Till we gain this direct experience of the Self, whatever we discuss about the scriptures, whatever discourses we hear or give, are, at best, indirect knowledge, a mere blabber, no matter how eloquent the talks may be.

When I go there, 'I' cannot exist; when I come back, 'I' cannot explain. What happens to you at that time? The mind becomes exactly like the hailstone fallen in the ocean.

Just as in an undisturbed lake the heavens are reflected honestly, so is this state of samādhi, a state where there is no more any contact with the outer objects, a state where you are well-settled in Ātman. There you experience that supreme State from which nothing has ever come. This greatest bliss is based upon the realization of the Self. It is peace, identical with liberation, indescribable and unborn.

When one transports oneself into the experience of Infinitude, nobody can say how long the experience will last. There is no count of time. To remain in the

State of Perfection — in the State of Thoughtlessness (nirvikalpa samādhi) — and to enjoy its bliss constantly for a long period of time, is the result of one's own inner purity and merit. Willing or wishing, desiring or determining, cannot make us stay there for any longer period of time. It is not an amphitheater where self-effort has any play. For an ordinary seeker, long periods of nirvikalpa samādhi are impossible. The one who is plunged in samādhi for long periods of time is indeed one who is to be congratulated. In case there be one who is experiencing this State of Beatitude constantly for a long period of time, he is indeed enjoying the results of endless merits he had acquired in the past. In its own logic, the individual is pushed out of its frontiers back into the relative fields. Even when one comes back to the realm of change, the individual is constantly conscious of his own Infinitude, but to remain in the Self as the Self, completely merged in the infinite Peace and absolutely resting in It, is not in the hands of the individual himself.

When you touch one live wire, you are in contact with universal electricity all over the world. With one drop of the Arabian Sea on the tongue, you have tasted the seven seas around the world. Eternity is experienced at the sacred depth of the present moment. To live in the present, independent of the past and the future, is to experience samādhi, the revealing culmination of meditation.

The supreme State experienced by the mystics, pointed out in all the great scriptures of the world, is the state that has been indicated by a most popular term in Hinduism, Śivarātrī. Śiva means auspiciousness. That State of Supreme Auspiciousness, the State of Perfection and Beatitude, is a state an individual experiences when all other usual fields of perception are transcended. Just as in the night, when the darkness closes in, every object becomes imperceptible to the human eye, a time when the usual world of plurality is blanked away from our awareness — such moments of pure, infinite, subjective Experience are that which is indicated as Śivarātrī.

Contemplation replaces the wrong thought with the right thought at the vāsanā level:

Swami Advayananda: Gurudev's commentary in *Ātma Bodha,* verse 37, had a deep impact on me. I began to understand that tackling erroneous notions about ourselves at the level of the mind alone was not enough. The change had to be brought about at the much deeper level of vāsanās, the layer beneath even our subconscious, for it to be effective. This was a totally new strain of psychology which I had not thought about! So long as the vāsanā of one being the BMI is not 'roasted' and obliterated, no real change can happen. Also, I realized only in nirvikalpa samādhi, the brahmākāra-vṛtti, the thought "I am Brahman," can be completely transfigured into the vāsanā "I am Brahman." The vāsanā of "I am the body–mind–intellect" cannot be annihilated by the thought "I am Brahman," but only by the vāsanā "I am Brahman," for one vāsanā alone can nullify another, since vāsanās are at the causal level and thoughts are at the subtle level. In nididhyāsana (contemplation) and savikalpa samādhi, the thought "I am Brahman" still remains a thought. It has not yet become the corresponding vāsanā. Even though the process of the "I am Brahman" vāsanā begins in the state of contemplation, nididhyāsana and savikalpa samādhi, where this thought-flow becomes effortless, it is only in nirvikalpa samādhi that this vāsanā reaches its perfection and has the muscle to put an end to the vāsanās — "I am the BMI," "I am but a doer and an enjoyer," and so on (which are termed 'viparīta-bhāvana,' that is, notions contrary to the knowledge "I am Brahman"). Thus, it becomes imperative for the seeker to reach nirvikalpa samādhi in his spiritual pursuit.

Are time and duration relevant in the state of samādhi?

***Anjali Singh**:* One day, I asked Swamiji, "How long does one have to remain in nirvikalpa samādhi? A highly evolved person told me that it should be a few hours at least!" Swamiji said, "Time itself is a concept of the intellect and the time-space world alone has the ego. Whether it is for one minute or many hours, this calculation is in this world of time and space. If you have once tasted one drop of water of the Bay of Bengal, what do you taste? — All the seven seas are in your mouth now!"

Difference between the thought-less-ness of deep sleep and nirvikalpa samādhi:

Swami Advayananda: During 1992, when Gurudev took the entire *Vivekacūḍāmaṇi* in Sidhbari, our Sandeepany Mumbai batch was lucky enough to be sent there. Gurudev often referred to the ocean of difference between thoughtlessness in nirvikalpa samādhi and the deep-sleep state. One is reached when overpowered by tamas, whereas the other is reached by the fullness of sattva. After waking up from deep sleep, one knows one has slept; after getting up from nirvikalpa samādhi, one does know quite well that one has not slept!

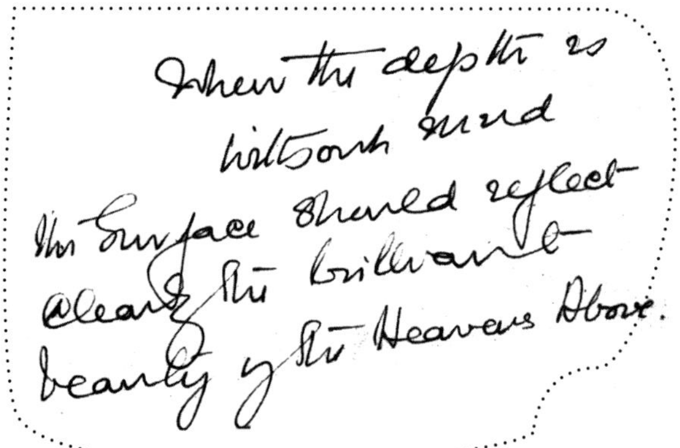
When the depth is
without wind
the surface should reflect
clearly the brilliant
beauty of the Heavens Above.

*N*o amount of study is of any avail. Fulfill the reading with meditation. Through meditation, crawl up to the arena of Joy and Peace. There in the Topmost Tower, we shall meet away from all disturbances. Come. I am waiting for you.

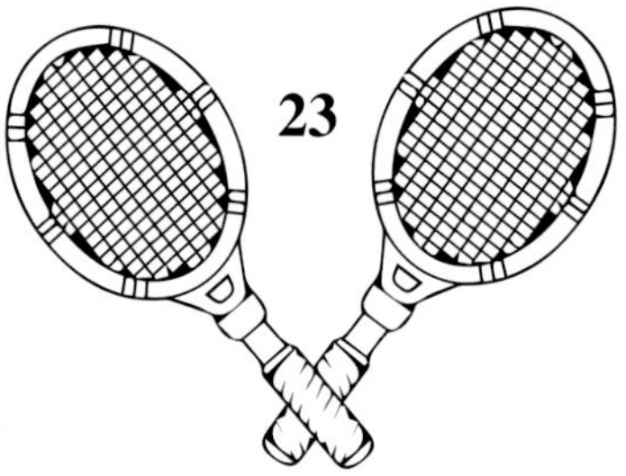

23

Grand Slam!

Swamiji looked at the player on the TV screen and said, "The Winning Post is yet far away!" A devotee wondered: "How far? One year? Two years? How many years… or lifetimes? One gets discouraged if it seems far!" Looking at the player, Swamiji said, "If you tell some people that it is difficult and far away, they get inspired and take it as a challenge. There is the other type, the one who needs to be told that it's not far. This one is the type that needs encouragement. Yes, I will encourage him."

The "Winning Post" is the absolute Knowledge, through Realization of the Self, to which a person awakens. Realization is spontaneous and natural — like realizing that one is looking at a rope and not a snake on the ground. Ignorance as to the nature of the Self goes away totally. The seeker and the sought — indeed the whole world — are realized as One. The mind becomes like a frail cobweb that has suddenly dissolved into nothingness. The mind that continues thereafter, since the body has to continue, is a mind that no longer has the power to persecute one as it did before. It is now like a genie that serves the Master.

This Awareness about the nature of the Self frees one from the identification with the body–mind–intellect, and their modifications, and is called the state of Jīvanmukti, the State of Liberation — even while living. In Yoga Vāsiṣṭa, which is a treatise on contemplation, three further stages are mentioned even after the Realization of the Self, the fifth, sixth, and seventh stages of spiritual evolution. But it is to be noted that these are only the degrees to which the mind dwells in the Knowledge of the Self. The Knowledge itself remains the same throughout, irrespective of how much the mind dwells on it, or the bliss it derives from it, that is occasioned with the absence of the perception of the world. Having gained this Self-knowledge, one attains Jīvanmukti, after which there are no more births in the world of becoming.

There are two types of seekers who reach this far to the doorway of jīvanmukti. One is the seeker of Knowledge who has pursued the path by following the steps of śravaṇa, manana, and nididhyāsana that are given in Vedānta sādhanā. This seeker "takes it as a challenge" and follows the sādhanā prescribed. He is not daunted by the difficulties. The other type is the devotee who has total devotion to God or Guru and has surrendered everything completely into the hands of God. The "encouragement" that Swamiji refers to is assistance, which God or the Guru surely gives because of the devotee's love and total surrender.

Both types receive Knowledge. One expands his notion of the Self and proclaims, "I am Brahman," and in the fullness of his comprehension attains the state of Jīvanmukti. The other shrinks his ego into extinction and declares, "I don't exist; whatever is, is only God." In the case of such a devotee, the omnipresent and compassionate God assists ("encourages") him to look within and realize the Self. The final goal, call it Self-realization or God-realization, is one and the same and is thus achieved by both — the seeker of liberation and the devotee of the Lord.

THE JOY OF REALIZATION

Once the recognition of the Self, or the dawn of Knowledge, takes place, which happens effortlessly and spontaneously, the mind, the now flimsy ego-veil disappears like a thin cobweb. The PFT (perceiver–feeler–thinker) disappears into the all-pervading Self and realizes with complete certainty that "I am the timeless, spaceless Self." The 'knower' becomes Knowledge itself, since the knower and the object of Knowledge coalesce. 'I' realize that the world of multiplicity is 'I the Self.' This is the State of Consciousness called Jīvanmukti — liberated in life. This Consciousness is full of Bliss and it IS. It is neither a void nor nothingness, but one cannot say it exists in the same way as an object exists. It cannot even be called as a 'State' with reference to the mind. This Reality is the only Reality. The objects that we, in ignorance, consider as real and on which we thus bestow existence and reality are truly ephemeral and do not stand the test of time. When the recognition happens for the first time, one is taken aback — first, because of the ease with which it takes place and one wonders why the Self was not recognized earlier since it was always there; and, second, because the experience of Bliss, the sense of total freedom, and the sense of fulfillment are overwhelming.

Swami Chinmayananda:

The Indescribable:

"Oooo Aah! Oooo Aah!!" cannot be understood in the context of the ego. It is the divine roar of a person who has reached the summit of his evolution, breaking all the shackles of his attachments, and has escaped from the gruesome dungeon in the castle of matter. The cry of wonderment is a declaration when I come face to face with the vastness and splendor of the effulgent One. It is also a revelation, because normally wonder is an emotion that comes to me whenever I apprehend something that is beyond my intellect to comprehend and beyond my mind to feel. At all such experiences, when my reasoning faculty is benumbed and my feelings frozen at the onslaught of an experience, I cry out, "Ha! — the wonder!"

I know no Sanskrit. I know no Hindi. I know no language to express what I know. In brief, I know that I know not how to make you know what I know. I know that I know not, yet I know what I know. My Gurus know that I know, but I know not how to make you know what my Gurus know. Knowledge is unknowable, yet the unknowable becomes known when a knower explains it to be the knower's own Self, which illumines for him the very urge to know. Beneath the waves is the eternal, still silence of majesty and fullness. Light rays are blasted into a million fragments only when they strike the agitating bosom of the restless waves. The dim, green light that filters through the depths seems to be coiled up there upon itself … for in the womb of the ocean, the reflections caused by the precious gems of the deep, dance no more, but merge themselves to be one with the mellow blaze of light. The Light of Knowledge is split into shreds only when it strikes the surface of life: plurality begins in and ends with the phenomenon. Serene in the recesses of the bosom, when Knowledge comes to know itself, the Wisdom Light is one homogeneous whole, in which the unknown becomes known without the distorting intervention of a knower knowing the knowledge. In short, unless you are ready to take a plunge into your own within and move up beyond the mind and the intellect to the very source of all light, power, and wisdom, I know not how to make you know what I know. (Written by Swamiji in Uttarkashi, 1951.)

An individual, when he comes to discover even an ordinary joy or beauty, almost goes mad and strives to explain the experiences to his fellow men. Thus, we have the sons of bards in every language, besides the various columns of literature, on every branch of knowledge. Instances are not wanting where scientists have almost gone mad when they suddenly, during their deep study, discovered for themselves one more secret of nature. Newton, certainly, could not have felt so much the pain of the apple falling on his nose as the joy of his thoughts over a gravitational force that draws everything toward the earth! Archimedes ran naked directly from his bathtub, crying "Eureka! Eureka!" through the streets of the city when he discovered for the first time how volumes can be measured by measuring the water displaced by material objects!

Give a piece of jaggery to a dumb man, he enjoys it, his eyes sparkle, his lips smile, and he cries out, "Aah, Aah!" Now you ask him, "Is it good?" "Aaah!!" …. He replies and makes signs and sounds to express himself — but he cannot. Then you ask him, "Please explain, what is the taste?" The poor man is silent. To taste a piece of jaggery in any part of the world is sufficient to give us an experience of the taste of all the jaggeries of every part of the world, in all the periods of time. Similarly, when the great sages of old, in their silent contemplation upon Truth, came to realize the godliness that is eternally their nature, they roared forth their joy calls and victory trumpets to their generation in their joy of the absolute Perfection. The wave has merged in the ocean. The pot has been crushed and has become the mud. The dreamer has awakened. The Liberated-in-life is the supreme Self-in-action. Manhood has ended in sheer Godhood..

Self-realization is the unveiling ceremony of the Ātman within. An instrument, other than the Self, is not necessary in experiencing the Self-hood. Realization is only possible in the state of samādhi. One who has awakened to the supreme State, to him alone, there is total Liberation from the bondages of saṁsāra. The persecutions of a dream end when the dreamer wakes up!

Once successful, the Self-realized individual remains ever liberated from all bondages. This egoless state becomes natural to him. In the beginning, such a state can be frighteningly shocking, confusing to those who have no devotion to the Lord. It is a new dimension of experience: no ego — yet, we experience with the 'no-experiencer' in us! One is then no more in the objective world of things and beings, but within a realm where the objective world is not, and yet is fully included. Nothing is excluded from the Self. Wonder is a sentiment that the human heart feels when the intellect comes in contact with a problem that it cannot solve itself. The mute intellect, trying to express its burning experiences through a choked heart, is the expression of supreme wonderment in the shock of realization when a man suddenly rediscovers that he is God!

All pleasures enjoyed by all living creatures and the celestial beings in all periods of time are only an infinitesimal fraction of the bliss experienced by the Man of Self-realization. The bliss of God-realization is of such magnitude that it is inconceivable by the human intellect. Scripture says, "There is nothing like It" in the range of our experiences today; therefore, it is incomparable.

This state, which is indescribable in terms of words, can be indicated by the Teacher only by giving us an analogy. Each student will understand it only according to his capacity. The example given is: Watch the heaving, seething, dancing, rolling, jumping, frisking waves of the roaring, thunderous ocean, ever frothing and fuming in the continuous clash of waves. When you see the undulating waves of the ocean, your mind also moves with them. Imagine then that the rising wave has suddenly frozen and the wave behind it has also come to an immediate halt. It is as though all the waves of the ocean have suddenly stopped at the magic wave of a wand, as though they have been stunned into freezing! All the waves have frozen suddenly into utter stillness. The awesome beauty of that silence, the majesty of that stillness perhaps could convey to your mind a vague picture of the boundless state of hushed joy that the realized one experiences when the mind becomes totally absorbed in the bliss of the silent Self. The student's mind halts.... He is pushed into a voiceless state of awe-filled joy and inexplicable peace. Try. If you can imagine this, you will come to experience a peculiar peace and silence. The whole world of plurality suddenly disappears totally — away from the sorrows of the world, ever liberated from the thralldom of the BMI — "That Thou Art"!

Point of no return:

Knowledge, as used in philosophy, is not the same as we use in our ordinary discourse of life. In the world-of-objects, by 'knowledge' we mean the knowledge of things which changes from object to object; we understand awareness only as the awareness of the existing mental waves. The attempt is to define the Awareness as such. Here, knowledge is meant the Knowledge Absolute, which is all-pervading. With the rise of Knowledge of Spiritual Bliss, the dreary darkness of ignorance ends and the ego, too, comes to a total extinction from which it cannot restart its career again.

When all selfish activities and thoughts dry up, there we come to 'experience,' 'live in,' and 'reach' Brahman. Any verb is wrong. At this stage, 'reach' if you say, "Where were you before?" Can the dreamer 'reach' the waker? The dreamer 'arrives' at? Wrong! 'Recognizes?' Wrong! Any verb is wrong. At this stage verbs end, because no verb is really suitable! Will I, at that time, 'see' Paramātma? How can I? — without the body! At that time, will I 'embrace' Paramātma? How can I? — without two hands! Just as a dreamer rediscovers himself to be the waker, you — who was the little ego — 'rediscover' your identity with Brahman.

There is no other example by which we can indicate this great Consciousness, which is all-pervading and eternal. It can only be compared with space. Space itself is not the ultimate Reality. It is the nearest indicative illustration, inasmuch as it is the subtlest of all elements. Space is often taken as an example for Consciousness. Since it has the property of sound, it becomes a substance. Things which have properties and are substances, are finite, ever-changing objects. Since space is an object, it has a beginning and an end. Ātman is not space, but is like space for the purpose of intellectual understanding. A Self-realized one testifies to a depth — a dimension in experience — that defies speech and thought and yet provides a more realistic experience than any sense-impressions.

From there he never comes down again under any circumstance, having established wherein there is not an iota of sorrow; even the heaviest sorrow disturbs him not. Like the prophet on the cross nailed five times, he cries: "Father, forgive them, for they know not what they do!" — a state of total satisfaction. Understand that to be yoga, which is a divorce from our wedlock to sorrow. Once the State of Self is reached, the Man of Realization lives that experience all the time. He can never come out of it because it is timeless and therefore endless.

Rare indeed is the man who is completely established in his identity with the Higher. Such a rare one sits ever merged in the Self, extremely relaxed and completely happy as a result of the infinite merits acquired in the many, many lives in the past. When he thus lives established in his divine Self, he is the most revered one on the surface of the earth.

When such a saint functions in our world of plurality, to him it is a sport with his own Self, because he sees nothing but the Self, playing as plurality. When the saint, tired of sporting with his own Self in the many, folds up the mind and enters into his meditative inner poise, he revels in the pure Self as the Self.

Till you have got it, you've not got it; but when once you've got it, you've got it! Till this moment of fulfillment, a devotee seeks, strives, and learns to surrender totally to the Infinite all his egocentric finite passions and appetites. When once this identification with the higher Self is complete, then there is no more any sense of separation between the seeker–devotee and his Love. He melts to become his love for his Love. Such a pure love, such devotion in its entire fulfillment, comes to manifest or express itself in some rare bosoms of only a very rare set of individuals. Based upon this same eternal truth, Lord Kṛṣṇa explains in the *Gītā* why this divine Love comes to manifest Itself very, very rarely: "At the end of many births, the wise man comes to Me, realizing that all this is Vāsudeva (the innermost Self). Such a Mahātmā (great soul) is very hard to find."

A devotee in the parabhakti (supreme devotion) stage, at the culminating point of his love, comes to ask a question unto himself: "All around I see the all-pervading Lord. I am His love, He, my Beloved. I see nothing else, I see only Him, I see Him everywhere, but then who am I?" This is the flame that comes to be applied to the prepared pile of emotions, and in a blinding flash of Illumination Supreme, the entire bundle of māyā (illusionary or ignorant) disturbances and equipment gets forever blasted into nothingness. With this supreme question, the devotee looks within. At that stage of devotion-prepared intensity, he can see nothing but the Lord, whether inside or outside, and in that inward gaze, he meets himself, his own devoted Beloved: he, the devotee, ends in the conflagration — the Lord alone thereafter exists, as eternally full as ever.

A description is not possible since it is not an experience; also, there is no connection between the two states:

In a letter to ***Susheela Purushottam:*** The final stage is NOT an experience. Due to lack of words, which the student should understand, we borrow this word. The dreamer is not experiencing waking. The waker can never experience sleep. Dreamer ends. Waker ends. Not into zero! That is OM!

Letter to ***Swamini Kaivalyananda:*** At such a moment when the individual ego gets sucked into the higher State of Consciousness, he experiences perfect Knowledge. His mind then is zero, just as in sleep your mind is zero.

One wondered how there could be a doubt in anyone's mind whether Swamiji was realized or not; yet he was asked this question many times, and never did he say, "I am realized":

Swami Chidrupananda: Someone asked Gurudev, "Are you realized"? Gurudev smiled as he read out the question in a Q&A session and said: "I am waiting at the threshold. I can walk into vaikuṇṭha at any time. But I am not walking into it alone. Poor Viṣṇu is lying inside without any inspiration, because only occasionally someone walks into Vaikuṇṭha and greets Him. Viṣṇu has never seen too many entering vaikuṇṭha in one go, so let us enter His abode together as a large group and surprise Him."

STEP 7

HOW TO LIVE WITH WISDOM

*O*ne who has reached the peaks to become one with the Highest, there is nothing for him to gain as his desires have all ended. He enjoys endless freedom from the castle of matter. No more can the vehicles of flesh enslave him, nor the shackles of emotion chain him, nor can the whip of desire lash him. He has ended all vāsanās and crossed over the morass of ignorance. Out of the mortal has emerged the immortal; from darkness he has walked into light.

-Swami Chinmayananda

24

World Number One

World Number One: "The God-man functions as a true 'sportsman' in his playfield, where the very enjoyment is in the sport and not in the score!"

Swamiji himself was a perfect example of a Man of Perfection ("a true sportsman"). He was always joyous, bubbling with laughter. All those who came to him felt happy being in his presence — such was the aura around him. He worked twenty hours a day and loved his work. To him, life was like a game of sport, where one should put in one's best, while enjoying the entire process, and without worrying over the results ("the score"). That's the real purpose of a game.

There are so many instances when, despite dire circumstances, Swamiji's reactions were so natural, unflustered, and full of ease. In October 1991, he was in a precarious condition in the ICU of Yol Cantonment Hospital near Sidhbari. When asked how he was, he said that he had left the body twice and had then come back. "What was the experience?" He answered, "Param Ānanda! [Supreme Happiness]." When asked, "What pulled you back into the body?" He said that it had just happened on its own. One assumed that it was samaṣṭi prārabdha — the destiny of the totality. Since he had talked longer than doctors had advised, he said, "Now I am going to sleep. Do you know the art of sleeping?" He yawned. We waited. Even in that condition, after a heart attack, when his heart had stopped beating twice, he was the teacher. He said, "You have to struggle to sleep at first, but then you must let go of the struggle and let sleep happen." Then he lay back and shut his eyes and the devotees left the room. He had just given an important instruction in meditation: You have to make the effort at first; then you need to let go of the effort and let meditation happen.

A DIFFERENT LENS

The State of Jīvanmukti (State of Liberation while living) is not only a deliverance from the oppression of pain but a positive experience of bliss. A Jīvanmukta, or a Man of Perfection, gets liberated from the thralldom of matter, from the conditionings that made him feel troubled. He had been suffering needlessly all his life, searching for happiness, and now he finds himself in permanent bliss! The Man of Perfection no longer views the world from the limited viewpoint of a PFT. His is the larger vision — seeing through a different lens. He roams about the world in complete freedom. Identified with the Totality, he is not capable of doing wrong. The Man of Perfection lives in the firm conviction that he is sat-cit-ānanda, that he is the ever conscious, all-pervading, blissful Reality and needs no reminders about it! He is the one who truly lives the meaning of his name. While interacting with the world, he is ever conscious of its false diversity and impermanent nature, and because of this understanding, the world can pose no threat.

Swami Chinmayananda:

It is not that something different is seen, but that one comes to see everything differently. It is as though a new dimension changed the spatial act of seeing. A Jīvanmukta has severed his contact with the world of becoming, where things are constantly changing to become something else.

When a description like 'unborn' or 'undying' becomes a description of me, then I have known the Truth; otherwise, it is an intellectual experience of an idea.

This is the last stage of the pilgrimage — the termination of all efforts, the fulfillment of all seeking, and the end of all evolution, the Goal Divine. After realizing this inner state of fulfillment, no more is that Man of Perfection a victim of the world of plurality, nor is he, thereafter, ever afraid of the flux of matter. Within and without, he is the Lord of the vehicles and the objects of his experience. Drawing his inspiration from the omnipotent Infinitude, the Sage walks the earth in the strides of a God — as a liberated soul, free from the paltry viewpoints of selfish individuality. His are the joys of perfection; his, the powers of the Divine; his, the freedom of the soul. Ever a God-man, he moves among man-Gods.

With such a peaceful and conquered mind and intellect within, the Man of Perfection lives in the world like an uncrowned king, a sovereign of sovereigns. He sometimes sports with all enjoyments, and sometimes he is seen retired to the mountain retreats, on the Ganges banks, and there he lives lost in samādhi. To a Man of Realization there is nothing to gain or to lose — either by the practice of meditation or by working in the world. He may serve mankind through any form of activity in the world outside, or he may accomplish this through meditation and prayer. Periods of history reflect the tempo of man and his social activities. He may serve the era of his time due to the pressure of the total vāsanās of the community, or he may withdraw into his own inner experience. If the world is peopled by a generation that requires the services of a Master, the total demand of the community works through him.

It is a criminal misrepresentation of Vedānta to say that a Man of Realization should run away from life into the dead jungle. Vedānta would not have been a self-surviving philosophy in all these periods of history if the perfection conceived was to send people away from the world and its joys — from the great scheme of nature, the reveling beauty, and the gorgeous extravagance of light and color, which smile ecstasy into a dull and dreary darkness. Be it in Jerusalem or in Mecca, call him the Son of the Lord or a Prophet, a messenger of the Highest — all of them, after realization, lived and worked for mankind and reveled in themselves constantly in their inward Perfection. In fact, they alone brought into our life the flashes of love and light, life and liveliness, which constitute the glory of all civilizations.

A Man of Realization acts inspired in any field of endeavor that comes to him as his lot without ever getting himself shackled by the duties attached to it. To him, all activities become an engaging sport, a joyous relaxation, an entertaining play.

The liberated one who has ended his ego and has 'become' the Self is no more under any injunctions and laws of right conduct or ideal behavior prescribed by the Vedas to the ego in man. He cannot be touched by the laws of duties and responsibilities projected and maintained by the mind-in-disturbance. He is a law unto himself, and all injunctions in the scriptures upon the right code of conduct are ordered by such a perfect man's motive, attitude, and behavior. His life itself is a scripture, his words are hymns, and his actions are blessings upon the world. He is the fulfilled, the perfect. In such an accomplished man, we watch God and His play. He is also at all times, on all occasions, under all situations, a master of himself and a dynamic force to be reckoned with. He is the man who will guide the destinies of the world, not only in his own times but also in the days to come.

When the final Beatitude is experienced, man is unruffled by the painful experiences that he may have to live thereafter in the world. Once the State of Self is reached, the Man of Realization lives that experience all the time — he can never come out of it — because it is timeless and therefore endless. With his equipment he also suffers his joys and sorrows. But he has an extra smile on his face, seeing which the world is tempted to put him on the cross.

His supreme balance-of-mind, under all conditions outside, is the final test to know a liberated person. Neither the beloved of the dream, nor the tiger of the dream can ever bring any mental disturbance in one who has awakened from his dream! For such a mind, death has no ferocity; love, no enchantment. Power has no satisfaction; wealth has no charm — for the true Man of Wisdom.

This can be observed in life when we observe a devotee closely. A Christ in rags, a Buddha under a Bodhi tree, a Ramakrishna in the Kali temple, a Vivekananda on the cold railway platform in America, a Guru Gobind Singh encircled with danger and threat to his life at every moment, a Rama Tirtha in the valleys of Himalayas ... none of them could, in any sense of the term, be conceived as having been provided with any reason to be happy or joyous. Yet, these are the rare ones who wore their eternal smile at the perfection achieved, the contentment gained, and the tranquility discovered.

A great musician, accepted as the greatest in the world cannot, while singing, miss a beat or break the tunes or topple the rhythm, and future artists imitate him as the ideal. In the same way, a Man of Perfection, who has eliminated from himself his ego and its desires, can never come to look upon the world as we do and set up a relationship with the world based upon passions and attachments, which are the delusory methods of an egocentric man of ignorance. What he does is thereafter the ethics and morality for his generation to follow. Even the Vedas are but a compendium of how such Men of Perfection felt and acted under various circumstances. A Sage of Perfection is a creature of inspiration, an artist of life who cannot go wrong. The earth comes to be blessed and shines out in diviner glory in the Great Man who beams out divinity all around. The most blessed people in the world respect and revere him. A Man of Realization is the conclusion of the product of millions of lives of noble work. He is the holiest of the holy.

He who has experienced the Higher refuses to remember and relive the past. Like a signature on running waters, nothing can stay in a God-realized person to leave behind a vāsanā. The Man of Realization can only act; he will not be ever found to react.

Even if we meet a realized One, we will not recognize him or accept him. He cannot be intelligible to us. He is unique. He is understood only by yet another Sage! To the extent we grow within ourselves, to that extent alone we will be able to understand the perfect Man's beauty and glory. An infant child will not be able to recognize, appreciate, or make use of a brilliant nuclear scientist.

Query *from a Postal Lesson Course student:* Swamiji, does a person who has realized the Truth work in this worldly life?

Swamiji: Activity is the insignia of life. Where all activities have ended, life has ceased and that is the state of death. Truth is very much alive; It is the very life in all creatures. A man who is realizing the Truth is not courting death but is a seeker of life itself. Therefore, when he realizes It, he becomes irresistibly vibrant with a roaring life. In divine spontaneity, activity gurgles through him with a staggering velocity, with a breathtaking beauty, and with a never-to-forget efficiency. A physical equipment of BMI is generally too frail a reed to stand the blazing gush of love and work; and, therefore, such prophetic Masters generally fold up in a blinding flash of brilliant service to mankind, carried on for a short duration of perhaps twenty or thirty years.

Your question is "Why should he work?" Can you tell me why the sun is illumining, why fire is hot, sugar sweet, oceanic waters salty, birds fly, flowers bloom, mirrors reflect, air moves, and earth revolves? Are they not their essential nature? The realized Saint is one with life. And life expresses itself in action. Can a person who has achieved the higher Consciousness, become a businessman, considering that a businessman has to suppress others by foul means in order to survive? That is, can business and spiritual life go together? Every prophetic sage, recorded history tells us, was an efficient and effective businessman! He did his business with efficiency and profit for all. The 'shops' that he opened in his lifetime rarely got closed down. Two thousand years ago, a petty carpenter's son started the business of 'interior decoration' and selling flowers of love and seeds of charity. The business has not yet folded!! Are you comparing these mighty men with the modern businessman whom you see in the world around you? … With a heart of love and selflessness, Men of Wisdom pursue the pure business of rehabilitating man into a nobler State of Peace and Purity.

How to recognize a saint:

Swamini Kaivalyananda: During the Vivekacūḍāmaṇi Camp at a satsaṅga, Br. Aniket asked Gurudev how to identify a saint. His concern was that because around that time some well-known saints had attained Mahāsamādhi — the saint population was getting scarce! Gurudev said, "India is a land which will always have saints. They could be anyone — a person who is making cow dung cakes [patties for fuel], or just sitting silently near a garbage pit, or even sitting under a tree. If you want to recognize saints, you should reach their level."

How to gauge whether we have reached the destination:

Anjali Singh: In 1992, I spent two-and-a-half months in Sidhbari when Swamiji taught the entire *Vivekacūḍāmaṇi* text. When I returned home to Delhi, I found that my domestic staff had run away with 90 percent of all my silver articles. I felt really bad for two minutes. But because of the euphoria of Swamiji's talks still in my head, I recovered quickly from the shock of the loss. I laughed out loud, finding it so funny that the *Vivekacūḍāmaṇi* lesson on dispassion had been put to the test so soon! At that time, Isabel Taylor was with me. She was quite astounded and reported the incident to Swamiji when we met him that evening. He asked, "Did you really feel bad only for two minutes?" I was feeling happy that Swamiji had appreciated my quick bounce back, but then he continued, "When you don't feel bad for even two minutes, then you can consider that you have reached the destination!" That time has still not come!

May the Lord of Smiles
Smile through you at the Sad
Suffering world around. The
Confused man wrapped up in
his false values creates, all for
himself, a miserable world of
pains and conflicts, tensions
and struggles.

In joyous abandon
listen to His enchanting Flute
within. Get mad with Love
and Beauty that floods from
Him within you. Embrace
everyone with this gushing bliss
of His Glory. Live Love Love,

Chinmaya

THE AWESOME POWER OF HUMAN LIFE

If human beings understood that the rare God-given chance to fulfill their ultimate purpose is waiting for them in this life itself, they would wake up and not waste so many years in non-productive endeavors. If the 'Sampras' in us understands that this wakeup call is the Guru's compassion and grace, our lives will be fulfilled to an extent we cannot imagine possible. This wonderful human life holds the capacity for great achievement. Each human being has the capacity to understand his true nature — his identity with God, Brahman — to realize that he is immortal, ever aware, forever blissful, and unconditionally happy. After the State of Jīvanmukti, as he abides more and more in the Self, a deeper quietude and shine comes to his mind. These are the fifth, sixth, and seventh stages of spiritual evolution expounded in the *Yoga Vāsiṣṭha*. The divinity that manifests itself in a Saint, rooted in his divine Self, is the divinity that is attributed to Godhood. This divinity has the power to influence an entire era to embrace a better system of values in life. This is seen in the lives of the Saints and Sages in history. Christ's teachings have influenced the morality of generations for over two millennia; Buddha's message of compassion for over two-and-a-half millennia; Veda Vyāsa's compilations for seven millennia; and Ādi Śaṅkara's works for about one-and-a-quarter millennium. These are a few among the many who have preserved sanity in the human race.

Swami Chinmayananda:

Man alone of all the species of the living kingdoms, can hasten his own evolution by cooperating with the great eternal scheme of things around him. If in this life you come to know this great Truth — great is the gain. One does not realize the enormity of the loss, if, after trillions of lives, you come to gain a human birth and you do not utilize it to fulfill your life and reach the Goal.

We have the inimitable philosophy, the likes of which the world had never seen before, wherein the sacred embraces the secular. In the eyes of the Realized, there is nothing but perfection reveling in disorder and confusion. A little self-discipline, a few little adjustments in the valley of life, will make the very same world of agitations, passions, and sorrows into a heaven of perfect joys.

Truly great souls are, indeed, at any given period of history, very rare; therefore, it is not always possible for all people to come into contact with them. And even if we do, it is extremely difficult to recognize their greatness and to tune ourselves fully to them. And yet, in case we meet and recognize a Master and learn to diligently come under his beneficial influences, he is unerringly infallible. When he lives established in his divine Self, he is the most revered one on the surface of the earth.

It is only the unique ones — a Buddha, a Christ, a Śaṅkara, a Vivekananda, and other Masters — who have blessed the world, and it is only they who have molded the human character into its nobility. They bring into this ugly, animal human nature a dose of love, an embrace of brotherhood, a sprinkling of tolerance, mercy, goodness, kindness, and thereby bring about a general purification of the total vāsanās of the world. The mental and the intellectual behavior of the entire world thereby improves. In place of a life of strife, hate, quarrels, and war, there comes the reign of peace, tranquility, and prosperity on earth. One such life inspires a whole world to strive for such an ideal existence.

Many are the stories in our treasure houses which indicate how even a passing word of a great Master has come true in the end. There is nothing strange in it. When a radio is tuned up to Delhi, it cannot but relay the songs sung in the Delhi broadcasting room. Similarly, a God-man, who in his realized Self-perfection, has totally tuned himself to That, will not and cannot express himself in futile words. All his thoughts are the thoughts of the Total Mind. His words are always the immutable words of the divine Will. This ought to be the intelligent understanding of every disciple if he is to profit from the grace of a Guru in the spiritual field.

It is these mighty Men of Realization, who move about tenderly serving humanity, who add a secret glory and meaning to all actions, making karma a sukarma, and who lend the compelling authority to the scriptural texts. The scriptures would have had no authority — or authenticity — had it not been for these great ones and their exemplary lives. Because of them, we have been able to have and understand, at least a little, the sacred scriptures. Otherwise, the scriptures would have been only a glorious vision. The very destiny of man is directed thus by their mere presence. When such a Man of Realization lives established in his divine Self, he is the most revered one on the surface of the earth. By the very existence of such an individual, his tribe becomes blessed, his family purified, his mother fulfilled, and the entire world rendered blessed.

If a single-pointed mind wishes for anything to the exclusion of any contending thoughts or desires, it shall at once be fulfilled. One who has complete control over his mind is a God upon earth, whose wishes become, as they cross his mind, accomplished facts. Continued love and dedicated loyalty gives to the Lover a certain secret authority over his beloved. When a devotee has lived sufficiently long, a full life of divine pursuit, his expanding heart of purity and faith gurgles up a flood of confidence and assurance in its own nobility and in the Lord's infinite kindness. In this confidence, the devotee dares even to command the Supreme to serve him in dire moments. This power to command comes to him as a privilege of love, in the authority of faith, sanctified by the moral dignity that comes to him as a result of his chaste life of tapas.

When a devotee rises to the level where his heart overflows with love, when his body shivers in joyous horripilation, and when he bathes in a constant pool of blissful tears, then the mothers and fathers (ancestors) in the worlds, rejoice. The gods dance in ecstasy in the presence of such lovers of the Lord living in the world. Intoxicated with their love, these people move about in the world. The serenity of their purified presence sanctifies the places already considered holy and sacred. It is not because of the place that a man becomes great, but the places are made holy because of the men who have occupied them. People go to Gaya to prostrate at the Bodhi tree, not because the tree is great but because the Buddha sat there and rediscovered his Immortality there. When mighty men live in a place, that spot becomes a pilgrim center.

Such a Self-realized Master's mere existence in the world is in itself a blessing to the people and their whole era. The contemporaries, not realizing the contributions of such men, invariably punished them through neglect, slander, insults, and persecutions. In Bharat, we had recognized this truth long ago, and when others were forcing their philosophers to empty a cup of poison, or were dragging their prophet to the cross, or were defeating and routing their messengers from God, we, in this country, had an endless tradition of serving such men with reverence and devotion. In the language of our own dynamic Yogis, we can say that such Men of Realization become channels conveying the Super-consciousness into life. They bring down the higher Life to enrich and nourish the base life of everyday cravings that we live through ordinarily. It is they who discovered things, revealed values, unveiled visions, inaugurated movements, which all ended in revolutionizing life. If man can today claim the glories of his civilization and culture, if the concepts of love, beauty, and freedom have come to us, all these are the gifts to man from such silent men of contemplation in the past.

While we think or act, at that moment that thought or act would seem as private, personal, limited, insignificant. But it moves, gathering a fresh momentum every moment, spreading its message, which grows more eloquent as it moves round the earth!! STRANGE!

The impact of the ṛṣis' words have reverberated down the centuries:

Bina Sutarwala: *Māṇḍūkya Upaniṣad* is an incredible text, and Gurudev took it extremely seriously. However, during the yajña in Sidhbari, he became very ill and had to end his last class midway. As he was being taken by ambulance to the hospital, he took off the ventilator, recited the last verse, and said, "I have now completed the text and many will gain, since it is out there in the Universe!"

Communication can take place even without the communicator's physical presence:

Swami Siddhananda: A Yuva Kendra couple moved from India to Philadelphia. They started coming to the āśrama, attending all the programs. On a 'Guru Pūrṇimā' day, I asked them to offer flowers and akṣata (food offering) to Gurudev's pādukās (sandals) while I chanted the aṣṭotharas. The young wife felt uneasiness and her eyes filled with tears. Actually she conceived on that day. All throughout the pregnancy they attended the classes, especially Gurudev's *Vivekacūḍāmaṇi* video lectures. In due time, a beautiful baby boy was born. After a few months, the couple had to move to another place. Unhappy, they desperately wanted to return. On August 3, 2013, Gurudev's Mahāsamādhi day, both of them received appointment orders for jobs near our place. A wonder, indeed! The child is very fond of Gurudev and always goes near the Pādukā Shrine. After all, he listened to the whole *Vivekacūḍāmaṇi* while in his mother's womb! In another incident, an American lady ordered a set of *Bhagavad-gītā* books for her classes. Curious, I asked her about the class. She revealed her story. She was a nurse at the San Diego hospital where Gurudev's samādhi took place. Seeing some divinity, she obtained a small sample of Gurudev's blood and kept it in her home. It completely changed her. She started learning the *Bhagavad-gītā* and became a teacher. It was a miracle for her.

I was at CIF Adi Sankara Nilayam (birthplace of Ādi Śaṅkarācārya) when we heard the news of Gurudev's Mahāsamādhi. On the day after, I received a letter from him — written from Washington, D.C. With trembling hands, I opened it. In that, he wrote "May Gurudev (Swami Tapovanji Maharaj) bless all at Adi Sankara Nilayam."

What another equally great saint had to say:

Dr. Shailaja Nadkarni: When Pūjya Gurudev was at Sharp Hospital in San Diego, California, in August 1993, many devotees gathered in the waiting area and chanted the Mahā-mṛtyuñjaya-mantra for him. That night, after everyone had left, I stayed back. The phone was ringing continuously with queries about Gurudev's health. At about 3:45 A.M., the phone rang once again. My heart was heavy and I was exhausted and feeling sad. The voice on the phone said, "This is Chidananda; how is Chinmaya? I have come from India to meet him." I told him that Gurudev was in critical condition and was in intensive care. Swami Chidanandaji Maharaj, who was head of the Divine Life Society and Pūjya Gurudev's Guru-bhāī (spiritual brother with the same Guru), said, "The Guru is never critical. Take your shoes off, go to his room, and bask in the presence of Brahman. Anyone who has a glimpse of Swami Chinmayananda has had total Īśvara-darśana."

Swami Chidananda and Swami Chinmayananda at 'Guru Niwas' in Rishikesh, 1985

Anjali Singh: When Swami Chidanandaji Maharaj had come to Sidhbari in 1994 for the 'First Mahāsamādhi Anniversary' of Swamiji and had looked at the pictures of Swami Sivanandaji Maharaj and Swami Tapovanji Maharaj by Gurudev's bedside table, he told us that when he had visited Swamiji at the San Diego hospital in August 1993, he had invoked the presence of both Gurus by Swamiji's bedside. Although it makes no difference to a great Mahātma, who has already merged with God in his lifetime, in what circumstances he leaves his body, but from the point of view of his devotees, it was a grand end to a great journey that all these holy men were there (in body and in spirit) in the last hours of Gurudev's human life!

A wealth of meaning can be derived from the statements of great saints. Hinting at the agami karma, which the devotees of saints receive as inheritance, Gurudev's gurubhai had this to say while taking a parikramā around his samādhi sthala (place) in Sidhbari. He said, "A bit of Swami Chinmayananda is in the hearts of each one of all his devotees, without exception!"

Truth manifest in a Master speaks to the faithful of all religions:

Swamini Radhikananda: The first time I saw Gurudev walking up to the dais, I heard his words, "Friends, this is not a lecture. It is a discussion between you and me." The quality of his voice reverberated unmistakably from the depths of his own spiritual experience, having true power to effect a change in my thinking. I realized what the Gospel writer meant about Jesus when he said: "For he spoke as one with authority, and not as the scribes and Pharisees do." (Matthew 7:29) Listening to him was the unforgettable turning point of my life. The last time I met Gurudev was in 1993 when he flew to San Diego, where he became gravely ill and was admitted to Sharp Hospital and underwent emergency heart surgery. At the hospital, doctors were allowing, very briefly, only two people at a time, to go into Gurudev's room. What I saw was the exact image of Christ crucified. The impact was too much to bear. The end came the next day. Later, another devotee described her experience of Gurudev in the hospital as the "Sleeping Buddha." I was meant to see him as Christ. But, why? The beneficent Lord knew that only one who reflected so literally the life and image of Christ could inspire enough faith in me to receive the sublime message of Vedānta.

A rare acknowledgement by Gurudev in Hong Kong — recalls ***Swami Swaroopananda:***

An extremely rare Master is one who not only serves society but is also a visionary who has plans for generations to come. Such an extraordinary rare Master was our Gurudev. The sun had just set beyond the horizon, and Gurudev sat surrounded by some devotees in Hong Kong. A question from our youth classes in Hong Kong seemed to be one without answers: "Why does a realized Person come back to this world? He knows, 'I alone am' and sees the world as an illusion. If so, to save whom or for what would he come back?" We knew the common answer was that we come into this world to exhaust our vāsanās; the realized Master comes back to serve the world, not out of desire but out of love. Our individual world comes to an end on Realization, Īśvara's creation continues. But… if God's creation is also an illusion and the world is an illusion, why would the Master come back?

Gurudev discerned that we were not going to give up our 'logical' reasoning. He placed his hands on his knees and bent forward toward us: "When a person realizes, he, the individual, has merged and gone. Through the shell of his body, the total vāsanās express themselves. Īśvara Himself expresses Himself. God finds that 'Here is a ready-made equipment. I don't have to go through the play of birth, growth, and be now and then spanked by the mother. Why not continue through this body?' That is why we say, 'gururbrahmā, gururviṣnuḥ, gururdevo maheśvaraḥ.'"

Before we could think of how to corner him further, Gurudev looked straight into our eyes; his own eyes turned within, the fingers of his hands turned toward his heart, and tapping his chest, in a deep voice he said, "The meditator who meditated is merged and gone; it is Nārāyaṇa functioning through this body, my children; it is Nārāyaṇa functioning through this body."

Some of the achievements possible in human life as seen in Gurudev:

Vinay R. Nair: Will you call him a *Visionary* because the projects he had envisioned materialized even after he left his mortal body? Will you call him a *Saint* because he learned, taught, and lived in the way prescribed in the scriptures? Will you call him *Leader* because wherever he went; he had a lot of followers? Will you call him *Spiritual Dynamo* because he could inspire the youth even when he was 77? Will you call him *Administrator* because he could head more than 200 centers worldwide, manage 80 schools, and administer hundreds of projects at the same time? Will you call him *Writer* because he wrote so many books and commentaries on the scriptural texts? Will you call him *Speaker* because leaving the audience mesmerized by his speeches was a common phenomenon? Will you call him *Psychologist* because he could understand the psyche of almost anybody? Will you call him *Architect* because he could give structural designs (even though he did not have an Engineering background for the institutions he built)? Will you call him *Guru* because he was a teacher to millions of people? Will you call him *Friend* because whenever you need him, the moment you think of him, he's there for you? Will you call him *Mother* because he loved everyone more than any mother would love her child? Will you call him *Father* because he shaped your personality? Will you call him *Military General* because he could give orders and put anyone to task without even pointing a gun at them? Will you call him *Scholar* because he was an expert in the scriptures? Will you call him *Storyteller* because no one could tell stories instantly as he did? Will you call him *Patriot* because every single task he took on would be to uplift the country? Will you call him *Humanitarian* because his love for mankind was the same, irrespective of which background they came from? What will you call a man who had experienced the blissful state of the Self and could have stayed in the Himalayas, but came down only to uplift the downtrodden people whom he never knew? What will you call him who lived every moment of his life for the welfare of humanity? What will you call him whose every breath was a teaching? What will you call him who worked eighteen hours a day, despite having heart and other ailments, only to serve humanity? What will you call him who would answer every letter any devotee would write to him, thus ending up writing an average of 40–50 letters every day throughout his life? What will you call him who showed you the right direction and purpose of your life? What will you call him who loves you more than anyone else could ever do? What will you call him who was all of the above and much more? You can call him by no other name but *Swami Chinmayananda*!

The power of the blessings of great saints:

K. Aiyappan Pillai *(101 years old in 2016, he has met the great saint Śrī Chattambiswami):* The Diwan of Koshi, Mr. Rama Iyer, arranged a meeting between Swami Vivekananda and Śrī Vidyadhiraja Chattambiswami. At first, Vivekananda was a little indifferent, seeing the swami in white clothes, but later his attitude changed to one of great respect. After Chattambiswami satisfactorily explained a query, Swami Vivekananda prostrated, touched his feet, and exclaimed, "You are indeed a great sannyāsī. Only now have I found the answer to my nagging questions." Placing both his hands on Vivekananda, the great saint blessed him, saying, "You will become one of the greatest figures of the world." Soon thereafter, in 1893, Swami Vivekananda addressed the World Parliament of Religions in Chicago. The saint Chattambiswami was also a frequent visitor to Poothampalli House, the home where Swami Chinmayananda was born. He was very fond of the baby Balakrishnan and used to shower him with lots of love and affection by placing him on his lap and singing bhajans to him. Thus, Chattambiswami blessed both Swami Vivekananda and Swami Chinmayananda. One became the renowned saint of the nineteenth century, and the other rose to become the illustrious sage of the twentieth century.

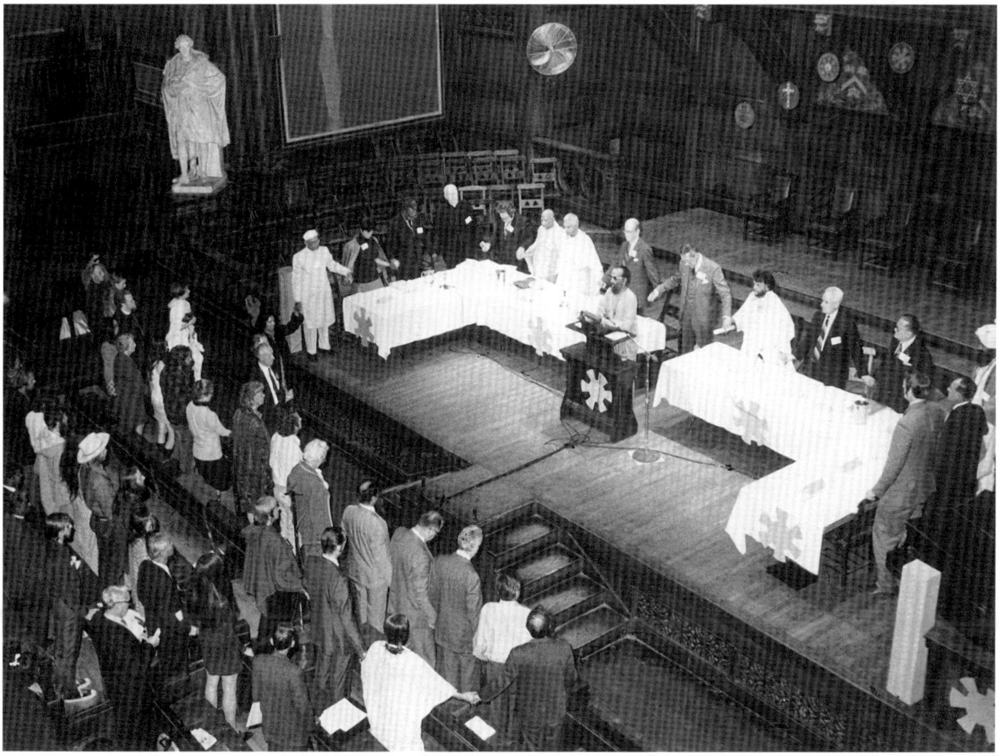

Swami Chinmayananda leading the prayer of all faiths at Harvard University

STEP 8

THE GRACE THAT IS THE GURU

When you are entering the inner realms of contemplation, you think you can do so without a Guru. Even in the outer activities, you need a teacher for everything. For this great Knowledge, a Guru is unavoidable. You have to have a Guru — have no doubt about it. This Knowledge is too sublime and subjective. Here, a Teacher is really necessary. We have to prepare our minds for him to work on. The mind must have the least ego; it must have devotion, faith, and reverence.

-Swami Chinmayananda

25

No Player?

In June 1993, one of the devotees who had watched the French Open on television with Swamiji, wrote to him (Swamiji was now in the U.S.A.): "Wimbledon starts the day after. I am sure I won't enjoy it as much as the French Open!! Riddle for you: Why does a tennis ball sometimes get stuck in the air, like a satellite in space, as if moving neither forward nor backward?" Swamiji replied on the letter itself: "There is no body to hit it!"

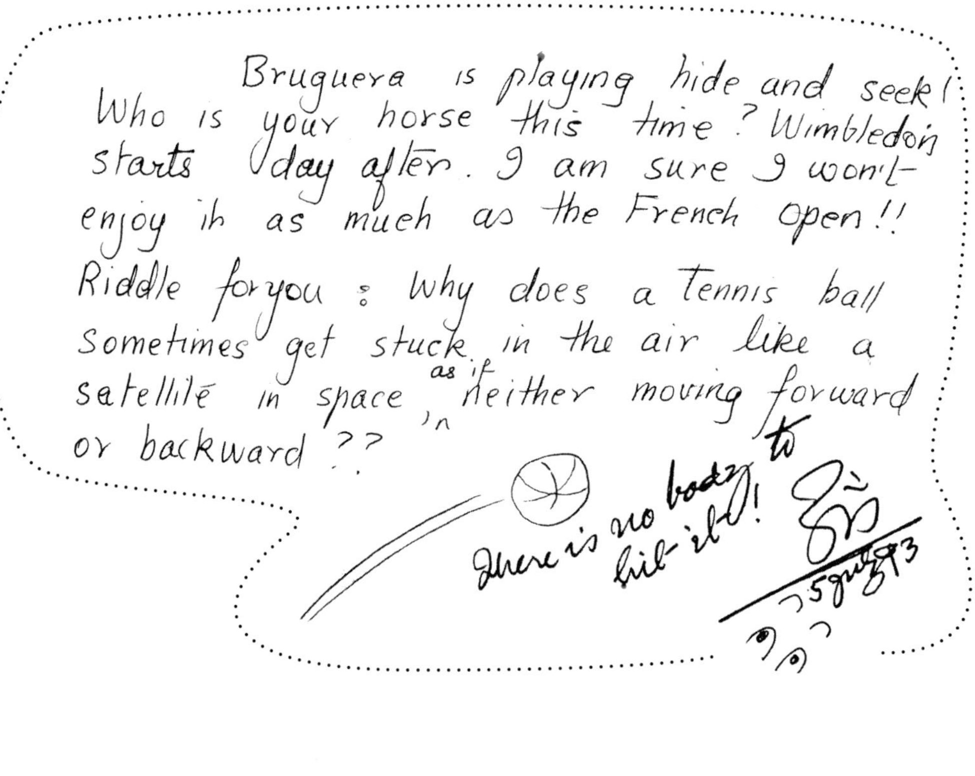

Bruguera is playing hide and seek!
Who is your horse this time? Wimbledon starts day after. I am sure I won't enjoy it as much as the French Open!!
Riddle for you: Why does a tennis ball sometimes get stuck in the air like a satellite in space as if neither moving forward or backward??

There is no body to hit it!

5 Jul 93

When the ego disappears ("there is no body to hit it"), the individuality recognizes its oneness with Brahman, which is infinite like space and timeless like eternity — an entity unto Itself, as no other entity exists. Brahman is not space, but the nearest example approximating It — as it is the substratum of even space, which is the subtlest of all elements.

So, this is how the knack of playing tennis in the court of life was imparted to the players and lovers of tennis in a Grand Slam played simultaneously in Roland Garros, Paris, and in Sidhbari in June 1993. Two days later, Swamiji left via Mumbai, Paris, and London for the U.S.A. and on August 3, 1993, he left his mortal frame in San Diego, California.

But for devotees, he has not gone anywhere. He is still sitting in his Samādhi Mandir in Sidhbari — as infinite Brahman, an ever-willing coach for players ready to come forward and play the game. Many devotees have experienced how, when they sit alone with him in Sidhbari or anywhere in the world to 'play the game,' they receive 'balls' of grace. He used to do this playfully, after a bhikṣā or a Pādukā Pūjā, when he would throw fruit (like tennis balls) at the devotees. The knack really is to be able to catch the ball (of grace). For that, all we have to do is take a leap of faith — with love.

The play has not stopped.
Next player, please… The score is Love All!

A UNIQUE RELATIONSHIP

A Guru is not needed for those who are still exploring. The right type of Guru will come to them when the search has ended and they are ready for the seeking. In the Guru's life itself, we see the ultimate proof of Self-knowledge. Just as in science, all previous discoveries are handed down to the next generation of scientists so as to retain the knowledge discovered, so, also, in the science of Self-discovery, spiritual Knowledge is handed down to fit students, who, in turn, become teachers to the next generation of seekers. This is called Guru-śiṣya-paramparā (Teacher-disciple lineage). Spiritual culture has survived in India because Self-realization has been an enduring goal of the nation. In particular, the relationship of Guru-śiṣya is crucial for the transmission and, thus, preservation of spiritual culture. Without this direct relationship, the essential medium for passing the torch is not there. In the spiritual search, a Guru is most essential and the Guru's relationship with each student is unique. The Guru will teach the student according to the student's personality and needs. In order to pass on the Knowledge of the Self, which is beyond explanation, a Guru, even if he is realized, needs to be well versed in the scriptures, which alone can give the method of conveying the profundity of the Self-knowledge to the students. Of course, there are exceptions where seekers can gain the Knowledge through silent transmission from the Teacher.

> No Guru can give; but we can endlessly take from him. Hence the glory of Guru Upasana: the Worship of the teacher. With devotion and reverence when we invoke the Grace of the Guru, the inner equipment in us becomes tuned up to recieve the Experience of the Self — expounded in the Upanishads, and explained by the Guru.

Swami Chinmayananda:

Gaṅgā stands for spiritual Knowledge for the Hindu — the eternal river of the Knowledge of the Self that has been kept up till today, flowing from Teacher to the taught in an unbroken perennial stream. To sip a drop of this spiritual flow is to enjoy the serenity and fullness of the inner kingdom. Some positively decry this belief — "What is there sacred in a river?" — Ask some! What a colossal ignorance of the symbolism! What is there in your national flag as such, except three colored pieces stitched together with a wheel-figure in the center? The sanctity of my country's flag is not in the material contents or the form of it, but in the significance that I have given to it. So, too, Mother Gaṅgā is sacred, for she signifies the spiritual wisdom and the flow of it along the Teacher-taught unbroken stream.

Vedānta is the foundation of all theories of Self-perfection though the techniques may differ from place to place and from Master to Master.

When one sheep has jumped over the stream, the whole flock jumps across on each other's heels.

A true Teacher is one who has both the ability to explain (Brahma-śrotriya) and who is also well established in the infinite Experience (Brahma-niṣṭha). When such a perfect Teacher and a true student have met, the student must strive to establish a true, deep, and intimate spiritual relationship with the Teacher. This is neither a mere intellectual appreciation of his philosophy, nor is its content a mere emotional love for him. A combination of these two — appreciation and love — when offered at any altar, is termed as *reverence*.

Guru is not a person; he is a personality, an institution. He is the radio through which the Lord contacts the student. When a student meets his Teacher, it is always a miracle. In fact, it is love at first sight. The student is immediately attracted to him and his words ring a bell. Another speaker may speak better, but only his Teacher will attract him. If you get the rare privilege of meeting such a Master and you happen to really understand a little of what he says, then progress has to happen. It is unfailing. It is very productive. Whenever anyone meets his Teacher, it is always a miracle. If in case you are benefitted, do not forget that the Teacher was brought to you by Īśvara (total vāsanās, of which a part were yours) — and remember, there is no difference between God and Guru, the corporeal entity before you. Therefore, be on the lookout when you meet a Master. Search! Seek! And fulfill!

The one in whom you have *faith* is your Guru. No individual mortal is ever a preceptor. The Lord alone is the Teacher everywhere, at all times. Seekers should not misuse the Teacher and discuss with him secular questions or domestic problems. It is almost prohibited. He should be asked only about the special Knowledge of the Self in which he is perfect. If you find peace in the presence of a Mahātma; if you are inspired by his speeches; if he is able to clear your doubts; if he is free from greed, anger, and lust; if he is selfless and loving; with whom if you compare your own life you feel ashamed of your own weaknesses — you can take him as your Guru.

To students of Vedānta, the Guru is the embodiment of their Goal. The Guru is nothing but pure Consciousness, absolute Bliss, and eternal Wisdom. Anyone who can elicit a continual feeling of faith and devotion in us is our Guru. If we expect a Guru to transform us to Godhood by a touch, we shall wait in vain. Self-redemption must come ultimately from within us. The external props, such as temples, idols, and Gurus, are all just encouragements. With inner purity, the student comes to be guided more and more by the intellect. In fact, the real Guru is the pure intellect within, whereas the purified, deeply aspiring mind is the disciple. When we come to deserve a Master, he shall reach us. Stick to your spiritual practices. Be good, kind, and sincere. Refine life's motives by building upon the enduring values of love, mercy, charity, and purity. Through constant remembrance of the Lord, rise in spirituality.

"O flower, you stay there; dance to the breeze and open up in the warmth of the sun and dance there." "But then there are no bees!" "Bees will come." "How are you so sure?" It is the Universal Law.

However much you may personally show devotion to the Guru, you will still be a stranger to him if you are not walking the spiritual path.

True disciples have to meet their Master but once. Even if the Master were not very perfect, the disciple's life pattern changes, and in his own inner maturity, he climbs the heights within. Hearing this Knowledge directly from the mouth of a Teacher is twenty times more powerful than if you read it.

A seeker must not lose chances of meeting known Mahāpuruṣas (great Spirits) and realized Ones. This doesn't mean unfaithfulness to your Teacher. You are a Vedāntic student seeking the Self in all. In the One, where is other? We visit and prostrate to every Master … to take what appeals, to rehear what has been heard, to draw fresh inspiration from such darśinas (those who see). It is a must. Fanatics had this rule — not to see anyone else except their own. This shows the limitation of their philosophy, their 'vision.' To the bird that flies in the Brahmic vastness, where is limitation, where is his boundary? Unlimited, boundless is he, his God, his Guru.

The Master can clearly see the spiritual destiny and the divine Perfection, which lie in the innermost core of the disciple. The impetuosity of the prārabdha of people makes a Mahātma function in the world in order to satisfy the demands of the disciples. The Teacher dies when the prārabdha of a disciple is over.

If a Guru takes you under his wings to guide you and protect you, it is a great blessing.

Swami Tapovanam, the Guru of Swami Chinmayananda, and Swami Chinmayananda at Tapovan Kuti, Uttarkashi, 1956

Don't forget the Creator when you see the product. Remember to be grateful to your Param-Guru when you feel grateful to me. All my life is the story of my love for him. Swami Tapovanji Maharaj was not a person. He was not just any historical entity; he was not a saint of the ordinary order, and he was indeed a miracle and a great blessing for the society that he lived in our times. The glory of what the Mission is doing is all his glory. It is that great Master who is your Grandsire in this organization and a silent Witness to what is going on here. We, his family of disciples, have a great responsibility to see that he finds an ample field in our individual bosoms to express himself. Swami Tapovanji Maharaj is a presence, a light, a fragrance, a glow. As such, it is impossible to communicate it. A light, a joy is something to be experienced. The only way to communicate is that you also study the *Gitā* and learn to live the righteous life and to experience what Swami Tapovanam is. Invoke His grace, a very powerful one, in order to make you an adhikārī (a seeker who is qualified) for study of the Upaniṣads and for help in meditation. Make use of Him — if you can.

***Query** from a Postal Lesson Course student:* When and by whom was the original Knowledge of the Vedic scriptures given out?

Swamiji: The ṛṣis who gave out this Truth from the white heat peaks of their transcendental experience, in their exquisite moments of total inspiration, away from their individuality, their ego consciousness, forgot to put their signature upon these declarations. They are Īśvara-prokta [divinely bestowed] and not mānuṣya-kṛta [man-made]. We know nothing about them — when, who, from where, or how. Those words were caught in the memories of the students, and they, in turn, having confirmed the veracity of the declarations in their own subjective direct experience, gave it out to the seekers who reached them. Thus, in the hierarchy of Guru-disciple [paramparā)] it came down to the times of Vyāsa. Vyāsa is the one who compiled, edited, and published these existing mantras into the four volumes which you and I today call the Vedas. Therefore, if you ask me the date of the Veda, I will have to refer to you the date of Vidyācārya Vyāsa; and this will be true only if you mean by the word 'Veda' the volumes, the written manuscripts, the textbooks that we call the four Vedas. The ṛṣis have shrouded themselves in a mystery so that their shadows may not fall to dim the clarity of the Truth that they expounded… THINK.

Letter to ***Kambham Suhasini:*** Just as an artist can easily slip from his contemplation of beauty to the flesh, which is beautiful, similarly, a devotee may slip to fall and love the idol and not the Ideal, you should not mistake the philosophy to be the philosopher — the māhātmya (greatness) of the Lord as the Mahātma. Gururdevo Maheśvaraḥ — see in the Guru the play and glory of the great Lord, Maheśvara. [Be] Careful. I love you, so I am taking time to explain. The teacher can never fall, but the disciple may; be forewarned.

Letter to ***Pranji Lodhia*** *dated July 23, 1993:*

Letter to ***Anjali Singh:***

As a teacher I have given you all you need. Now it is for you to apply it all in life and learn to live accepting everything, rejecting nothing, expecting all, yet keeping nothing. What is there in the world other than the expression of His glory?

Tender reminiscences of devotees and students:

Guru-śiṣya-paramparā ensures the continuity of cultural revival:

Swami Tejomayananda: Gurudev knew that more than one person was needed to do the work of cultural revival. If it had to continue, there has to be a paramparā (lineage). The two-year Vedānta courses in Sandeepanys, in different languages, have been going on continuously, maintaining this Guru-śiṣya sampradāya (tradition). I was supposed to teach a two-year course, but had to take many breaks because of health and travel. But was there any break in the course? No. Why? This is the strength of Guru-śiṣya-paramparā. Some Ācārya or the other came to take over — such is the power of the paramparā.

What one knows cannot be explained, yet what one may not know can be explained:

Swami Swaroopananda: Once, our eloquent Gurudev was asked to speak about marriage. "Who decided this topic? I have no direct experience of marriage, neither did my Guru have it!" he reproved. Yet he went on stage and gave an eloquent talk on marriage! But about Swami Tapovanam, he could not speak anything other than saying, "Tapovanji Maharaj is Brahman, and Brahman cannot be described."

The grace of the Master:

Swami Tejomayananda: Someone asked, "Who is the head of the Mission?" This was when I had just become the head. One Mission member pointed at me. The person said, "But he is so small! Our Gurudev was tall and had a presence; how will he do everything?" The Mission member later related this comment to me. I replied, "Yes, it is true that I am small." And then I pointed to a picture where I was standing by the side of Gurudev, and I added, "But what he does not see is that the one holding me is tall." I may not be tall, but He is! It is like the father who puts his child on his shoulders so that he can see."

Top left: Swami Chinmayananda and Swami Tejomayananda, the present head of Chinmaya Mission. ***Top right:*** Swami Tejomayananda and Swami Swaroopananda, the appointed future head of Chinmaya Mission. ***Bottom:*** Swami Swaroopananda and Swami Chinmayananda

***Swami Dheerananda's** words echo the feelings of all devotees:*

"I'll be there for you as long as you need me" — those words of Śrī Gurudev echoed inside me, fueling strength, courage, and determination. I never thought there would be a time when he would not be physically there for me. In Sidhbari, I would wake up at 3:00 A.M. and wait at the door of Gurudev's kuṭiyā to get a glimpse of the divine Vision. Gurudev would walk over to his writing desk and start his selfless service of the day, expressing genuine concern and providing positive hope through his writing. I would revel and enjoy the tender expressions dancing on his face as he pored over each letter with complete concentration. The quietness of the setting was transformed when the priest brought in tīrtham and vibhūti. The grace with which Gurudev's fingers would receive them reminded me of a perfect, harmonious symphony orchestra — Śrī Gurudev softly savoring the tīrtham, smoothly collecting the vibhūti, and smearing it across the forehead, leaving a straight line right above the chandan tilaka (mark made by sandalwood paste on the center of the forehead). It was a bold statement on focus, balance, and control. Watching Gurudev in utter silence was as much a feast to the eyes as observing his actions. The absolute peace and unconditional love that one felt in his presence had an overpowering magnetic effect.

One day, while nervously preparing for Ācārya's satsaṅga, I sought Gurudev's blessings. He said, "You prepare answers to questions that come to your mind. If those questions are not the ones asked of you, go ahead and confidently answer the questions that your mind asked." What a powerful inspiration!

The brilliance of Śrī Gurudev's stories never failed to fascinate me. He emphasized, time and time again, the importance of a quiet, alert, and vigilant mind. Once, Gurudev was given a cup of steaming hot tea. He remarked, "Let me check my nervous system," and proceeded to transfer the hot tea from the cup to the saucer in one flawless, sweeping motion. He then remarked, "Let me now check if my nervous system can transfer it back to the cup." We watched spellbound, as Śrī Gurudev transferred the entire tea back to the cup, spilling not a single drop! Every moment with him was a learning experience, not only through direct interaction, but also through the import of his message that one discovered much later after reflecting on his words.

After Gurudev's samādhi, I wondered, "Did my Guru leave because I spent more time in his physical presence than attending his teachings?" As I reflected, it all made sense, Gurudev is right here with me — be it preparing for classes or following a schedule, memories of his words and actions provide continuous guidance. Gurudev is there for us always! We just have to close our eyes, think of him, and receive his ever-flowing grace and blessings!

Seeing Gurudev always and finding his presence everywhere is what the teaching is all about:

Shankar Pillai: Every time I think of Gurudev, whom I met in 1956 as a teenager in Kerala, I get choked with emotion. He is constantly active in my thoughts, as the back screen of my mind. Whenever I try to write something down, I fail. It does not get translated. He has filled my life so much that I do not even miss him, not even a single moment in my life, because he is always there. I see his presence in our mission in Chicago, which has grown very big to become one of the major centers in the U.S., with two major centers in Chicago itself and supporting many satellite centers in nearby states and cities — Indiana, Wisconsin, Iowa, Missouri, Ohio, and more. I see Gurudev's grace in all his work — it is such a fulfilling life!

Catching the ball of grace:

Mimi Robins: To attend bhikṣās with Swamiji was always a delightful experience. After the meal, he would sit with the family and other guests and answer questions. Toward the end, a bowl of fruit would be presented to Swamiji. Swamiji would select a fruit for each member of the host family, hold it, bless it, and place it in their hands. However, with Swami Chinmayananda, the usual was often unusual. Sometimes, he would look around the room and pick and throw a fruit to a selected recipient. Apples, pears, peaches, mangos, oranges, even bananas, flew into the waiting hands of the chosen target. Once, Swamiji was giving talks in New York City. After the meal, he commenced his 'air-delivery' ritual. I was standing at the back, when suddenly a peach missile hit me on my forehead. On an impulse, I reacted. With a pained expression and exaggerated, dramatic movements, my hand went up to my forehead. I let out a sigh and staged a dramatic swoon. Swamiji roared with laughter. In a booming voice, he declared: "Very good. Fall and I will lift you!"

Indra Advani: In the early days, with childlike joy, he distributed prasāda to devotees sitting around him in a nontraditional way; he playfully tossed some apples to them instead of waiting for each to come to him for prasāda. Each devotee was eager and ready to receive an apple if it came his way. Here was a lesson. He transferred the joy of playing the game of life, the accepting of a win or a loss, at every interaction.

Those who make the effort get more:

Isabel Taylor: One time after a bhikṣā, Swamiji went to sit outside with hundreds of people in front of him. Next to him was a big basket of fruit. He took an apple and threw it at a young woman standing at the back. It bounced off her, and Swamiji threw another one at her. It, too, bounced off and fell away. And a third one met the same fate. So, Swamiji threw another piece of fruit toward the center of the crowd. A young brahmacārī sprang up and reached out and caught it! Swamiji kept throwing fruit in all directions and the young brahmacārī, whose legs were like a spring, would reach out and catch the fruit. Swamiji commented: "The Lord keeps throwing blessings at you and some people just let them fall away. And some people reach out and grab all the blessings!"

Teachings and blessings from the Guru pass on to the next generation:

Swami Mitrananda: In 1968, my father got Gurudev's autograph in the *Holy Gītā*. Gurudev wrote: "Read five verses daily and meet me after three years." Twenty years later, I gave the same book to Gurudev for his autograph during his yajña at Tirupati. He saw the old signature and asked, "Whose book is it?" When I told him about my father, he smiled and wrote on the same page: Son also, advice the same." To the people sitting around, Gurudev said "This is our culture; the book should be handed over to the next generation." In 1989, I joined the āśrama at Mumbai. On the day of my dīkṣā in 1991, I showed the book to Gurudev. He wrote: "Father missed it, but son got it." It has become a rare book with three signatures of Gurudev on the same page.

Rose Ann Blau*, formerly a nun for nineteen years, met Swamiji nine years after she left the convent:*
My friend Mavis and I attended a yoga class. The yoga instructor told us about a free Vedāntic lecture series that was about to start at the University of Wisconsin. From there, we signed up for a camp at Olivet, Michigan. Just before leaving for camp, we learned that the camp was going to be taught by Swami Chinmayananda. We did not know him, but since we were all paid up, we decided to go anyway. Several times, I had heard that when the student is ready, the Teacher comes. Dr. Apparo Mukkamala met us at the airport and asked us to wait because Swami Chinmayananda's plane was to arrive shortly and we could help to welcome him. Mavis and I laughed because we did not know who he was, but we did stay to welcome him. When Gurudev got off the plane, he looked down and did not look at anyone. Seeing him for the first time, I was overwhelmed and speechless. Years later, I heard Gurudev say several times that when you meet your Guru, it is love at first sight. When we got to the door of the building where he was staying, I walked a little faster so I could open the door, but Gurudev said, "No." As he opened the door, he did not tell me in words, but I clearly understood that he would open many doors in my life. When I look back over these thirty years, he has truly opened many doors in my life.

Noble intentions should be carried out immediately:

Ācārya Sharada Kumar: A group of us were at Detroit airport to see Gurudev off. We were all sitting around and feeling very sad that he was leaving as it was Guru-pūrṇimā the next day. We would miss doing pāda-pūjā for him. "Why don't you do it here? It is already Pūrṇimā now," he told us. So right there and then, without any materials, Bhargavi Raiji and I did mānasa-pūjā (mental worship). I chanted Gurudev's 108 names and he kept counting to check if I was missing any!

Is one ready to give what the Guru really wants?

Christine Grimmer: After meeting Gurudev, I just wanted to bask in his company. However, it took a much longer time to understand the unique relationship of the Guru and śiṣya. Mercifully, Gurudev tolerated my novice understanding and enthusiasm. Once, he asked me if I might give him some water. Thrilled, I said: "I will give you anything, Gurudev." "Anything?" "Yes." He said, "Give me your pancreas!" This kind of joke, in reference to his diseased pancreas, was typical of Gurudev. But it was a necessary jolt to me. I had to be more cautious about my declarations of devotion. I understood what giving up the ego might mean; I was no more ready to give that up than I was my pancreas.

Tape-recorded teaching is no substitute for hearing from the teacher directly:

Mimi Robins: As Swami Chinmayananda was about to speak, in front of a large classroom, a group of enthusiastic individuals rushed down to place tape recorders close to the speaker. Immediately, he asked for their removal, as it would disturb the audience. He added, "Recorded words do not convey the meaning of spiritual texts. The contents are carried through the aligned concentration of the Teacher and the taught."

The utmost reverence toward the Guru:

Swamini Kaivalyananda: In the 1992 camp in Sidhbari, one of our batch mates Br. Aniket asked Gurudev about the greatness of Tapovanji Maharaj. Gurudev became silent as a mild mist enveloped his eyes. He closed them, and, with an utmost reverential voice, said, "He cannot be described. He is an Ocean and I am the wave… waiting to merge back into Him." There was utter silence for almost five minutes.

True humility grounded in gratitude to Guru and God:

Swamini Umananda: After the Paris program in 1993, Swamiji went to London and announced that the Guru-dakṣiṇā (student's offering to the Teacher) collected would go to Chinmaya Mission France. A little later, I went to thank him for the help given to the French center. He was sitting in an armchair. I knelt beside him and handed a letter expressing my feelings, my gratitude, and my longing to contribute to his work, to his Mission. He read the words, put his arm around my shoulders, and said with great gentleness: "It is not my Mission; it is the Mission of my master, Swami Tapovanam. He is the one to be thanked."

Directing the mind to anchor itself in contemplation:

Swamini Amritananda: After completing the Vedānta course in Mumbai, I traveled to Goa with Gurudev. His loving advice to me before I left India was never to go far from Tapovanji Maharaj's veranda, as it was there that Gurudev received the highest Knowledge from his Guru. For me, the message meant keeping my heart on that veranda at all times, no matter what the challenges. It was to always remain in that quiet, contemplative atmosphere where Truth resides.

A reminder that we are never really apart from Guru and God:

Jyoti Madhavan: Once, I was feeling sad about an impending separation from Gurudev. I had not conveyed my emotion to anyone. However, Gurudev sensed my sadness and very sweetly and lovingly comforted me. He said, "We are all like logs floating in a river. We bump into each other and travel downstream together for some time. Then we separate for a while and again may bump into each other later. We must be at ease and flow with the stream." He also remarked, "God is ever present and keeping a watchful and protective eye on all." His words put my mind at ease.

Silence — the gift from the Guru:

Daniela Purchase-Schwarz: It is a fact that to the prepared student, eagerly looking for knowledge and direct experience, the Guru must come. All will then have their own story to tell. It is all about going to the source, that fountain of life, Brahman. To illustrate this I would like to share an incident that happened in Palghat, South India, in 1982. The Gītā Yajña had just come to an end. Gurudev closed the textbook and left the stage. An audience of 10,000 people — hard to imagine but quite possible in India — sat outside in the open grounds immersed in silence. Nobody got up. Nobody went home — 10,000 people remaining in utter silence, immersed in their own Self, a deep and unforgettable moment, indeed, never to be extinguished from my mind.

The Guru will always be there in the physical form as long as we need him:

Anjali Singh: St. Gallen in 1991, during an evening satsaṅga in Daniela Purchase's house, Swamiji said, "The Jīvanmukta [Man of Perfection] is dead, finished. The mystery is that his body remains to fulfill samaṣṭi prārabdha [total destiny]. If the Master falls sick, it is because the devotees need to go through the experience of pain and sevā. If he dies a painful death, it is not for himself but for the sins of others. Jesus was immaculate; the sins he died for were samaṣṭi sins. Samaṣṭi prārabdha deserved to see that kind of death for him. When the body passes away, it is because the devotee no longer needs it." On feeling relieved in hearing the last words, I said to Swamiji, "O good! That means you can't go because I will always need you!" He continued, "… and it is Nārāyaṇa who decides the need!"

Final advice of the Guru: ***Swami Chinmayananda:***

This is our culture. The great philosophy of Hinduism considers the glory of life lived as the only real wealth. May you grow to be the richest Hindu in living true Hindutva, the true Bhāratiya culture. Live Vedānta, and thus, let us all reach That Destination, where having met, we shall never part. Meet me there. Reach there through love, service, and purity.

Be regular in your pursuit. Be sincere in your studies. Be heroic enough to live what you have understood and pursue diligently, without compromises, the deep convictions that the irrefutable Vedānta has touched in you. Those who have now reached the precarious state in meditation, when you need my guidance almost regularly; you need not feel that I am now far away. You may continue your practices as though I am here; in fact, I shall be next to each one of you at your hour of meditation. With courage and confidence, continue the practice regularly. And those who are in the lower rudders should not also allow their fervor to cool down. The 'farther' I go, the nearer shall I be for each one of you. This is a promise.

This sādhu shall see you home — this is a solemn promise.

I have tried my best to impart what I had gained from my beloved Teachers to thousands around the world. This work has been my sport, my mission in life. You have all helped me always. We shall meet in our hearts.

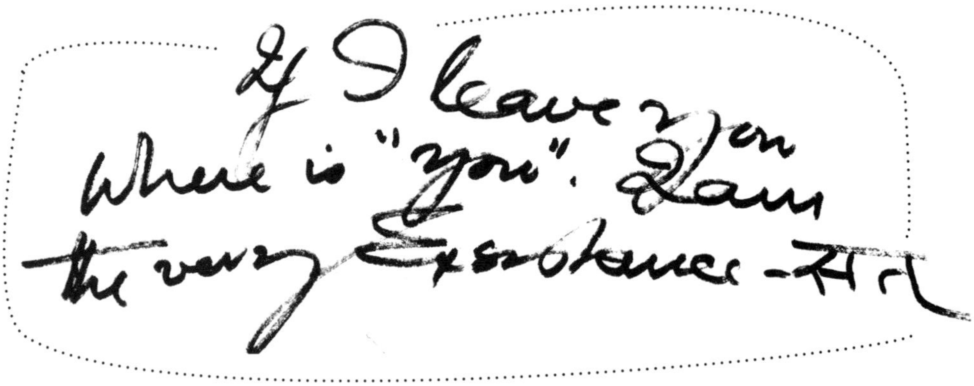
If I leave you
where is "you". I am
the very Existence -

May Śrī Jagadīśvara bless us always!

Realise this and live spreading all your love always everywhere.

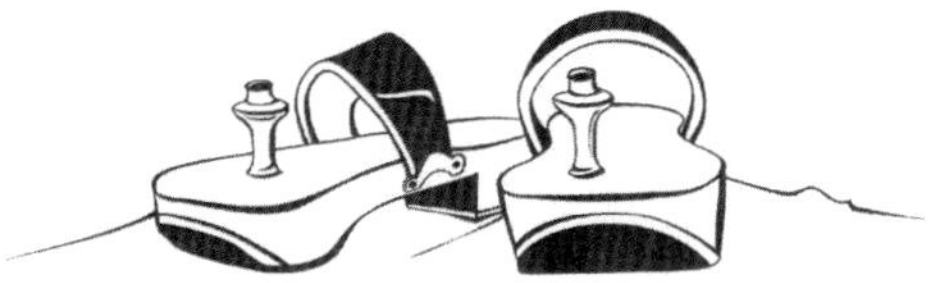

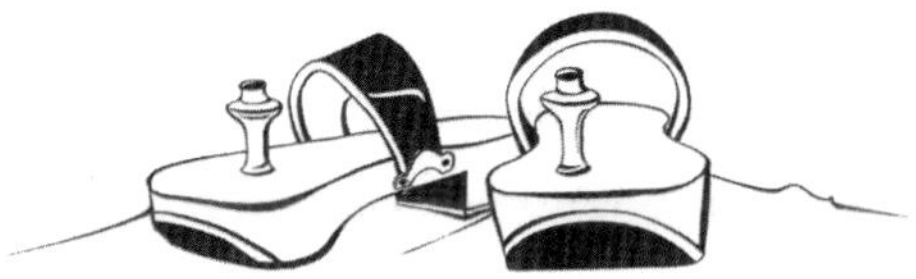

Appendix: List of Devotees Who Contributed to the Book

List of devotees who contributed to the book their experiences with Pūjya Gurudev:

In alphabetical order by first name:

Swami Advayananda: Ācārya Chinmaya International Foundation (CIF).

Col. Ajit Sukhtankar: Member Chinmaya Mission Belgaum, Karnataka.

Swamini Amritananda: Head of Chinmaya Mission, New Zealand.

Anant Narayan (Uncle Mani): Ācārya, Chinmaya Mission Chicago, Chicago, Illinois, 1991–1994.

Anjali Singh: Unofficial photographer of Pūjya Gurudev; compiled Chinmaya Photo Archives and several books; former editor of "CM News Bulletin Delhi."

Anil Choudhary: COO, Delhi Chinmaya Sewa Trust; member of Executive Committee, Chinmaya Mission Delhi and member of Board of Management, Chinmaya Vidyalaya-Delhi.

Anil Sachdev: Trustee and President of Chinmaya Mission Gurgaon; former Secretary and President of Chinmaya Mission Delhi.

Dr. Anita Raina Thapan: Study Group Leader and former Vice President of Chinmaya Mission Delhi; author.

Dr. Apparao Mukkamala: Director and past President, Chinmaya Mission West (CMW) U.S.A.; coordinated Gurudev's medical care in the U.S.A.

Ashlesha Madhok: Past President of Chinmaya Mission, Minneapolis, Minnesota, U.S.A.

Bharati Sukhtankar: Author of *Bala Bhagavatam* and *Bala Ramayana*.

Bina Sutarwala: Founder of Chinmaya Mission Ottawa, Ottawa, Canada; traveled with Gurudev for two years all over the world as his secretary and nurse, 1988–90.

Mata Brahmjyoti: Sannyāsī (also known as Munni Mai) who did sādhanā in Uttarkashi at the same time as Gurudev; at the writing of this book, she is 95 years old and lives in Haridwar.

Cate Hallpike: Member Chinmaya Mission Melbourne.

Swami Chidrupananda: Ācārya Chinmaya Mission Noida and Director of All-India Chinmaya Yuva Kendra (youth wing of Chinmaya Mission).

Christine Grimmer: Past Bala Vihar Coordinator, Chinmaya Mission, Melbourne and Sydney, Australia; former Secretary and Study Group Coordinator, Chinmaya Mission Sydney.

Daniela Purchase-Schwarz: Organized Gurudev's yajñas in St. Gallen, Switzerland, from the mid-1980s onward; associated with the Chinmaya satsaṅga group in Switzerland.

Swami Dheerananda: Ācārya Chinmaya Mission Washington Regional Center (CMWRC), metropolitan area of Washington, D.C., U.S.A.

Gaurang and Darshana Nanavaty: Ācāryas Chinmaya Mission Houston, Texas, U.S.A.; **Darshanaben** is the author of Bala Vihar teaching manuals.

Swamini Gurupriyananda: Head of Chinmaya Ranjan Center in New Delhi; she started Chinmaya Mission Bhakti Sandhya (Indian Classical Music and Dance) programs in Delhi.

Indra Advani: Member of the Board of Directors of Chinmaya Mission San Jose, San Jose, California, U.S.A.; published the *Amar Chitra Katha* Illustrated Classic issue on Swami Chinmayananda.

Isabel Taylor: Conceived and executed the professional video recording of Pūjya Gurudev's *Bhagavad-gītā* talks in 1991 at Krishnalaya, Piercy, California, U.S.A.

K. C. Patnaik: General Manager, Chinmaya Prakashan (Publication Division of CCMT).

K. P. Daswani: Trustee, Central Chinmaya Mission Trust; Trustee, Chinmaya Foundation, Hong Kong; organized yajñas for Gurudev all over Southeast Asia, including China.

Jyoti Bharucha Madhavan: Served Gurudev as his secretary and nurse while traveling with him in India and the U.S.A., 1990–1993.

K. Aiyappan Pillai: A 101-year-old devotee, who met the saint Śrī Vidyadhiraja Chattambiswami.

Swamini Kaivalyananda: Co-author of *Yours Forever*; has been collecting Gurudev's to-be-archived material.

R. Krishnamoorthy (Tatha): Former Secretary and President of Chinmaya Mission Delhi; associated with Hanuman Mastaka Abhishekam in Sidhbari for over three decades; also associated with Dhanwantari (Medical Wing) in Chinmaya Vibhooti.

Dr. Kshama Metre: National Director and Trustee of CORD (Chinmaya Organization for Rural Development); received Padma Shri prize in 2008 for comprehensive integrated rural development work in India.

Ācārya Dr. Kuntimaddi Sadananda: Former Trustee of Chinmaya Mission Washington Regional Center; Secretary and Treasurer of SEVA, Inc., a philanthropic organization for Chinmaya Mission before CORD was formed.

Laju Chanrai: Trustee, Central Chinmaya Mission Trust, Tara Cultural Trust, CORD, Chinmaya Foundation Trust Lagos, Nigeria and Chinmaya Mission Durban, South Africa; President, Chinmaya Foundation Trust Lagos, Nigeria. Director, Chinmaya International Residential School, Coimbatore.

Leela Nambiar: Trustee, Central Chinmaya Mission Trust; publisher, *Tapovan Prasad* (spiritual monthly of Chinmaya Mission worldwide); helped establish the first Chinmaya Vidyalaya in Chennai.

Manisha Khemlani: CEO, Central Chinmaya Mission Trust, with headquarters in Mumbai, India.

Margaret Dukes: Editor of *Mananam* since 1987.

Mimi Robins: Official photographer of Pūjya Gurudev at the U.S.A. jñāna yajña camps.

Swami Mitrananda: Ācārya-in-charge Chinmaya Mission Chennai and publisher of *Chinmaya Udghosh*; former President of the Youth Wing of Chinmaya Mission (CHYK) in India; he wrote the script for the movie "On a Quest" about Pūjya Gurudev Swami Chinmayananda.

Neeru Mehta: Member, Chinmaya Mission since 1973 in Mumbai, now Ahmedabad; compiled and published *Scraps & Bits* in English and *Swamin Namaste* in Hindi.

Nirmal Bharvani: Hon. Secretary of Chinmaya Seva Centre Singapore; runs Bala Vihars in Singapore.

Parvathy Raman: Editor of *Tapovan Prasad*, author of *Words to the Wordless*, and co-author of *Yours Forever*; served in Sidhbari Ashram in the mid-1980s and at a Chinmaya Vidyalaya in the early 1990s.

Pranji Lodhia: Member of the CMW Board of Directors, Treasurer of CMW, and member of the Board of Directors, Chinmaya Mission San Jose, California, U.S.A.

Prarthna Saran: President of Chinmaya Mission Delhi; she holds regular classes on Vedānta and gives talks to various associations in New Delhi.

Purnima Daulat Singh: Trustee, CORD (Chinmaya Organization for Rural Development).

Swami Prashantananda: Head of the Senior Citizens' Chinmaya Mission Ashram in Rewa; author of several books.

Swamini Radhikananda: President, Chinmaya Mission St. Augustine, St. Augustine, Florida, U.S.A.

Col. Rakesh Sachdeva: Member of Executive Committee, Chinmaya Mission Pune.

Ram and Sheela Kirpalani: Original members of Chinmaya Mission New York, New York City, New York, U.S.A.; **Ram:** Head Engineer, Sidhbari in the early 1990s; **Sheela:** songwriter; started the Alcoholics Anonymous program in Sidhbari in the early 1990s.

Swami Ramananda: Prior to becoming a monk of Chinmaya Mission, he was a manager of the Sidhbari Ashram.

Dr. Rashmi Singh: Member of the Board of Directors, Chinmaya Mission Los Angeles, Tustin, California, U.S.A.; past member of the CMW Board of Directors; Gurudev's doctor during the Krishnalaya Camp in 1991.

Rose Anne Blau: Author of *My Children*; started the Chinmaya Mission Center in Milwaukee, Wisconsin, U.S.A.

Ruchi Nanavaty Vasa: Member of Chinmaya Mission Toronto, Brampton, Ontario, Canada.

Rudite J. Emir: Founding member of CMW Board of Directors, founding editor of *Mananam;* author of *At Every Breath A Teaching*, and editor of *Self-Unfoldment*; for many years, held Vedānta lectures and camps in her native Latvia.

Sarv Singh: Member, Chinmaya Mission Los Angeles, Tustin, California, U.S.A.

Ācārya Dr. Shailaja Nadkarni: Member of the Board of Directors, Chinmaya Mission Orlando, Casselberry, Florida, U.S.A.

Shankar Pillai: Ācārya, Chinmaya Mission Chicago and member of CMW Board of Directors.

Swami Shantananda: President CMW; Head of Tri-State Center, Cranberry, New Jersey, U.S.A.; served as secretary to Gurudev; served as Brahmacārī-in-charge of Chinmaya Mission Taipei.

Sharda Chawla: Bala Vihar Sevika; Study Group facilitator; member of the Managing Committee, Chinmaya Vidyalaya, Delhi, India.

Ācārya Sharada Kumar: Head of Chinmaya Mission Ann Arbor, Ann Arbor, Michigan, U.S.A.; sang the Sanskrit ślokas during the *Vivekacūḍāmaṇi* video recording in Sidhbari.

Som Oberoi: Past member of Chinmaya Mission Kuwait, now a member of Chinmaya Mission Gurgaon, India.

Swamini Shivapriyananda: Senior Ācārya Chinmaya Mission Toronto, Brampton, Ontario, Canada.

Swami Siddhananda: Ācārya-in-charge of CMW's Chinmaya Publications Division, Langhorne, Pennsylvania, U.S.A.; Ācārya Chinmaya Mission Philadelphia, Morrisville, Pennsylvania, U.S.A. (CM Philadelphia includes satellite sites: Chinmaya Kedar, Chinmaya Madhuvan, Chinmaya Exton, and Chinmaya Harrisburg).

Swami Swaroopananda: Regional Head of Chinmaya Mission Australia and the Far East, London, and Africa; member of the Board of Directors of Chinmaya International School, Coimbatore; author of *Ik Onkaar* and several other books and CDs and the interactive self-development course "Make it Happen." ™

Swami Tejomayananda: Gurudev's successor and Head of all Chinmaya Mission Trusts worldwide; author of many books, musical CDs, and DVD discourses.

Swamini Umananda: Head of Chinmaya Mission France, Paris, France; translated several books of Gurudev into French, including the *Holy Gitā*.

Ācārya Uma Jeyarasasingam: A devotee of Pūjya Gurudev since 1971, she served in the San Francisco Bay area, becoming an Ācārya in 1996 at CM San Jose. She now lives in Virginia, U.S.A., but continues to supervise the Bala Vihar movement at CMSJ.

Uma Shergill: Past Trustee of Chinmaya Tapovan Trust, Sidhbari, and Past President of Chinmaya Mission, Amritsar.

Viji Sundaram: Editor of *Tapovan Prasad* 1977–1981; author of *Chinmaya Mission – Transforming Lives*.

Ācārya Vilasini Balakrishnan: Served Gurudev as his personal secretary for several years, traveling with him in the U.S.A, Canada, and India; she is a member of the Board of Directors of CMW and CMWRC and is Regional Director of Bala Vihar in metropolitan Washington, D.C.

Swamini Vimalananda: Ācārya-in-charge of Chinmaya Mission Coimbatore; spearheads the CCMT Education Cell and 100 Chinmaya Education Institutions; authored several books.

Vinay R. Nair: Head of the School of Vedic Maths and author of the CIF Vedic Mathematics Course. Author of *Journey to the Himalayas* and *The Teacher who Taught us to Think*.

Devotees whose letters from Gurudev were used from the Chinmaya Letter Archives:

In alphabetical order:

A. Balakrishnan, Anjali Singh, Divakaran Namboodiri, Erica Proels, Ācāryas Gaurang and Darshana Nanavaty, Gauri Menon, Hemlata Rajan, H. P. Eshwar, Jujhar Singh, Kamala Chidambaram, Dr. Kambham Suhasini, Prof. Lakshmi Reddy, Madhuri Jhala, Margaret Dukes, Meenambal, Nanki Singh, Neeru Mehta, Padma Jaisinghani, Pravin Gandhi, Premila Modi, Rudite Emir, Sarla Birla, Shakuntala Bindra, Sharda Chawla, Sheila Sharma, Shri Trivedi, Sneh Chakraburtty, Srichand Krishnani, Susheela Purushottam, Swami Swaroopananda, Tarachand Chawla, Swami Tejomayananda, Dr. Thangamma Ganapthy, T. N. Parthasarthy, Vinita Asrani, Vrinda Chidambaram.

Glossary

A

Ādi Śaṅkarācārya	one of Hinduism's greatest seers, who propounded the Advaita Vedānta school of philosophy
ārati (**ārtī**)	ritual of showing light in front of a deity, represents burning of the ego
āśrama	the residence and teaching center of a spiritual teacher, which often includes lodgings for his or her students
Ātman (Ātma)	the Self, pure Consciousness, the immanent aspect of the supreme Reality; this same Consciousness, when regarded as transcendent, is called Brahman.

B

Bala Rāmāyaṇam	the epic narrative dealing with Rāma's life and his defeat of the evil Rāvaṇa
Bhagavad-gītā	"Song of God"; a major scriptural poem in eighteen chapters, contained in the *Mahābhārata*. It is a dialogue between Lord Kṛṣṇa and Arjuna, his friend and disciple, on the battlefield of the dynastic war between the Pandavas and Kauravas.
bhakta	one who follows the path of devotion (see yoga)
bhakti yoga	the path of devotion, one of the four main paths to liberation
Bhārat (Bhārata)	The name Bhārat came from emperor Bharata, and it has been used as a self-ascribed name by people of the Indian subcontinent.
bhikṣā	offering of food, especially to a renunciate
Bhishma Pitahma	the central figure in the great epic Mahābhārata, had taken a vow never to marry and to always support whoever sat on the Hastinapur throne. Because of his vow, he had to put up with the unrighteous behavior of his grand nephews, the sons of the Regent.
brahmacārī	a seeker of the knowledge of Brahman; one who has taken the first monastic vows. The first of the four stages of life, the others being the life of the householder, the life of retirement, and the life of renunciation

D

darśana	auspicious sight of a deity or holy person
dharma	the inherent quality of anything, such as the heat in fire and sweetness in sugar; also righteousness; duty
dīkṣā	a ceremony of initiation whereby a disciple is inducted into the spiritual path or order, often with a special mantra

G

gopī	'milkmaid'; the gopīs were devotees of Lord Kṛṣṇa, exemplifying the most intense love for the Divine.
guṇa	thought quality or texture; the three types of guṇas are: sāttvika (pure and serene), rājasika (passionate and agitated), and tāmasika (dull and inactive)

I

Īśvara	the supreme Lord, God; Consciousness functioning through māyā

J

Jagadīśvara	Lord of the World
japa	repeating one of God's names, a mantra, with the help of a *mālā*, a rosary
jīva	the individual soul; the individuality or ego in a human being
jñāna	divine Knowledge, wisdom
jñāna yajña	a series of lectures on Vedānta
jñāna yoga	the path of knowledge, one of the four main paths to liberation

K

karma yoga	the path of action, one of the four main paths to liberation
kṣaya	diminish, wane, exhaust; hidden vāsanās
kuṭiyā	small house, hut

M

Mahā Śivarātrī Day	sacred night of worship of Lord Śiva
Mahābhārata	a long epic poem, attributed to Vyāsa, relating to the events of a dynastic war between the Pandavas and Kauravas; it illustrates the truths of the *Vedas* and includes the great philosophic poem, the *Bhagavad-gītā*.
Mahāmṛtyuṃjaya mantra	— 'Great Death-Conquering Mantra'; chanted when a person is close to death
Mahāsamādhi	end of the physical existence of a great Master
manana	reflection upon and careful analysis of the knowledge gained from the teacher and the scriptures to internalize that knowledge, free from doubt

N

Nachiketas	a child extolled in the *Kaṭhopaniṣad* for his rejection of material desires and for his single-minded pursuit to realize Brahman
namaskāra	a pleasant greeting; an offering of respect or reverence; also, a prostration of surrender
Nārada	the celestial sage devoted to spreading the name of the God Nārāyaṇa
nididhyāsana	meditation; the flow of like thoughts related to Brahman, to the exclusion of all other thoughts

nirvikalpa samādhi	the transcendental State of Consciousness in which the mind becomes totally absorbed in the supreme Reality, with all sense of individuality and duality lost (see savikalpa samādhi)
O	
Om Namaḥ Śivāya	prostrations to Lord Śiva
P	
pāda-pūjā	worship of the Master's feet, symbolic of his ideals and the Knowledge he stands on
Paramātma	the Supreme
parikramā	circumambulating, circling around; roaming about; walking through
pāyasa	rice pudding, boiled in milk with sugar
Prahlāda	a great devotee of Lord Viṣṇu; one filled with joy
prakaraṇa grantha	introductory texts that explain concepts of Vedānta for lay persons
prārabdha	destiny/results of past actions
prasāda (prasad)	that which is accepted as a token of the Lord's blessings after worship; an offering to a deity or a Master, or the remnants of such an offering returned as blessing to the worshiper
pūjā	ritualistic worship
Pūjya	honorable; to be worshiped
puruṣārtha	self-effort, a faculty unique to human beings, which helps them to choose their actions regardless of their inborn tendencies (vāsanās)
R	
rājasika	one of the three thought textures (guṇas) that characterize qualities of the human personality; rājasika is characterized by activity, passion, and agitation (see guṇa)
ṛṣi (rishi)	ancient sage, seer
S	
sādhanā	any spiritual practice, such as reading the scriptures, meditating, distributing one's wealth to the needy
samādhi	oneness, integration; 'tranquil mind'; state of absorption or thoughtlessness in which a person experiences his identity with the supreme Reality
saṁsāra	the endless cycle of births and deaths, which human beings experience before they realize their identity with the supreme Reality
saṁsārī	persons entangled in this material world; materially contaminated
sannyāsa	renunciation; the monastic life; the last of the four stages of life, the others being: (1) student life (brahmacarya), (2) married householder life (gṛhastha), and (3) the life of retirement and contemplation (*vā*naprastha)

sannyāsī	a renunciate; one who has taken the vow of sannyāsa
śāstra	scriptures, including both those considered to be revealed by God (Śruti) and those written by sages (Smṛti)
sat-cit-ānanda	absolute Existence–Knowledge–Bliss, an epithet for Brahman
satsaṅga	'good company'; maintenance of contact with the higher values of life by association with noble persons or with inspiring writings and ideas
sāttvika	clarity, luminosity; a fundamental essence of nature, or guṇa; one of the three thought textures (guṇas) that characterize the human personality; the sāttvika quality is characterized by purity and serenity (see rājasika and tāmasika)
savikalpa samādhi	the state of consciousness in which the mind experiences its essential divinity; at this stage, a trace of individuality still lingers to experience that divine vision (see nirvikalpa samādhi)
sevā	service done in a spirit of selflessness
sevikā (sevak)	one who is serving
siddhi	accomplishment; a power acquired (usually after penance of yoga)
Śiva	'the Auspicious'; also, God in the aspect of Destroyer; one of the Hindu Trinity, the other two being Viṣṇu and Brahma
śravaṇa	listening to scriptures
Śrī	title of respect used before the name of a deity, a holy book, or a man
sthiti	'staying in a particular condition,' referring to Arjuna, who developed a neurotic state of mind on the battlefield
sukarma	action that causes no material karma (reaction) either good or bad
T	
tāmasika	one of the three thought textures (guṇas) that characterize the human personality; the tamasic quality is characterized by dullness and inactivity, expresses as ignorance and stupor, and causes nonapprehension of Reality (see *rā*jasika and *sā*ttvika)
tapas	austerity
tapasvin	ascetic; a person of penance
tat tvam asi	"That thou art" found in the *Chāndogya-upaniṣad*, one of the four grand pronouncements of the Upaniṣads. The meaning of the phrase is that the Self, in its pure State, is identical with the ultimate Reality
tīrtham	holy water given to devotees in a temple (often flavored with tulsī leaves)
tulsī	an aromatic plant used for religious and medicinal purposes
Turīya	the fourth state: the State of Consciousness, which transcends the three ordinary states of consciousness — the waking, dreaming, and deep-sleep states

U

upadeśa	instruction; teaching
upāsana	act of sitting or being near or at hand; worship

V

vaikuṇṭha	'Place of Not Hindrance'; Lord Viṣṇu's celestial home
vairāgya	dispassion, nonattachment; indifference to worldly things
vana-māla tulsī	garland of forest flowers
vānaprasthi	one who is in the vānaprastha stage of life
vāsanās	inborn dispositions and motivating urges deep in the unconscious; the impressions formed in the personality when one acts in the world with egocentric desires
Vaśiṣṭha Manu	one of the great ṛṣis
Vāsudeva	the innermost Self; also, a popular name of Kṛṣṇa
Vedānta	'end of the Vedas'; the end portion of the Vedas, which consist of the Upanisads: Vedānta can also denote 'the end of knowledge' or 'the most profound knowledge'; Vedānta teaches that the purpose of life is to realize the supreme Reality
Vedāntin	one who identifies with and follows the teachings of Vedānta
vibhūti	sacred ashes smeared on the forehead; also, Lord's Glory
vicāra	insight, reflection
vikṣepa	agitation; veiling due to ignorance
viveka	discrimination between the ephemeral objects of the world and the eternal Principle of Life
Vivekacūḍāmaṇi	'The Crest-Jewel of Discrimination'; an introductory text to the entire theory of Vedānta, the "Science of Life," written by Ādi Śaṅkarācārya
vratam	vow, commitment

Y

yajña	worship; cooperative activities that integrate (see jñāna yajna)
yoga	the word *yoga* comes from the root *yuj*, meaning 'to join, to yoke'; the joining of the self to the supreme Self

TRANSLITERATION AND PRONUNCIATION GUIDE

In the book, Devanāgarī characters are transliterated according to the scheme adopted by the International Congress of Orientalists at Athens in 1912. In it, one fixed pronunciation value is given to each letter; f, q, w, x, and z are not called to use. An audio recording of this guide is available at www.chinmayamission.com/scriptures.php. According to this scheme:

	sounds like		*sounds like*
a	u in f*u*n	m	m in i*m*provise
ā	a in c*a*r	ṁ	*see below*
ai	i in h*igh*	n	n in *n*umber
au	o in n*ow*	ṅ	n in thu*n*der
b	b in *b*ut	ṅ	an in si*n*g
bh	bh in a*bh*or	ñ	ny in ba*ny*an
c	ch in *ch*unk	o	o in *o*ver
ch	ch in mat*ch*	om	oam in f*oam*
d	th in *th*is	p	p in *p*urse
ḍ	d in *d*og	ph	ph in sap*ph*ire
e	ay in pl*ay*	ṛ	r in *r*ig
g	g in *g*ate	ṝ	long ṛ
gh	gh in *gh*ost	s	sir
h	h in *h*appy	ś	sh in *sh*ovel
ḥ	*see below*	ṣ	sh in bu*sh*el
i	i in d*i*fferent	t	t in *th*ink
ī	ee in f*ee*t	th	th in pa*th*etic
j	j in *j*ustice	ṭ	*t* in tank
jh	dge in he*dge*hog	ṭh	th in an*th*ill
jñ	gn in *gn*osis	tr	tr in *t*ree
k	k in *k*ind	u	u in f*u*ll
kh	kh in *kh*an	ū	oo in b*oo*t
kñ	tio in ac*tion*	v	v in *v*ery
kṣ	ksh in wor*ksh*eet	y	y in *y*oung
l	l in *l*ove	’	unpronounced *a*
ḷ	l in wor*l*d	”	unpronounced ā (long a)

ḥ aspiration of preceding consonant
ṁ nasalization of preceding consonant

PATRONS AND DONORS

Grateful acknowledgment and special thanks are given to the following:

DAVID & MARGARET DUKES

| TORONTO, ONTARIO, CANADA |

DANIELA PURCHASE–SCHWARZ

| ST. GALLEN, SWITZERLAND |

ARVIND & MEENA MATHUR

| SINGAPORE |

CHINMAYA MISSION ST. AUGUSTINE

| FLORIDA, U.S.A. |

ROSE ANNE BLAU

| HARTFORD, WISCONSIN, U.S.A. |

SHARDA CHAWLA

| NEW DELHI, INDIA |